0 kilometers   50

0 miles   25

**MOLOKA'I AND
LĀNA'I**
Pages 94–105

MAUI
Pages 106–129

MOLOKA'I

LĀNA'I

● Kahului

MAUI

KAHO'OLAWE

HAWAI'I ISLAND
Pages 130–155

● Kailua-Kona

Hilo ●

HAWAI'I
ISLAND

EYEWITNESS TRAVEL

HAWAII

EYEWITNESS TRAVEL

HAWAII

LONDON, NEW YORK,
MELBOURNE, MUNICH AND DELHI
www.dk.com

PROJECT EDITOR Helen Townsend
ART EDITOR Anthony Limerick
EDITOR Freddy Hamilton
DESIGNERS Tessa Bindloss, Tim Mann
US EDITORS Mary Sutherland, Michael Wise
MAP CO-ORDINATORS Emily Green, David Pugh
PICTURE RESEARCH Ellen Root
DTP DESIGNER Ingrid Vienings
SENIOR REVISIONS EDITOR Esther Labi

CONTRIBUTORS
Gerald Carr, Bonnie Friedman, Rita Goldman, Clemence McLaren,
Melissa Miller, Alex Salkever, Stephen Self, Greg Ward, Paul Wood

PHOTOGRAPHERS
Rob Reichenfeld, Mike Severns

ILLUSTRATORS
Robert Ashby, Richard Bonson, Gary Cross, Chris Forsey, Stephen Gyapay,
Claire Littlejohn, Chris Orr & Associates, Robbie Polley, Mike Taylor,
John Woodcock

Printed and bound in China by L.Rex Printing Co. Ltd

First American Edition, 1998
13 14 15 16 10 9 8 7 6 5 4 3 2 1

Published in the United States by DK Publishing,
375 Hudson Street, New York, New York 10014

**Reprinted with revisions 1999, 2000, 2001, 2002,
2003, 2004, 2005, 2006, 2007, 2009, 2011, 2013**

Copyright © 1998, 2013 Dorling Kindersley Limited, London

Published in Great Britain by Dorling Kindersley Limited.

A catalog record for this book is available from
the Library of Congress.

ISSN 1542-1554
ISBN 978-0-75669-489-0

Front cover main image: Waikiki Beach, Hawai'i

MIX
Paper from
responsible sources
FSC
www.fsc.org   FSC™ C018179

◁ Beautiful, lush Mākaha ("ferocious") Valley on O'ahu's remote Wai'anae Coast

Waikīkī Beach and Diamond Head

CONTENTS

HOW TO USE
THIS GUIDE 6

INTRODUCING
HAWAI'I

Ali'iōlani Hale, the state judiciary
building in Honolulu

The rugged, sharply incised Nā Pali Coast on Kauaʻi's North Shore

SURVIVAL GUIDE

Dancer at the Polynesian
Cultural Center at Lāʻie, Oʻahu

Yellow *ʻilima*, a Hawaiian hibiscus
relative and Oʻahu's official flower

Historic cape made with the
feathers of thousands of birds

Geological diagram of
the Hawaiian Islands
(see pp18–19)

HOW TO USE THIS GUIDE

This guide helps you to get the most from your visit to Hawai'i. It provides both detailed practical information and expert recommendations. *Introducing Hawai'i* maps the island chain and sets it in its historical and cultural context. The five island chapters, plus *Honolulu and Waikīkī*, describe important sights, using maps, photographs, and illustrations. Tips for hotels, restaurants, shops, entertainment, and sports are found in *Travelers' Needs*. The final section, *Survival Guide,* contains practical advice on everything from personal security to using public transportation.

HONOLULU AND WAIKĪKĪ

This chapter is divided into three areas: Downtown Honolulu, Waikīkī, and Greater Honolulu. Each area has its own section that opens with a list of the sights described. All sights are numbered and plotted on the chapter's *Area Map*. Information on each sight is easy to locate as it follows the numerical order on the map.

Sights at a Glance lists the chapter's sights by category: Cathedrals and Churches, Museums and Galleries, Historic Streets and Buildings, Parks and Gardens, Cemeteries and Memorials.

Each area has colour-coded thumb tabs.

A locator map shows where you are in relation to other areas on the island of O'ahu.

1 Area Map
For easy reference, the sights in each area are numbered and plotted on a map. The sights are also shown on the Honolulu and Waikīkī Street Finder *(see pp76–9).*

2 Street-by-Street Map
This gives a bird's-eye view of the key areas in each chapter.

A suggested route for a walk is shown in red.

3 Detailed information
The sights in the three main areas are described individually. Addresses, telephone numbers, opening hours, admission charges, tours, photography, and wheelchair access are also provided, as well as public transportation links.

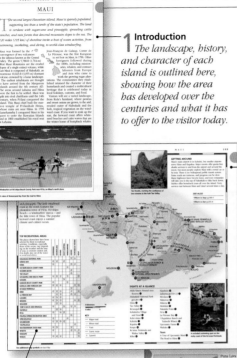

1 Introduction
The landscape, history, and character of each island is outlined here, showing how the area has developed over the centuries and what it has to offer to the visitor today.

HAWAI'I AREA BY AREA
Apart from an initial section on Honolulu and Waikīkī, the state has been divided into five island groups, each of which has a separate chapter. The most interesting towns and places to visit are numbered on a *Regional Map* at the beginning of each chapter.

2 Regional Map
This shows the main road network and gives an illustrated overview of the whole island group. All interesting places to visit are numbered and there are also useful tips on getting around the region.

Each area of Hawaii can be quickly identified by its colour coding, shown on the inside front cover.

A Recreational Areas Chart shows where to head for the top activities on each island.

3 Detailed information
All the important towns and other places to visit are described individually. They are listed in order, following the numbering on the Regional Map. *Within each town or city, there is detailed information on important buildings and other sights.*

A Visitors' Checklist provides the practical information you will need to plan your visit.

4 Hawai'i's top sights
These are given two or more full pages. Museums and galleries have color-coded floor plans to help locate the most interesting exhibits; national parks have maps showing facilities and trails.

INTRODUCING HAWAI'I

DISCOVERING HAWAIʻI

The only island state in the United States, each one of the major six Hawaiian islands has its own distinctive character. From the spectacular sun-drenched beaches and world-renowned surf enjoyed on Oʻahu to Maui's rugged coastlines,

Native hibiscus flower

Hawaiʻi Island's active volcano, peaceful Molokaʻi and Lānaʻi, and Kauaʻi's awe-inspiring lush beauty, this is a land of breathtaking extremes. The following pages are designed to help visitors pinpoint the highlights of each unique and fascinating island.

High-rise buildings bordering the famous beachfront at Waikīkī

HONOLULU AND WAIKĪKĪ

- World-class beaches
- Historic Capitol District
- Vibrant Chinatown
- Pearl Harbor

Honolulu is the state capital as well as Hawaiʻi's largest city. This sprawling urban metropolis includes **Waikīkī** *(see pp62–3)*, the center of the tourist industry, with thousands of high-rise hotels, restaurants, boutique stores, and nightclubs. The world famous golden sand and clear blue ocean in Waikīkī lure millions of visitors each year. Be sure to visit the statue on **Kūhiō Beach** *(see p65)* of Duke Kahanamoku, the father of modern surfing. Honolulu's Capitol District is a treasure of architecture, history, and culture. Highlights include the **State Capitol** *(see p55)*, **Kawaihaʻo Church** *(see p54)*, and, most glorious of all, **ʻIolani Palace** *(see p55)*. The state's most important

art collection is housed at the **Honolulu Museum of Art** *(see p71)*, and the nearby **Bishop Museum** *(see pp68–9)* offers a fascinating insight into Hawaiian culture. **Chinatown** *(see pp58–9)* is well worth exploring for the food markets, ethnic restaurants, *lei* sellers, antique shops, and art galleries. The relics and memorials of the infamous World War II site **Pearl Harbor** *(see p73)* draw 1.5 million visitors each year and should not be missed.

OʻAHU

- Snorkeling at Hanauma Bay
- Polynesian Cultural Center
- Legendary surf on the North Shore

Visitors who remain in Waikīkī miss much of Oʻahu's scenic and cultural beauty as well as its history.
 Snorkeling in shallow water with Hawaiʻi's myriad variety of reef fish is the major attraction at popular

Hanauma Bay *(see p65)*. The **Polynesian Cultural Center** *(see p92)* is Hawaiʻi's top visitor attraction. **Haleʻiwa** *(see pp92–3)* is the quaint town at the core of the surfing community. There are surf shops galore, boutiques, and a surfing museum. The town is also home to **Matsumoto's** *(see p199)* – Hawaiʻi's most famous shave ice spot. The North Shore is the site of some of the most spectacular surf in the world and each winter many world-class surf meets are held here. North Shore beaches are for extremely experienced and skilled surfers only.

Powerful breaks on Oʻahu's North Shore attract world-class surfers

MOLOKAʻI AND LĀNAʻI

- Enchanting Hālawa Valley
- Remote Kalaupapa
- The lunar landscape of Lānaʻi's Garden of the Gods

The idyllic islands of Molokaʻi and Lānaʻi provide a serene and remote retreat. **Kaunakakai** *(see p98)*, Molokaʻi's main town, is a charming location for a stroll. The untouched east side of the island is where visitors can experience Hawai'i's striking natural beauty. Sheltered **Hālawa Valley** *(see p99)* and **Kalaupapa National Historical Park** *(see pp100–1)* boast spectacular and haunting landscapes.

Once known as The Pineapple Isle, **Lāna'i** *(see pp104–5)* offers visitors a host of wonders. The **Garden of the Gods** *(see p105)* is a lunar-like landscape filled with rocks of every shape and size, formed by wind erosion over many millennia.

Sun-drenched 'Anaeho'omalu Bay, Hawai'i Island

Glowing red boulders at Garden of the Gods, Lāna'i

MAUI

- **The thriving town of Lahaina**
- **Hiking in 'Īao Valley**
- **Haleakalā National Park**
- **The rugged Hāna Coast**

The second largest island in the chain, Maui is the destination of choice for more than two million visitors each year. **Lahaina** *(see pp110–13)*, once the capital of the Hawaiian Islands, is packed with shops, galleries, restaurants, and tourists.

The Central Valley town of **Wailuku** *(see p118)* merits a visit. See Maui's largest collection of Hawaiian artifacts at Bailey House Museum and continue on to picturesque Kepaniwai Gardens. Nearby **'Īao Valley** *(see p119)* has excellent

hiking trails. To escape the crowds, **Upcountry Maui** *(see pp122–3)* offers incredible vistas, rolling pastureland, artistic **Makawao** *(see p123)*, and Maui's only winery, **Tedeschi Winery** *(see p121)*. Head to the magnificent and diverse slopes of **Haleakalā National Park** *(see pp128–9)* for a spectacular sunrise. The scenery along **The Road to Hāna** *(see pp124–5)* is stunning, with the ocean crashing against the cliff faces of the rugged coast.

HAWAI'I ISLAND

- **Lava flows at Hawai'i Volcanoes National Park**
- **Stunning beaches**
- **World-famous Kona coffee**

Experience the extraordinary thrill of seeing a continuously erupting volcano in **Hawai'i Volcanoes National Park** *(see p152–5)*. Extensive hiking trails give visitors a close-up view of the lava flows. Sun worshippers should head to Makalawena, a stunning beach on the Kona Coast near **Kekaha Kai State Park** *(see p134)*, **Hāpuna Bay** *(see p140)* on the Kohala Coast, or to the popular coconut-fringed white sand beach of 'Anaeho'omalu Bay, **Waikoloa Coast** *(see p137)*. Visit **Waimea** *(see p134)* to glimpse the tradition of *paniolo* (cowboy) culture. Kona district farms, famous for **Kona Coffee** *(see p135)* also merit exploration.

Nearby **Pu'uhonua O Hōnaunau National Historical Park** *(see pp138–9)* is one of the most sacred places in the Hawaiian island chain.

KAUA'I

- **The lush North Shore**
- **Magnificent Nā Pali Coast**
- **Dramatic Waimea**

Kaua'i's lush and tropical landscape is breathtaking. Visit the amazing North Shore, the nature preserve near **Kīlauea Point** *(see p164)*, atmospheric **Princeville** *(see p165)* and **Hanalei** *(see p166)*, and the Nā Pali Coast with **Kalalau Trail** *(see pp168–9)* winding through **Kalalau Valley** *(see p169)*. **Waimea Canyon and Kōke'e State Park** *(see pp170–71)* offers spectacular views.

Soaring cliffs lining Kaua'i's verdant Nā Pali coast

Putting Hawai'i on the Map

Hawai'i is an isolated archipelago in the middle of the
Pacific Ocean and is one of the United States. It consists
of eight main islands covering 6,425 sq miles (16,650 sq km).
Most visitors arrive in Honolulu, the state capital, and travel
to the other islands by inter-island flights or cruises.

Princeville

KAUA'I

Kapa'a

• Pu'uwai   Waimea   Līhu'e

Hanapēpē •   • Po'ipū

NI'IHAU

O'AHU

Waimea •   • Kahuku
        Hale'iwa   • Hau'ula
Mākua •
Mākaha •   • Wahiawa

Pearl City •   Kāne'o

⚓HONOLL

• Waik

← *Asia*

↓ *Australasia*

Satellite View of the Hawaiian Islands
*This image, from the north looking south, shows
the string of Hawaiian islands in the Pacific Ocean,
with Kaua'i and tiny Ni'ihau at the bottom right.*

← *Asia*

HAWAIIAN ISLANDS

| 0 kilometers | 1,500 |
| 0 miles | 1,000 |

• Seattle

CANADA

UNITED STATES
OF AMERICA

• San Francisco

• Los Angeles

MEXICO

CUBA

BELIZE
GUATEMALA / HONDURAS

NICARAGUA
COSTA RICA
PANAMA
COLOMBIA

⚐ ECUADOR

Isolated Archipelago
*Hawai'i is the most isolated
archipelago in the world,
lying 2,500 miles (4,000
km) from the nearest landmass – the west coast of
North America. In 1959 it
became the 50th state to
join the United States. It
has a population of over
1.3 million, with nearly 70
percent living on O'ahu.*

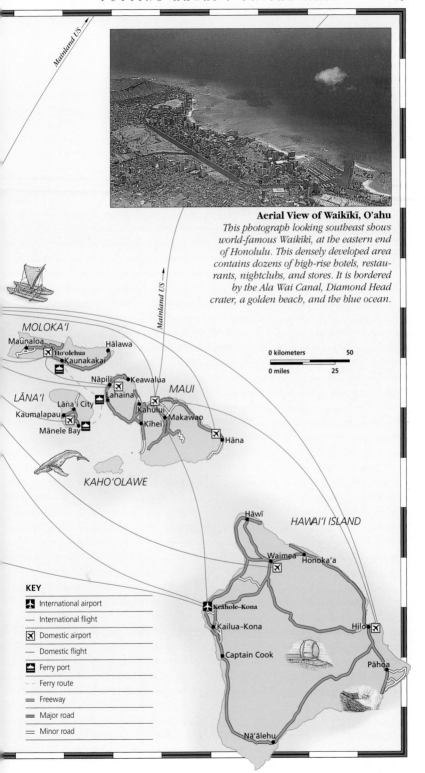

Mainland US

Aerial View of Waikīkī, O'ahu
*This photograph looking southeast shows
world-famous Waikīkī, at the eastern end
of Honolulu. This densely developed area
contains dozens of high-rise hotels, restaurants, nightclubs, and stores. It is bordered
by the Ala Wai Canal, Diamond Head
crater, a golden beach, and the blue ocean.*

MOLOKA'I

Maûnaloa
Ho'olehua
Kaunakakai
Hālawa

Nāpili
Keawalua
LĀNA'I
Lāna'i City
Lahaina
MAUI
Kaumalapau
Kahului
Mānele Bay
Kīhei
Makawao
Hāna

Mainland US

KAHO'OLAWE

0 kilometers   50

0 miles   25

Hāwī
HAWAI'I ISLAND

Waimea
Honoka'a

Keahole–Kona

Kailua–Kona
Hilo

Captain Cook

Pāhoa

Nā'ālehu

KEY

✈	International airport
—	International flight
☒	Domestic airport
—	Domestic flight
⛴	Ferry port
- -	Ferry route
═	Freeway
═	Major road
═	Minor road

A PORTRAIT OF HAWAI'I

Hawai'i is, quite simply, America's paradise. Its long stretches of white sand, crystal blue waters, swaying palms, and lush tropical rainforests dotted with pristine waterfalls attract millions of visitors each year. Hawai'i represents an ever-growing population encompassing a myriad of ethnic groups, development and tourism, agricultural diversity, and it is the homeland of a rich cultural heritage.

The most isolated land masses and the longest island chain on earth, the Hawaiian Islands were all formed by volcanic eruptions deep beneath the sea and are, technically, the summits of submerged volcanoes. Of the archipelago's numerous islands and atolls, the six main islands are O'ahu, Moloka'i, Lāna'i, Maui, Hawai'i Island, and Kaua'i. The state's unique topography is most vividly apparent on Hawai'i Island where the world's most active volcano, Kīlauea, has been erupting constantly since 1983. As Kīlauea's lava empties into the sea, the island continues to grow and change shape. The isolation of the Hawaiian islands and their diverse habitats have resulted in spectacular native flora and fauna. These impressive and fragile ecosystems are home to more endangered species than anywhere else in the world. Climates vary considerably, with 12 of the earth's 13 climactic zones represented. Windward coasts to the north and west receive more rainfall and are characterized by jagged cliffs, lush valleys, and dense foliage. The sunnier leeward sides to the south and west are drier and make ideal locations for popular tourist resorts.

Modern hula dancer

A pristine stretch of beach on Maui's north shore, with the West Maui mountains in the background

◁ Kīlauea volcano spewing molten lava, Hawai'i Island

Tourists flock to the clear blue waters of O'ahu's North Shore

TOURISM AND ECONOMICS

Tourism is, by far, the islands' biggest industry and it continues to grow annually. More than seven million people from around the globe visit the Hawaiian islands each year. Resort hotels, restaurants, retail outlets, and operators that organize sports activities dominate the industry. Military installations, including Pearl Harbor, are the second leading source of outside income. The agricultural industry remains an

One of Hawai'i's many surf schools

important facet of Hawai'i's economy. Major agricultural products include coffee, macadamia nuts, tropical flowers, cane sugar, pine-apples, bananas, and papayas. In addition to these larger agricultural ventures, small farmers are making a resurgence and are today driving a diversified agriculture movement thanks, in large measure, to their partnerships with island chefs. A myriad variety of vegetables, herbs, beef cattle, and locally grown and produced foodstuffs now appear on restaurant menus throughout the islands.

Hawai'i's strategic location in the Pacific Rim also fuels the state's modern economy. Hi-tech companies and financial institutions establish themselves here, the closest place in the United States to the markets of Asia.

PEOPLE AND SOCIETY

To call Hawai'i an ethnic melting pot is an understatement. Immigration to these islands started more than six

Pineapple plantation, West Maui

centuries ago, with the arrival of the first Polynesian settlers, and continued during the plantation era with waves of Chinese, Portuguese, Japanese, Filipino, Korean, German, and Puerto Rican laborers. Today, more ethnic and cultural groups are represented in Hawai'i than in any other state. Each group has brought traditions that have been tightly woven into the fabric of modern Hawaiian life.

The tradition of removing one's shoes before entering a home, the annual O-Bon and Floating Lantern Festival which honors ancestors,

Crafting of a canoe using traditional methods

the proliferation of sushi restaurants, and the extreme reverence for elders are all Japanese customs that today know few ethnic boundaries. The roots of the cattle industry, ranches, rodeos, 'ukulele music, and sweet bread lie in the influx of Portuguese immigrants in the 19th century.

CULTURE AND THE ARTS

Hawai'i's cultural renaissance began in the late 1970s and continues to grow strongly and steadily to this day. There are many organizations and workshops dedicated to the preservation and perpetuation of the Hawaiian culture. Most important is the revival of the Hawaiian language in recent years.

Traditional Hawaiian chanter

A lively contemporary music scene also flourishes throughout the islands which blends mainstream reggae, rock 'n' roll, and jazz with more traditional sounds, including Hawaiian slack key guitar. It is still possible to see traditional *hula* performances, and the arts of Polynesian navigation and *lua,* a Hawaiian martial art, are also thriving. Hawaiian crafts – such as the making of hula implements, feather *lei* (garlands), and weaving – are also experiencing a welcome revival. And, of course, the ancient sports of surfing and canoe paddling are more popular than ever.

Artists from all over the world have been inspired by the people and beauty of Hawai'i, and Western and Asian visual and performing arts are very well represented. Honolulu boasts two world-class art institutions – the Honolulu Academy of Arts and The Contemporary Museum – and all of the islands are home to a number of galleries and artists' studios.

Floating lanterns at the annual O-Bon festival, Honolulu

Formation of the Hawaiian Islands

The Hawaiian Islands are the tips of a large chain of volcanoes stretching almost 3,100 miles (5,000 km) from Hawai'i Island to the Aleutian Trench in the north Pacific. Most are now underwater stumps, fringed by coral reefs, but many were once great shield (dome-shaped) volcanoes. The oldest, northernmost volcano is slowly disappearing into the Aleutian Trench. The youngest volcano – Kīlauea – today spews out basaltic lava, creating new land on Hawai'i Island. This cycle of destruction and creation, driven by the conveyor-belt movement of the Pacific plate over a stationary hot spot of magma, has been occurring for 70 million years.

Moloka'i's sea cliffs (see pp100–1) *constitute the back wall of giant landslide scars formed when half of the Wailau shield volcano slumped into the sea. Marine erosion keeps the cliffs steep by undercutting the bases.*

The areas of undulating ocean floor are deposits of giant landslides. Little is known about them because they sit in deep water, and their precise age of formation is unknown.

O'AHU

KAUA'I

NI'IHAU

Stretching almost halfway along O'ahu, the spectacular Nu'uanu Pali (cliffs) formed when a large section of the Ko'olau shield volcano slumped into the sea.

Ocean floor

The Pacific plate moves northwesterly at a rate of 2–3.5 in (5–9 cm) a year.

Kaua'i's *amazing Waimea Canyon (see pp170–71) is carved into the Wai'ale'ale shield volcano. The layers of lava flows that created the volcano are visible. Large canyons of this nature are typical of Hawaiian volcanoes in their late erosional stage.*

CONVEYOR BELT

As it moves, the Pacific plate – the huge slab of earth's crust underlying the Pacific Ocean – rides over a stationary hot spot (mantle plume) that feeds heat and basaltic magma toward the surface. Mauna Loa, Kīlauea, and the "new" underwater volcano Lō'ihi, are presently over the hot spot. As the plate moves to the northwest, volcanoes are gradually pulled off the hot spot while new volcanoes grow in their place.

O'ahu's Hanauma Bay (see p88) *is a late-stage volcanic crater, one of several forming a line of cones, craters, and vents caused by an eruption at least 10,000 years ago. The ash cones are the result of explosive interaction of rising magma with sea water. Either the bay's present shape is due to breaching of the crater wall or, more likely, the wall was never complete.*

Maui's Haleakalā (see pp128–9), *in its erosional, middle to late stage, is Hawai'i's only active shield volcano outside Hawai'i Island. Its last lava eruption was in 1790. Young cones and lava flows occur in and around the misnamed crater – actually an erosional depression formed where two large valleys coalesced.*

VOLCANO LIFE CYCLE

Shield volcanoes form while over a hot spot. As they move off it, volcanic activity decreases and erosion begins. Late stage volcanoes occur from a magma source deeper than the hot spot. Eventually volcanoes disappear under the ocean surface.

1. Formation below sea level

2. Shield-building stage

3. Caldera stage

4. Erosional stage

5. Post-erosional late stage volcano

6. Atoll stage

MOLOKA'I
KAHO'OLAWE
LĀNA'I
MAUI
HAWAI'I ISLAND
Mauna Kea
Rift zone

Kīlauea, a growing volcano perhaps calved off Mauna Loa some 200,000 years ago, has been erupting since 1983 and shows no sign of stopping *(see pp152–3)*. During this period lava has extended the coastline and formed about 2 sq miles (5 sq km) of new land.

Volcanic material

Lō'ihi, Hawai'i's newest shield volcano, lurks nearly 1 mile (1.5 km) below the ocean surface and is not expected to emerge for 100,000 to 200,000 years. It has all the features of a Hawaiian shield volcano, but none of its eruptions has broken the surface.

Main conduit   Vent   Lithosphere   Underplating
Hot spot

Magma reservoir

Mauna Loa *(see p147)* makes up over one-half the volume of Hawai'i Island.

Hawai'i Island's Mauna Kea *(shown here) and Mauna Loa, a pair of giant shield volcanoes, are hard to distinguish at their base beneath the sea. Mauna Kea (see p146) is older, in its post-shield stage with many smaller cones, giving it a rough appearance. Bulkier Mauna Loa's mass is so heavy that it has depressed the ocean floor. Together they make up the earth's largest single volcanic structure.*

Flora of the Hawaiian Islands

Prior to human settlement, the location of the Hawaiian islands in the middle of the Pacific Ocean was a natural barrier to the colonization of plants from other parts of the world. In prehistoric times, fewer than 300 immigrant flowering plant species – seeds borne by wind, carried by birds, or drifting on the ocean – colonized the islands. Extreme isolation produced a limited flora in comparison with continental floras; for example, Hawai'i has only three native orchids out of a worldwide family of 20,000 species. Some species evolved into new forms able to exploit a wide variety of habitats. Thorns and other defensive adaptations have largely been lost in Hawaiian plants as they conferred no advantage in a flora isolated from natural predators. As a result, native flora is unique, with 89 percent of its flowering species found only in Hawai'i.

Koa *is one of the most important forest trees in the Hawaiian islands. The largest specimens can attain heights of over 115 ft (35 m), and their huge trunks were used by Hawaiians to make voyaging canoes.*

Grasses are found in virtually all vegetation zones, occasionally as the dominant species. In dry, lowland areas *pili* grasslands provided thatching material for early Hawaiians *(see p69).* About 150 native and naturalized species of this important and large family occur in Hawai'i.

'Ōhi'a lehua, *probably the most common tree in the Hawaiian flora, occurs from near sea level to elevations of 7,200 ft (2,200 m). It is also one of the most variable, with mature forms ranging from a few inches in bog habitats to 80 ft (24 m) or more in forest habitats. Epiphytes and a tree fern understory also characterize wet 'ōhi'a lehua forests.*

Iliau, a relative of the silversword

Hibiscus, *a favorite flower, is represented here by* koki'o, *one of seven native species and hundreds of ornamental varieties and hybrids in Hawai'i.*

Palm trees imported from Polynesia

Bougainvillea imported from Brazil

Pōhuehue, a typical beachfront plant

Naupaka *is a dune-binding shrub with distinctive "half" flowers. Ocean currents have dispersed its buoyant fruits throughout the Pacific Basin. Scientists believe that two separate colonizations account for eight endemic species growing in a variety of upland habitats.*

'Ākala, *or native Hawaiian raspberries, appear to have lost an unnecessary defense mechanism (thorns in this case) that was present in their continental ancestors.*

The silversword, *or 'āhinahina (see p129), occurs on Maui and Hawai'i Island in alpine desert habitats to elevations of over 12,000 ft (3,650 m). This species, together with the bog greensword and 25 other shrubs, trees, and a liana, actually evolved in the Hawaiian islands from one single ancestral immigrant.*

VEGETATION ZONES

Alpine vegetation, *a sparse array of shrubs dominated by silverswords and kūpaoa, occurs at 9,850–11,150 ft (3,000–3,400 m). A harsh, dry zone, it may freeze at night.*

Subalpine communities *occur in a relatively cool, dry zone from about 5,575–9,850 ft (1,700–3,000 m). Vegetation varies from grassland or shrubland to stunted trees.*

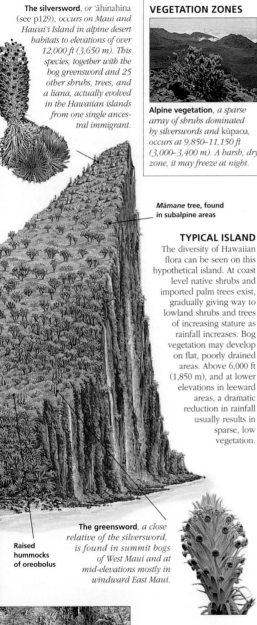

Māmane tree, found in subalpine areas

TYPICAL ISLAND
The diversity of Hawaiian flora can be seen on this hypothetical island. At coast level native shrubs and imported palm trees exist, gradually giving way to lowland shrubs and trees of increasing stature as rainfall increases. Bog vegetation may develop on flat, poorly drained areas. Above 6,000 ft (1,850 m), and at lower elevations in leeward areas, a dramatic reduction in rainfall usually results in sparse, low vegetation.

Raised hummocks of oreobolus

The greensword, *a close relative of the silversword, is found in summit bogs of West Maui and at mid-elevations mostly in windward East Maui.*

Montane dry areas *are characteristic of leeward slopes at an elevation of 1,650–8,850 ft (500–2,700 m). Vegetation varies from dry grasslands to dry forests with a canopy 10–65 ft (3–20 m) high.*

Montane wetlands, *in areas of high rainfall at elevations of 3,950–7,200 ft (1,200–2,200 m), include wet herblands, sedgelands, shrublands, bogs, and forests with canopies up to 130 ft (40 m) high.*

Lowland and coastal communities *include a diverse array of dry, medium, and wet herb, grass, shrub, and forest vegetation occurring below 5,000 ft (1,500 m) elevation.*

Tropical plants *from around the world thrive in Hawai'i. This lush planting on O'ahu includes giant aroids and bananas. Alien plants pose a real threat to native species by displacing them and preventing their regeneration.*

Marine Life of Hawai'i

Parrot fish

Hawai'i's remote location in the middle of the Pacific Ocean supports a rich population of marine life and a relatively undisturbed coral reef habitat. This dynamic reef ecosystem is home to more than 7,000 marine species, of which approximately one third are unique to the Hawaiian Islands. It is also home to many endangered species which are protected under the 1973 Endangered Species Act, including Hawaiian monk seals and green sea turtles. In 2006, the Northwestern Hawaiian Islands National Monument was created in order to protect 140,000 sq miles (360,000 sq km) of this precious marine habitat, including ten islands and atolls, making this the largest area dedicated to marine conservation in the world.

Humuhumunukunukuāoua'a (reef triggerfish) *is the designated state fish of Hawai'i. Its name means "triggerfish with a snout like a pig". With sharp teeth and powerful jaws, it feeds off molluscs and crustaceans.*

Cauliflower coral has heavy, leaf-like branches.

Corals are living animals that eat, grow, and reproduce.

Urchins inhabit crevices in the coral reef.

Antler coral, *common in Hawai'i, is usually found in depths of 35 ft (11 m) to 150 ft (46 m). Its branches resemble moose antlers.*

The seven eleven crab *has seven prominent spots on the top of its shell and four more along the bottom for a total of eleven. It is most commonly seen at night.*

The pencil-slate sea urchin *is bright red and has large, blunt, pencil-thick spines.*

The green sea turtle *measures more than 3 ft (1 m) across and weighs up to 220 lbs (100 kg). Once a food source for islanders, it is now a protected species.*

SHARKS OF THE COASTLINE

There are about 40 species of sharks found in Hawaiian waters, ranging in size from the deep-water pygmy shark, about 0.7 ft (0.2 m) long, to the whale shark, up to 50 ft (15 m) long. The most frequently encountered near Hawaiian reefs are the whitetip reef, hammerhead, and, occasionally, tiger sharks. Sharks are essential in maintaining the balance of the ecosystem.

Whitetip reef shark

Hammerhead shark

CORAL REEFS

Hawai'i's coral reefs are home to thousands of fish and other sea animals and plants that come in every size, shape, and color imaginable. The reefs house the majority of coral found in U.S. waters. They grow only 0.25 inches (0.6 cm) each year.

Moorish Idols are brightly-colored and move gracefully through the water feeding off the coral.

Butterfly fish live in depths of less than 20 ft (6 m). There are 25 species in Hawaiian waters.

The octopus *is a master of camouflage. It escapes detection by changing its color to match its environment.*

The Hawaiian stilt *is a rare and threatened species. This slender wading bird with long pink "stilt" legs is endemic to the Hawaiian island chain. It can grow up to 1.3 ft (0.4 m) tall.*

Spinner dolphins *are the most common dolphin species in Hawai'i. They can be observed daily off the coast of O'ahu.*

Hawaiian monk seals*, so named because their folds of skin resemble a monk's hood, are the most endangered marine mammal in the U.S. Adults can grow to 600 lbs (272 kg).*

Voices of Hawai'i

David Malo

Ancient Hawai'i produced a wealth of oral literature and myth, which was passed down from generation to generation. A 12-letter alphabet, the smallest in the world, was developed by the missionaries in the early 19th century. Notable literary visitors wrote accounts of the islands and completed other works during their stays. Today, a new generation of Hawaiians is creating modern native literature, while maintaining a profound respect for the myths and chants that perpetuate the old ways of Hawai'i.

The demigod Maui fishing the Hawaiian islands out of the sea

ORAL TRADITION

The oral traditions of pre-contact Hawai'i played a vital role in island life. The literature, committed to memory, was often chanted to the accompaniment of music and dance. There were *oli* (chants), *mo'olelo* (stories and narratives), *mele* (songs), and *'ōlelo no'eau* (proverbs). The *kāhuna* (priests) composed and recited poetry to preserve history, genealogies, and the knowledge of traditional crafts. *Haku mele* (composers) often composed verses for special occasions, such as the birth of an *ali'i* (royal) child; such songs were considered sacred.

The *haku mele* took advantage of the fact that many words sound alike, building on repetitions and word play. The similarity of words was not considered accidental; if a sea creature's name matched that of a geographical feature, these phenomena were considered *kino*, manifestations of the same spiritual force.

The most famous creation chant, the *Kumulipo*, tells of life and the islands growing up gradually, on their own initiative. The progenitors of

19th-century image of Kū

humans were the male *Wākea* (the Heavens) and the female *Papa* (the Earth). Hawaiians venerated four main gods: Kāne (light, life, water), Lono (productivity of the land), Kū (war, courage), and Kanaloa (sea). Each had numerous manifestations, all with names, and their deeds were visible in everyday nature. Stories tell of Pele, the fiery-tempered volcano goddess who migrated from *Kahiki* (Tahiti, or simply the distant homeland) seeking a dry place for her eternal fires. Tracing the geological evolution of the islands, she resided first on Kaua'i and then O'ahu before settling for a time in Maui's Haleakalā Crater. She now lives in Hawai'i Island's Kīlauea Caldera (*see pp152–3*).

Myths are told of Pele's entire clan, especially of her jealous relationship with her beautiful youngest sister, Hi'iaka, the first dancer of the *hula*. Pele's opponent in many stories is the shape-shifting pig-man Kamapua'a, a carnal, violent manifestation of Lono. Representing the productivity of the mountains and fields, his unending quest is to tame and fertilize the destructive goddess of lava. A cinder cone near Hāna on Maui is called Ka Iwi o Pele, or Pele's bones (*see p125*), because the two titans met there for a cataclysmic battle.

Other stories tell of Maui, the Prometheus of Hawaiian mythology, who brought fire to the human race, lifted the roof of the heavens, slowed the speed of the sun, and fished the islands out of the sea with a magic hook.

EARLY RECORDS

The first written words about Hawai'i are found in the logbooks and journals of the early visitors. Thomas Manby, on an expedition in 1791, wrote candidly of the seamen's amorous relations with Hawaiian women and gave a humorous portrait of Kamehameha I's first sight of a cow – startled, the great warrior knocked over half his retinue fleeing for his life.

The first missionaries kept more restrained records. The Reverend Hiram Bingham, leader of the first mission in

An 1834 edition of *Ka Lama Hawaii* (The Hawaiian Luminary)

1820, set the pattern with his *Missionaries versus Man-of-Warsmen*. Within 14 years of their arrival the missionaries had created a Hawaiian alphabet, translated the Bible, established a printing press, and put out the first Hawaiian language newspaper, *Ka Lama Hawaii*.

Native oral tradition was suppressed but never lost during this time. Traditional songs *(mele)* passed through the filter of hymns *(himeni)* and the introduction of the guitar and *'ukulele* to emerge as "Hawaiian music." King Kalākaua (1874–91) started a renaissance of Hawaiian culture by calling for a revival of the *mele*, chants, and *hula*. In the same era, scholarly converts such as Samuel M. Kamakau and David Malo wrote invaluable records of life in precontact Hawai'i.

Jack and Charmian London on Waikīkī Beach in 1915

Portrait of Robert Louis Stevenson by Girolamo Piero Nerli (1892)

LITERARY VISITORS

In the opening chapter of Herman Melville's *Moby Dick*, Ishmael says, "I love to sail forbidden seas and land on barbarous coasts." This urge to explore exotic realms was an echo of that felt by Ishmael's creator and many other writers, and in the 1800s the lure of the South Seas was particularly strong. In 1843, Melville himself spent four months in Hawai'i, working in a Honolulu bowling alley and beachcombing in Lahaina.

Following in Melville's footsteps, the 31-year-old Mark Twain explored the islands in 1866 as a correspondent for the *Sacramento Union*. While touring, he wrote a series of *Letters from the Sandwich Islands* and later put several chapters about Hawai'i in his book *Roughing It*. Though he never visited again, he wrote that "no other land could so lovingly and so beseechingly haunt me, sleeping and waking, through half a lifetime, as that one has done."

In 1889, the Scottish writer Robert Louis Stevenson dined with King David Kalākaua. Suffering from tuberculosis, the author of *Treasure Island* traveled the South Seas from 1888 until his death in 1894. In Hawai'i he befriended the royal family, studied the language, and visited Kalaupapa leprosy colony *(see pp100–1)*. Stevenson worked at fever pitch during his five-month visit, finishing *The Master of Ballantrae*, conceiving his novel *The Wrecker*, roughing out a collection of sketches about Hawai'i called *The Eight Islands*, and writing numerous poems and letters. Two of his best stories, "The Bottle Imp" and "The Isle of Voices," were also penned here.

Jack London arrived in Honolulu aboard his yacht *Snark* in 1907. The islands became his second home and

where he wrote some of his famous works, such as *The Call of the Wild* and *White Fang*. He was the first literary figure to call himself a *kama'āina* (child of the land). His volumes of island-set stories, *On The Makaloa Mat* and *The House of Pride*, angered the authorities by depicting racial snobbery and the cruelty of official responses to leprosy.

HAWAI'I CALLS

Twentieth-century tourism produced a new mythology, casting the islands as a "paradise" filled with relaxed, *'ukulele*-strumming natives. A surge of interest in 1916 stimulated songs such as "Oh, How She Could Yacki Hacki Wicki Wacki Woo (That's Love In Honolu)." A second wave in the 1930s prompted a string of Hollywood Waikīkī fantasies, including the 1936 film *Honolulu*, which turned *hula* into a form of tap dance.

Today, the Hawai'i Visitors and Convention Bureau continues to romanticize Hawai'i. However, island-born writers such as Oswald A. Bushnell and Milton Murayama are creating a wealth of native literature. With support from local intellectuals, many now write in pidgin, the hybrid language that evolved on the plantations so that different ethnic groups could communicate. The stories of Lois-Ann Yamanaka, for example, have received international acclaim.

Wild Meat and the Bully Burgers, a novel by Lois-Ann Yamanaka

Hula and Hawaiian Music

Traditional *'uli'uli* rattle

Hula began, it is believed, as a form of religious ritual to honor the ancient gods and chiefs while providing entertainment for the ruling classes. The traditional *hula kāhiko* was accompanied only by the human voice through chants *(oli)* or song *(mele)*, and by percussion instruments. In the early 19th century the missionaries tried to abolish *hula* but succeeded only in driving it underground. King Kalākaua, the Merrie Monarch, encouraged the revival of *hula* in the late 19th century, giving rise to the modern *hula 'auwana*. This style was influenced by Western music and clothing – women wore, and still do, long-sleeved, floor-length dresses *(holokū)*. The 1930s ushered in the "Sweet Leilani" era when dancers in cellophane skirts and flower *lei* greeted the ocean liners bringing tourists to Honolulu. Today *hula* enjoys great respect.

This 19th-century engraving *is a European interpretation of a native woman with traditional tattoos dancing* hula noho *(sitting hula) in a* kapa *skirt.*

The earliest hula *was, some say, the domain of men, although there is no documented evidence. However, there has been a great resurgence of male* hula *in recent years.*

Knee-length *ti*-leaf **skirts** are worn in *hula kāhiko*. The flat leaves rustle with the dancers' movements.

Dog-tooth leg ornaments, *or* kūpe'e niho 'ilio, *were traditionally worn exclusively by male dancers. Only four teeth from each dog were used, and it took nearly 3,000 dogs to make some ornaments.*

The 'uli'uli is a small gourd containing seeds and fitted with a handle. It is often decorated with feathers.

The ipu heke *is a percussion instrument made of two gourds. It is the most common accompaniment for* hula kāhiko. *The* kumu *(teacher) here is wearing a dried* ti-leaf *cape, which originally would have functioned as a raincoat.*

The standing pahu drum *is traditionally made from a section of coconut tree covered with shark skin, played with the hands. Pahu are often used in conjunction with the smaller* pūniu – *a drum made of coconut, lashed to the chanter's right thigh and played with a thong of braided fiber.*

WHERE TO ENJOY HULA AND MUSIC

Merrie Monarch Festival *(p37)*
Polynesian Cultural
Center *(p92)*
Moloka'i Ka Hula Piko *(p34)*
Prince Lot Hula Festival *(p35)*
Nā Mele O Maui *(p36)*

Pū'ili are made of bamboo; one end is a handle and the other is split into a narrow "fringe" that makes a rattling sound.

This group of kūpuna *(respected elders) dressed in* mu'umu'u *are singing and playing instruments that typically accompany* hula 'auwana – 'ukulele, guitar, and standing bass. The *ipu heke and* 'uli'uli *lying in the foreground are used for* hula kāhiko.

The 'ukulele is one of many instruments brought to Hawai'i by immigrants, in this case the Portuguese. It is integral to contemporary Hawaiian music.

Flower lei are not authentic to *hula kāhiko*; dancers traditionally wear fern anklets and bracelets.

Maui's Keali'i Reichel *is a well-known chanter, hula dancer, singer, composer, and teacher dedicated to the preservation of the culture.*

HULA KĀHIKO

This old form of *hula* is shown here with contemporary twists. The *ti*-leaf skirts, *pū'ili*, and *'uli'uli* are traditional, while the plumeria flower *lei* and colorful fabric tops are modern. Visitors can see this combined style of old and new elements on all the Hawaiian islands.

THE REVIVAL OF HULA AND HAWAIIAN MUSIC

Today *hula kāhiko* is pursued by hundreds of students performing the same chants and using the same instruments as their ancestors, and *hula 'auwana* is more popular than in King Kalākaua's time. *Hula*'s connection to Hawaiian music is inextricable. The "music" accompanying traditional dancers took the form of musical poetry – chants and song. When Western musical influence became widespread, *hula* embraced it in the *'auwana* style. In the early 19th century missionaries brought sober hymns to Hawai'i, and increased sea traffic brought musicians from Europe and Asia with their varied secular music. The era from 1900 to the Hawaiian Renaissance of the 1970s saw an explosion of *hapa haole* – Hawaiian music influenced by ragtime, Tin Pan Alley, and even orchestrations from films and television shows. The instruments brought by immigrants – *'ukulele*, Hawaiian guitar, standing bass, piano – were stirred into the musical pot. The ongoing Hawaiian Renaissance has brought an enthusiastic revival of early Hawaiian music.

Child dancing hula kāhiko

Traditional Hawaiian Crafts

What we consider crafts today – woven baskets, feather *lei* (garlands), *poi* (taro paste) pounders, wooden bowls – were integral to the lives of ancient Hawaiians. They were made with care from readily available sources, such as coconut fronds, feathers of the *mamo* bird, local stone, and native *koa* wood. Many crafts are still made in the old, precontact ways. Even the ancient, almost lost art of beating and printing *kapa* (bark cloth) is undergoing a revival. Traditional implements are often favored over the modern, but certain tools have been updated. For instance, metal needles for stringing *lei* have replaced those made from coconut palm frond midribs. Not all crafts are indigenous. The missionaries introduced quilting, an art that is still passed from generation to generation *(see p68)*. Both the ancient and modern crafts are time-consuming pursuits requiring patience and skill – not unusual attributes among Hawaiians.

Netting *was the most efficient method of fishing in old Hawai'i. The best nets were made with a netting needle and mesh gauge, using cord from the* olonā *shrub.*

These two wooden bowls*, connected by a human figure crowned with feathers, were probably used by an ali'i (chief) for Poi (taro paste) or 'awa (a ceremonial drink).*

THE STARBUCK CAPE

This superb 19th-century 'ahu'ula (cape) with a unique geometric pattern was made with the feathers of thousands of birds, which were released after giving up just a few feathers each. It was probably given to Captain Starbuck by Kamehameha II, who with his wife sailed to London on the captain's ship in 1824.

Feathers were arranged by size, tied together at the quills, and attached to the net with *olonā* thread.

Decorating *kapa* cloth

KAPA CLOTH

Common garments (*'a'ahu*) in ancient Hawai'i were made of *kapa* (bark cloth). The *wauke* (paper mulberry tree) produced the best cloth, which was pounded with wooden *kapa* beaters. Using dyes from native plants in every imaginable hue, bamboo implements were used to stamp patterns on the cloth. Today *kapa* is still made for certain ceremonies and is highly regarded for its variety of textures and beautiful, intricate designs.

This late 18th-century pe'ahi *(fan) is made out of coconut leaves, human hair, cordage, and dyes. Fans with this distinctive shape were probably used exclusively by the ali'i (chiefs).*

Gourds with tubular necks *were used in ancient Hawai'i to hold drinking water. It is believed that dyes created with infusions of bruised leaves, bark, or black mud were used to make the dark patterns on gourd bowls and water containers. Gourds of different shapes and sizes were also used as percussion instruments (see pp26–7).*

HAWAIIAN LEI

Lei are wreaths or garlands, made of flowers, leaves, shells, nuts, or feathers, which are worn around the neck. They range from simple strings of blossoms to complex woven garlands of native leaves and plants. *Lei* have always been important symbols of affection in Hawai'i and are bestowed frequently with a kiss. They are worn by everyone with pride on Lei Day *(see p34).*

Two-ply cord made from the bark of the *olonā* shrub was used in the net foundation and the fasteners.

The irregular black shapes are made from the feathers of the '*ō'ō* bird. Black feathers were rarely used.

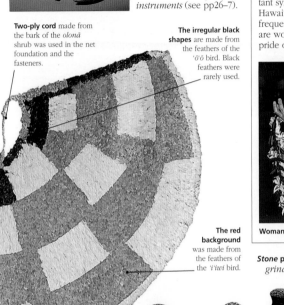

The red background was made from the feathers of the '*i'iwi* bird.

Woman with colorful flower *lei*

The '*ō'ō* bird also provided the bright yellow feathers.

Stone poi pounders *were used to grind taro (see p125), a vital food source, into poi (a thick paste eaten with the fingers). It was heavy work, done by men who sat at a wooden pounding board, which was moistened with water, and mashed the cooked taro.*

TRADITIONAL BRAIDING

In ancient Hawai'i, braiding or weaving was an important method of creating everyday objects, such as floor coverings, sleeping mats, pillows, baskets, and fans. *Lauhala* – the large leaves *(lau)* of the pandanus tree *(hala)* – were one of the most common materials. Sedge grass, including the coveted fine sedge *makaloa*, and certain palms were also used. The most extraordinary sleeping mats were made of *makaloa* on the island of Ni'ihau. In preparing the leaves for braiding, the weaver had to be careful because their edges and spines were sharp. Today, coconut palm fronds are commonly woven into hats and baskets. Generally speaking, the tighter the weave, the more valuable the item.

Coconut frond hat

Stiff, sharp leaves used as braiding material

Surfing in Hawai'i

Sign for Hale'iwa, O'ahu's surf town

Past and present, surfing has occupied an honored place in Hawaiian culture. Though its exact origins are unclear, *he'e nalu* (wave sliding) has been practiced here for centuries. The sport was dominated by the *ali'i* (chiefs), who had their own surf breaks that commoners were not permitted to enjoy; Kamehameha the Great himself was an avid wave rider. In the 19th century the sport went into decline after the missionaries discouraged it. A revival started in the early 20th century when Waikīkī became an international playground. Today the islands remain the ultimate place to surf.

Hawaiian surfers *ride the waves in this 19th-century engraving. In ancient times, entire villages flocked to the beach when the surf was up.*

The face of the wave, just before it breaks, is where the energy is most concentrated.

Duke Kahanamoku, *shown here with fellow surfers in front of the Moana Hotel c.1915, was the father of modern surfing (see p65). The Duke was a gifted surfer and the epitome of the carefree Waikīkī Beach life in the early 20th century.*

The surfer keeps knees bent and arms out for balance and to control speed and movement.

Most modern surfboards *are made of lightweight fiberglass and range in length from 6–12 ft (2–4 m). They usually have three fins attached to the underside of their tails, though longer boards may only have one.*

BANZAI PIPELINE

This spectacular wave on O'ahu's North Shore shows an expert surfer engulfed in a tube of water. He must maintain an exact position inside the "barrel" or risk being thrown over the "falls."

Long boards may be wide for riding gently sloped waves, like those of Waikīkī, or narrow for riding steep, very large waves, like those of Waimea Bay.

Short boards, the most maneuverable boards, are used for steep small- to medium-size waves. They are more difficult to stand on than long boards.

Fins add stability and maneuverability. They come in different shapes and sizes. In big waves, the fin would be backward and in small waves, it would be forward.

Boogie boards are small foam boards coated with fiberglass used to surf steep waves, often in shallow water. Riders lie flat on the boards and kick with fins to gain enough speed to catch the waves.

O'ahu's **North Shore** *sees towering waves from October to April, when storms sweep across the North Pacific producing powerful swell lines. Waimea Bay (above) has always been known for the largest waves that can be surfed.*

In the 1960s *daredevil surfers like American Mike Doyle, seen here with Duke Kahanamoku, came to Hawai'i in search of challenging surf. They found it on Oahu's North Shore, which soon became the surfing capital of the world.*

The wave breaks just behind the surfer, creating a cascade of spray and foam.

Special techniques *in surfing can involve the use of foot straps for aerial tricks, exotic board shapes, and towing by jet skis to surf giant waves.*

TRIPLE CROWN OF SURFING

Every year for three weeks in late November to mid-December O'ahu's North Shore is transformed into a surf carnival. During this time the Triple Crown of Surfing, the world's most prestigious series of surfing contests, takes place at Banzai Pipeline and Sunset Beach near Waimea, and at Ali'i Beach Park in Hale'iwa *(see p92)*. Giant waves and spectacular rides create a level of excitement and performance found almost nowhere else in surfing. The contests attract surfers from around the globe for competitions that often decide the world championship. The highlight is the PipeMasters at the Banzai Pipeline – the most coveted title in surfing. Live commentary makes the events accessible even to spectators watching surfing for the first time. Food is not generally available at the beach parks so spectators take a picnic.

Winners of O'ahu's famous Triple Crown, which is contested on waves bigger than 20 ft (6 m)

Scuba Diving and Snorkeling

Diving and snorkeling in Hawai'i is an experience like no other. The warm, crystalline waters teem with an incredible array of fish, coral, and other marine life. Visibility often exceeds 100 ft (33 m). Below the ocean's surface, the spectacular scenery includes reefs, lava formations, caves, and sandy plains. Beginners quickly get the hang of snorkeling. You can rent or buy a mask, snorkel, and fins on every island; if you go on a snorkeling boat excursion, instruction and gear are provided. Scuba diving usually takes place on the calmer, leeward sides of the islands. Instruction and gear are provided by dive shops and charter boats. Most offer introductory dives and internationally recognized certification courses. A wet suit is always recommended for scuba diving.

Snorkeling *is a popular pastime on each of the islands and there are many sites to choose from. It offers the chance to see schools of tropical fish and colorful marine life at close range.*

Kaua'i (see pp156–73) *has some of the best protected reef lagoons. Po'ipū Beach Park offers a sheltered, shallow cove ideal for novice snorkelers. Kaua'i is known for its rugged and pristine diving. Popular sites include General Store, a reef 65–80 ft (20–24 m) deep with a 19th-century sunken steamship.*

Brennecke's Ledge is best viewed from below, to spot long nose hawk fish and Hawaiian lionfish.

Mahi Shipwreck is a former minesweeper where lemon butterflyfish and other tropical species practically pose for photographs.

0 kilometres   50

0 miles   50

DIVE SITE RATINGS

There is a good variety of dive sites around the Hawaiian island chain. Divers should find out the level of experience required at any dive site before braving the waters.

	SNORKELING	NOVICE DIVING	ADVANCED DIVING	EXPERT DIVING
PO'IPŪ BEACH PARK ①	●	■		
GENERAL STORE ②			●	
BRENNECKE'S LEDGE ③			●	
HANAUMA BAY ④	●	■	●	■
HALE'IWA BEACH PARK ⑤	●	■	●	■
MAHI SHIPWRECK ⑥			●	
MURPHY'S BEACH ⑦	●	■		
FISH BOWL ⑧			●	■
HULOPO'E BEACH ⑨	●	■		
CATHEDRALS ⑩			●	
MOLOKINI ⑪	●	■	●	■
CARTHAGINIAN ⑫			●	
RICHARDSON'S BEACH PARK ⑬	●	■		

O'ahu (see pp84–93) *has dive sites that range from lava formations to shipwrecks. Hanauma Bay, the most popular snorkeling destination, is a natural "fish bowl". Originally the cone of a volcano, depths range from 15 ft (5 m) to 70 ft (21 m). Hale'iwa Beach Park is also good.*

Moloka'i (see pp94–103) *boasts the longest barrier reef in Hawai'i. The best snorkeling spots are between mile markers 18 and 20, heading east from Kaunakakai along Kamehameha V Highway, such as Murphy's Beach. Sites like Fish Bowl offer superb scuba diving, but are seldom visited due to weather and sea conditions.*

GETTING TO THE DIVE SITES

Organized diving excursions include equipment and transportation by boat or motor van. If you are certified and wish to dive on your own, you can get directions and maps at any dive shop when you pick up your equipment.
Getting there: *Each island has at least one major airport, and there are limited ferry services between Maui and the islands of Lāna'i and Moloka'i. See pages 12–13 for the location of airports, ferry ports, and major roads.*

Hulopo'e Beach on Lāna'i (see pp104–5) *is renowned for its snorkeling; it is edged by tide pools full of tiny fish and anemones. The most popular scuba site is Cathedrals, named for the size of its lava tubes and the stained-glass effect created by the sun's rays coming through holes in the lava ceiling.*

Most dive sites in Maui (see pp106–29) *are located off the west coast, including Molokini. Maui's newest scuba diving attraction is the Carthaginian, a replica of a double-masted brigantine, which was sunk in 2005 off Lahaina to create an artificial reef.*

Molokini *(see p121) is perfect for snorkelers and learner divers. Charter boats drop anchor here so both can view the abundant trumpetfish, octopus, and other marine life.*

On Hawai'i Island (see pp130–55), *Richardson's Beach Park, east of Hilo, is a good place for beginner snorkelers. The more adventurous can swim around the lava rock outcroppings to a reef with fish and sea turtles.*

HAWAI'I THROUGH THE YEAR

Contrary to popular belief, Hawai'i does have distinct seasons but only two: summer and winter. To residents, the distinctions are clear. It is summer if the mango tree in the garden is weighed down with fruit, or the intoxicating aroma of white ginger wafts in the air. Sudden rains or storms mean the onset of winter, as do the big waves that surfers eagerly await.

Statue decorated for King Kamehameha Day

Residents in the cooler upcountry areas of Kaua'i, Maui, and Hawai'i Island spend Christmas Eve gathered around the fireplace. A fair generalization for visitors is that May to October is hot and dry; November through April is slightly cooler and wetter. Happily for visitors, though, there are very few days during the year when Hawai'i's fine beaches do not beckon.

SUMMER

By May the winter rains have ceased and summer bursts into life all over the Hawaiian islands with blooming flowers and myriad festivals. **Lei Day** takes advantage of the abundance of scented flowers, with everyone donning a flowered garland. Hawai'i's oldest state holiday, **King Kamehameha Day**, dates back to 1872; there are many celebrations on all the islands to honor the great chief who united Hawai'i (see p41). All summer long there are cultural, music, and food festivals, as well as great sports competitions, from big rodeos to outrigger canoe races and the grueling **Ironman Triathlon**. The summer draws to a close with the grandest of all annual parties, the **Aloha Week Festivals**.

MAY

Lei Day (May 1), all islands. Everyone is adorned with at least one of these traditional Hawaiian garlands; lei-making contests are held on the islands of O'ahu and Kaua'i.
Moloka'i Ka Hula Piko (3rd Sat), Pāpōhaku Beach County Park (see p103), Moloka'i. This celebration of the birth of hula features music, dancing, food, and traditional crafts.
Hawaiian Steel Guitar Festival (early May), Kā'anapali, Maui. Concerts and workshops featuring the Island's only indigenous stringed instrument.
Memorial Day (last Mon), all islands. This national holiday commemorates soldiers who lost their lives in battle.

JUNE

Dolphin Days Summer Festival is a weekend of food, golf, and fun held at the Hilton Waikoloa Village Resort (see p189) on Hawai'i Island.
King Kamehameha Day (Jun 11 and surrounding days), all islands. This state holiday is celebrated with parades, hula and chant performances, crafts festivals, and much more. The biggest celebration is held at the Neal Blaisdell Center in Honolulu (see p219).
Hawaiian Slack Key Guitar Festival (June to Jul), Maui, O'ahu, and Hawai'i. This uniquely Hawaiian guitar tuning is used in performances by the state's best guitarists.
O-Bon Festivals (late Jun to end Aug), all islands. At every Buddhist temple in Hawai'i, Japanese Bon dancers honor their ancestors. There are spectacular floating lantern ceremonies in Lahaina, Maui, (Jul) and at Honolulu's Ala Wai Canal (Aug).

Dancers at the traditional Buddhist O-Bon Festival in Honolulu

JULY

Pu'uhonua O Hōnaunau Cultural Festival (weekend closest to Jul 1), Pu'uhonua O Hōnaunau National Historical Park (see pp138–9), Hawai'i Island. A royal court and demonstrations of traditional Hawaiian crafts.
Makawao Rodeo (weekend closest to Jul 4), Makawao (see p123), Maui. Hawai'i's biggest rodeo, where paniolo, Hawaiian cowboys (see p143), demonstrate their skill.

Crowd-pleasing bull-riding at the annual Makawao Rodeo

AVERAGE NUMBER OF SUNNY DAYS PER MONTH

Days

Jan Feb Mar Apr May Jun Jul Aug Sep Oct Nov Dec

Sunshine Chart
*Hawai'i has few days with-
out at least some sunshine,
with leeward (southwest)
coasts being, on the whole,
sunnier than windward
(northeast) ones. Blue skies
and warm days are thus
a fairly consistent feature,
except at higher altitudes,
which are often misty. The
chart gives the number of
days per month with little
or no cloud cover, aver-
aged across the islands.*

Parker Ranch Rodeo *(weekend closest to Jul 4)*, Waimea
(see p137), Hawai'i Island.
Set in the ranching heartland.
Prince Lot Hula Festival
(3rd Sat), Moanalua Gardens,
O'ahu. Local *hālau hula* (*hula*
schools) honor Prince Lot
(Kamehameha V) with both
the ancient and modern styles.
Kōloa Plantation Days *(late
Jul)*, Kōloa, Kaua'i. A parade
and other celebrations which
commemorate one of the first
sugar plantations to be
established in Hawai'i.

AUGUST

**Hawaiian International
Billfish Tournament**
*(late Jul to early Aug, or
1st half of Aug)*, Kailua-Kona
(see p134), Hawai'i Island.
The world's leading international marlin fishing
tournament. Fishermen
and avid fans are drawn
to this renowned event
from all over the world.

SEPTEMBER

Aloha Week *(mid-Sep to
late Oct)*, all islands. Dozens
of music and dance events,
craft fairs and demonstrations,
floral parades, delicious food,
and even a royal ball make
up this grandest of Hawai'i's
annual celebrations. The
festival begins on O'ahu and
continues on each of the
other main islands, lasting
a week on each island.
Kaua'i Mokihana Festival
(Sep or Oct), Lihu'e *(see
pp160–61)* and island-wide,
Kaua'i. This weeklong celebration showcases contemporary
Hawaiian music and *hula*,
with concerts and competitions.

Traditional costumes and flower-decked float at an Aloha Week parade

Nā Wahine O Ke Kai *(late
Sep)*, Hale O Lono, Moloka'i.
The most important women's
outrigger canoe race of the
year; finishes on O'ahu.

OCTOBER

**Princess Ka'iulani Keiki Hula
Festival** *(date varies)*, Princess
Ka'iluani Hotel, O'ahu. More
than 200 children, aged
between 5 and 12, from local
hula schools perform here.
Ironman Triathlon *(Sat
closest to full moon)*,
Kailua-Kona *(see p134)*,
Hawai'i Island. The ultimate
physical challenge for the
1,250 participants, this race
combines a
2.4- mile (3.8-km)
swim with a
112-mile (180-km)
bike ride before
finishing with
a grueling
26-mile (42-km)
marathon.
Coconut Festival
(early Oct),
Kapa'a Beach
Park *(see p163)*,
Kaua'i. The

cultural, social, and historical
importance of the versatile
fruit is celebrated with
coconut food items, crafts,
games, contests, and
entertainment.
Nā Moloka'i Hoe *(mid-Oct)*,
Hale O Lono, Moloka'i. More
than 50 men's teams from
around the world compete in
this outrigger canoe race to
O'ahu. It has become the
most important annual event
in the sport in the world.
**Halloween Mardi Gras
of the Pacific** *(Oct 31)*,
Lahaina *(see pp110–13)*,
Maui. The streets are closed
to all traffic for this rollicking
Halloween party.

Start of the Ironman Triathlon in Kailua-Kona

AVERAGE MONTHLY RAINFALL

MM · Inches

200 — 8
175
150 — 6
125
100 — 4
75
50 — 2
25
0 — 0

Jan Feb Mar Apr May Jun Jul Aug Sep Oct Nov Dec

Rainfall Chart
This two-tiered chart gives average figures for all of Hawai'i. The dark blue indicates rainfall on the sheltered, leeward coasts, while the light blue indicates the higher rainfall on the exposed windward coasts. The winter months, from November through April, receive the most rainfall, while the summer months, May to October, receive the least.

WINTER

In ancient Hawai'i, winter was the time of Lono, the god of agriculture and peace (*see p24*). Lono made himself known with extreme weather that could change from minute to minute. Traditionally, wars were concluded by the onset of winter, and it was time for the people and the land to rest from the year's labors.

November, December, and January are the most unpredictable months, but Hawaiian winters are generally mild, and there are many sports and cultural events. The remarkable **Triple Crown of Surfing** displays feats of great skill and courage, while major Pro-Am golf tournaments are held statewide. Winter ends with the famous **Merrie Monarch Festival** of *hula*.

NOVEMBER

Kona Coffee Cultural Festival, Kona district (*see p135*), Hawai'i Island. With parades, arts and crafts, gourmet tasting, and a coffee-picking contest, the Kona district pays homage to the bean that made it famous.

Float at the Kona Coffee Cultural Festival

Hawai'i International Film Festival (*early to mid-Nov*), all islands. Dozens of screenings, workshops, and symposia starting on O'ahu, and then running concurrently on the other islands. Except for some films on O'ahu, screenings are free.

Triple Crown of Surfing (*late Nov to mid-Dec*), North Shore (*see p92*), O'ahu. The world's most prestigious surfing competition, which spans three weeks (*see p31*), waves and weather permitting.

Thanksgiving Day (*4th Thu*), all islands. National holiday celebrated with family feasts.

Mission Houses Museum Annual Christmas Fair (*last weekend in Nov*), O'ahu. An open-air market features artists and crafts-people showing and selling Christmas-related handicrafts.

DECEMBER

Honolulu City Lights and Festival of Trees (*early Dec to early Jan*), Honolulu. A must-see display of lights and one-of-a-kind trees, all created by employees of different county and city departments.

Nā Mele O Maui (*1st weekend*), Kā'anapali (*see p114*), Maui. Cultural celebration of music featuring a student song contest to help preserve the knowledge and love of Hawaiian traditions.

Honolulu Marathon (*2nd Sun*), Honolulu. One of the most popular and scenic marathons in the US, it stretches 26 miles (42 km) from the Aloha Tower to Kapi'olani Park, drawing 15,000 runners.

Christmas (*Dec 25*), all islands. National holiday.

Sheraton Hawai'i Bowl (*Dec 25*), Aloha Stadium, O'ahu. Annual event contended by college football teams.

Lion dancer at the Narcissus Festival in Honolulu's Chinatown

JANUARY

Narcissus Festival (*Jan–Mar, lasting 12 weeks*), all islands. This celebration of the Chinese New Year features lion dances, fireworks, a coronation ball, and traditional food. Honolulu's Chinatown (*see pp58–9*) hosts the best parties.

Ka Moloka'i Makahiki (*late Jan*), Kaunakakai (*see p98*), Moloka'i. Week-long cultural festival beginning with a fishing contest in outrigger canoes. There are traditional Hawaiian games, sports, *hula*, and music.

Pacific Island Arts Festival (*Jan*), Kapiolani Park, Waikīkī. Annual exhibit of works by native artists.

AVERAGE MONTHLY TEMPERATURE

Temperature Chart
Hawai'i has consistently warm temperatures year round, with little variation between summer and winter. The coastal areas are warmest, particularly the leeward coasts, which are more sheltered from wind and rain. The upcountry and mountainous areas can be much cooler, with a marked difference in the mornings and evenings.

Sony Open in Hawai'i
(mid-Jan), Wai'alae Golf and Country Club, O'ahu. Major tournament on the PGA tour.

FEBRUARY

Cherry Blossom Festival
(late Jan or early Feb to Mar or early Apr), all over O'ahu. Japanese festival with tea ceremonies, cooking and flower arranging demonstrations, *mochi*-pounding, and traditional Taiko drumming.
Panaewa Stampede Bud Light Pro-Am Rodeo *(mid-Feb)*, Equestrian Center next to zoo outside Hilo *(see p148)*, Hawai'i. Professional and amateur cowboys and cowgirls compete for prizes.
NFL Pro Bowl *(early Feb)*, Aloha Stadium, O'ahu. NFL stars play a post-season game. Reserve tickets early.

The annual NFL Pro Bowl game at O'ahu's Aloha Stadium

MARCH

World Championship of Women's Bodyboarding
(mid-Mar–mid-Apr), Banzai Pipeline, north shore O'ahu. Pro women bodyboarders compete for prize money.

Hula dancers with their flower *leis* at the Merrie Monarch Festival

Ocean Arts Fest *(mid-Feb to early Mar)*, Banyan Tree Lahaina *(see pp110–13)*, Maui. Celebration of marine life and the humpback whales that spend winters in Maui's coastal waters *(see p115)*.
Prince Kūhiō Day *(Mar 26)*, all islands. Holiday in celebration of Hawai'i's first delegate to the US Congress and a well-liked "people's prince." There are ceremonies at the Federal Building in Honolulu.
Windward Orchid Society Annual Spring Show *(late Mar)*, O'ahu. Beautiful orchids on display in every imaginable hue. Demonstrations on plant care and plant sale.

APRIL

Easter Sunrise Service *(Easter Sun)*, National Memorial Cemetery of the Pacific *(see p71)*, Honolulu. An inspiring ceremony held at "Punchbowl" crater with views of the city.
Merrie Monarch Festival *(week starting Easter Sun)*, Hilo *(see pp148–9)*, Hawai'i Island. This week-long Hilo festival honoring King David

Kalākaua culminates with the "Olympics" of *hula*. Plan well in advance for this extremely popular event, as tickets sell out almost immediately.

PUBLIC HOLIDAYS

New Year's Day (Jan 1)
Martin Luther King Day (3rd Mon in Jan)
Presidents' Day (3rd Mon in Feb)
Prince Kūhiō Day (Mar 26)
Memorial Day (last Mon in May)
King Kamehameha Day (Jun 11)
Independence Day (Jul 4)
Admission Day (3rd Fri in Aug)
Labor Day (1st Mon in Sep)
Columbus Day (2nd Mon in Oct)
Election Day (1st Tue in Nov)
Veterans' Day (Nov 11)
Thanksgiving Day (4th Thu in Nov)
Christmas Day (Dec 25)

THE HISTORY OF HAWAI'I

Spanning less than 2,000 years, Hawaiian history is one of the briefest in the world, with much of it shrouded in legend. And yet it equals the world's best for bloodshed, irony, and heroism. Hawai'i has had to adapt to waves of invasion and immigration, and now supports one of the world's most ethnically diverse cultures.

The islands were formed by volcanic eruptions in the Pacific Ocean, more than 2,500 miles (4,000 km) from the nearest landmass. Life on the isolated Hawaiian archipelago evolved from wind-borne spores and seeds, corky fruits that drifted in the sea, and the occasional hardy bird blown off course by a storm. Sea creatures had difficulty reaching the islands, as the North Pacific currents push life-rich plankton away from Hawai'i. As a result, the unspoiled island ecosystem consisted of thousands of unique species that evolved by adapting to the new environment.

Ancient petroglyph from Hawai'i Island

The Polynesians, whose culture was established in the island clusters of Samoa and Tonga between 2,000 and 1,500 BC, possessed a remarkable seafaring technology. They traveled in twin-hulled voyaging canoes that carried up to 100 passengers plus planting stocks of crops (taro, coconut, sweet potato, banana) and pairs of domesticated animals (pigs, dogs, and chickens). These explorers colonized the Society Islands (Tahiti) and the Marquesas Islands in the first century AD. Around AD 300 the Marquesans dared the 3,000-mile (5,000-km) ocean crossing to discover the Hawaiian islands. Archaeologists have based this date on excavations of habitation sites at Waimānalo (O'ahu), Hālawa Valley (Moloka'i), and Ka Lae (Hawai'i Island). Hawaiian ancestral chants, which were rigorously preserved in oral tradition, carried family lines back further, to the first century.

Map from 1862 showing the Hawaiian archipelago and its location in the middle of the Pacific

◁ Early Hawaiians gathered around a thatched *hale* (house)

KĀNAKA MAOLI ("REAL PEOPLE")

The early Hawaiians established an advanced, spiritual culture. Dedicated farmers and stone-builders, they were the first to alter a landscape that had evolved in isolation for millions of years.

Hawaiian men dancing in front of a crowd

They divided the land into *ahupua'a*, pie-shaped wedges running from the mountaintop to the sea, providing each district with access to the full range of island resources. They also built monumental *heiau* (temples) and some of the largest irrigation systems in Polynesia.

Life centered on the *'ohana* (extended family) of 250 to 300 people, in which everyone from *keiki* (child) to *kupuna* (grandparent) was vital to the whole. Cultural values included *aloha 'āina* (love of land), *laulima* (cooperation), and *pa'ahana* (hard work).

INVASION OF THE ALI'I

During the 12th and 13th centuries, new waves of Polynesian settlers came from the Society Islands (Tahiti). According to oral tradition, the invasions were cruel and bloody. Casting themselves as reformers of a weakened Polynesian race, they established a rigid class system with themselves as

Traditional *ali'i* attire, as worn in the 13th century

ali'i (chiefs) who regulated the lives of the *maka'āinana* (commoners) through the harshly enforced *kapu* system. Derived from the Tahitian term "taboo," *kapu* designated any activity that was forbidden because it interfered with the apportionment of *mana* (supernatural power). Women, for example, were forbidden to eat with men. Commoners could not touch the clothes or shadows of the nobility, or lift their heads higher than the chiefs'. Punishment for infractions was quick and fatal, and the *ali'i* rededicated temples as *luakini heiau*, for human sacrifice.

The chief figure in this reform was the Tahitian priest Pā'ao, who probably made several journeys between the two archipelagos. He established a line of *kuhina nui* (high priests) and brought a chief named Pili, probably from Samoa, to consolidate political power. For unknown reasons, these voyages ceased after the 13th century.

CONTACT

Although British sea captain and explorer James Cook is credited with the "discovery" of Hawai'i in 1778, convincing evidence suggests that Spanish ships preceded him by more than 200 years. In the mid-16th century, Spanish galleons made annual voyages across the Pacific between their colonies in Mexico and recently established bases in the Philippines. In 1542 a fleet commanded by Ruy Lopes de Villalobos and led by Portuguese navigator Joao Gaetano stumbled onto islands they named the Isla de Mesa group. Navigators were ordered not to mention

TIMELINE

AD 300 Marquesans discover and settle Hawaiian islands

Hawaiian stone idol

1250 Arrival of Tahitian priest Pā'ao, who rededicates *heiau* (temples) for human sacrifice

Early hale (house)

| AD 300 | 600 | 900 | 1200 | 1500 |

Early voyaging canoe (c.300)

AD 1100–1300 Tahitians invade Hawai'i

1542 Spanish expedition, led by Joao Gaetano, finds Hawai'i and suppresses the information the islands in their logs for fear that knowledge of them would fall into British hands. In 1742, the British burst into the Pacific with their man-of-war *Centurion*, commanded by Lord Anson, and captured a Spanish galleon in its annual crossing. They seized its treasure and a chart showing the Isla de Mesa group; Cook must have had a copy of that chart.

Confrontation at Kealakekua Bay, Hawai'i Island, in 1779

The timing of Cook's arrival at Hawai'i Island's Kealakekua Bay constitutes one of history's oddest ironies. His ships the *Resolution* and *Discovery* appeared at the height of the annual *makahiki* festival honoring the Hawaiian god of agriculture, Lono. The British ships bore a startling resemblance to Hawaiian prophecies that said that one day Lono would return on a floating island. Much to Cook's surprise, the Hawaiians greeted him with reverence beyond anything he had experienced in the Pacific.

All went well until his departure in February 1779, when a storm snapped a mast, forcing Cook back to Kealakekua Bay. By now the Hawaiians surmised that the *haole* (Westerners) were less than divine, and a series of squabbles, including the killing of a chief, escalated into violent confrontation over a stolen boat. Cook was knifed to death in the fray.

Kamehameha the Great, ruler from 1795 to 1819

Other explorers followed, including Frenchman La Pérouse in 1786, the first Westerner on Maui. Four years later, American Simon Metcalf ordered the slaughter of dozens of Maui natives in the Olowalu Massacre. In 1792 British captain George Vancouver introduced cattle, goats, and sheep to Hawai'i. Within a generation of "discovery," domestic animals had begun to denude the forests, and imported diseases were killing large numbers of Hawaiians.

KAMEHAMEHA THE GREAT

An ambitious chief from Kohala (Hawai'i Island), Kamehameha could claim a direct kinship to the powerful chief Pili, who lived 500 years earlier. A skilled warrior and shrewd opportunist, he managed to quell centuries of internecine warfare by systematically conquering each of the islands. In 1790 he demoralized the Hawai'i Island chiefs by constructing Pu'ukoholā Heiau *(see p140)* and sacrificing his key rival on its altar. In 1795 he stormed Maui, terrifying the enemy with cannon plundered from an American ship. O'ahu fell the same year after bloody fighting along the Nu'uanu *pali* (cliffs). Twice he tried to invade Kaua'i, but storms turned back his fleet. Kamehameha then invited chief Kaumuali'i to visit him on O'ahu.

1750	1760	1770	1780	1790

1758 Kamehameha I born

1778 British captain James Cook first sights Ni'ihau and Kaua'i

1779 Cook killed at Kealakekua Bay

1795 Kamehameha conquers Maui, Moloka'i, Lāna'i, and O'ahu

1790 Hundreds killed in Olowalu Massacre

1786 La Pérouse explores Hawaiian islands

1791 Kamehameha begins conquest of islands

Captain Cook (1728–79)

Through threats and rewards, he forced the chief to cede Kaua'i, and Hawai'i became a united kingdom in 1809.

When the old conqueror died in 1819, he left a leadership void that his son Kamehameha II was unable to fill. The

Mid-19th-century painting of an enormous whale effortlessly destroying a whaling boat

drunken youth was coerced that same year to abandon the strict *kapu* system. The crucial moment came when he shared a meal with women – his mother Keōpūolani and his father's favorite wife, Ka'ahumanu. This act of *'ai noa* (free eating) was taken as a symbolic deed that invalidated all traditional rules. Thus the kingdom was reduced to a class of leaders with no precise set of laws.

MISSIONARY YEARS
The American Board of Foreign Missions provided relief just six months later. On April 19, 1820, the brig *Thaddeus* landed in Kailua Bay *(see p135)* carrying 23 Congregationalists, the first of 12 such groups to come to Hawai'i over the next three decades. In 1823 the second group established a church in Lahaina, Maui, which was by now the whaling capital. The missionaries had running battles with rowdy whalers. They also baptized

Missionary preaching to Hawaiians on Kaua'i, 1840

Keōpūolani, the dying queen mother, who commanded her people to embrace Christianity.

Kamehameha II had bankrupted the kingdom by now, despite stripping the native forests to sell Hawaiian sandalwood to China. To distract himself from his problems, he and his wife sailed to England where they arrived unannounced and unrecognized. Instead of meeting King George IV as they had hoped, they both contracted measles and died of the disease in July 1824. This misfortune left Kamehameha III, the king's 11-year-old brother, to rule. Power, however, was wielded by the formidable regent, Queen Ka'ahumanu. By the time of her death eight years later, Ka'ahumanu had engineered the peaceful conversion of the entire kingdom to Christianity.

THE RISE OF AMERICAN BUSINESS
Generally speaking, the missionary children showed a greater appetite for commerce than for religion. They and other Western entrepreneurs began to experiment with agribusiness ventures, particularly plantation-style production of sugar. In 1832 Kamehameha III leased land in Kōloa, Kaua'i for this purpose.

The king's unenviable job was to push ancient Hawai'i into the Western-dominated world. Guided by his *haole* (Western) advisors, he developed a constitution in 1840. Then, needing an infusion of revenues for the monarchy and maintaining that the *maka'āinana* (commoners) deserved to own land, he announced the Great *Mahele* (land division) in 1848. This released millions

TIMELINE

1809 Kaua'i joins united Hawaiian Kingdom

Kamehameha III (1814–54)

1820 First missionary party arrives in Kailua-Kona

1840 Kamehameha III proclaims Hawai'i's first constitution

1825 Kamehameha III becomes king, with Ka'ahumanu as regent

1800	1810	1820	1830	1840

A blubber pot used in the whaling trade

1819 Kamehameha I dies; Kamehameha II discards *kapu* system. Whaling commences

1825 Sugar and coffee plantations begun on O'ahu

1842 US recognizes independence of Hawaiian Kingdom

THE HISTORY OF HAWAI'I

Sugar plantation workers gathered around a steam plow in the mid-19th century

of acres for sale to private owners. Ironically, the *maka'āinana* possessed a weak understanding of "owning" land, and most of the deeds went to Western planters. For the next 100 years, sugar ruled the Hawaiian economy.

Large plantations required a labor force willing to endure long hours, poor pay, and cruel treatment, and native Hawaiians, demoralized by social change and crippling foreign plagues, largely declined. Instead, the planters began importing contract laborers, first from China in 1852. Later recruitments drew from the Portuguese islands of Madeira and the Azores, Japan, Puerto Rico, Korea, and the Philippines. As workers finished their contracts, a great number assimilated into island life. Many Chinese married into Hawaiian families. The Portuguese came, with their families, intent on settling. Other workers, particularly Japanese men, saw little incentive for returning to their former lives of hardship; they opted to

Queen Kapi'olani and Princess Lili'uokalani, wife and sister of Kalākaua, visiting the White House in 1887

pioneer lands leased in the Hawaiian wilderness, eventually writing home for brides and family members to join them. By 1900, over half the population of Hawai'i was of Japanese origin.

THE ENDANGERED MONARCHY

After Kamehameha III's death in 1854, a succession of short-lived rulers did what they could for the rapidly dwindling native population. Kamehameha IV and his wife Queen Emma established Queen's Medical Center to help stave off the effects of contagious disease on Hawaiians. Kamehameha V issued a new constitution in 1864 that strengthened the power of the monarchy, and introduced laws to protect the rights of foreign laborers. Lunalilo ruled only a year. By 1873 high tariffs on sugar were causing the planters to talk openly of annexation to the US. In 1874 David Kalākaua took the throne. Called the "Merrie Monarch," he initiated a cultural renaissance by promoting a revival of the *hula* and ancient chants, spending lavishly to build 'Iolani Palace (*see p55*), and planning a Polynesian empire with Hawai'i as its capital. The tide of history, however, had turned against him. Pressure applied by armed *haole* planters forced the king to secure a reciprocity treaty with the US. It eliminated tariffs on Hawaiian sugar, creating an economic dependency on agribusiness and US imports. In 1887 a league of planters forced Kalākaua to sign the Bayonet Constitution, which restricted the power of the monarchy.

Kamehameha III proclaims Great *Mahele*. Imported diseases kill 10,000 Hawaiians

Father Damien (1840–89)

1866 Leprosy patients taken to Moloka'i's Kalaupapa Peninsula

1876 H.P. Baldwin completes Hāmākua Ditch, bringing wide-scale sugar production to Maui. Reciprocity Treaty with US

1850	1860	1870	1880	1890

1863 Kamehameha IV dies

45 Seat of government moves m Lahaina to Honolulu

1864 Kamehameha V issues constitution strengthening the monarchy

1874 Kalākaua ascends the throne

1873 Lunalilo reigns for a year

1887 Royal power curtailed by Bayonet Constitution

The king's sister Lili'uokalani took the throne in 1891 and attempted to broaden constitutional powers, but was deposed in 1893 by the all-white "Committee of Safety" backed by illegally requisitioned American troops. Queen Lili'uokalani turned to the United States government for justice. President Grover Cleveland examined the facts and demanded that the queen be restored. However, the Provisional Government, led by missionary son Sanford P. Dole, refused.

Hula dancers accompanied by musicians at Waikīkī, with Diamond Head in the background (c.1920)

THE STOLEN KINGDOM

The Provisional Government established itself as the Republic of Hawai'i in 1894, but its clear intention was to be absorbed into the United States. Cleveland refused to annex the pirated kingdom, but his successor McKinley did so gladly in 1898. In 1900, Hawai'i became a US territory. The territorial government was largely an oligarchy of white Republicans who controlled every aspect of island life from their positions as directors of Hawai'i's five main agribusiness companies. Attempts to unionize plantation labor in the

1930s were firmly squelched. Ironically, it took the threat of Japanese invasion to force democracy on the nearly feudal institutions of territorial Hawai'i.

On December 7, 1941, Japanese bombers crippled US military installations on O'ahu, sinking or severely damaging 18 battleships at rest in Pearl Harbor, destroying or disabling nearly 200 aircraft, and killing more than 2,000 officers and men. Within 24 hours, Hawai'i's government was replaced by a military one that stayed in power throughout World War II. Five years of direct federal involvement forced territorial leaders to adopt more democratic methods. After the war, a strike – violent, but ultimately effective – shut down the plantations for 79 days. At the same time, Hawai'i's underclass began wielding the power of the ballot, and soon the children of the plantation camps were being swept into positions of political power. In 1959 the US Congress offered to make Hawai'i the 50th state of the union, and a majority of citizens voted to accept, led by a strong endorsement from the Japanese population.

Celebration of the US annexation of Hawai'i in 1898

TIMELINE

	1890	1900	1910	1920	1930	1940	1950
	1893 Monarchy is overthrown		**1922** Dole creates world's largest pineapple plantation on Lāna'i	**1936** *Hawai'i Clipper* flies from San Francisco to Honolulu, initiating commercial air traffic to Hawai'i		**1949** Strikes cripple Hawai'i, shifting political power away from "Big Five" companies	
	1894 Hawai'i is declared a republic		**1917** Lili'uokalani dies				
		1898 Hawai'i annexed by US		**1927** Royal Hawaiian Hotel is built, catering to cruise liner trade	**1941** Japan attacks Pearl Harbor; many Japanese-Americans sent to mainland internment camps	**1954** Labor-backed Democrats swamp Republicans in Territorial elections	
		1895 Citizens attempt an armed insurrection	*US Territory seal*				

Japanese bombing of US naval base at Pearl Harbor in 1941, bringing the United States into World War II

The invention of air travel has changed Hawai'i perhaps more than any other imported technology, not only because it turned O'ahu into the center of US military defense in the Pacific but also because it opened the door for mass tourism. Commercial flights had begun in the 1930s with Pan Am's *Hawai'i Clipper*, but it was the introduction of jet travel in 1959 that brought the world to the islands. Suddenly, Hawai'i, especially Waikīkī, was an affordable four-and-a-half hour flight from the US mainland. Hotel development and population growth hit O'ahu first; by 1959 more than half the people in the state lived in Honolulu. Soon the large agribusiness landholders on all islands began diversifying. During the 1960s, the development of West Maui's Kā'anapali as a resort community signaled a new era for island economy. Whereas the plantations were once the driving economic force, many of the great sugar and pineapple fields now lay fallow, and Hawai'i's fortunes began to rise and fall with the moods of tourism and the price of real estate.

Anniversary of the monarchy's overthrow (1993)

At the same time, some 140,000 resident Hawaiians have started taking political action to reclaim autonomy in their ancient homeland. During the 1970s, Hawaiians began demanding the release of Kaho'olawe from the grip of the US military, which had been using the island for target practice for 50 years. A renewed interest in Hawaiian culture, language, and crafts culminated in 1976 with the building of the *Hōkūle'a* – the first authentic voyaging canoe to be built in over 500 years *(see p57).* In 1993 the US government apologized for any complicity in the wrongful overthrow of the monarchy, and the "nation of Hawai'i" began a movement to reestablish its own sovereignty.

Today the Hawaiian islands support a population of over 1 million, with Hawaiians accounting for 12.5 percent, and each year over 6 million tourists visit. The island chain accommodates one of the most ethnically diverse and tolerant populations in the world, where over 15 entrenched cultures jostle for position with an embattled heritage. No matter where you go in the islands, however, Polynesian roots grow very close to the surface.

The crowded golden sand of Waikīkī Beach, Hawai'i's most popular visitor destination

	"Statehood" newspapers	1983 Kīlauea begins present eruption	1992 Closure of Hāmākua Sugar, Hawai'i Island's last plantation. Hurricane Iniki devastates Kaua'i	2006 The US Government announces the Northwestern Hawaiian islands as a national monument; it is the largest marine sanctuary in the world
59 wai'i comes h US state	1982 Hurricane Iwa devastates Kaua'i			
60	1970	1980	1990	2000	2010	2020

1977 Activists George Helm and Kimo Mitchell die while trespassing on Kaho'olawe

1986 John Waihe'e becomes first Hawaiian governor

1996 Citizens vote to convene on the issue of sovereignty

2008 Hawai'i-born Barack Obama elected president of the US

2002 Linda Lingle is elected as the first woman governor of Hawai'i

HONOLULU
AND WAIKĪKĪ

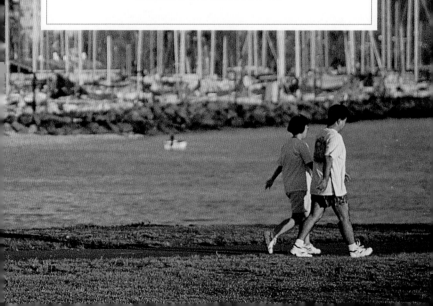

Honolulu and Waikīkī at a Glance

Hawai'i's capital city has two focal points, the historic and business district of Downtown Honolulu and the world-famous resort of Waikīkī. The downtown area first gained prominence as a trading port in the early 19th century. Waikīkī, by contrast, was still a swamp when its first luxury hotel went up in 1901. With Honolulu's best beach, however, the resort's success was guaranteed.

'Iolani Palace (see p55) *was built in 1882 and served as home for Hawai'i's last two monarchs, King Kalākaua and Queen Lili'uokalani.*

Chinatown (see pp58–9) *is a lively district. The streets are lined with exotic emporia, religious shrines, and lei stands.*

| 0 meters | 500 |
| 0 yards | 500 |

Mission Houses Museum (see p54) *preserves three mission buildings from the early 1800s.*

DOWNTOWN HONOLULU
(see pp50–59)

The Aloha Tower (see p56), *built in 1926 to a height of 184 ft (56 m), was at the time Honolulu's tallest building. A street-level marketplace contains shops and restaurants.*

Hawai'i Theatre (see p57) *closed in 1984 after years of decline. Reopened in 1996, this historic Art-Deco theater has been beautifully renovated. Its neon sign has become a Honolulu landmark.*

HONOLULU AND WAIKĪKĪ

O'AHU

0 kilometers   2

0 miles   1

The Royal Hawaiian Hotel (see p62), or "Pink Palace," affords tranquil respite from Waikīkī's incessant bustle. This landmark hotel, opened in 1927, has played host to Roosevelts and Rockefellers.

International Market Place (see p64), a huge open-air plaza, offers an amazing array of handicrafts and souvenir items.

King's Village (see p65) is a Victorian–theme shopping mall.

WAIKĪKĪ
(see pp48–53)

Kūhiō Beach (see p65) features a statue of Duke Kahanamoku, the "Father of Surfing."

The Waikīkī Beach Front (see pp62–3) is lined by high-rise hotels, restaurants, and nightclubs, with the distinctive Diamond Head crater at the far end. Every day of the year this 2-mile (3-km) stretch of golden sand attracts sun-seekers by the thousands.

The Moana Surfrider Hotel (see p64) dates from the early 20th century. The seaside Banyan Court bar is the perfect spot for sipping cocktails while watching glorious sunsets over the ocean.

DOWNTOWN HONOLULU

Seal on the gates of the State Capitol

Once a fishing village called Kou, Honolulu was described in the 1820s as "a mass of brown thatched huts looking like haystacks." In the course of that century, however, it became a vital port of call for fur traders and whaling vessels visiting Oʻahu, and in 1866 the novelist Mark Twain commented that every step in the city revealed a new contrast. This is no less true today. In a relatively small and compact area, downtown Honolulu manages to squeeze together towering skyscrapers, Japanese shrines, New England-style missionary houses, a cathedral, a royal palace, former opium dens, strip joints, and fish markets.

This bustling capital has a strong ethnic mix, and the downtown streets mirror the diversity. Hawaiian businessmen in three-piece suits, children in school uniforms, and Samoans in bright sarongs mingle in harmony.

SIGHTS AT A GLANCE

Historic Streets and Buildings
Aloha Tower Marketplace 8
Chinatown pp58–9 11
Fort Street Mall 7
Hawaiʻi Theatre 9
ʻIolani Palace 4
State Capitol 5

Museums and Galleries
Hawaiʻi State Art Museum 10
Mission Houses Museum 3

Cathedrals and Churches
Kawaiahaʻo Church 2
St. Andrew's Cathedral 6

Monuments
King Kamehameha Statue 1

GETTING THERE

Downtown Honolulu is 3 miles (5 km) *ʻEwa* (to the west) of Waikīkī. From Waikīkī, take *TheBus* 2, 13, 19, 20, or 47 westbound, or the Aloha Tower Trolley or Waikīkī Trolley. For more details, see inside back cover.

KEY

Street-by-Street map
See pp52–3

Street-by-Street map
See pp58–9

Main bus terminal

Taxi stand

— Pedestrian street

◁ **The King Kamehameha Statue, draped with dozens of *lei* in celebration of Kamehameha Day (June 11)**

Street-by-Street: Capitol District

'Iolani Palace crest

The architectural contrasts in this compact area mirror Hawai'i's cultural medley and trace its fascinating history. A short walk takes you from clapboard missionary homes to a sophisticated, Victorian-style palace where Hawaiian kings hosted lavish parties and the last queen of the islands was imprisoned. This majestic survivor of the island monarchy soon gives way, though, to a nearby symbol of 20th-century democracy – one of the few domeless state capitol buildings in the United States.

The 'Iolani Barracks were built in 1871 to house royal soldiers.

Chinatown (see pp58–9)

Hawaii State Art Museum

★ **'Iolani Palace**
The only royal residence in the United States, 'Iolani ("Royal Hawk") Palace was completed in 1882. The interior has an elegant koa-wood staircase ❹

Hawaiian Electric Company building

The Royal Bandstand, set in the shaded grounds of 'Iolani Palace, was built for the coronation of King Kalākaua in 1883. It is still used for official functions.

Post Office

King Kamehameha Statue
The king's bronze statue stands proudly in front of Ali'iōlani Hale ❶

RICHARDS STREET

MERCHANT STREET

SOUTH KING STREET

MILILANI STREET

QUEEN STREET

PUNCH

Waterfront

STAR SIGHTS

★ 'Iolani Palace

★ Kawaiaha'o Church

★ Mission Houses Museum

Ali'iōlani Hale ("House of the Heavenly King") was designed as a palace and built in 1874. It now houses the Supreme Court and the Judiciary History Center.

St. Andrew's Cathedral
Built in 1867, this cathedral features a large window of vivid stained glass **6**

Washington Place, a Georgian-style frame house built in 1846, is now a museum for Hawai'i's last queen, Lili'okulani.

LOCATOR MAP
See Street Finder, map 1

Eternal Flame War Memorial

State Capitol
The design of this unique building represents the formation of Hawai'i's volcanic islands **5**

The Statue of Queen Lili'uokalani commemorates Hawai'i's last monarch, who took the throne in 1891 but was deposed by the "Committee of Safety" just two years later *(see p44).*

LILI'UOKALANI

★ Kawaiaha'o Church
Prior to the completion of this New England-style church in 1842, missionaries used to preach from thatched huts on the same site. Sunday services are conducted here in both English and Hawaiian **2**

SOUTH BERETANIA STREET
MILLER STREET
PUNCHBOWL STREET
SOUTH KING STREET
KAWAIAHA'O STREET

Kawaiaha'o Cemetery

0 meters 100
0 yards 100

KEY
– – – Suggested route

★ Mission Houses Museum
This excellent museum is housed in three buildings, including a printing house, erected by missionaries between 1821 and 1841 **3**

Bronze statue of the king, his hand extended in a gesture of welcome

King Kamehameha Statue ❶

Corner of King St & Mililani St.
Map 1 B3. 🚌 2, 13.

Kamehameha the Great, who ruled the islands from 1795 to 1819, is Hawai'i's most revered monarch. This Hawai'i Island chief turned the islands from chiefdoms riddled by inter-necine warfare into a respected monarchy. As a young warrior, Kamehameha met illustrious foreigners, including Captain Cook in 1778. He soon grasped the importance of Western technology and incorporated ships and cannons into his conquest of the war-ring chiefs. After consolidating the kingdom, Kamehameha I turned his attention to looking after his people.

With its gold-leaf feathered helmet and cloak, the bronze statue in front of Ali'iōlani Hale is one of the most famous sights in Hawai'i. The original statue was lost in a storm, and this replica was unveiled by King Kalākaua in 1883. The original was recovered by divers the same year and erected in Kapa'au (see p141).

Kawaiaha'o Church ❷

957 Punchbowl St. **Map** 1 B3. **Tel** (808) 522-1333. 🚌 2. 🕐 8:30am–4pm daily. 🌐 public hols. ♿ 🎥 by appt.
www.kawaiahao.org

This imposing edifice is a monument to Hawai'i's missionary days. With the collapse of the old Hawaiian religion around 1820 – shortly after Kamehameha I's death – the missionaries soon gained influential converts, including the formidable Ka'ahumanu, the king's favorite wife. In earlier thatched churches on the site, the Reverend Hiram Bingham preached to as many as 2,000 penitent Hawaiians, who would attend in what one missionary wife described in 1829 as "an appalling state of undress." With their first exposure to Western clothing, some wore just a shirt or a top hat. By the time the present church was built in 1842, the women wore deco-rous *mu'umu'u* (long dresses), and most worshipers sported shoes due to the planting of thorn-shedding *kiawe* trees.

King Lunalilo's Gothic-style mausoleum

The church's New England-style architecture is softened by the coral-block construction. The upper gallery has 21 portraits of the Hawaiian monarchs and their families, most of whom were baptized, married, and crowned here.

Outside are two cemeteries for missionaries and their early converts, and a mausoleum where King Lunalilo is buried. Apart from Kamehameha I, whose bones were hidden so that no one could steal his *mana* (spiritual power), most of the other royalty lie in the Royal Mausoleum (see p70).

Mission Houses Museum ❸

553 South King St. **Map** 1 C3.
Tel (808) 531-0481. 🚌 2, 13.
🕐 10am–4pm Tue–Sun. 🌐 public hols. 🎥 ♿ first floor only. 🎥
www.missionhouses.org

This bucolic enclave of the past contains the oldest timber frame house in Hawai'i, a testament to the persuasive powers of the New England missionaries. In 1821, one year after their arrival, Kamehameha II allowed Reverend Bingham to build a Christian house and to establish Hawai'i's first printing press. A more elegant house followed, part of which contains a replica press. The interiors have been lovingly preserved. Especially interest-ing are the clothes worn by the mis-sionaries, including long underwear.

The missionaries were so good at converting the rowdy whalers and Sandwich Island heathens that in 1825 a Russian visitor described Honolulu as follows: "streets deserted, games pro-hibited [and] singing, dancing [and] riding horseback on Sun-days all punishable offenses."

Elegant coral-block house at the Mission Houses Museum

South façade of 'Iolani Palace, with steps up to the main entrance

'Iolani Palace 4

King St & Richards St. **Map** 1 B3. **Tel** (808) 522-0832. 🚌 2, 13. ◐ 8:30am–4pm Mon–Sat. 🌣 Jan 1, Jul 4, Thanksgiving, Dec 25. 🎟 ⊘ 🚹 🎫 recommended (except at gallery). **www**.iolanipalace.org

King David Kalākaua was inspired by English Victorian architecture when he commissioned this royal residence on the site of an earlier palace. Drawing heavily on sugarcane profits, Hawai'i's "Merrie Monarch" tried to recreate the pomp and circumstance of the English court in the palace's luxurious interiors.

The only royal palace in the US, 'Iolani ("Royal Hawk") Palace served that function for just 11 years. Kalākaua took up residence in 1882, followed by his sister, Lili'uokalani, who reigned for only two years before the monarchy was overthrown in 1893 (see p44).

The palace became the seat of government, and in 1895, Lili'uokalani was imprisoned here for nine months. The first governor used Kalākaua's bedroom as his office, and the legislature met in the chambers downstairs. After the government moved to the Capitol building, the palace became a set for Jack Lord's office in the television series *Hawaii Five-0*. Fans will recognize the arched floor-to-ceiling windows. Children under five are not admitted to the palace.

The grounds make a pleasant place for a stroll. The barracks of Kalākaua's royal guard, which date from 1871, serve as a gift shop and visitor center.

The grass near Kalākaua's coronation bandstand makes an ideal picnic spot, and every Friday at noon – except in August – the Royal Hawaiian Band gives a free concert.

State Capitol 5

Beretania St & Richards St. **Map** 1 B2. **Tel** (808) 586-0221. 🚌 2, 13. ◐ 7:45am–4:30pm Mon–Fri. 🌣 public hols. 🚹 🎫 by appointment. **Washington Place** 🎫 Mon–Fri; reservations required: (808) 586-0248.

Crossing beneath the canopy of banyans from 'Iolani Palace to the back of Hawai'i's State Capitol is a trip from old to new, from Victorian monarchy to contemporary crossroads of the Pacific.

America's youngest state boasts the most imaginative statehouse, its architecture symbolizing Hawai'i's majestic environment. The building rises from a reflecting pool just as the islands rise from the blue Pacific. Fluted columns, suggesting lofty palms, circle the veranda, and two volcano-shaped chambers contain the houses of the legislature. At the rear, by the Capitol veranda, stands a statue of Queen Lili'uokalani, holding the music to "Aloha 'Oe," a famous ballad she composed. The words mean "may you be loved or greeted." The statue is often decked with flower *lei*. In front of the building is a modern statue of Father Damien (see p101) by Marisol Escobar.

Across Beretania Street ("British" street in Hawaiian), is the **Eternal Flame**, a memorial to World War II soldiers. Farther down the street is **Washington Place**, formerly the governor's mansion and Hawai'i's oldest continuously occupied dwelling. This Georgian-style frame house was built by John Dominis, Queen Lili'uokalani's father-in-law, in 1846. After release from imprisonment in the palace, the queen lived out her days in this house and it is now a museum in her honor.

The Eternal Flame, a war memorial across from the State Capitol

St. Andrew statue at the cathedral

St. Andrew's Cathedral **6**

229 Queen Emma Square. **Map** 1 B2. *Tel* (808) 524-2822. 2, 13. 9am–5pm daily. **www**.saintandrewscathedral.net

The oldest Episcopal edifice in Hawai'i, St. Andrew's was built as an Anglican cathedral in 1867. (It turned Episcopalian in 1898, when Hawai'i became an American territory.) Alexander Liholiho (Kamehameha IV), Hawai'i's most Anglophile king, brought Anglicanism to Honolulu following a trip to England during which he was enchanted by English church rituals. His wife Queen Emma, the grand-daughter of Englishman John Young, an advisor of Kameha-meha the Great, was baptized by the first Anglican clergymen to arrive in the islands.

After the death of the king in 1863, Emma traveled to England to raise funds and to find an architect for the cathe-dral. Her husband's brother and successor, Kamehameha V, laid the cornerstone four years later. Much of the stone was imported from England, although the arched walkways are more suggestive of Gothic churches in France.

The cathedral was not consecrated until 1958, when the final phase of construction,

Detail of stained glass at St. Andrew's

including a huge stained-glass mural, was completed. Outside, a statue of St. Andrew appears to preach to fish rising from a surrounding pool. The carved message reads "Preach the Gospel to every creature."

Fort Street Mall **7**

Fort St. **Map** 1 A3. 2, 13.

This street was named after the former Kekuanohu fort. Kamehameha I decided to build a harbor fort after he fought off a Russian bid to colonize the islands in 1816. John Young, the king's advisor, supervised the work, and the whitewashed walls stood until 1857. According to early documents, the stronghold also functioned as a prison. By the 1860s the adjacent street was a thriving business center, with a dressmaker, milliner, hardware store, and lumberyard. Some small shops remain today, but the four-block street has been turned into a pedestrian mall. At the *mauka* end (toward the moun-tains) is **Our Lady of Peace**, an austere Catholic cathedral built of coral in 1843. Father Damien *(see p101)*, the "Martyr of Moloka'i," was ordained here in 1864. Opposite is the contemporary **Hawai'i Pacific University** building. Eating places nearby reflect the uni-versity's international student body – Vietnamese, Korean,

Chinese, French gourmet, and even a Filipino-Polish restau-rant. Midway down the mall, the benches are often occupied by retired Filipino grandpas who spend their time people watching, strumming 'ukulele, and chatting away in Tagalog. The mall affords interesting views both *mauka* and *makai* (toward the sea).

View down Fort Street Mall, lined with diverse eating establishments

Aloha Tower Marketplace **8**

Pier 9, Honolulu Harbor. **Map** 1 A3. *Tel* (808) 528-5700. 19, 20, 47. 10am–7pm Mon–Sat, 10am–6pm Sun; observation deck: 9:30am–sunset daily. **www**.alohatower.com

Originally known as the "Gateway to Fort Street," the Aloha Tower was constructed in 1926, in the days when tourists arrived by steamship. Locals flocked to the tower

View of Aloha Tower Marketplace and the Honolulu Harbor

and terminals to sell *lei* to the arriving passengers, dance the *hula*, dive for coins, and partake vicariously of the excitement of travel only few could afford. Departing passengers threw multicolored streamers from the decks while the Royal Hawaiian Band played the famous and much loved ballad, "Aloha 'Oe" *(see p55)*.

Standing ten stories high, with four clocks facing the four points of the compass, what was once Honolulu's tallest building is now dwarfed by gleaming skyscrapers. An elevator carries visitors to an observation deck, which delivers a 360° view of Honolulu Harbor and the mountains.

Today the tower is the hub of a tasteful complex that houses upscale stores, and restaurants offering sheltered outdoor seating, perfect for sunsetwatching. Local musicians play throughout the complex. Cruise liners still pull up at the pier, as do working ships from all over the world. Some naval vessels welcome visitors free of charge during designated hours. Sightseeing vessels run harbor tours, and **Navatek I** offers whale-watching cruises from January to April.

Clock face at the top of the Aloha Tower

Hawai'i Theatre ❾

1130 Bethel St. **Map** 1 A2. *Tel (808) 528-0506.* 🚌 2, 13. ☐ 9am–5pm *Tue–Sat (box office).* ◑ *most public hols.* ♿ **www.**hawaiitheatre.com

Opened in 1922 to present vaudeville, musicals, plays, and silent movies, the Hawai'i Theatre was dubbed "The Pride of the Pacific". Hawaiian architects Walter Emory and Marshall Webb created a Neoclassical exterior with a variety of decorative elements – Byzantine, Corinthian, and Moorish – and a lavish interior with plush carpets, ornate columns, marble statuary, and a gilded dome. When talking pictures took off in the 1930s, the Hawai'i became an upscale movie theater, but eventually it went into decline, finally closing down in 1984. A local campaigning group raised funds to save the building and restore it to its former glory. It reopened in 1996 as a multi-purpose venue offering films, concerts, and stage performances. Exterior renovations were completed in 2005. In recognition of its historic importance, the theater is listed on the US National Register of Historic Places.

Model of a sailing canoe in Hawai'i State Art Museum

Hawai'i State Art Museum ❿

2nd floor, No.1 Capitol Building, 250 South Hotel St. **Map** 1 A2. *Tel (808) 586-0900.* ☐ 10am–4pm *Tue–Sat.* ◑ *public hols.* 🖾 🛍 ♿ **www.**hawaii.gov/sfca

This museum, housed in a handsome Spanish-Mission-style building, is dedicated to Hawaiian art, including bark cloth items, embroidery, quilts, and pottery. Many items blend Western forms and traditional folk art. The museum is also home to Art in Public Places, which brings together over 5,000 works of art by more than 1,400 Hawaiian artists.

THE HŌKŪLE'A

Hawai'i's first modern reconstruction of an ancient sailing canoe, the *Hōkūle'a* sailed to Tahiti and back in 1976 without radar or compass. This feat proved that the first Hawaiians arrived in these islands thanks to their mastery of celestial navigation, rather than by chance, and helped to spark off a full-blown renaissance of Hawaiian culture.

Ancient navigators were carefully chosen as infants for a lifelong training to read the stars, ocean currents, and flights of birds. Because this knowledge had been lost to modern Hawaiians, the *Hōkūle'a* relied on a Micronesian, Mau Pialug, to steer that first voyage. Over the years he has passed on his wisdom to a young Hawaiian, Nainoa Thompson, who, with Hawai'i's Polynesian Voyaging Society, is training new generations in the ancient arts of canoe building and navigation. Since 1976 the society has sponsored further voyages of rediscovery.

The *Hōkūle'a* ("Star of Joy") at sea with billowing sails

Street-by-Street: Chinatown

Hawai'i's first Chinese arrived on merchant ships in 1789, followed in 1852 by large numbers who came to work on O'ahu's sugar plantations. On completion of their contracts, many gravitated to downtown Honolulu to build restaurants, herb shops, and clubhouses. Chinatown also developed a flourishing opium trade. A fire in 1886 destroyed the area, and in 1900 another was started by health officials to wipe out bubonic plague. By this time Chinese immigration was a divisive political issue, and some believe the fire was intended to ruin the area. However, Chinatown rose from the ashes and today is a thriving community.

★ **Izumo Taisha Shrine**
The oldest Japanese Shinto shrine in Hawai'i, this was built in 1923 without nails. Facing the Nu'uanu Stream is a traditional gate.

Footbridge

Nu'uanu Stream

Dr. Sun Yat-sen (1866–1925), the Chinese statesman who became the first president of the Republic of China, is honored with this statue next to the Nu'uanu Stream. On the other side of the stream is a statue of Jose Rizal (1861–96), a Filipino hero.

Maunakea Market Place

The Wo Fat building, with its pagoda-style roof, was once a landmark Chinese restaurant. Mr. Wo Fat, a baker, opened the original establishment in the 1880s. The present pink building dates from 1936.

At O'ahu Market you can haggle for fresh fish, exotic fruits and vegetables, and delicacies such as pigs' heads.

STAR SIGHTS

★ Izumo Taisha Shrine

★ Open-Air Markets

★ Hawai'i Theatre

★ **Open-Air Markets**
Chinatown's abundant open-air markets sell everything from duck and salmon heads to fresh ginger.

0 meters 100
0 yards 100

For hotels and restaurants in this region see pp178–81 and pp196–9

Foster Botanical Gardens

Kuan Yin Temple

DOWNTOWN HONOLULU

LOCATOR MAP
See Street Finder, map 1

The Lum Sai Ho Tong Temple is a small Taoist temple above a store, where members of the Lum clan worship.

Chinese Cultural Plaza contains shops and a stage where Chinese dances and plays are performed.

★ **Hawai'i Theatre**
This lovingly renovated Art Deco theater on the edge of Chinatown has elaborate plasterwork on the exterior and also boasts an elegant interior.

At the entrance to Chinatown sit two marble lions. They were donated by Honolulu's sister city, Kaohsiung in Taiwan, in honor of the 200th anniversary of Chinese settlement in Hawai'i.

KEY
– – – Suggested route

Chinatown ⓫

Map 1 A2. 🚌 2, 13. 🛈 HVCB, Waikīkī, (808) 924-0266. 🎎 Chinese New Year (early Jan–Mar). **Foster Botanical Gardens** 50 N Vineyard Blvd. **Map** 1 A1. **Tel** (808) 522-7066. 🚌 4. 🕘 9am–4pm daily. ● Jan 1, Dec 25. 🎫 ♿ 🏬

This exotic neighborhood is full of colorful flower *lei* (garlands worn around the neck) stands, open markets with hanging ducks and tropical fish, herbal medicine shops displaying dried snakes and rats, trendy art galleries, and acupuncture and tattooing emporia. There are also less salubrious saloons with topless dancing, especially on Pauahi and North Hotel streets, downtown Honolulu's red light district – the legacy of World War II soldiers on leave.

The twin lions on Bethel and North Hotel streets, the gateway to Chinatown from the adjacent business district, are symbols of a major rejuvenation project. Many buildings, such as the Hawai'i Theatre, have been beautifully restored.

Visitors to Chinatown may be lucky enough to witness a Chinese wedding with full percussion orchestra and a prancing lion dance. At the Maunakea Market Place, you can sample food from all over Asia, and the noodle shops along River Street are much favored by local residents.

At the edge of Chinatown, the **Foster Botanical Gardens** are an oasis of tranquillity in the heart of a fast-paced city. They contain some protected trees and a prehistoric plant exhibit. The gift shop sells plants that can be sent home.

Chinese herbalist in a North King Street shop weighing his goods

WAIKĪKĪ

Waikīkī Trolley sightseeing bus

Waikīkī was a nondescript place of taro patches and fish ponds when Kamehameha I, the chief who united the Hawaiian islands, landed here to launch an invasion in 1795 *(see p41)*. After conquering the chiefs of O'ahu, he built a bungalow facing the ocean, not far from the present Royal Hawaiian Hotel. Now Waikīkī has one of the world's famous beaches, a sliver of people-packed sand against the backdrop of Diamond Head crater.

Waikīkī's "golden mile" of glass and concrete skyscrapers is a hectic hodge-podge of Western, Asian, and Pacific cultures bustling with some 65,000 tourists a day. The streets are packed with T-shirt vendors, sunburned honeymooners, Japanese matrons with Christian Dior bags, and barefoot boys carrying surfboards on their bikes. Local people strum 'ukulele at beachfront bars, music throbs from nightclubs, and a band of performers roams the streets.

The turquoise water is dotted with swimmers and multicolored inflatables. Beyond them, outrigger canoes cut swaths through the ranks of surfers, and farther out, red and yellow sailboats bob on the horizon.

SIGHTS AT A GLANCE

Historic Hotels
Moana Surfider ❸
Royal Hawaiian Hotel ❶

Shopping Areas
International Market Place ❷
King's Village ❹

Beaches
Kūhiō Beach ❺

GETTING THERE
From the airport, take *TheBus* 19 or 20, "Waikīkī Beach & Hotels" (hand luggage only), or one of the many shuttle buses or taxis. From downtown Honolulu, catch *TheBus* 2, 13, 19, or 20, "Waikīkī Beach & Hotels," or the Aloha Tower or Waikīkī Trolleys. Buses 4, 8, 22, and 58 also serve Waikīkī. For more details, see inside back cover.

| 0 meters | | 250 |
| 0 yards | | 250 |

◁ **Vacationers relaxing on the terrace of Waikīkī's "Pink Palace" – the Royal Hawaiian Hotel**

Beachfront façade of the Royal Hawaiian Hotel, known to countless tourists as the "Pink Palace"

Royal Hawaiian Hotel ❶

2259 Kalākaua Ave. **Map** 4 D5.
Tel *(808) 923-7311.* 🚌 *many buses.*
www.royal-hawaiian.com

An oasis in the high-rise surroundings of Waikīkī, the Royal Hawaiian Hotel occupies 10 acres of land in a former coconut grove where Kamehameha V built a summer cottage in the 1870s. Some of the hotel's palms are thought to survive from that period. Paths meander across emerald green lawns under cathedral-size banyan trees to arrive at this Spanish-Moorish-style gem, known affectionately as the "Pink Palace." Almost everything here is coral pink, from the rooftop cupolas to the telephones, and carpets.

When it opened in 1927, the Royal Hawaiian Hotel was hailed by the *Honolulu Star-Bulletin* as "the finest resort hostelry in America." It soon became famous for its rollicking parties and was

Waikīkī Beach Front

This world-famous sandy beach actually encompasses several individually named, smaller beaches stretching 2.5 miles (4 km) from the Hilton Hawaiian Village (*see p181*) to Diamond Head. The whole beach is open to the public.

Thousands of tourists *flock to Waikīkī Beach daily to sunbathe on the golden sand, swim in the sheltered water, and surf the gentle waves.*

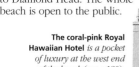

The coral-pink Royal Hawaiian Hotel *is a pocket of luxury at the west end of the beach* (see p180).

The Sheraton Waikīkī Hotel's Hanohano Room, on the 30th floor, offers stupendous views, especially at sunset (*see p180*).

Outrigger Waikīkī on the Beach (*see p179*).

The International Market Place is a popular center for vacation souvenirs (*see p64*).

Moana Surfrider, a Westin Resort and Spa (*see p180*).

Royal Hawaiian Shopping Center

Hawai'i Visitors and Convention Bureau

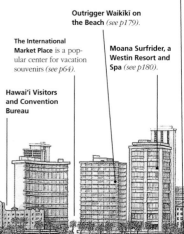

patronized by the wealthy and fashionable. Some guests even brought along their own servants and Rolls Royces.

The Depression of the 1930s slowed business down, and during World War II the hotel was leased to the US Navy as a center for rest and recreation for sailors in the Pacific Fleet. After refurbishment, the hotel was reopened in 1947. It was closed again in 2008 for a $110 million restoration that includes a new lobby, new pools, renovated guest rooms, and the addition of spa suites.

The aura of Hollywood glitz still lingers. On the beach, the "beautiful people" can be seen tanning and attracting all sorts of local commerce.

Behind the hotel, covering three city blocks, is the **Royal Hawaiian Shopping Center**. This modern arcade contains dozens of upscale shops, boutiques, and fast-food places.

EARLY TOURISM IN WAIKĪKĪ

Prior to the development of tourism, Waikīkī was a swampy marshland, consisting mainly of taro patches (see p125) and rice paddies. The land was reclaimed in the early part of the 20th century; large areas were filled in and the Ala Wai Canal was dug to drain the area by diverting streams from the hills above Waikīkī to the sea. Tourism began gradually around 1901 with the building of the Moana Hotel (now the Sheraton Moana Surfrider), which included a wooden pier that extended 300 ft (90 m) into the sea. Tourism accelerated in the 1920s with the opening of the Royal Hawaiian Hotel, which was host to movie stars and millionaires.

A view toward the gracious Moana Hotel in April 1920

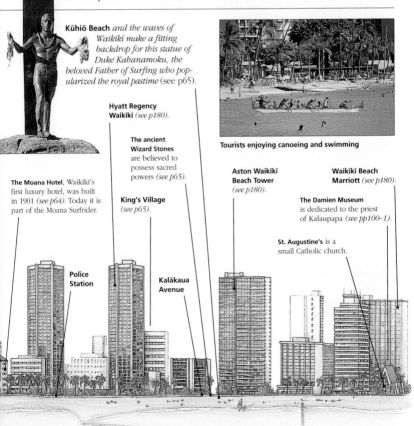

Kūhiō Beach and the waves of Waikīkī make a fitting backdrop for this statue of Duke Kahanamoku, the beloved Father of Surfing who popularized the royal pastime (see p65).

Hyatt Regency Waikīkī (see p180).

The ancient Wizard Stones are believed to possess sacred powers (see p65).

King's Village (see p65).

The Moana Hotel, Waikīkī's first luxury hotel, was built in 1901 (see p64). Today it is part of the Moana Surfrider.

Tourists enjoying canoeing and swimming

Aston Waikīkī Beach Tower (see p180).

Waikīkī Beach Marriott (see p180).

The Damien Museum is dedicated to the priest of Kalaupapa (see pp100–1).

St. Augustine's is a small Catholic church.

Police Station

Kalākaua Avenue

The façade of the Moana Surfrider Hotel, the "First Lady of Waikīkī," restored to its original splendor in 1989

International Market Place **❷**

2330 Kalākaua Ave. **Map** 4 E5.
Tel (808) 971-2080. 🚌 many buses.
🕐 10am–9pm daily. ♿

Situated across the street from the Royal Hawaiian Shopping Center (see p63), the open-air International Market Place occupies a city block between Kalākaua and Kūhiō Avenues. This theme-park shopping plaza is a labyrinth of food stalls (on the Kūhiō Avenue side) and souvenir-crammed carts. Choose from shell sculptures, funky cigarette lighters, and racks of identical chains and watches, or pick up an "island" candle or silk flower *lei* – often manufactured in Korea, unfortunately.

Typically vivid Hawaiian shirt on sale at International Market Place

Elsewhere in the market, visitors can watch local sculptors at work, ship home a painted coconut, have their fingernails painted with tropical scenes, or even consult the on-site palm reader. They can have their pictures taken in grass skirts, with green and red parrots, in front of a waterfall, or next to a fiberglass wave.

Just like the wave, this shopping plaza is plastic Polynesia at its worst, but it is a good, central place to shop for T-shirts and colorful island wear. Bargaining is *de rigueur*, and it is always wise to

Souvenir plate at International Market Place

check the prices of similar merchandise around the market. When the going gets too hot, you can rest in the shade of the huge banyan tree in the middle. If you get lost, follow the yellow stripe on the floor to get back to the street.

Moana Surfrider Hotel **❸**

2365 Kalākaua Ave. **Map** 4 E5.
Tel (808) 922-3111.
🚌 many buses. 🕐 daily. ♿ 📷
www.moana-surfrider.com

The colonial-style Moana, Waikīkī's oldest hotel, opened in 1901 to cater to an international steamship crowd. It became famous for gala events attended by movie stars. In 1920, the Prince of Wales stayed at the hotel and was given outrigger canoe and surfing lessons from local hero Duke Kahanamoku.

An award-winning restoration project, begun in 1986, returned the hotel to something approaching its original look. Restorers used original drawings and templates that were found in the hotel basement. Memorabilia now on display throughout the hotel include a 1905 guest register, photos of famous visitors, and monogrammed woolen swimsuits that were issued to guests in the 1930s. There are free daily tours.

Although nowadays the Moana is part of the Starwood Group's Westin Resort and Spa chain (see p180), the hotel's quiet luxury still seems a world away from brash and bustling Kalākaua Avenue, just outside the grand entrance. On a front porch bedecked with rocking chairs, visitors are greeted with *lei* by South Seas beauties dressed in Victorian attire. The nostalgic lobby is decorated with period furniture and huge vases of anthuriums, while over on the ocean side, guests are served high-tea on the airy veranda.

King's Village ❹

131 Ka'iulani Ave. **Map** 4 E4.
***Tel** (808) 237-6344.* 🚌 *many buses.*
🕐 *9am–10pm daily.* ♿

King's Village is a cobble-stone shopping mall that recreates the period of David Kalākaua, ruler of the islands from 1874–91. Kalākaua was the last Hawaiian king and is known as the Merrie Monarch, thanks to his revival of the *hula*, which had been banned by the missionaries as a "lewd and lascivious dance." As the first Hawaiian monarch to travel the world, Kalākaua was particularly impressed with the British Empire and modeled 'Iolani Palace *(see p55)* and his guards' uniforms on what he saw in Victorian London.

King's Village itself consists of mock 19th-century shops selling souvenirs, clothing, jewelry, and fabrics. There are various food stalls and themed restaurants. Local street artists gather here at night to provide impromptu entertainment.

Every day at 6:15pm the center puts on a changing-of-the-guard ceremony, set against the backdrop of a Victorian-style Burger King! This is followed three nights a week by a *hula* show that demonstrates both ancient and modern styles *(see pp26–7)*.

Changing of the guard at King's Village

The area where King's Village and the Princess Ka'iulani and Hyatt hotels now stand was once a royal estate called 'Āinahau, famous for its lush gardens and flocks of peacocks. Here, in a grass hut, Robert Louis Stevenson told tales of England and Scotland to Ka'iulani, a half-Scottish, half-Hawaiian princess who was next in line to the Hawaiian throne. Later, distressed by the US annexation of Hawai'i *(see p44)*, Stevenson left the islands, heading farther into the Pacific, to Samoa. Princess Ka'iulani died in 1899 at the age of 23, some say from a broken heart caused by the loss of her beloved land.

Lifeguard keeping watch over water activities at Kūhiō Beach

Kūhiō Beach ❺

Map 4 F5. 🚌 *many buses.*

Wide Kūhiō Beach stretches eastward from Duke Kahanamoku's statue in central Waikīkī. Near the statue are four sacred boulders, known as the **Wizard Stones**, that represent healers who came from Tahiti before the 16th century. The healers are said to have passed their powers to the stones before returning home. The beach is a calm haven amid Waikīkī's swirling crowds. It is often rich in local color – grandmas in *mu'umu'u* (long, loose dresses) string *lei* garlands and weave coconut fronds, locals play back-gammon, and *hula* schools entertain in the evenings.

DUKE KAHANAMOKU

Duke Kahanamoku (1890–1968) first swam into fame at the 1912 Olympics, when he broke the world record for the 100-yard freestyle. It was as the father of modern surfing, though, that "the Duke" really made his name. He popularized the Hawaiian pastime, called *he'e nalu* (wave sliding), by giving demonstrations in the US, Europe, and Australia, and has been credited with putting Hawai'i on the map almost single-handedly. Back home, the popular hero was sheriff of Honolulu and unofficial goodwill ambassador. When he danced the *hula* with Queen Elizabeth, the photos were captioned "royalty dancing with royalty." At his funeral in 1968, 10,000 people turned out to see his ashes scattered in the seas off Waikīkī. His statue on Kūhiō Beach, always draped with *lei* from devoted fans, stands with its back to the sea. Some say it should be turned around so that the Duke can face his beloved ocean.

Sports hero Duke Kahanamoku receiving an award from Mayor Hylan of New York in 1920

GREATER HONOLULU

The landscape around Honolulu and Waikīkī is dominated by the peaks of the Ko'olau Range. Here, wild boar roam freely and hiking trails lead to waterfalls splashing into mountain pools. Set in these wooded hills, the Lyon Arboretum offers the chance to marvel at Hawai'i's botanical heritage, while nearby, the Queen Emma Summer Palace provides respite from the city heat, just as it did for the Queen herself back in the 1850s.

Closer to the city, the extinct craters of Diamond Head and Punchbowl stand guard. Kapi'olani Park, which sprawls beneath Diamond Head's

Rhinoceros at Honolulu Zoo

famous profile, is home to the Honolulu Zoo and Waikīkī Aquarium. The National Memorial Cemetery of the Pacific, in Punchbowl Crater, contains the graves of thousands of US war dead, and the horror of war is also remembered to the west, at Pearl Harbor. Here, on the site of the infamous 1941 attack, visitors tour the memorials and pay their respects to those who died.

Many of Honolulu's museums and galleries are situated on the outskirts of the city. Most significant among them is Bishop Museum, which houses the world's finest collection of Hawaiian and Polynesian artifacts.

SIGHTS AT A GLANCE

Museums and Galleries
Bishop Museum pp68–9 **1**
Honolulu Museum of Art **6**
Honolulu Museum of Art Spalding House **7**

Historic Buildings
Queen Emma Summer Palace **4**

Parks and Gardens
Kapi'olani Park **9**
Lyon Arboretum **8**

Cemeteries and Memorials
National Memorial Cemetery of the Pacific **5**
O'ahu Cemetery **2**
Pearl Harbor **10**
Royal Mausoleum **3**

KEY
	Main sightseeing areas
	Urban area
	Military/restricted area
✈	Airport
	Freeway
	Major road
	Minor road

0 kilometers 5
0 miles 3

Bishop Museum ❶

Princess Bernice Pauahi Bishop

Considered the world's finest museum of Polynesian culture, Bishop Museum was created as an American businessman's farewell to his beloved wife. When Princess Bernice Pauahi, the last royal descendant of Kamehameha the Great *(see p41)*, died in 1884, she left all her family heirlooms to her husband, Charles Bishop. Her cousin, Queen Emma, died shortly afterward and bequeathed her own Hawaiian artifacts to Bishop. He immediately set about building a home for the priceless collection, and Bishop Museum opened in 1902. Designated the "State Museum of Natural and Cultural History," it has over a million Pacific artifacts, plus millions of specimens of regional fauna and flora.

Third floor

STAR EXHIBITS

★ *Pili*-grass *Hale*

★ Tamate Costume

KEY

- ☐ Hawaiian Hall
- ☐ Polynesian Hall
- ☐ Picture Gallery
- ☐ J.M. Long Gallery
- ☐ Kāhili Room
- ☐ Nonexhibition space

★ Tamate Costume
Worn in dances involving a mock chase of women, this Melanesian shredded-fiber costume is a very rare artifact, as most are burned after the dance.

Entered from outside only, this vine-covered pavilion leads to a shell collection.

TRADITIONAL HAWAIIAN QUILTS

The Hawaiians' style of quilting reflects both their own tradition with *kapa* (bark cloth) and the quilting methods of missionaries. The designs, which are said to have been inspired by the shadows cast by breadfruit leaves on a piece of cloth, often honor the Hawaiian monarchy or depict the natural beauty of the islands. The habit of stitching Hawaiian flags into quilts began in 1843, when a British admiral ordered all flags to be destroyed.

The Bishop Museum has a fine collection of old and contemporary quilts.

Traditional Hawaiian quilt

Kāhili Room
Feather standards, or Kāhili, which accompanied high chiefs, are exhibited here in this room. They were made from feathers of forest and sea birds.

★ Pili-grass Hale
The timbers of this full-sized hale (traditional house), thatched with pili grass, were brought from Kaua'i in 1902. It sits on a platform to discourage dampness, has woven floor mats and a low doorway.

Second floor

Fern Stem Top Hat
A Hawaiian adaptation of Western fashion, this top hat was made in the early 19th century from local ferns.

Kū, the War God
This large sacred image of the war god Kū, carved from 'ōhi'a wood, dates from the early 19th century. It probably came from a heiau (temple) on Hawai'i Island.

First floor

Planetarium and Science Adventure Center

Moai
This Moai looms large on the lawn at the museum. It is a life-size replica of an Easter Island Rapanui, and was a gift from Japan.

MUSEUM GUIDE
The Hawaiian Hall has three floors: the first covers pre-contact Hawaiian culture, including a replica heiau; the second illustrates the importance of nature to Hawaiians in daily life and culture; and the third deals with Hawaiian gods, ali'i and history. Artifacts from the whole Pacific region can be seen in the Polynesian Hall, while the Kāhili Room displays the treasures of Hawai'i's monarchy. Other parts of the complex include a Science Adventure Center, planetarium, a library, and the Castle Building, which usually houses contemporary traveling exhibitions.

Castle Building

Main entrance

Three tiers of galleries overlooking the heart of the impressive Hawaiian Hall

Tombstones at Oʻahu Cemetery, established in 1844

Oʻahu Cemetery ❷

2162 Nuʻuanu Avenue. *Tel (808) 538-1538.* 4. 7am–6pm daily. only 5 or 6 times a year. **www**.oahucemetery.org

Oʻahu Cemetery (1844) was one of the first cemeteries established in Hawaiʻi. It was created to bury foreigners who did not belong to Kawaiahaʻo Church *(see p54)*, including members of prominent 19th-century missionary and merchant families. The cemetery is still in use, and many notable people of Asian, European, and Hawaiian descent are buried here. Among them are A.J. Cartwright, the "father of baseball"; Martha Root, spokesperson for the Bahaʻi faith; and several of Hawaiʻi's governors. Veterans of the Civil War are laid to rest here, as are casualties of the bombing of Pearl Harbor on December 7, 1941 *(see p44)*.

Royal Mausoleum ❸

2261 Nuʻuanu Avenue. *Tel (808) 587-0300.* 4. 8am–4pm Mon–Fri. public hols, except Mar 26 & Jun 11.

A few hundred yards from Oʻahu Cemetery is the Gothic-influenced Royal Mausoleum, enclosed by a wrought-iron

fence with gold crowns on each post. The final resting place of the kings and queens of Hawaiʻi, and their families, their bodies lie in tombs placed about the lawns.

Only two royal names are missing from this sanctuary: Kamehameha the Great (1758–1819), who was buried in the traditional way – in secret, his whereabouts unknown to this day – and Lunalilo (1835–74), who is buried in the grounds of Kawaiahaʻo Church *(see p54)* in downtown Honolulu.

Other people buried at the Royal Mausoleum include John Young, the English advisor to Kamehameha the Great, and Charles Bishop, the founder of the Bishop Museum *(see pp68–9)*. The original mausoleum building (1865) is now a chapel. The interior is made entirely of rich, dark *koa*-wood.

Queen Emma Summer Palace ❹

2913 Pali Highway (Hwy 61). *Tel (808) 595-3167.* 4, 55, 56, 57. 9am–4pm daily. public hols. **www**. queenemmasummerpalace.org

Built in the 1840s, this airy retreat in the Nuʻuanu Valley was used as a summer home by Queen Emma and her husband, Kamehameha IV. More modest than its name implies, it is a unique combination of Greek Revival architecture and local touches, such as the long *lānai* (porch). Emma's uncle, John Young II, left the palace to her in 1850.

Set in extensive gardens, it is still a cool oasis surrounded by huge trees, some planted by the royal family over 100 years ago. The mango trees planted at their wedding in 1856 are now 100-ft (30-m) tall and still bear fruit. The tamarind tree was planted by the couple's only son, Prince Albert, who died soon afterward, at the age of four.

The building houses many of the royal couple's personal belongings, including valuable period pieces, jewelry, household items, and artifacts from their Hawaiian heritage. Among the beautiful *koa*-wood furniture is the couple's large bed and their son's cradle, famous for its wave design.

The gift shop is run by the Daughters of Hawaiʻi, a group of women descended from missionary families, who rescued the house from demolition in 1913, restored it and then reopened it two years later. They also give daily tours to groups of ten or more.

The elegant façade of Queen Emma Summer Palace

The Honolulu Memorial at the National Memorial Cemetery of the Pacific

National Memorial Cemetery of the Pacific ❺

2177 Pūowaina Drive. **Map** 1 C1.
Tel (808) 532-3720. 🚌 15, then short
walk. ◯ 8am–5:30pm daily. 🅿️

Looming above downtown
Honolulu is Punchbowl, an
extinct volcanic crater. Within
it lies a 116-acre US military
cemetery, dedicated in 1949.
By 1991 the plot was filled to
capacity with over 33,000
graves, nearly half of them for
World War II dead, including
victims of the Pearl Harbor
attack in 1941 *(see p44)*.
There are also casualties from
the Korean War (1950–3) and
the Vietnam War (1964–75).
    Dominating the grounds
is the **Honolulu Memorial**
(dedicated in 1966), which
consists of a chapel, marble
slabs bearing the names of
over 28,000 soldiers missing in
action, and a staircase topped
by **Columbia**, a huge memorial statue. South of here a
short walk leads to a great
viewpoint over the city.

Honolulu Museum of Art ❻

900 S Beretania St. **Map** 2 D2.
Tel (808) 532-8700. 🚌 2, 13.
◯ 10am–4:30pm Tue–Sat, 1–5pm
Sun. 🅿️ public hols. 🅿️ 🛗 Ward
Ave Gate. 🅿️ 🖥️ 11:30am–2pm
Tue–Sat. **www**.honolulumuseum.org

In 2012, the Honolulu Academy
of Art, founded by Mrs.
Charles Montague Cooke in
1922, and The Contemporary

Museum combined to form the
Honolulu Museum of Art. The
galleries are located in two of
Honolulu's most beautiful
buildings. Visitors can enjoy
the cafés, gardens, concerts,
and films in both locations for
a single admission fee.
    The permanent collection
includes more than 20,000
works of Asian art, with the
highlight being the James A.
Michener Collection of more
than 10,000 Japanese *ukiyo-e*
woodblock prints.
    The collection also features
European art, notably Italian
Renaissance paintings and
works by Van Gogh, Monet,
and Picasso. American works
on display include pieces by
Mary Cassatt and Winslow
Homer among others.
    A tour to the Shangri La,
home of American heiress
Doris Duke, starts at the
museum. This architectural
landmark houses an extensive
Islamic art collection from Iran,
India, Morocco, and Syria.

Honolulu Museum of Art Spalding House ❼

2411 Makiki Heights Drive.
Tel (808) 532-8700. 🚌 15.
◯ 10am–4pm Tue–Sat; noon–4pm
Sun. 🅿️ public hols. 🅿️ 🛗 🖥️ 📷
www.honolulumuseum.org

Honolulu's only museum
dedicated to modern art was
formerly known as The
Contemporary Museum. It
started life in the downtown
News Building and moved to
the present site in 1988, when
the now defunct daily newspaper, the *Honolulu Advertiser*,
donated the luxurious estate
as a permanent home.
    Housing a permanent collec-
tion of sculptures, ceramics,
paintings, prints, photos, and
videos by national and international artists, spanning the
years from 1940 to the present.
There are also numerous
temporary exhibitions. The
Cades Pavilion displays
L'Enfant et les Sortilèges
(1983), David Hockney's
walk-through installation
based on his set for Ravel's
opera, staged by New York's
Metropolitan Opera.
    The estate that surrounds
the museum has innovative
sculpture, huge trees, sloping
lawns, orchids, bromeliads,
and a path that encourages
meditation as it winds among
grottoes designed by a local
minister turned gardener.
    The Spalding House Café,
set in a secluded corner, has
delicious food *(see p197)*.

Hockney's *L'Enfant et les Sortilèges* at Honolulu Museum of Art Spalding House

Lyon Arboretum ❽

3860 Mānoa Rd. *Tel (808) 988-0456.* 🚌 5. ⏰ *8am–4pm Mon–Fri, 9am–3pm Sat.* ⚫ *public hols.*
Donation 🎥 ♿ www.hawaii.edu/lyonarboretum

Only a short drive from busy Waikīkī, this retreat is an ideal tonic for the weary sightseer. Short, verdant trails wind through the trees and reveal botanical delights at every turn.

Founded in 1918 in an effort to reforest land made barren by cattle grazing, the Lyon Arboretum is now home to over 5,000 plant species, both native and introduced. It is nationally recognized as a center for the conservation of Hawaiian plants, and its 194 acres support over 80 endangered and rare species. These include the state flower, *ma'o hau hele* (a yellow hibiscus), and the tree gardenia, *nānū*, whose

scientific name, *Gardenia brighamii*, honors W.T. Brigham, the first director of the Bishop Museum *(see pp68–9)*. The arboretum now features around 600 varieties of palm, more than any other botanical garden in the world.

A substantial part of the arboretum is open to the public; the rest is set aside for research. The on-site hybridization program has resulted in more than 160 new cultivars, including hybrids of hibiscus and rhododendron.

There are three quiet memorial gardens and an aromatic spice and herb patch near the main building. A little farther away, the Beatrice H. Krauss Ethnobotanical Garden displays plants that have been used by native Hawaiians as medicine, food, and building materials.

View of Kapi'olani Park from Diamond Head

Kapi'olani Park ❾

Map 4 F5. 🚌 *4, 8, 19, 20, 47.* ⏰ *daily.* ♿ **Zoo** 151 Kapahulu Ave. *Tel (808) 971-7171.* ⏰ *9am–4:30pm daily.* ⚫ *Dec 25.* 🎥 ♿ www.honoluluzoo.org **Aquarium** 2777 Kalākaua Ave. *Tel (808) 923-9741.* ⏰ *9am–5pm daily.* ⚫ *Dec 25.* 🎥 ♿ www.waquarium.org

This 300-acre expanse of green offers a 2-mile (3-km) jogging path, tennis courts, barbecues, and special areas

HONOLULU'S MAKIKI-TANTALUS TRAILS

Forming a loop around lush Makiki Valley 3 miles (5 km) north of Waikīkī, Round Top Drive and Tantalus Drive offer fine views of the city. The trails that lace between the roads delve deep into the rain forest and teem with bird life and exotic flora. Weekday mornings are quietest, but weekend hikes run by the Sierra Club or Nature Conservancy *(see p235)* are informative and tackle the more challenging areas. On any hike, be well prepared: dress for comfort, wear sturdy shoes, bring a flashlight and plenty of water and food, and stick to the main trails. Most importantly, never hike alone. The Hawai'i Nature Center, off Makiki Heights Drive, provides maps and good advice.

View from Pu'u 'Ōhi'a Trail

KEY
═ Road
- - Hiking trail
🌟 Vista
🅿 Parking

for softball, archery, and kite-flying. It is also the site of crafts fairs and many celebrations.

The north end of the park is devoted to **Honolulu Zoo** whose highlight is an extensive African savanna section. On Sunday mornings, local artists display their works on the zoo fence facing Monsarrat Avenue.

The **Waikīkī Aquarium**, on the southwest side, features the usual sea life as well as a special exhibit on the endangered Hawaiian monk seal and a hands-on tide pool. The aquarium also organizes reef walks, some specially for children.

The park acts as a gateway to **Diamond Head**. To see the extinct volcano, either take the scenic circle drive to Diamond Head lighthouse, whose lawn is a favorite spot for tourist weddings and sunset watching, or you can hike to the summit from a parking lot in the crater. Entrance to the crater is marked by a sign on Diamond Head Road, the continuation of Monsarrat Avenue. The trail is quite steep, but the sweeping view is worth the hour-long ascent. Part of the hike involves climbing a staircase in a tunnel; take a flashlight if you are claustrophobic.

Pearl Harbor ⓾

7 miles (11 km) NW of downtown Honolulu. 🚌 20, 42. **USS Arizona** 1 Arizona Memorial Drive. *Tel* (808) 422-0561. ⏰ 7am–5pm daily. ⬤ Jan 1, Thanksgiving, Dec 25. ♿ ▓ www.nps.gov/usar **USS Bowfin** 11 Arizona Memorial Drive. *Tel* (808) 423-1341. ⏰ 8am–5pm daily. ⬤ Jan 1, Thanksgiving, Dec 25. ▓ ♿ museum only. www.bowfin.org **USS Missouri** and **Battleship Missouri Memorial** 11 Arizona Memorial Drive. *Tel* (808) 423-2263. ⏰ 8am–4pm daily. ⬤ Jan 1, Thanksgiving, Dec 25. ▓ ▓ www.ussmissouri.com

When Honolulu was made capital of Hawai'i in 1845, a major reason was its proximity to one of the world's best

The white-marble USS *Arizona* Memorial in Pearl Harbor

natural harbors – Pearl Harbor. In the time of Kamehameha the Great, the inlet supported oysters that were farmed for their pearls. Later, the port was crucial for whalers, trade with China, and both the sugar and pineapple industries. Leased to the US in 1887 as part of a trade treaty, it was first used militarily in the Spanish-American War of 1898. Today it houses modern warships, military museums, and memorials. Most significant among these is the **USS Arizona** Memorial, perched above the sunken ship of that name. The ship went down with hundreds of its crew during the Japanese attack on December 7, 1941 that brought the US into World War II. For many people the visit to this site is a pilgrimage, so appropriate dress is requested.

A huge Galapagos tortoise at Honolulu Zoo

On busy days tickets may all be allocated by 1pm, and there is often a wait of up to 2 hours for the boat to the offshore memorial. It is best to get your ticket first and then browse in the museum, which features details of the attack and histories of the ships, planes, and personnel involved, both US and Japanese. It offers a balanced and personal view of the participants. Near the ticket desk is a panel describing the volunteers for the day. They are usually Pearl Harbor survivors and are available to answer questions and share their stories. Ceremonies are held here on important days. Another place to visit during

a day at Pearl Harbor is the nearby award-winning **USS Bowfin Submarine Museum and Park**, a tribute to the role of the submarine in war and peacetime security. The museum covers the history of submarines, beginning with the first attempt to build one in 1776. Visitors can view the inner workings of a Poseidon missile, and they can also inspect control panels from retired submarines and see how the crew whiled away their time in cramped quarters.

The USS *Bowfin* submarine is moored nearby and is open for public viewing. The park itself contains a memorial to the crews of the 52 US submarines lost in World War II.

The **USS Missouri**, opened to the public in 1999 as the **Battleship Missouri Memorial**. On September 2, 1945, General MacArthur, aboard this ship, accepted the Japanese surrender that ended World War II. Check the website for additional information and images from the ship's history: (www. ussmissouri.com).

The crew's tightly packed bunks inside the USS *Bowfin* submarine

STREET FINDER

The map references given for sights, shops, and entertainment places in Honolulu and Waikīkī refer to the four pages of maps in this section. The key map below shows the area of the city that is covered, with the two major sightseeing districts color-coded red. All the principal sights mentioned in the text are marked as well as useful information such as transit stations, parking lots, tourist offices, and post offices; a full list is given in the key. Map references are also given in the Travelers' Needs section for the hotels *(see pp178–81)* and restaurants *(see pp196–9)* in Honolulu and Waikīkī.

KEY

▦ Major sight	🚓 Police station	← One-way street
▦ Other building	🚕 Taxi stand	▬ Pedestrianized street
🚌 Bus terminal	✝ Church	
⛴ Ferry terminal	🛕 Temple	**SCALE OF MAPS 1–4**
P Parking	⊠ Post office	
ℹ Tourist information	⛳ Golf course	0 meters 250
✚ Hospital with emergency room	▬ Freeway	0 yards 250

0 kilometers   1

0 miles   1

A

'A'ala Street	**1 A1**
'Ahana Street	**3 A2**
'Āhui Street	**1 C5**
'Ākala Lane	**2 F2**
Akoko Street	**2 F2**
Ala Moana Boulevard	**1 B4 & 3 A4**
Ala Wai Boulevard	**3 B4**
Alakea Street	**1 A3**
Alapa'i Street	**1 C3**
Alder Street	**2 F3**
Alexander Street	**3 B1**
Algaroba Street	**3 B2**
Aloha Drive	**4 D4**
Aloha Tower Drive	**1 A3**
'Alohi Way	**2 E3**
'Āmana Street	**3 A3**
Artesian Street	**3 B1**

Artesian Way	**3 B1**
Atkinson Drive	**3 A4**
Auahi Street	**1 B4**
Avon Way	**2 D1**

B

Barron Lane	**1 B1**
Beach Walk	**4 D4**
Bethel Street	**1 A3**
Beverly Court	**2 E2**
Bingham Street	**3 B1**
Birch Street	**2 F3**
Bishop Street	**1 A3**
Bowers Lane	**1 B2**

C

Captain Cook Avenue	**1 C2**
Cartwright Road	**4 F5**
Cary Circle	**2 D3**

Cedar Street	**2 F3**
Channel Street	**1 A5**
Chapin Street	**2 D3**
Chaplain Lane	**1 A2**
Church Lane	**4 E2**
Citron Street	**3 B2**
Clark Street	**3 A1**
Clayton Street	**2 D3**
Cleghorn Street	**4 E4**
College Walk	**1 A1**
Cooke Street	**1 C5**
Coolidge Street	**4 D2**
Coral Street	**1 B5**
Coyne Street	**3 B1**
Cummins Street	**2 D4**
Curtis Street	**1 C3**

D

Date Street	**3 C2**

Davenport Place	**2 E1**
Davenport Street	**2 E1**
Dewey Court	**3 C5**
Dole Street	**3 A1**
Don Ho Street	**4 D5**
Dreier Street	**1 C3**
Dudley Street	**3 C4**
Dudoit Lane	**3 C4**

E

'Ekela Avenue	**4 F3**
Elm Street	**2 E3**
Elsie Lane	**3 A2**
Emerson Street	**2 D1**
Emma Lane	**1 B2**
'Ena Road	**3 B4**
Enos Lane	**3 A1**
Ernest Street	**2 E2**
Evelyn Lane	**3 B1**

F

Farrington Street	3 C1
Fern Street	3 B3
First Avenue	4 F1
Fort Street	1 A3
Fort Street Mall	1 A3
Frear Street	1 C2

G

Green Street	2 D2
Griffiths Street	3 C1

H

Hakuhaku Street	2 E4
Halekauwila Street	1 B3
Halekula Way	3 A1
Hale Māka'i Street	2 D3
Haleumi Place	2 E1
Hassinger Street	2 E1
Hau'oli Street	3 B3
Hausten Street	4 D2
Helumoa Road	4 D5
Heulu Street	2 F1
Hi'aloa Street	1 B1
Hīhīwai Street	4 D3
Hoawa Lane	3 C1
Hobron Lane	3 B4
Holomoana Street	3 A4
Ho'ola'i Street	2 E3
Ho'onanea Street	3 C1
Hopaka Street	2 E4

I

Ilalo Street	1 B5
Ilaniwai Street	1 C4
'Iolani Avenue	1 B1
Isenberg Street	3 C2

K

Ka'aha Street	4 D2
Ka'aloa Street	4 D2
Ka'ipu'u Street	4 E2
Kahakai Drive	3 A4
Kāheka Street	3 A2
Kahoaloha Lane	4 E2
Kahūnā Lane	4 D2
Kai'ali'u Street	4 D1
Kaihe'e Street	2 F1
Kaimukī Avenue	4 F2
Kai'olu Street	4 D4
Kaio'o Drive	3 B4
Ka'iulani Avenue	4 E4
Kālaimoku Street	4 D4
Kalākaua Avenue	3 A2
Kalākaua Circle	3 A2
Kalauokalani Way	3 A3
Kalei Road	4 E1
Kālia Road	3 C4
Kalo Place	4 D1
Kāluawa'a Street	4 F1
Kamaile Street	2 F3
Kamakee Street	2 E4
Kamakini Street	4 F1
Kamāmalu Avenue	1 B1
Kamani Street	1 C4
Kamoku Street	4 D3
Kānekapōlei Street	4 E4
Kāneloa Road	4 F5
Kānewai Street	4 F1
Kanunu Street	2 F3 & 3 A3
Kapa'akea Lane	4 D2
Kapahulu Avenue	4 F2

Kapili Street	4 F4
Kapi'olani	
Boulevard	1 C3 & 3 A3
Kapuni Street	4 F4
Karratti Lane	2 E1
Kawaiaha'o Street	1 C3
Kealohilani Avenue	4 F5
Keauhou Street	1 B4
Keawe Street	1 B4
Ke'eaumoku Street	2 F1
Kelikoi Street	1 B5
Kemole Lane	3 C1
Keoniana Street	3 C4
Kewalo Street	2 F1
Kīhei Place	4 F2
Kinalau Place	2 D2
Kīna'u Street	1 C2
Koa Avenue	4 E5
Koali Road	4 F1
Kolo Place	4 D1
Kona Iki Street	2 F4
Kona Street	2 E4 & 3 A3
Kō'ula Street	1 C5
Kuamo'o Street	3 C4
Ku'ikahi Street	3 A2
Kuilei Street	4 D2
Kūhiō Avenue	3 C4

L

Lā'au Street	4 E3
Lana Lane	1 C5
Lauhala Street	1 C2
Lauiki Street	4 D3
Laulā Way	2 E3
Launiu Street	4 D4
Lau'ula Street	4 D4
Leialoha Avenue	4 F2
Leilehua Lane	1 B1
Lemon Road	4 F5
Lewers Street	4 D5
Liholiho Street	2 F1
Likelike Street	1 B3
Lili'uokalani Avenue	4 F5
Lime Street	3 B3
Lincoln Avenue	4 F2
Liona Street	2 F3
Līpe'epe'e Street	3 B4
Lisbon Street	1 C2
Lōkahi Street	3 B2
Lower Campus Road	4 D1
Lukepane Avenue	4 F2
Lunalilo	
Freeway	1 B1 & 3 A1
Lunalilo Street	1 C2
Lusitana Street	1 B1

M

Magazine Street	2 D1
Magellan Avenue	1 C1
Mahi Place	4 D1
Mahi'ai Place	4 E2
Māhukona Street	3 A3
Makahiki Way	3 C2
Makaleka Avenue	4 F3
Makaloa	
Street	2 F3 & 3 A3
Makaoe Lane	3 B3
Makiki Street	2 F2
Malanai Street	3 B2
Maluhia Street	3 C4
Mānalo Street	3 B2
Mānele Street	1 C2

Manukai Street	4 D4
Marmion Street	1 C3
Matlock Avenue	2 F2
Mauna'ihi Place	2 D1
Maunakea Street	1 A2
Maunawai Place	4 E2
McCully Street	3 B1
Merchant Street	1 A3
Metcalf Street	3 B1
Mililani Street	1 B3
Miller Street	1 B2
Mission Lane	1 C3
Moku Place	2 F1
Momi Way	3 C1
Mott-Smith Drive	2 E1
Mountain View	
Drive	4 F4

N

Nāhaku Place	4 E2
Nāhua Street	4 E4
Nāko'oko'o Street	4 D2
Nāmāhana Street	3 C4
Nanea Street	3 B3
Nehe Lane	1 B1
Nimitz Highway	1 A3
Niu Street	3 C4
Nohonani Street	4 E4
North Beretania	
Street	1 A2
North Hotel Street	1 A2
North King Street	1 A2
North Kukui Street	1 A1
Nu'uanu Avenue	1 A3

O

'Ohe Street	1 C5
'Ōhua Avenue	4 F5
Oliver Street	3 B1
'Olohana Street	4 D4
Olokele Avenue	4 F3
Osorio Place	2 D2

P

Pā'ani Street	3 C2
Pali Highway	1 B1
Palm Drive	2 F2
Paoa Place	3 C5
Paoakalani Avenue	4 F5
Papakū Place	2 E2
Pau Lane	3 B4
Pau Street	3 C4
Pauahi Street	1 A2
Pāwa'a Lane	3 B2
Pele Street	1 C1
Pensacola Street	2 E1
Philip Street	3 A2
Pi'ikoi Place	2 E1
Pi'ikoi Street	2 E1
Pohā Lane	3 C1
Pohukaina Street	1 B4
Poni Street	3 A3
Prince Edward	
Street	4 E4
Priory Lane	1 B2
Prospect Street	1 C1
Pua'ena Place	4 D1
Pualani Way	4 F4
Pualoke Place	3 A3
Pumehana Street	3 B2
Punahou Street	3 A1
Punchbowl Street	1 B4

Q

Queen Emma Square	1 B2
Queen Emma Street	1 B2
Queen Street	1 A3
Quinn Lane	1 B4

R

Reed Lane	1 B4
Richards Street	1 B3
River Street	1 A2
Roland Lane	1 C3
Royal Hawaiian	
Avenue	4 D4
Rycroft Street	2 E3 & 3 A3

S

Saint Louis Drive	4 F1
Saratoga Road	4 D4
Seaside Avenue	4 D4
Sheridan Street	2 F3
Smith Street	1 A2
South Beretania	
Street	1 A2 & 3 A2
South Hotel Street	1 A2
South King	
Street	1 A3 & 3 A2
South Kukui Street	1 A2
South School	
Street	1 A1
South Street	1 B5
Spencer Street	2 D2
Spreckels Street	3 A1

T

Thomas Square	2 D2
Thurston Avenue	2 D2
Tusitala Street	4 E4

U

Uluniu Avenue	4 E5
Union Mall	1 B2
University Avenue	4 D1

V

Varsity Circle	4 E1
Varsity Place	4 D1
Victoria Street	2 D2
Villa Lane	3 B1
Vineyard Boulevard	1 A1
Vineyard Street	1 B2

W

Wai Nani Way	4 F5
Wai'aka Place	4 E2
Wai'aka Road	4 E2
Wai'alae Avenue	4 E1
Waiau Place	3 A1
Waikolu Way	4 D4
Waimanu Street	2 D4
Waiola Street	3 B2
Walina Street	4 E4
Ward Avenue	2 D4
Whitney Street	3 A1
Wilder	
Avenue	2 F1 & 3 A1
Wiliwili Street	3 C2
Winam Avenue	4 F2
Wong Ho Lane	2 E2

Y

Young Street	2 D2 & 3 A2

HAWAI'I ISLAND BY ISLAND

The Hawaiian Islands at a Glance

The Hawaiian Islands offer an outstanding array
of natural beauty spots and places of cultural
interest. The landscape is incredibly diverse, from
beach-fringed coastal shores to lush, grassy uplands
and alpine summits. Visitors may experience volcanic
eruptions, see world-class surfing, explore the fascinating cultural heritage of Polynesia, or simply relax
in the sea and sun.

Princeville (see p165), *a resort
community on Kaua'i's lush
North Shore, is a favorite with
golfers for its excellent courses.*

KAUA'I
(see pp156–73)

NI'IHAU

0 kilometers   50

0 miles   25

Kaua'i's Nā Pali Coast
(see pp168–9) *features
stunning, sharply incised
cliffs, slender beaches, and
deep blue seas. Enthusiastic
hikers can see the scenery
up close by following the
rugged Kalalau Trail.*

O'AHU
(see pp84–93)

*Honolulu
and Waikīkī*

**Waimea Bay on O'ahu's North
Shore** (see p31) *is home to some of
the world's biggest waves. Expert surfers
flock here from around the world to
demonstrate their skill and courage
in front of appreciative onlookers.*

The Polynesian Cultural Center (see
p92) *in Lā'ie on O'ahu's windward shore
displays Polynesian heritage. Through
dances and craft demonstrations,
visitors witness the traditional cultures
of Tonga, Hawai'i, Samoa, Tahiti, Fiji,
the Marquesas, and New Zealand.*

Kalaupapa National Historical Park (see pp100–1) *commemorates the more than 8,000 victims of leprosy who suffered and died on this remote Moloka'i peninsula, and the saintly work of Father Damien who tended the sick. He was buried in the garden of St. Philomena.*

Wailea Beach *is one of a string of beautiful sheltered beaches on South Maui's leeward coast (see p127). Visitors flock here to relax on the golden sands and in the calm coastal waters, and to take advantage of the ideal swimming, snorkeling, and diving conditions.*

MOLOKA'I AND LĀNA'I *(see pp94–105)*

MAUI *(see pp106–29)*

KAHO'OLAWE

Maui's sheltered coastal waters are home to wintering whales.

Mauna Kea, snow-capped for part of the year, is Hawai'i's tallest mountain.

Hawai'i Volcanoes National Park (see pp152–3), *with its active East Rift Zone, is the site of both spectacular fire cones and lava flows. Billowing steam plumes, such as this one at Lae'apuki at sunrise, form when fiery lava enters the ocean.*

HAWAI'I ISLAND *(see pp130–55)*

Pu'uhonua o Hōnaunau National Historical Park (see pp138–9), *an ancient place of refuge, provides a unique glimpse into traditional Hawaiian culture and its laws.*

O'AHU

The third largest island in the archipelago with an area of 600 sq miles (1,550 sq km), O'ahu was born of two volcanoes that formed the Wai'anae Mountains to the west and the Ko'olau Range to the northeast. Three-quarters of Hawai'i's million residents live here, mostly in the greater Honolulu area or nestled in the deep valleys that cut between the mountains. This island also receives the largest number of visitors.

O'ahu was conquered in 1795 by Kamehameha the Great, whose forces chased rival chiefs Kai'ana and Kalanikūpule and their men back into Nu'uanu Valley, forcing them off a precipice at the top. Kai'ana was killed outright, and though Kalanikūpule escaped, he was later captured and sacrificed by the great king. The battle was an important victory in Kamehameha's campaign to unify the islands *(see pp41–2)*.

In the 1800s, farmers began growing pineapples in the highlands, and by the middle of the century sugar-cane plantations had become big business. Workers came from China, Japan, Portugal, and elsewhere – the origin of Hawai'i's ethnic diversity. But increasingly, as both the sugar and pineapple industries have declined, much of central O'ahu has been given over to malls and nondescript housing complexes, crammed together on expensive acreage. Some residents now link tourism with overdevelopment and the resultant threat to ancestral lands. Many local people live in relative poverty.

Beautiful scenery, however, is never far away. From Wahiawā the road rolls through undulating fields of pineapple down to the bohemian North Shore surfing town of Hale'iwa. From here to Makapu'u Point on O'ahu's southeast corner, the narrow highway skirts a chain of green velvet, mist-draped mountains. Islets dot the turquoise sea as you pass seaside villages and one deserted beach after another. Along the way are fruit stands, sparkling waterfalls, and Buddhist temples. In the west, the old town of Waipahu is a living museum of plantation history, and the arid Wai'anae Coast offers perfect sunsets and a chance to see an unspoiled slice of Hawaiian life.

Traditional dancing at the Polynesian Cultural Center in Lā'ie, a popular tourist attraction

◁ Fearless surfers riding the record-breaking waves of Waimea Bay, on O'ahu's legendary North Shore

Exploring Oʻahu

Hawaiʻi's most visited island, Oʻahu has much
to offer besides the clamor of humanity in
Honolulu, Waikīkī, and the central ʻEwa plain.
The rest of the island is amazingly rural, with
large areas of sugarcane fields and rain forest
where wild boar still roam. It is easy to escape
into Oʻahu's spectacular scenery as jungle-clad
roads and trails transport you from the high-rises
of Honolulu. The Waiʻanae Mountains and the
Koʻolau Range form the backbones of the island,
while tropical beaches line the shimmering coast.
The snorkelers' paradise of Hanauma Bay and
the world-class surf breaks on the North Shore
draw the crowds, but the Waiʻanae Coast
is peaceful. Cultural attractions
range from the popular
Polynesian Cultural
Center to the tranquil
Byodo-In Temple.

Byodo-In Temple, a Buddhist Shrine

SIGHTS AT A GLANCE

Byodo-In Temple ❸
Dole Plantation ❽
Haleʻiwa ❼
Hanauma Bay ❶
Hauʻula Trails ❹
Hawaiʻi's Plantation Village ❾
HONOLULU & WAIKĪKĪ pp46–79
Kaʻena Point ⓫
Makapuʻu Point ❷
Polynesian Cultural Center ❺
Waiʻanae Coast ❿
Waimea Valley ❻

SEE ALSO

• **Where to Stay** pp182–3
• **Where to Eat** pp199–200

KEY

═ Freeway
— Major road
┅ Minor road
-- Track
— Scenic route
△ Summit

Sheltered Hanauma Bay, a favorite with snorkelers

For additional map symbols *see back flap*

TOP RECREATIONAL AREAS

The places shown here have been selected for their recreational activities. Conditions, especially those of the ocean, vary depending on the weather and the time of year, so exercise caution and, if in doubt, stay out of the water or seek local advice.

	SWIMMING	SNORKELING	DIVING	BODY-SURFING	WINDSURFING	HIKING	HORSEBACK RIDING	GOLF
ALA MOANA BEACH COUNTY PARK	●	●		●				
ALI'I BEACH PARK	●			●				
DIAMOND HEAD				●	●	●		
HANAUMA BAY		●	●					
HAU'ULA TRAILS						●		
KA'ENA POINT						●		
KAHUKU AND KUILIMA	●						●	●
KAILUA BEACH COUNTY PARK	●				●			
KOKO HEAD CRATER						●		
MAKAPU'U POINT				●				
MĀNOA FALLS						●		
MAUNAWILI						●	●	
MOKULĒ'IA	●			●		●		
NORTH SHORE	●	●	●	●	●	●	●	
TANTALUS						●		
WAI'ANAE COAST	●	●	●	●	●	●		●
WAIKĪKĪ	●	●		●				
WAIMĀNALO	●		●	●			●	

GETTING AROUND

O'ahu is served by Honolulu International Airport. There is a good road network, and the best way to get around is by rented car. Three freeways radiate out from Honolulu: H1 takes you to the Wai'anae Coast, H2 veers north toward Hale'iwa, and H3 crosses to the windward (northeast) coast. *TheBus* company runs two routes (52, 55) that link Honolulu with central O'ahu, the windward coast, and the North Shore *(see inside back cover)*.

0 kilometers 5

0 miles 5

Trained dolphins performing graceful maneuvers at Sea Life Park

Remove your shoes before entering the shrine, where a 9-ft (3-m) gold and lacquer Buddha presides.

Visiting the temple just before sunset provides a tranquil experience. You will not be able to see the Buddha (the temple closes at 4pm), but the profound silence will be punctuated only by the singing of birds. The sun setting behind the cliffs gives off pink and mauve hues, and, if you are lucky, you may have the scene all to yourself.

Hanauma Bay ❶

Honolulu Co. Kalaniana'ole Highway (Hwy 72), 10 miles (16 km) E of Waikīkī. **Tel** (808) 396-4229. 🚌 ◯ 6am–6pm Wed–Mon. ● Dec 25. 📷 ♿🖥️📷

Snorkeling in this sheltered bay is like swimming in a gigantic aquarium with more than 400 species of fish, some of which exist only here. A sandy-bottomed hole in the reef is perfect for first-time snorkelers. Fish-feeding, once a popular tourist activity, is no longer allowed since this is a conservation district. A Marine Education Center presents an orientation video and offers restrooms, a snack bar; and a tram service to the beach. To avoid the crowds, visit early in the morning.

Makapu'u Point ❷

Honolulu Co. Kalaniana'ole Highway (Hwy 72), 14 miles (23 km) E of Waikīkī. 🚌 Sea Life Park.

It is worth stopping at the lookout below the Makapu'u lighthouse for humbling views of sky and sea, with rock islets artistically arranged. You can watch the action on nearby **Makapu'u Beach**, a pocket cove that boasts the island's best body-surfing waves. Local kids make the wave-hopping look easy, but it requires precise timing to avoid being dragged onto the rocks.

Hiking trails lead upward into black mountains, but you do not need to climb beyond the first 100 ft (30 m) or so for spectacular photos. Hikers can continue to the hang-glider launch site at 1,250 ft (380 m) and watch the intrepid fliers.

Facing Makapu'u Beach, the educational **Sea Life Park** features a huge Hawaiian reef tank and regular performances by penguins, sea lions, and dolphins. The park has spectacular views of O'ahu's breathtaking coastline. Buses link up with Waikīkī.

🎭 **Sea Life Park**
41-202 Kalaniana'ole Hwy (Hwy 72). **Tel** (808) 259-7933. ◯ 10:30am–5pm daily. 📷 ♿📷 **www.sealifeparkhawaii.com**

Byodo-In Temple ❸

Honolulu Co. 47-200 Kahekili Highway (Hwy 83), Kāne'ohe. **Tel** (808) 239-8811. 🚌 on Kahekili Hwy (Hwy 83), then 10-min walk. ◯ 9am–5pm daily. ● Dec 25. 📷♿ **www.byodo-in.com**

This replica of a 900-year-old Japanese temple cannot be seen from the highway. The only marker is a Hawai'i Visitors and Convention Bureau sign for a historic sight. Once you turn into the Valley of Temples – a nondenominational cemetery – the road winds into the valley to reach this hidden treasure, its walls red against fluted, green cliffs. After crossing the curved vermilion footbridge, you can ring a three-ton bell to assure long life and to receive the blessings of the Buddha.

Hau'ula Trails ❹

Honolulu Co. Kamehameha Hwy (Hwy 83), 20 miles (30 km) NW of Kāne'ohe, approximately 2 miles (3 km) past Punalu'u. **Tel** (808) 973-9782. ◯ weekends and holidays. **www.hawaiitrails.ehawaii.gov**

The three trails that make up the Hau'ula Trails area – Hau'ula Loop Trail, Ma'akua Ridge Trail, and Ma'akua Gulch Trail – provide everything that hikers love best about Hawai'i's finest trails. They are wide with excellent footing and offer spectacular mountain, valley, and ocean views. You should allow approximately two hours for a round-trip of any of the trails, all of which begin beyond the end of Ma'akua Road, off Hau'ula Homestead Road which is just beyond the tiny town of Hau'ula.

The beautifully crafted Buddha, centerpiece of the Japanese Byodo-In Temple

Beaches of Southeast O'ahu

From Makapu'u Point at the southern tip to the com-
muter suburbia of Kāne'ohe, O'ahu's southeast
coast features a range of delightful beaches, with free
access to the public. Waimānalo Beach offers lazy
swimming in calm seas, Lanikai Beach is exclusive
and quiet, and the tree-lined community of Kailua has
extensive beach facilities. To discourage break-ins
in the area, do not leave items of value in your car.

O'AHU

Kāne'ohe

HONOLULU

0 kilometers   4

0 miles   2

Kāne'ohe Bay, *protected
by a barrier reef, features
two prominent islands:
Mokoli'i (Chinaman's Hat)
and Moku o Lo'e (Coconut
Island). Kāne'ohe itself
is a bedroom town for
the local military base.*

MŌKAPU PENINSULA

● He'eia State Park

● He'eia

836

● KĀNE'OHE

H3

836

83

630

630

63

KAILUA ● Kailua
Beach

HONOLULU

H3

61

83

61

Kāne'ohe Bay

Kailua Bay

Kahekili Hwy

Kalaniana'ole Hwy

● Lanikai

Lanikai Beach

Lanikai Beach *is one of the
most beautiful beaches on
O'ahu. The white sands
stretch for a little over a mile
(1.5 km) and are overlooked
by the beachfront mansions
of affluent Lanikai.*

● Bellows Field
Beach Park

72

● Waimānalo Bay
State Recreation Area

● Waimānalo Bay

● Kaupō Beach
County Park

● Sea Life Park
● Makapu'u Beach
Makapu'u Point

72

HONOLULU

At Kailua Beach, a 30-acre
park with full facilities, you
can rent a kayak or a sail-
board for windsurfing, snorkel
to a deserted island, or just sit
back and enjoy the scenery.
The reef-protected waters are
popular with local families.

KEY

▬	Freeway
▬	Major road
▬	Minor road
🏌	Golf course
⚓	Vista

Waimānalo Beach, *the longest on
O'ahu at 3 miles (5 km), has safe
seas and gently sloping sand.*

Couple riding bikes at Kualoa Ranch, East O'ahu ▷

Polynesian Cultural Center ❺

Honolulu Co. 55-370 Kamehameha
Highway (Hwy 83), Lā'ie. **Tel** (808)
293-3333. 🅿 🕐 noon–9pm
Mon–Sat. ● Thanksgiving, Dec 25.
📷 ♿ www.polynesia.com

The village of Lā'ie was
founded by Mormon mis-
sionaries in 1864 after a failed
attempt to settle on the island
of Lāna'i. Lā'ie now contains
a Mormon temple, a branch
of Brigham Young University,
and a 42-acre educational
theme park known as the
Polynesian Cultural Center.

At the Center, students from
all over the Pacific demonstrate
crafts and dancing in seven
Polynesian "villages":
Tongan, Hawaiian, Samoan,
Tahitian, Fijian, Maori, and
Marquesan. The instruc-
tion, whether it be
Tongan drumming or
Samoan fire-making,
is delivered in almost
continuous minishows,
and audience participation
is encouraged. The
afternoon show,
Rainbows of Paradise,
presents legends from
all the islands with
singing, dancing, and
martial arts performed
on double-hulled canoes.

Matsumoto's
shave ice

The Center is worth the hefty
admission fee. However,
some critics question the
authenticity of the exhibits and
shows – not all the "islanders"
in the villages are the real
thing. Despite this, the PCC
remains Hawai'i's most popular
paid attraction, with 900,000
visitors a year. Regular shuttle
buses connect with Waikīkī.

Waimea Valley ❻

Honolulu Co. 59-864 Kamehameha
Highway (Hwy 83), Waimea. **Tel** (808)
638-7766. 🚌 52, 55. 🕐 9am–5pm
daily. ● Jan 1, Thanksgiving, Dec
25. 📷 ♿ www.waimeavalley.net

One of a few intact examples
of an *ahupua'a* – a Hawaiian
land division from mountain
to sea – Waimea Valley is a
beautiful, unspoilt environment, a sacred place for
native Hawaiians, and
an important educational
resource. After periods as an
attraction, with glitzy *hula*
shows and cliff divers, and as
a facility run by the Audubon
Society, it is now operated by
the Office of Hawaiian Affairs.

The 1,875-acre (759-hectare)
area includes a waterfall,
a 5,000-plant botanical
collection, a refuge for
endangered wildlife,
and archaeological sites,
including a 15th-century
heiau (temple) dedicated
to Lono, god of peace,
agriculture, and music.

Walking tours and
cultural activities such
as *lei* making, *hula*
lessons, and storytelling
are included in the cost
of admission. Bring binoculars,
as the park has great opportunities for bird-watching. After
your visit, enjoy a swim or a
snorkel at **Waimea Beach Park**
across the street.

Environs: Set above Waimea
Bay at an elevation of 300 ft
(90 m), **Pu'u O Mahuka Heiau
State Monument** offers fine
views. Here the ruins of three
sacred rock terraces make up
the largest *heiau* (temple) on

O'ahu. Ironically called "hill of
escape" in Hawaiian, this was
once a site of human sacrifice.

🏯 **Pu'u O Mahuka Heiau
State Monument**
Off Pūpūkea Road, half a mile
(800 m) E of Kamehameha Hwy
(Hwy 83), just N of Waimea.

Hale'iwa Beach Park on the North
Shore, a sheltered spot for a swim

Hale'iwa ❼

Honolulu Co. 🚶 4,000. 🚌 🚻 🛈
HVCB, Waikīkī, (808) 924-0266. 🎎
O-Bon Buddhist Festival (Jul or Aug).

Once a plantation town
and more recently a hip-
pie hangout, Hale'iwa is now
the hub for the North Shore
surfing community. Graced by
local color from these subcul-
tures, the town has a single
main street with art galleries,
boutiques, general stores,
restaurants, and coffee shops.
Tin-roofed **Matsumoto's** is the
best place to try a Hawaiian
specialty known as shave ice
(thinly shaved ice flavored
with exotic syrups and toppings, such as adzuki beans).

Flanking a picturesque boat
harbor are well-appointed
public beaches. **Ali'i Beach
Park** is famous for big waves
and surfing contests *(see p31)*,
but the adjacent **Hale'iwa
Beach Park**, protected by a
breakwater, is one of the few
North Shore spots where it is
usually safe to swim in winter.

The town's biggest event, the
O-Bon Festival, is held every
summer at a seaside Buddhist
temple. It involves folk dancing
and the release of thousands
of floating lanterns into the
sea, a truly enchanting sight.

Dancers performing aboard a canoe at the Polynesian Cultural Center

For hotels and restaurants in this region see pp182–3 and pp199–200

Environs: Driving west from Hale'iwa, you pass a former sugar plantation at Waialua and arrive at **Mokulē'ia**, where polo fields border on empty, white-sand beaches. Here you can spend a pleasant afternoon watching parachutists from nearby Dillingham Airfield float down across the surf like clouds of colorful butterflies.

Dole Plantation ❽

Honolulu Co. 64-1550 Kamehameha Highway (Hwy 99), 2 miles (3 km) N of Wahiawā. **Tel** (808) 621-8408. 🚌 Wahiawā. ⏰ 9:30am–5:30pm daily. ⬤ Dec 25. ♿ ▣
www.dole-plantation.com

The Dole Cannery, built by James Dole in 1903 next to his Wahiawā pineapple plantation, was at that time the world's largest fruit cannery. In 1907 operations moved to Honolulu, eventually closing in 1991 due to increasing competition from Asia. The original Dole Cannery in Wahiawā now functions as a distribution warehouse.

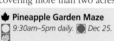
Dole's famous company logo

Across from the warehouse is Dole Plantation, a gift shop selling a range of pineapple products and a demonstration garden showing the different stages of the fruit's growth.

The Plantation is also home to the **Pineapple Garden Maze** which is the largest maze in the world, with 1.7 miles of paths and covering more than two acres.

♣ Pineapple Garden Maze
⏰ 9:30am–5pm daily. ⬤ Dec 25.

Hawai'i's Plantation Village ❾

Honolulu Co. 94-695 Waipahu Street, Waipahu. **Tel** (808) 677-0110. 🚌 Waipahu. ⏰ 10am–2pm Mon–Sat. ⬤ public hols. 📷 ♿ 📹
www.hawaiiplantationvillage.org

This $3 million restored village portrays over 100 years of sugar plantation culture. It

Interior of the Chinese Cookhouse at Hawai'i's Plantation Village

shows how plantation owners segregated workers along strict ethnic lines and how, in spite of this, a common pidgin language developed *(see p25)*.

The village contains some recreated buildings from the major ethnic groups that worked the plantations, from the Korean, Puerto Rican, and Japanese homes to a Japanese bathhouse and a Shinto shrine. Personal objects placed in the houses give the impression that the occupants have just left.

Wai'anae Coast ❿

Honolulu Co. 🚌 Nānākuli, Wai'anae and Mākaha Beach. ℹ HVCB, Waikīkī, (808) 924-0266.

With no souvenir stands and very few restaurants, O'ahu's sunny leeward coast is home to a population of native Hawaiians and other Pacific islanders. One of the coast's prettiest beaches is **Pōka'ī Bay**, where a breakwater shelters an aquamarine lagoon with sand as soft as cloth under your feet.

Farther northwest is **Mākaha Beach**, famous for its 30-ft (9-m) waves. In Mākaha Valley is **Kāne'ākī Heiau**, with thatched houses and *ki'i* (carved idols). It was used as a war temple by Kamehameha I. Mākaha means "ferocious," and the valley was once notorious for bandits. The area still has a reputation for car break-ins; camping is not advised.

⛩ Kāne'ākī Heiau
Off Mākaha Valley Rd.
Tel (808) 695-8174. ⏰ Tue–Sun.

Ka'ena Point ⓫

Honolulu Co. Beyond end of Farrington Highway (Hwy 930), 7 miles (11 km) N of Mākaha.

O'ahu's western extremity, Ka'ena Point has a stark, mountainous coastline and spectacular sunsets. A hot but relatively easy 2-mile (3-km) trail leads to the point.

Legend tells that the rock off the point is a chunk of Kaua'i that the demigod Maui pulled off when he was trying to unite the two islands. On clear days Kaua'i can be spotted to the north. You may also see rare monk seals, green turtles, and humpback whales *(see p115)*. The world's highest waves slam against the rocks here. So far no one has been suicidal enough to surf them. The point can also be reached from the road's end in Mokulē'ia. The two roads do not connect.

Ka'ena Point, reached by the exposed trail in the foreground

MOLOKA'I AND LĀNA'I

The small island of Moloka'i tends to be overlooked by vacationers scurrying between O'ahu and Maui. Far less developed for tourism than its neighbors, Moloka'i is the place to get away from it all, and most visitors are enchanted by its gentle pace. Across the Kalohi Channel to the south lies the smaller island of Lāna'i. This former pineapple plantation is now an exclusive tourist destination.

Moloka'i is formed from two extinct volcanoes that were once, along with Lāna'i and Kaho'olawe, attached to Maui. Its higher eastern peak, at some 5,000 ft (1,500 m), is topped by dense rain forest. The north shore is lined by the world's highest, steepest sea cliffs and indented by vast green valleys. The sheltered southern slopes traditionally held the bulk of the inhabitants, who planted crops along the coastline and raised fish in artificial enclosures just offshore. The western volcano, Mauna Loa, has been eroded to a smooth, rounded monolith, which receives so little rain that it is technically desert. Until recently this end of Moloka'i was barely populated, but since the 1970s, thanks to guaranteed sun and beaches like vast Pāpōhaku, it has been the site of what little development Moloka'i has seen. Despite repeatedly falling to invading armies from O'ahu, Maui, and Hawai'i Island, Moloka'i acquired a reputation for great spiritual power. Partly thanks to that sense of mystery and isolation, the Kalaupapa Peninsula was set aside in the 1860s as a leprosarium. The work of the Belgian priest Father Damien (canonized in 2009) in tending its exiled patients became famous, and pilgrims now flock to the peninsula from all around the world.

Lying in the rainshadow of Moloka'i and Maui, Lāna'i is now largely owned by the Castle & Cooke Corporation, and its luxury resorts have begun to shift the island's economy from agriculture to tourism. Visitors will find an open, sun-baked terrain, spectacular sea cliffs, unpopulated beaches, and the haunting remains of ancient native Hawaiian settlements.

Moloka'i's isolated Kalaupapa Peninsula, backed by the world's highest sea cliffs

◁ Native *kauna'oa* vine growing along Polihua Beach on Lāna'i's northern shore

Exploring Moloka'i and Lāna'i

Most of Moloka'i's accommodations are in the resort of Kaluako'i at the island's sunnier west end. Kaluako'i offers wonderful beaches. Kaunakakai, on the south coast, has a few charming hotels and most of the island's restaurants. No visitor should miss a drive along the flower-decked south coast to Hālawa Valley or a trip to Kalaupapa National Historical Park, backed by the north shore's huge sea cliffs. Lāna'i, Moloka'i's smaller and drier neighbor to the south, has luxury hotels, deserted beaches, and ancient ruins. Most residents live in the island's one small town, Lāna'i City.

SIGHTS AT A GLANCE

The golden sands of Polihua Beach on Lāna'i's remote north coast

TOP RECREATIONAL AREAS

The places shown here have been selected for their recreational activities. Conditions, especially those of the ocean, vary depending on the weather and the time of year, so exercise caution and, if in doubt, stay out of the water or seek local advice.

	SWIMMING	SNORKELING	DIVING	BODY-SURFING	WINDSURFING	HIKING	HORSEBACK RIDING	GOLF
DIXIE MARU BEACH	●	■						
HĀLAWA VALLEY	●			■				
HULOPO'E/MĀNELE BAY (LĀNA'I)	●	■	●					■
KALAUPAPA NAT'L HISTORICAL PARK						■	●	
KAMAKOU RAIN FOREST						■		
KAWA'ALOA BAY	●			■				
KAWĀKIU BAY	●	■						
KEPUHI BAY	●			●		●		
KŌ'ELE (LĀNA'I)						■	●	■
MO'OMOMI BEACH	●	■						
ONE ALI'I BEACH PARK	●							
PĀPŌHAKU BEACH						■		
TWENTY-MILE BEACH	●	■						

KEY

— Major road

=== Minor road

-- Track

— Scenic route

△ Summit

For additional map symbols *see back flap*

The road to Kalawao on Kalaupapa Peninsula, with 'Ōkala Island and Moloka'i's northern cliffs behind

Kalaupapa Peninsula
KALAUPAPA NATIONAL HISTORICAL PARK ❹
Kalaupapa
Kalawao
Mōkapu Island

ka'i Musuem Cultural Center
Kala'e
LAPU'U
K A ' I
Waikolu Lookout
KAMAKOU RAIN FOREST ❺
KAUNAKAKAI
450
Kawela
One Ali'i Beach Park
St Joseph's Church ❷
Kamalō

HĀLAWA VALLEY ❸
Moa'ula Falls
Pu'u o Hōkū Ranch
Cape Hālawa
Twenty Mile Beach
Kamakou △ 4961ft
'Ili'ili'opae Heiau
Our Lady of Sorrows Church
Pukoo
Kalua'aha
'Ualapu'e
'Ualapu'e Fishpond
TOUR OF EAST MOLOKA'I
Pailolo Channel

Kalohi Channel

GETTING AROUND

Neither Moloka'i nor Lāna'i has public transportation, so renting a car is essential. Car rental firms operate at Moloka'i's Ho'olehua airport and in Lāna'i City. A 12-mile (19-km) drive west of Ho'olehua gets you to Kaluako'i, while Hālawa Valley is 35 miles (56 km) east, on a road that steadily narrows beyond Kaunakakai. Lāna'i is best explored in a four-wheel-drive vehicle since the island has only 30 miles (48 km) of paved road and more than 100 miles (160 km) of red-dirt "pine roads" and rocky trails to the sea.

Shipwreck Beach
libua ach
Federation Camp
Garden of the Gods
LĀNA'I ❿
Pu'u Mahana 4714ft
430
Kane Pu'u Forest Preserve
LĀNĀ'I
Keone Bay
Kō'ele
Lana'i City
MUNRO TRAIL
Keōmuku
Lāna'ihale 3370ft
Hauola Gulch
'Au'au Channel
Luahiwa Petroglyphs
440
Pālāwai Basin
malapau Harbor
440
Lōpā
Pōka'i
Naha
Mākole Point
Kaunolū
Hulōpo'e Bay
Mānele Bay

0 kilometers 10
0 miles 5

Kaunakakai ➊

Maui Co. ⟪⟫ 3,500. ⟪⟫ Ala Malama St and Kamehameha V Hwy (Hwy 450), (808) 553-3876. ⟪⟫ Ka Moloka'i Makahiki (cultural festival; late Jan).

The main town on Moloka'i, Kaunakakai was built at the end of the 19th century as an administrative center and port for the local sugar plantations. During the 1920s, pineapple production took over from sugar, but these days commercial agriculture has all but disappeared from the island, and Kaunakakai looks its age. The wooden boardwalks of its principal thoroughfare, Ala Malama Street, are lined with false-fronted stores, such as the **Kanemitsu Bakery** (see p201), famous throughout the islands for its sweet Moloka'i bread. Dotted along the same street, homey diners reflect Moloka'i's broad ethnic mix. At the eastern end, tiny **St. Sophia's Church** is all but obscured behind an African tulip tree with its orange blossoms.

About half a mile (800 m) from the town center, the long stone jetty of of **Kaunakakai Harbor** juts out into the ocean. It was built in 1898 with rocks taken from a destroyed *heiau* (temple). To the ancient Hawaiians this place was known as Kaunakahakai, or "beach landing." A break in the coral reef made it a natural place from which to launch canoes. The harbor is often busy with local fishermen and divers.

During the 1860s, Chief Kapuāiwa, who later became King Kamehameha V, had a home near here. Its remains can still be seen just west of the road leading to the jetty.

Environs: Chief Kapuāiwa was also responsible for planting the soaring palms of the **Kapuāiwa Coconut Grove**, sandwiched between the highway and the ocean 2 miles (3 km) west of Kaunakakai. Well over 1,000 in number, the trees are a majestic sight when silhouetted against the setting sun. Visitors should take care, however, not to stand in the way of falling nuts. Opposite the grove is Kauanakakai's **Church Row**, a set of small wooden chapels belonging to different sects.

Ala Malama Street, Kaunakakai's main street

A Tour of East Moloka'i ➋

The coastal highway that nestles beneath the peaks of eastern Moloka'i is among the most beautiful drives in Hawai'i. Ancient sites and picturesque churches lie tucked away amid tropical flowers and luxuriant rain forest, while the slopes of West Maui are visible across the water. Few people live here now, so the villages often feel like ghost towns. The road finally twists to a halt at ravishing Hālawa Valley, one of Hawai'i's most stunning "amphitheater" valleys.

Old gas pump en route

Fishing boats and yachts in Kaunakakai Harbor

KEY

▬ Tour route

🌿 Vista

Kaunakakai

Kamehameha V Highway (450)

TIPS FOR DRIVERS

Tour length: 55 miles (88 km) round trip.

Stopping-off points: Allow a full day to visit the ancient fish ponds and pretty churches, to have a picnic at Twenty-Mile Beach or One Ali'i Beach Park, and even to fit in a hike through Hālwa Valley.

One Ali'i Beach Park ➀
At One Ali'i Beach Park, the small expanse of lawn, scattered with coconut palms, is ideal for picnics and also provides a perfect launching point for kayak trips. One Ali'i is a modern misspelling of the ancient Hawaiian name Oneali'i, meaning "Royal Sands."

St. Joseph Church ➁
Built in 1876 by Father Damien (see p101), this tiny church was painted a dazzling white in 1995 to celebrate the return of the priest's right hand to Kalaupapa. His statue, permanently garlanded with fresh *lei*, stands in the colorful garden.

Hālawa Valley ❸

Maui Co. End of Kamehameha V Highway (Hwy 450), 27 miles (43 km) E of Kaunakakai. 🔲 *Kaunakakai, (808) 553-3876.*

Hawai'i's original Polynesian settlers were established in beautiful Hālawa Valley by AD 650, and for over 1,000 years they grew taro *(see p125)* in an elaborate network of terraced fields. The ruins of nearly 20 ancient *heiau* (temples), including two dedicated to human sacrifice, lie hidden in the undergrowth on both sides of the valley. Hālawa was all but abandoned after the 1946 tsunami, but new generations of farmers grow taro now.

Visitors get their first glimpse of Hālawa from an overlook near mile marker 26. Though its farthest reaches are often obscured by mountain mists, the dramatic shoreline lies spread out 750 ft (230 m) below. The placid, unhurried

Waterfall in Hālawa Valley, seen from a roadside overlook

meanderings of the main stream as it approaches the ocean are in sharp contrast to the roaring surf just ahead.

The highway switchbacks down the hillside, reaching the valley floor at a quaint wooden chapel. A little farther along, the road ends at a low ridge of dunes, knitted together by

naupaka, a white-flowered creeper. Surfers launch themselves into the waves from the small gray beach just beyond.

In summer, visitors wade across the river mouth to reach a nicer beach on the far side; in winter it's safer to follow the dirt road that curves from beside the chapel. Shaded by imposing palm trees and sheltered from the full force of the sea by a stony headland, the beach is idyllic for swimming.

An intermediate, spectacular two-hour trail, which involves wading through the stream, leads through the rain forest to the 250-ft (75-m) **Moa'ula Falls**. Hawaiians claim that the pool at its base is home to a *mo'o* or giant lizard. Hikers traditionally throw a *ti* leaf onto the water before swimming; if it sinks, the *mo'o* is lying in wait. The trail is accessible only by guided hikes. Contact the Moloka'i Visitors Bureau (808) 553-3876 for information.

Hālawa Valley ⑦
With its soaring walls, lush vegetation, and shimmering waterfalls, Hālawa Valley is regarded as the most scenic spot on Moloka'i.

0 kilometers   5

0 miles   3

Twenty-Mile Beach ⑥
This thin strip of pristine sand at mile marker 20 is shaded by overhanging trees. Sheltered from the open ocean, it's great for snorkeling, but beyond the reef the sea can be dangerous.

'Ili'ili'ōpae Heiau ⑤
This huge structure, Hawai'i's second largest *heiau* (temple), witnessed human sacrifices in the 18th century. It is on private land, but hikers can follow the five-minute trail that runs inland halfway between mile markers 15 and 16.

'Ualapu'e Fish Pond ③
Of the 50 or so ancient fish ponds that line Moloka'i's southeast coast, 'Ualapu'e, just after mile marker 13, is one of the largest. Created by erecting a stone wall on top of a submerged reef, it encloses a vast area of shallow ocean and was used to raise mullet for the chief's table.

Our Lady of Sorrows ④
Father Damien took his first short break from Kalaupapa in 1874, to build the church of Our Lady Of Sorrows at 'Ualapu'e. Below lush mountain slopes, its red-tiled roof is shaded by the tousled coconut palms that surround it.

Kalaupapa National Historical Park ❹

A local stone landmark

Millions of years after Moloka'i emerged from the sea, a volcanic afterthought created the remote Kalaupapa peninsula *(see pp18–19)*. In 1865, when the imported disease of leprosy seemed to threaten the survival of the Hawaiian people, the peninsula was designated a leprosy colony. Bounty hunters rounded up those with even minor skin blemishes to be exiled at the original settlement of Kalawao. In the beginning, food and medicine were in short supply, and condemnation to the peninsula was seen as a death sentence. The settlement eventually relocated to the more sheltered Kalaupapa. The last patients arrived in 1969, when the policy of enforced isolation ended. The park now serves as a permanent memorial.

View from Pālā'au State Park
Sealed off from the rest of Moloka'i by a mighty wall of cliffs, this remote peninsula was an obvious choice for a leprosy colony.

★ Kalaupapa
All of the peninsula's residents, consisting of aging patients who chose to live out their lives here and state and federal employees, live on its sheltered western side in the village of Kalaupapa. It has three churches and a bar – Elaine's Place.

The Moloka'i Light from Kalaupapa Lighthouse was one of the most powerful in the Pacific when it was built in 1908.

Kalaupapa airstrip

SS *Kā'ala*, wrecked in 1932, remains a rusting hull stranded on the reef just offshore.

The Damien Monument, a Celtic cross, was paid for by public donations in England (1890) and erected in 1893.

★ Kalaupapa Trail
Hikers and mule riders alike pick their way down the 26 switchbacks of this precipitous trail, enjoying stupendous views during the 3-mile (5-km) journey.

Pālā'au State Park
(see p102)

PHALLIC ROCK

KŪALAPU'U
KAUNAKAKAI

STAR SIGHTS

★ Kalaupapa

★ Kalaupapa Trail

★ St. Philomena Church

0 kilometers   1

0 miles   1

Offshore Islands
From the peninsula's exposed eastern side, small islands can be seen poking out of the sea next to staggering 2,000-ft (600-m) cliffs – the tallest sea cliffs in the world.

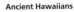

★ St. Philomena Church
The church was shipped from Honolulu in 1872 and later modified by Father (now Saint) Damien, whose grave lies nearby. In 1936 his body was returned to Belgium, but his right hand was later reinterred here.

Ancient Hawaiians used to jump off Leinaopapio Point for fun, with palm leaves as parachutes.

Judd Park

Kalawao, the original settlement, had a peak population of 1,174 in 1890, but it was abandoned in 1932.

Kauhakō Crater, what's left of the volcano that formed the peninsula, has an 800-ft (245-m) deep lake at its center.

KEY

═══ Minor road

══ Dirt or four-wheel-drive road

■ ■ Hiking trail and mule track

🅿 Parking

☀ Vista

ST. DAMIEN OF MOLOKA'I (1840–89)

Joseph de Veuster, born in Belgium, went to Hawai'i as a Roman Catholic missionary in 1864, and was ordained as Father Damien at Our Lady of Peace *(see p56)* in Honolulu. In 1873, he volunteered to serve the original leprosy colony of Kalawao, on the isolated Kalaupapa Peninsula. Hailed as a hero by the Honolulu press, he embraced his destiny willingly. He built hospitals, churches, and homes with his bare hands and nursed patients without fear for his own life. Father Damien finally succumbed to leprosy in 1889. The dedication of the "Martyr of Moloka'i" won him universal acclaim. His beatification as the "Blessed Damien" in 1995 preceded his canonization by Pope Benedict XVI in 2009.

Father Damien statue in Honolulu

Path through the dense vegetation of the Kamakou Rain Forest

Kamakou Rain Forest ❺

Maui Co. Reached by four-wheel-drive road E of Maunaloa Hwy (Hwy 460), 4 miles (6.5 km) NW of Kaunakakai.
🛈 Kaunakakai, (808) 553-3876.

The remote mountain-top ridges of eastern Moloka‘i preserve one of the least spoiled tracts of rain forest in Hawai‘i. It is reached by four-wheel-drive vehicle or mountain bike on a rutted dirt road.

This region saw its one brief flurry of activity early in the 1800s, when native Hawaiians were sent up here in search of sandalwood to sell to foreign merchants (see p42). Near the top of the island's central ridge is a grooved depression in the shape of a ship's hold. This so-called **Sandalwood Boat** was where the cut logs were piled.

The higher you climb, the wetter and lusher the forest becomes, and the more the road deteriorates. Native fauna and flora increasingly predominate, with colorful ‘ōhi‘a trees erupting amid vivid green foliage. Ten miles (16 km) in, superb views open out all the way to the north shore valleys. Here, Waikolu Lookout stands above the 3,700-ft (1,150-m) drop of Waikolu Valley.

Just beyond, the Pēpē‘ōpae Trail climbs along a wooden walkway through otherwise impenetrable rain forest. Every tree is festooned with hanging vines and spongy moss, while orchids glisten in the undergrowth. This misty wonderland is the last refuge of endangered birds like the Moloka‘i thrush (oloma‘o) and Moloka‘i creeper (kākāwahie). After crossing an eerie, windswept bog, the trail traverses a series of gulches to emerge at an astonishing overlook above Pelekunu Valley.

Kualapu‘u ❻

Maui Co. 🏠 1,900.
🛈 Kaunakakai, (808) 553-3876.

The former plantation village of Kualapu‘u is now home to Moloka‘i's first coffee plantation, whose products can be tasted at the friendly, roadside espresso bar. Two miles (3 km) northeast of town, the **RW Meyer Sugar Mill** preserves the remains of the area's short-lived dabble in the sugar business. The mill machinery, now beautifully restored, was in use for just 11 years from 1878 to 1889. It now forms part of the adjoining **Moloka‘i Museum**

and Cultural Center, an interesting little collection of artifacts that illustrates the island's varied history.

Environs: Four miles (6.5 km) northeast of Kualapu‘u, Kala‘e Highway (Hwy 470) comes to an end at **Palau‘au State Park**, which combines superb views over the Kalaupapa Peninsula (see pp100–1) with a legendary site. Stop at the viewpoint to gaze eastward along the awesome cliffs to Kalaupapa village and beyond. From the vista's parking lot a hiking trail leads through the forest to **Phallic Rock**. As ancient legend has it, women who sleep beneath this outcrop will wake up pregnant. Its lifelike appearance is in part the work of human hands.

🏛 **Moloka‘i Museum and Cultural Center**
Kala‘e Highway (Hwy 470).
Tel (808) 567-6436. ⏰ 10am–2pm Mon–Sat. 🔵 public hols. 🈂 ♿

Legendary Phallic Rock, Pālā‘au State Park

Mo‘omomi Beach ❼

Maui Co. At the end of Mo‘omomi Rd, 5 miles (8 km) NW of Ho‘olehua.

Mo‘omomi Beach, the only stretch of Moloka‘i's north shore accessible to casual visitors, belongs very much to the drier western end of the island. The coastline here is made up of ancient sand dunes that have become lithified (turned to rock). The area is rich in the bones of flightless birds, which may have been hunted to extinction by the early Polynesian

RW Meyer Sugar Mill, the smallest in Hawai‘i

The dirt road serving Moʻomomi Beach

settlers. A 5-mile (8-km) dirt road from Hoʻolehua leads to Moʻomomi Bay, a surfing and fishing beach popular with local residents.

Kaluakoʻi ❽

Maui Co. Off Maunaloa Hwy (Hwy 460), 5 miles (8 km) NW of Maunaloa. ⓘ *Kaunakakai, (808) 553-3876.* ▣ *Molokaʻi Ka Hula Piko (May).*

The gentle slopes of Mauna Loa, Molokaʻi's western volcano, have always been far too arid to sustain a significant human presence. The island's west coast was known to the ancients as Kaluakoʻi, "the adze pit," for its valuable basalt deposits. This area had a population of just one person in the 1970s. Since then, it has become Molokaʻi's only resort, home to a large hotel and condo complexes.

Environs: The island's most spectacular expanse of sand, broad **Pāpōhaku Beach** starts about a mile (1.5 km) down the coast. Colossal waves render the beach unsafe for swimming, so it is often empty, with a splendid sense of romantic isolation.

Every May, **Pāpōhaku Beach County Park** hosts the Molokaʻi Ka Hula Piko festival, which celebrates the birth of *hula* with music and dance. There are *hālau hula* (*hula* schools), contemporary musicians, and local crafts. Lectures and storytelling take place across the island in the week before the festival.

Beyond Pāpōhaku's southern end, secluded **Dixie Maru Beach** offers sheltered swimming and good snorkeling.

Maunaloa ❾

Maui Co. ⚿ *400.* ⓘ *Kaunakakai, (808) 553-3876.*

When the Molokaʻi Ranch specialized in cattle and pineapples, tiny Maunaloa, on the flanks of the mountain, was the quintessential Hawaiian plantation village. From wooded groves, the timber-frame houses of its farm workers and *paniolo* (*see p143*) faced right across the ocean to Waikīkī.

In the 1970s, the ranch switched to tourism, offering luxury camping, an upscale hotel, and outdoor activities. However, it was not successful and shut down in 2008. Today, a few homespun businesses still survive on the main street, including the **Big Wind Kite Factory**. Owner Jonathan Socher is happy to show visitors around his manufacturing area and discuss the many kite designs. He also offers kite-flying lessons in the adjacent park.

Molokaʻi was renowned in ancient times as *Molokaʻi pule oʻo* (Molokaʻi of strong prayers), the home of powerful priests and sorcerers. Dreaded "poisonwood gods" lived in the forests above Maunaloa; a sliver of wood cut from their favored trees could kill any foe. However, the *ʻōhiʻa* woods nearby played a more benign role in Hawaiian legend. Here the goddess Laka learned the *hula* and taught it to humans. This claim to be the birthplace of *hula* is disputed. Kēʻē Beach on Kauaʻi boasts the same distinction *(see p167)*.

Big Wind Kite Factory
120 Maunaloa Hwy (Hwy 460). *Tel (808) 552-2364.* **www.**bigwindkites.com

Colorful kites at the Big Wind Kite Factory in Maunaloa

Lāna'i ⑩

Sun-baked Lāna'i was once the world's largest pineapple plantation, owned by the Dole Company, but in 1991 it underwent an historic conversion. In that year, Lāna'i's new owner, the Castle & Cooke Corporation, opened two luxury resorts and reemployed the island's farm workers as hotel staff. This identity shift left the island open for exploration of its many beaches, cliffs, and ancient ruins.

Colorful Lāna'i City house backed by Cook Island Pine trees

Exploring Lāna'i

This relatively low island is topped by the Lāna'ihale ridge. The heart of the island, rural Lāna'i City, is perched below the ridge at an elevation of 1,600 ft (490 m). Roads, more often dirt than paved, radiate outward to reach the coast at a few remote, beautiful spots.

Lāna'i City

Home to virtually all of the island's 3,200 residents, Lāna'i City offers a firsthand experience of the classic Hawaiian plantation town. Built in the early 1920s to house Dole's mostly Filipino laborers, this friendly town centers on rectangular **Dole Park**. The park is lined with frontier-style shops and the **Hotel Lāna'i**, a vintage wooden inn *(see p183)*. At the northeast corner

of the town, on the site of the former headquarters of Lāna'i Ranch (1874–1951), is **The Lodge at Kō'ele** *(see p184)*. This award-winning resort offers respite from the island's coastal heat. The attractions here include an 18-hole golf course, an orchid house, stables, and manicured grounds. The fine restaurant is open to the public.

🌶 Luahiwa Petroglyphs

Off Hō'ike Rd, 2 miles (3 km) S of Lāna'i City, near the water tower on the ridge.

The broad, softly hazy expanse of Pālāwai Basin is actually the remains of Lāna'i's extinct and worn-down volcanic crater. Its eastern wall bears one of Hawai'i's richest collections of petroglyphs. Visible from quite a distance, a cluster of 34 black boulders stands out against a steep red hillside dotted with dry white patches of *pili* grass. Some of these stones were thought to possess the *mana* (sacred power) of the rain gods Kū and Hina. Starting at least 500 years ago, Hawaiians decorated them by carving enigmatic figures representing humans and dogs. More recent images of horses, surfers, and leashed dogs were carved by students from Maui's Lahainaluna School during the 1870s. The petroglyphs are best viewed early or late, when the sun is not overhead.

🌶 Mānele and Hulopo'e Bays

End of Mānele Rd (Hwy 440), 8 miles (13 km) S of Lāna'i City.

Together, these adjacent bays form a marine life conservation district, home to Hawaiian spinner dolphins. Mānele Bay is Lāna'i's only small boat harbor. The misleadingly named **Four Seasons Lāna'i at Mānele Bay** *(see p184)* spreads over the hillside above Hulopo'e Bay, the island's best swimming and snorkeling spot. The resort, even with its interior opulence and fragrant gardens, harmonizes with its savage location. The bay is off-limits to all boats except those of Maui's oldest sailing excursion company, **Trilogy**. Camping is permitted here.

Between the bays lies **Pu'u Pehe**, or Sweetheart Rock. According to legend, lovely Pehe was kept by her jealous husband in a nearby cave until one day, while he was away, she drowned in a storm. He buried her on this rock island and then jumped to his death.

Pu'u Pehe, or Sweetheart Rock, in the waters off Mānele Bay

🌶 Kaunolū

Kaunolū Trail, a dirt track off Kaupili Rd, which leaves Mānele Rd (Hwy 440) 4.5 miles (7 km) S of Lāna'i City.

Few sites evoke the drama of ancient Hawaiian life like the ruins of this seldom-visited fishing village, abandoned in the mid-19th century. The rough drive to this naturally fortified cliff top, with its dizzying views of Lāna'i's southern coast, takes a full hour from Lāna'i City and requires a four-wheel-drive vehicle.

The early Hawaiians excelled in the art of building with un-mortared stone, and here at

The beautifully maintained grounds of The Lodge at Kō'ele in Lāna'i City

For hotels and restaurants in this region see pp183–4 and pp201–2

LĀNAʻI'S COOK ISLAND PINE TREES

Groves of Cook Island Pine, which give the island its characteristic look, were planted in the early 1900s by New Zealander George C. Munro, the manager of what was then the Lānaʻi Ranch. Freshwater is Lānaʻi's most precious resource, and Munro realized that these trees increase the island's water-drawing capacities. Mountain mists collect in the trees' tightly leaved branches and drip onto the thirsty ground – on a good day, as much as 40 gallons (150 liters) of water per tree.

An impressive row of Cook Island Pines at The Lodge at Kōʻele stables

VISITORS' CHECKLIST

Maui Co. 🏘 3,100. ✈ 4 miles
(6.5 km) SW of Lānaʻi City. ⛴
Mānele Bay. 🛈 431 7th St, (808)
565-7600. 🎭 Aloha Week (mid-
Oct). www.gohawaii.com/lanai

Kaunolū you can see several well-preserved examples, including the stone platform of the large **Halulu Heiau** on Kaunolū Bay's west side. On the east side there is a cliff-side platform that was once the home and fishing retreat of Kamehameha the Great. There are also ruins of a canoe house and a large fishing shrine.

One way in which ancient Hawaiians showed their bravery was by cliff-jumping, and just west of Kaunolū Bay there is a suicidal diving platform. At **Kahekili's Leap**, the former chief of Maui, Kahekili, proved his mettle by hurling himself more than 60 ft (18 m) down – clearing a 15-ft (4.5-m) wide outcrop of rocks – into water just 10 ft (3 m) deep.

🏞 The Munro Trail

Turn off Mānele Rd (Hwy 440) 5 miles
(8 km) S of Lānaʻi City.
This pine-studded drive along the volcanic ridge of Lānaʻihale,

whose summit reaches 3,370 ft (1,050 m), offers sensational views of five of the Hawaiian islands. Because the Kōʻele end of the road can be alarmingly muddy, best taken downhill, the drive should begin at the other end. At the concrete stripe on Mānele Road just after the Pālāwai Basin, turn left onto a dirt road and then follow the most worn track up the hill. Allow at least two hours by jeep for this rugged 20-mile (32-km) jaunt.

🏞 Garden of the Gods

Polihua Rd, 6 miles (10 km) NW
of Lānaʻi City.
The Garden of the Gods is a visual oddity, a reddish lunar landscape dotted with boulders made of compacted sand. They range in color from reds and oranges to browns and blues, and the effect is most intense at sunset, when the rocks seem to glow. This peculiar dry and rocky

landscape is reached by an easy 30-minute drive along a dirt road from Kōʻele, which passes through a hunting zone for axis, or spotted, deer and native dryland forest.

Continuing on, the road to the island's northern tip gets rougher, ending at long, wild **Polihua Beach**. At this remote strand, one hour from Kōʻele, a visitor's footprints may be the only ones of the day. The ocean currents can be dangerous.

Strange rust-red rock formations at the Garden of the Gods

🏞 Shipwreck Beach

Keōmuku Rd (Hwy 430), 8 miles
(13 km) NE of Lānaʻi City.
Lānaʻi's northern shore is lined with an 8-mile (13-km) stretch of beach that takes its name from the rusting hulk of a World War II supply ship that is wrecked on the reef. Many other ships have come to harm in these shallow, hazardous waters, including an oil tanker that is visible 6 miles (10 km) up the beach. To reach the beach, follow Keōmuku Road (Hwy 430) until the asphalt ends; then take the dirt road on the left that rambles over sandy ground for about a mile (1.5 km). From here, a beach-comber's trek offers isolation and beautiful views of Maui and Molokaʻi – a day's hike northward will bring you to Polihua Beach. Off Shipwreck Beach is an extensive reef, but swimming is dangerous here.

Shipwreck Beach, with the hulking 1940s wreck in the distance

MAUI

The second largest Hawaiian island, Maui is sparsely populated, supporting less than a tenth of the state's population. The land is verdant with sugarcane and pineapple, sprawling cattle ranches, and rain forests that descend mountain slopes to the sea. The 120 miles (195 km) of shoreline invite a host of ocean activities, from swimming, snorkeling, and diving, to world-class windsurfing.

Maui was formed by the convergence of two volcanoes at the isthmus known as the Central Valley. The green 5,788-ft (1,764-m) West Maui Mountains are the eroded slopes of a single extinct volcano, while East Maui is composed of Haleakalā, an enormous 10,023-ft (3,055-m) dormant volcano crowned by a lunar landscape.

The earliest inhabitants are thought to have arrived from the Marquesas Islands around the 4th century AD. The areas around Lahaina and Hāna were the first to be settled. Maui was split into rival chiefdoms until the 14th century, when Pi'ilani conquered the island. This Maui chief built the massive temple of Pi'ilanihale Heiau, whose ruins are near Hāna. In 1795 Kamehameha I conquered Maui in his quest to unite the Hawaiian Islands and in 1800 established his royal seat at Lahaina. Jean-François de Galaup,

Comte de La Pérouse, was the first European to set foot on Maui, in 1786. Other foreigners followed during the 1800s, including missionaries, whalers, and contract laborers from Europe and Asia who came to work the growing sugar plantations. The communities they established retained the character of their homelands and created a multicultural heritage that is celebrated today in local holidays, customs, and food.

Visitors will see a varied landscape, from Kula's farmland, where proteas and sweet onions are grown, to the arid, eroded crater of Haleakalā and the lush, tropical vegetation on the windward coast. If you want to soak up the sun, the leeward coast offers white-sand beaches and calm waters that are the winter home of humpback whales.

Windsurfers at Ho'okipa Beach County Park near Pā'ia, on Maui's north shore

◁ A view of Honomanū Bay from the road to Hāna

Exploring Maui

Maui is composed of two volcanoes connected by the Central Valley, the island's population hub and the site of several attractions. The West Maui Mountains (Kahalawai) are actually a single, extinct volcano that time has carved into steep canyons, accessible at just a few places, such as 'Īao Valley. A road skirting the mountain's southern flank leads to historic Lahaina and the coastal resorts of Kā'anapali and Kapalua. Haleakalā, a dormant volcano capped by a huge crater, makes up the larger region of East Maui. Its outer slopes are covered with cattle ranches and fields of sugarcane and pineapple. The lush windward coast in the north features the plantation town of Pā'ia, Ho'okipa Beach – a windsurfers' mecca – and the little town of Hāna. The popular leeward coast enjoys a sunnier climate and calmer ocean.

TOP RECREATIONAL AREAS

The places shown here have been selected for their recreational activities. Conditions, especially those of the ocean, vary depending on the weather and the time of year, so exercise caution and, if in doubt, stay out of the water or seek local advice.

	SWIMMING	SNORKELING	DIVING	BODY-SURFING	WINDSURFING	HIKING	HORSEBACK RIDING	GOLF
HALEAKALĀ NATIONAL PARK						●	●	
HĀMOA BAY	●	■		■				
HĀNA	●					■	●	
HO'OKIPA BEACH COUNTY PARK					●			
HOSMER GROVE						■		
'ĪAO VALLEY						■		
KĀ'ANAPALI AND KEKA'A POINT	●	■	●	●				■
KAHANA				■				
KANAHĀ BEACH COUNTY PARK	●				●			
KAPALUA AND HONOLUA BAY	●	■	●				●	■
KE'ANAE PENINSULA						■		
KĪHEI	●	■	●		●			■
LA PÉROUSE BAY		■	●			■	●	
LAHAINA	●	■	●					
MĀKENA	●	■	●				●	■
MOLOKINI		■	●					
'OHE'O GULCH AND KĪPAHULU	●			■		■	●	
OLOWALU		■	●					
PĀ'IA	●		●	■	●			
POLIPOLI SPRINGS RECREATION AREA						■		
SPRECKELSVILLE	●				●			
UKUMEHAME	●	■	●	■				
'ULUPALAKUA							●	
WAI'ĀNAPANAPA STATE PARK	●	■				■		
WAIHE'E	●					■	●	■
WAIKAPŪ								■
WAILEA	●	■	●					■

Honokōhau

④ NĀKĀLELE POINT

KAPALUA ③

Napili

Kahana

⑤ KAHAKULOA VILLAGE

Honokōwai

Waihe'e

KĀ'ANAPALI ②

WAILU

Lahainaluna

LAHAINA ①

'ĪAO VALLEY ⑧

Hanaula 4616ft   Waika

Launiupoko

Awalua Beach

Puu Anu 2972ft

Olowalu

Ukumehame

MĀ'ALAE

'Au'au Channel

MOLOKIN

KAHOOLAWE ⑭

0 kilometers   10

0 miles   5

KEY

— Major road

═══ Minor road

- - Track

— Scenic route

△ Summit

For additional map symbols *see back flap*

'Īao Needle, marking the confluence of
two streams in the lush 'Īao Valley

GETTING AROUND

Maui's main airport is in Kahului, but smaller airports serve
Hāna and Kapalua. Major resorts offer guests free shuttle
services to and from the airport and around the resort, but
most people explore Maui with a rental car or by tour.
There is a county bus with limited routes. Some roads
are tortuous, and progress can be slow. Many highways
have bicycle lanes, and tour companies will take you up
the slope of Haleakalā to bike back down. Stables offer
horseback tours all over the island. Ferry services run
between Maui and the islands of Lāna'i and Moloka'i.

SEE ALSO

• *Where to Stay* pp188–9

• *Where to Eat* pp206–8

SIGHTS AT A GLANCE

A secluded swimming spot on the
rocky coast of the Ke'anae Peninsula

Street-by-Street: Lahaina ❶

Statue outside
Pioneer Inn

Stroll the streets of Lahaina, and you
follow in the footsteps of scoundrels and
kings. Until 1845 this small harbor town
was the capital of the Kingdom of Hawai'i.
By the mid-19th century, during the peak of
the whaling era, it had a reputation as a
rowdy port-of-call. Missionaries sometimes
struggled to maintain control over the town
and the souls of its inhabitants. Today, it is
one of the most popular visitor attractions
on Maui. Front Street, lined with pioneer-
style homes and storefronts, is evocative
of Lahaina's past. The Lahaina Restoration
Foundation has restored a number of historic sites, and
a wealth of history can be found within a small area.

Front Street, once the haunt of
boisterous sailors after women and
whiskey, now offers souvenir shops
and colorful street stalls.

Wo Hing Temple

Masters'
Reading Room

★ Baldwin Home
*Maui's oldest Western-style
dwelling, dating from the 1830s,
has been faithfully restored
with period furnishings, including several original pieces.*

The Hauola Stone
was believed by
ancient Hawaiians
to calm and heal.

★ Pioneer Inn
*Built in 1901 by
an Englishman, the
Pioneer Inn was the
first hotel to open in
Lahaina. It remains a
hotel to this day and
is a favorite land-
mark in the town.*

KEY

 Suggested route

STAR SIGHTS

★ Baldwin Home

★ Banyan Tree

★ Pioneer Inn

The Old Lahaina Courthouse was built in 1859 and
was intended to be a palace for King Kamehameha III,
but was used instead as a post office, a courtroom and
jail. It now serves as a Visitor Center and Art Society
where local artists' pottery and paintings are displayed.

LAHAINA'S TRAGIC PRINCESS

Hawaiian culture once sanctified royal marriages between siblings; such alliances kept bloodlines pure and ensured offspring great *mana* (power). Ancient custom was cast aside with the arrival of Christianity, however. When Nahi'ena'ena and her brother Kauikeaouli (later Kamehameha III) fell in love, they were separated. Nahi'ena'ena still managed to bear their son, who lived only hours. Sick in body and soul, she died soon afterward.

Nahi'ena'ena, who died at 21

VISITORS' CHECKLIST

Maui Co. 🚶 11,700. ⛵ *Lahaina Harbor.* 🏛 *648 Wharf St, (808) 667-9193.* 🎭 *Ocean Arts Festival (Mar); 4th of July Fireworks; Halloween in Lahaina (Oct 31); Holiday Lighting of the Banyan Tree (Dec).* **www**.visitlahaina.com

0 meters	100
0 yards	100

Chapel in the prison grounds

Hale Pa'ahao, or "Stuck-in-Irons House," was the new prison built in the 1850s with bricks from the Lahaina Fort.

Lahaina Fort was built in the 1830s to jail rowdy whalers, but dismantled 20 years later. A small part has been reconstructed.

★ **Banyan Tree**
The tree is over a century old and is so large that special events, including arts and crafts fairs, are held beneath its many branches. The square is named after it.

Exploring Lahaina

Front Street is the hub of Lahaina. A low seawall opens up nearly a block of the street to scenic views of the sea and nearby islands, and makes strolling an old-fashioned pleasure. Whether you visit the historic Baldwin Home, the Old Lahaina Courthouse, or shop in the town's colorful stores, Lahaina offers a variety of interesting diversions. On most evenings, live music spills into the street from restaurants and bars.

Lahaina Harbor, against a backdrop of the West Maui Mountains

🏛 Baldwin Home
696 Front Street. *Tel (808) 661-3262.* ⬜ *10am–4pm daily.* ⬤ *Jan 1, Dec 25.* 📷 ♿ 🚶 *compulsory.* www.lahainarestoration.org

The four original rooms of this historic home were built in 1834 by the Reverend Ephraim Spaulding. The coral and stone walls were 24 in (60 cm) thick, perhaps a measure to minimize the sounds of revelry outside. At the height of the Pacific whaling trade, tensions often ran high between the seamen who frequented the port's brothels and grog shops and the missionaries who sought to establish Christian faith and law in the islands.

The Reverend Dwight Baldwin and his wife came to Hawai'i from the US in the early 1830s and were assigned to Lahaina's Waine'e Church. When Spaulding fell ill around 1836 the Baldwins moved into his house. As the family grew – to an eventual total of eight children – so did their home. A second-story dormitory was added in 1849, apparently to protect the daughters from the town's rowdier elements.

The first floor is open to the public. Many of the furnish-ings, which were donated by the Baldwin family, date from the 1850s. Original pieces in-clude an 18th-century sewing box, rocking chairs, and a four-poster bed made out of *koa* wood. Among the acquisitions is a quilt with a Hawaiian-flag design *(see p68)*, a gift to a Captain Born from Hawai'i's last queen, Lili'uokalani.

The two-story house next door was built around 1834 – the same time as the Baldwin Home. It takes its name, the **Masters' Reading Room**, from the second floor, which was designed to offer "suitable reading rooms for the accommodation of Seamen who visit Lahaina, as well as a convenient place of retirement from the heat and unpleasant dust of the market."

The Baldwin Home, set in a shady garden

The Reading Room, once housing the Lahaina Restor-ation Foundation, has been preserved in its original state but is closed to the public.

🌳 Banyan Tree
Canal St or Front St.

The Banyan Tree *(ficus benghalensis)* was all of 8 ft (2.4 m) tall when it was planted by Maui sheriff William O. Smith in 1873 to mark the 50th anniversary of the founding of Lahaina's first Christian mission. Lahaina was once the capital of the Hawaiian kingdom and the whaling capital of the world, and as the town grew and developed, the tree continued to grow – and grow. Today, it measures almost one-fourth of a mile (402 m) in circum-ference, stands 60 ft (18 m) high and covers two-thirds of an acre (2,700 sq m) in the courtyard outside the Lahaina courthouse. There are many celebrations and festivities held underneath its branches, such as the weekly He U'i Cultural Arts Festival and the annual holiday tree lighting ceremony in December.

The Banyan Tree attracts hundreds of people every day who come to take its picture and catch a glimpse of history. It has also been designated as a National Historical Landmark.

🏛 Pioneer Inn
658 Wharf St. *Tel (808) 661-3636.* ♿

Lahaina's best-known hotel was built by an Englishman called George Freeland. He had originally emigrated to Canada, where he joined the Mounties, but ended up in Lahaina in 1900, having pur-sued a criminal all the way to Maui. Freeland did not catch the fugitive, but stayed here, fell in love with a Hawaiian woman, and in 1901, built a hotel.

Pioneer Inn is a hotel to this day, on land still owned by the Freeland family. It has been renovat-ed but retains many of the original fea-tures. These include whaling memorabilia and a list of house

SCRIMSHAW – THE WHALERS' ART

Life aboard a 19th-century whaling ship had its moments of excitement, but these were the exception. For the average sailor, whaling meant months of boredom, bad food, and low pay. To pass the time, sailors made scrimshaw from whale ivory – carving and etching into the surface of whale teeth and bones. Their "dot-to-dot" technique involved puncturing the surface with a knife or sail needle, applying a mixture of soot and oil, and polishing the ivory with shark's skin. The results were often exquisite works of art. A scrimshander might just decorate the ivory, or else carve it into something useful, such as spoons or gun handles. Scrimshaw fetched a high price then and still does today, in stores along Lahaina's Front Street and at Kā'anapali's Whalers Village (see p114).

Decorative scrimshaw made from whale bones

formed mutual aid societies to maintain ties with China. One such was the Wo Hing Society, founded in 1909, which built the Wo Hing Temple in 1912.

As a museum, the temple provides a good insight into the local Chinese community. There are artifacts as well as a shrine; the altar is replenished with fresh offerings every day.

A separate cookhouse serves as a theater, showing old films about Hawai'i made by American inventor Thomas Edison in 1898 and 1906.

🏛 Hale Pa'i

End of Lahainaluna Road. **Tel** (808) 667-7040. ◯ 10am–4pm Mon–Fri. ● Jan 1, Dec 25. & ☑

The "house of printing" is situated on the grounds of the oldest high school west of the Rocky Mountains – the former Lahainaluna Seminary. When missionaries arrived in Hawai'i they lost no time in trying to convert the locals to Christianity, as well as teaching them to read.

The Lahainaluna Seminary was set up in 1831, and in 1834 the missionaries added the Hale Pa'i. Originally a thatched hut, the printing house was later replaced with a sturdier building made of stone and timber.

In 1982, the Hale Pa'i became a museum, tracing the history of the written word in Hawai'i. There is a working replica of the original printing press and facsimiles of early Hawaiian printing.

rules in the rooms, forbidding tenants from burning the beds and womanizing. You do not need to be a guest to explore the shopping arcade or enjoy the popular bar and grill overlooking the harbor.

🏛 Lahaina Courthouse

649 Wharf St. **Tel** (808) 667-9193. ◯ 9am–5pm daily. ● Jan 1, Dec 25. &

Completed in 1859, the Lahaina Courthouse on Wharf Street originally contained a governor's office, a customs house, a post office, a courtroom, and a jail. It was built with stones from the earlier courthouse and palace that were destroyed by gale-force winds in 1858.

Here too is the Lahaina Visitor Center, which sells souvenirs. Archive photos in the hallway give a glimpse of how the place once looked. The galleries of the Lahaina Arts Society are located in the old jail in the basement.

🏛 Hale Pa'ahao

Prison & Waine'e Streets. **Tel** (808) 667-1985. ◯ 10am–4pm Mon–Fri. ● Jan 1, Dec 25. &

Sailors and missionaries who arrived in the islands in the 18th and 19th centuries introduced Hawaiians to a host of new vices – and to codes of conduct unfamiliar to them.

This jail, whose name means "Stuck-in-Irons House," was built by convicts in the 1850s, using coral stone taken from the town's demolished fort.

It was used to incarcerate foreigners and natives alike for crimes ranging from murder to riding horses on the Sabbath or violating fish taboos.

A high stone wall encloses a grassy yard and the jailhouse. Visitors can peek into one of the cells, where a "convict" (actually a mannequin lying on a straw mattress) talks about 19th-century prison life.

Hawaiian papers in Hale Pa'i

🏛 Wo Hing Temple

858 Front St. **Tel** (808) 661-5553. ◯ 10am–4pm Sat–Thu, 1–8pm Fri. ● Jan 1, Dec 25.

The Chinese were among Hawai'i's earliest immigrants. They came to work on the plantations and many moved into commerce. They often

Taoist altar in the shrine room of the Wo Hing Temple

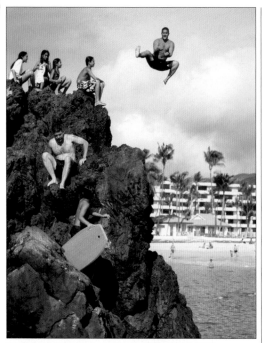

Locals demonstrating their courage at Puʻu Kekaʻa (Black Rock)

Kāʻanapali ❷

Maui Co. 🚶 1,400. ℹ Suite 1B, 2530 Kekaʻa Drive, (808) 661-3271. 🎏 Maui Onion Festival (early Aug), Na Mele O Maui (Dec). **www**.kaanapaliresort.com

Nestled between a 3-mile (5-km) beach and the West Maui Mountains, Kāʻanapali is Mauiʻs largest resort. It includes six beachfront hotels, five condominiums, two golf courses, 35 tennis courts, and a large shopping center.

Despite all the hotels, the resort maintains a sense of community by staging events like Na Mele O Maui ("the songs of Maui"), a celebration of Hawaiian culture, and the Maui Onion Festival, which honors the local crop.

Through the ages Kāʻanapali was a special place, the site of a *heiau* (temple), a taro patch, and a royal fishpond. In the early 20th century, it became a playground for Hawaiian royalty, complete with a horse-racing track. Free tours of sites throughout the resort are conducted by hotel employees each week.

Puʻu Kekaʻa, better known as Black Rock, towers above long, white Kāʻanapali Beach and overlooks one of the best snorkeling spots in Maui. Two centuries ago, when Maui chief Kahekili sought to encourage his troops, he would leap into the ocean from Black Rock. This involved spiritual, not physical, danger since it was believed that the dead jumped into the spirit world from here.

At the heart of Kāʻanapali is **Whalers Village**, an upscale shopping center with many stores and restaurants. In addition, the **Whalers Village Museum** explores in unhappy detail the demise of the whale through the whaling trade. Displays include tools and weapons used for whaling, old photographs, models of whaling ships, and products made from the carcasses. Even more fascinating is the insight given into a young whaler's life by letters, diaries, and official accounts.

West Mauiʻs most unusual means of transportation is the **Lahaina Kāʻanapali & Pacific Railroad**, whose steam locomotives chug the 6 miles (10 km) between Lahaina and Kāʻanapali. Steam engines were used in Hawaiʻi from the late 1800s until the 1950s to carry both sugarcane and plantation workers. Now the "Sugarcane Train" rides again, taking passengers along the same route as that used in earlier times. The scenic ride passes fields of cane and rises to cross the impressive Hahakea Trestle for a view of the ocean and the West Maui Mountains.

🏛 **Whalers Village and Whalers Village Museum**
2435 Kāʻanapali Parkway. **Tel** (808) 661-5992. ⬜ 9:30am–10pm daily. ♿ **www**.whalersvillage.com

Lahaina Kāʻanapali & Pacific Railroad
Lahaina Station: Limahana Place. **Kaʻanapali (Puʻukoliʻi) Station:** off Puʻukoliʻi Road. **Tel** (808) 661-0080. ⬜ daily. 🎏 ♿ **www**.sugarcanetrain.com

Steam "Sugarcane Train", Lahaina Kāʻanapali & Pacific Railroad

For hotels and restaurants in this region see pp184–7 and pp202–6

One of the pristine bays that line the coast at Kapalua

Kapalua **❸**

Maui Co. 🏠 350. ✈ 🛈 Lahaina,
(808) 669-0244. 🍷 Kapalua Wine &
Food Symposium (Jul), Celebration
of the Arts (March/April).
www.kapaluamaui.com

Twenty minutes' drive north
of Kāʻanapali lies Kapalua,
West Maui's second planned
resort, whose luxury rooms
and 54 championship fairways
are surrounded by a series of
exquisite crescent bays and a
pineapple plantation that carpets the lower slopes of the
West Maui Mountains.

Two of the bays, **Honolua**
and **Mokulēʻia**, have been
designated marine life conservation districts, where divers
and swimmers keep company
with reef fish and sea turtles.
The golf courses are Audubon
Society-approved bird sanctu-
aries, and the environmentally

sensitive lands above the resort
are under the stewardship of
the Nature Conservancy.
The resort also hosts a PGA
golf championship in January,
with prize money in excess of
$1 million, and a wine and
food symposium that attracts
vintners, chefs, and connois-
seurs from around the world.
The resort also offers a wedding package, complete with a
cake and Hawaiian performers.

Built in 1929 as a plantation
general store, **Honolua Store**
looks much the same today as
it did when it opened. Now
the merchandise is more upscale and clothing here sports
the Kapalua Resort butterfly
logo. A deli counter serves
breakfast and lunch.

🏠 Honolua Store
502 Office Rd.
Tel (808) 665-9105.
🕐 6am–8pm daily.

Nakalele Point **❹**

Maui Co. Hwy 30. 🛈 Maui VB,
Wailuku, (808) 244-3530.

This is the most northerly
point on Maui and the site of
Hawaiʻi's first lighthouse. Vivid
red-hued cliffs drop to the
ocean and the trails along the
bluffs offer terrific ocean views.
When the surf is right here,
sea water is forced as high
as 100 ft (30 m) into the air
through a hole in the shoreline lava tube. The blowhole
is a short walk down the hill
from the road, though you
can see it from the top. Be
careful if you approach it,
as both the waves and the
geysers are unpredictable.

Kahakuloa Village and Head **❺**

Maui Co. 🏠 25. 🛈 Maui VB,
Wailuku, (808) 244-3530.

For nearly 1,500 years families
have inhabited Kahakuloa,
growing taro (see p125) on
stone terraces and using
aqueducts to irrigate their
crops from mountain streams.
One of the most isolated
villages on Maui, it has no gas
stations or restaurants, and
the most prominent building
is a lovely small church. East
of the village, the monolithic
636-ft (194-m) Kahakuloa
Head rises majestically
from the water's edge.

HUMPBACK WHALES

Once the hub of the Pacific whaling
trade, Maui County is today an official
sanctuary for humpbacks. The whales
spend the winter here, bearing their
young in the warm, shallow waters.
Newborns are 10–12 ft (3–4 m) long
and weigh a svelte 1–2 tons. Adults
may reach 45 ft (14 m) in length and
weigh 30 to 40 tons. In the mating
season, males produce a hauntingly
beautiful "song" – a series of whistles, groans, creaks, and screeches
that are thought to help establish
territory or attract females. Although
regulations forbid boats from moving
too close, these intelligent creatures
may approach a boat, as passengers
on Maui's whale-watching cruises (see
p224) are often thrilled to discover.

The unforgettable sight of a humpback whale breaching

Snorkelers enjoying the shallow waters off palm-fringed Lahaina Beach, Maui ▷

Plants cultivated at Maui Tropical Plantation and Country Store

Wailuku

Maui Co. 15,000. MVB, 1727 Wili Pā Loop, (808) 244-3530.

Tucked into the foothills of the West Maui Mountains, Wailuku was in ancient times a royal center and the scene of many important battles. Today, it is a county seat and a thriving community. It has an intriguing mix of architectural styles, with several notable buildings along High Street. These include **Wailuku Library**, whose main structure was designed by noted Hawaiian architect C.W. Dickey, the old **Wailuku Courthouse**, the **Territorial Building**, and **Wailuku Union Church**. Also of interest is Market Street, with its antique stores, art galleries, cafés, boutiques, and the historic **ʻĪao Theater**.

🏛 Bailey House Museum
2375A Main St. **Tel** (808) 244-3326. 10am–4pm Mon–Sat. Jan 1, Thanksgiving, Dec 25. www.mauimuseum.org

Headquarters of the Maui Historical Society, this museum is a time capsule of mission life in 19th-century Hawaiʻi. From 1837 to 1849, the building housed the Wailuku Female Seminary, where New England missionary Edward Bailey and his wife, Caroline, taught. When the seminary closed, Bailey bought the house. Today, the museum contains a large collection of local artifacts, including *kapa* (tree bark) cloth, stone utensils, carvings, *lei* (see p29), and Bailey's own paintings of Maui.

Carving at Bailey House Museum

🏯 Kaʻahumanu Church
103 S. High Street. **Tel** (808) 244-5189. 9am Sun.

This Wailuku landmark was originally constructed in 1832 and is listed on the National Register of Historic Places. After several attempts at rebuilding, the New England-style structure and steeple we see today were erected in the 1880s. It is named for an important early convert to Christianity, Queen Kaʻahumanu, the powerful wife of Kamehameha I. The church was designed by the Protestant missionary Edward Bailey, whose home next door is now the Bailey House Museum. At this church, the Sunday services are conducted in the Hawaiian language and visitors are welcome to attend.

♣ Maui Tropical Plantation and Country Store
1670 Honoapiʻilani Hwy (Hwy 30), 2 miles (3 km) S of Wailuku. **Tel** (808) 244-7643. daily. tram only.

Some of the tropical plants displayed here, such as banana, coconut, breadfruit, and taro, were brought to the Hawaiian islands by the ancient Polynesians. Others were introduced more recently, such as orchids from Africa, papaya from South America, starfruit from Southeast Asia, and macadamia nuts from Australia. An informative open-air tram tour circles about half of the plantation's 112 acres. Various plants are sold in the shop.

🏯 Halekiʻi-Pihana Heiau State Monument
Hea Place, off Kūhiō Place, accessed from Waiehu Beach Rd. **Tel** (808) 984-8109. daily.

Important religious and civic affairs were conducted here, at the most significant pre-contact *heiau* (temple) in the Central Valley. Halekiʻi ("the House of Images") was probably a compound for chiefs. During religious ceremonies, *aliʻi* (royalty) would reside in thatched houses whose walls are still visible on the temple's eastern face. A reconstructed section of wall is all that remains of Pihana ("Fullness"), a *luakini heiau* (temple used for human sacrifices). Kamehameha I conducted a sacrifice here in order to give thanks for his victory in ʻĪao Valley in 1790.

Aerial view of Kahului harbor

Kahului ⑦

Maui Co. 26,000. MVB, Wailuku, (808) 244-3530.

Kahului is the commercial and industrial center of Maui. The island's biggest airport and principal shipping harbor are located here. It also offers beaches, large parks, historic sites, and cultural attractions.

The **Alexander and Baldwin Sugar Museum** is located 2 miles (5km) west of Kahului. Across from the Puʻunēnē Sugar Mill, built in 1902 by Alexander and Baldwin (see p123), the old supervisor's residence has been transformed into a museum about the industry that dominated Hawaiʻi's economy for more than half a century. It features historical exhibits, narrated

For hotels and restaurants in this region see pp184–7 and pp202–6

displays, and a model of a cane-crushing mill.

The **Kanaha State Wild-life Sanctuary**, once a royal fish pond, is home to many migratory and native birds. These include two endangered species, the slender, pink-legged Hawaiian stilt (*ae'o*) and the gray-black, ducklike Hawaiian coot (*'alae keoke'o*). To access the walking trails, visitors must obtain a permit from the **State Department of Natural Resources**. There is an observation pavilion on the ocean side of Hāna Highway.

🏛 **Alexander and Baldwin Sugar Museum**
3957 Hansen Rd. **Tel** (808) 871-8058. ☐ 9:30am–4:30pm daily.
☐ Jan 1, Thanksgiving, Dec 25. 💳
♿ www.sugarmuseum.com

💥 **Kanaha Pond State Wildlife Sanctuary**
Off Hāna Hwy, between Kahului Airport and Kahului town.
Tel (808) 984-8100.

State Department of Natural Resources
Division of Forestry and Wildlife, 54 S High St, Room 101.
Tel (808) 984-8100.

'Iao Valley ❽

Maui Co. 🚹 MVB, Wailuku, (808) 244-3530.

The 'Iao Valley Road leads into the West Maui Mountains, winding beneath sheer cliffs as it follows a river hidden by trees. As the road begins to climb, the air becomes cooler, and traffic noise is replaced by the green of 'Iao Valley, one of Maui's most sacred and historic sites. At one time, the bones of kings were buried here. In this valley in 1790, equipped with Western knowledge and weaponry, the forces of Kamehameha the Great trapped and annihilated those of Kahekili, the last independent chief of the island.

In a beautiful setting, about 2 miles (3 km) up the valley from Wailuku, you will find

Kepaniwai Heritage Gardens, a lovely county park with shaded picnic tables used by local families. Scattered about the park are smaller-than-life models showing the architectural styles brought to the islands by various ethnic and racial groups. A thatched Hawaiian *hale* (house), a Portuguese dwelling with its outdoor oven, a simple Japanese home, and a prim New England cottage are some of the structures that reflect Hawai'i's people – immigrants who come from the four corners of the world.

Statue of Japanese workers at Kepaniwai Heritage Gardens

Adjacent to the gardens, the **Hawai'i Nature Center** offers hikes and other outdoor activities for young and old. "Mud Scientists," "Tremendous Trees," and "Slugfest" are a few of the hands-on educational offerings for budding scientists as young as three years old. In 1997, the center opened a new building called the 'Iao Valley Interactive Science Arcade, an innovative museum featuring games and displays that serve to educate visitors about the plant and animal life that has reached these islands.

The paved road ends at 'Iao Valley State Park, at the foot of 'Iao Needle, a pinnacle of rock that towers 1,200 ft (365 m) above the valley floor. The Needle is a hard, volcanic rock that remained when softer rocks around it eroded away. Trails continue into the valley, but this is one of the wettest places on earth, and hiking here can be dangerous when heavy rains create flash-flood conditions.

🌺 **Kepaniwai Heritage Gardens**
'Iao Valley Road.
Tel (808) 270-7230. ☐ daily. ♿

💥 **Hawai'i Nature Center**
'Iao Valley Road. **Tel** (808) 244-6500. ☐ 10am–4pm daily. ☐ Jan 1, Thanksgiving, Dec 25. 💳
www.hawaiinaturecenter.org

🏞 **'Iao Valley State Park**
'Iao Valley Road, 3 miles (5 km) W of Wailuku. ☐ 7am–7pm daily.

Mā'alaea ❾

Maui Co. 🚹 400. 🚹 MVB, Wailuku, (808) 244-3530.

Nestled along the shoreline off Honoapi'ilani Highway, Mā'alaea has oceanfront condominiums, several restaurants, a shopping plaza, a few attractions, and a small boat harbor. Many snorkel and fishing boat charters depart from Mā'alaea Harbor and facilities here include an activity booth and a US Coast Guard station. Mā'alaea Bay, is a favorite of surfers and windsurfers. In the winter, humpback whales (*see p115*) frequent the bay and can easily be seen from shore.

On the seafront, **Maui Ocean Center**, a huge aquarium and marine park, has more than 60 indoor and outdoor displays, where it is possible to see marine life up close without getting wet. Exhibits include the Living Reef, Turtle Lagoon, and the Open Ocean. The Discovery Pool is an interactive exhibit, where visitors can handle creatures that inhabit tide pools, like sea stars and sea cucumbers. For a thrilling experience, try The Underwater Journey, on which visitors walk through a transparent tunnel set inside a 750,000-gallon tank that is teeming with colorful fish, sharks, rays, and other marine life.

💥 **Maui Ocean Center**
192 Mā'alaea Rd. **Tel** (808) 270-7000. ☐ 9am–5pm daily. 💳
www.mauioceancenter.com

Diving with spotted eagle rays, Maui Ocean Center

Kīhei ❿

Maui Co. 🏠 *17,000.* 🚌 ℹ️ *MVB, Wailuku, (808) 244-3530.*

One of the most populated areas on Maui, Kīhei lies on the island's sunny southern shore and boasts a vast stretch of sparkling white-sand beaches. Some of the island's best beaches for swimming, windsurfing, and snorkeling are found here, including Kalama Park and Kama'ole I, II, and III Parks. Just south of Kama'ole III, there is a boat ramp from which many ocean activity charters depart.

The **Hawaiian Islands Humpback Whale National Marine Sanctuary** encompasses most of the ocean around Hawai'i, but its administrative center is located in Kīhei, at the edge of an ancient fishpond. Here there is an observation deck with a large viewing scope, allowing visitors to enjoy whale watching at a safe and nonintrusive distance.

Covering 1.1 sq miles (2.8 sq km) of some of the last remaining natural wetland habitat in Hawai'i, **Kealia Pond National Wildlife Refuge** has wet and dry periods. It is home to more than 30 species of birds. Neighboring it is Kealia Beach, a nesting ground for the endangered hawksbill turtle.

🐋 **Hawaiian Islands Humpback Whale National Marine Sanctuary**
726 S Kīhei Road. *Tel (808) 879-2818.* 🕐 *10am–3pm Mon–Fri.*
www.hihwnms.nos.noaa.gov

🐋 **Kealia Pond National Wildlife Refuge**
Off Mokulele Hwy near Mile Marker 6. *Tel (808) 875-1582.*

Mākena ⓫

Maui Co. 🏠 *5,700.* ℹ️ *MVB, Wailuku, (808) 244-3530.*

At Mākena, Big Beach is separated from Little Beach by a rock outcropping that you have to climb over. When conditions are right, both beaches are good spots for

An alluring stretch of golden sand at Little Beach, Mākena

body surfing, boogie boarding, snorkeling, swimming, and sunbathing. Big Beach is the nickname of the long, white-sand, crescent-shaped Oneloa Beach, which lies to the south of Wailea Marriott Resort *(see p187)*. Facilities in the area are few so arrive prepared. Unofficially, Little Beach is known as a "clothing optional" beach.

The white, steepled **Keawala'i Church** stands beside the ocean in a tranquil, palm-tree-fringed cove. The spectacular setting of this quaint church make it a popular venue for weddings. Built in 1855, it has had a continuous and active congregation, which has lovingly renovated the building over the years. The church welcomes visitors, but asks that they remove their shoes before entering. Sunday services are held in the Hawaiian language.

🛐 **Keawala'i Church**
190 Makena Road. *Tel (808) 879-5577.* www.keawalai.org

Ahihi Kina'u Natural Area Reserve ⓬

Maui Co. At the end of Mākena Alanui, 5 miles (8 km) past Wailea. *Tel (808) 873-3506.* 🕐 *daily.*

About a mile and a half south of the Makena Beach and Golf Resort *(see p186)*, this preserve is unique in Hawai'i in that it protects both land and sea environments. To that end, some areas are closed to the public. The section on dry

land is a dramatic lava landscape created by the last eruption of Haleakalā *(see pp128–9)* in 1790. Underwater, fantastic snorkeling and diving is on offer. Because this area is protected, it is illegal to damage or remove any of the natural habitat.

La Pérouse Bay ⓭

Maui Co. ℹ️ *MVB, Wailuku, (808) 244-3530.*

South of Mākena, this bay was named for the first European to set foot on Maui, French explorer Jean Francis Gallup Comte de La Pérouse, who arrived in 1786. There is a monument marking the spot on the *mauka* (mountain) side of the road. When La Pérouse returned in 1790, he found that the communities he had visited before were abandoned and covered with lava. Today the bay is known for its fantastic kayaking, snorkeling, and diving.

Kayaking in the crystal clear waters of La Pérouse Bay

Kaho'olawe ⑭

Maui Co. No general access.

A dry, uninhabited island less than 11 miles (18 km) long, Kaho'olawe has at different times been host to exiled convicts, sheep and goats who eroded the soil, and the United States Navy, who used it for target practice. In the 1970s, native Hawaiians began a campaign to regain the island, and in 1994 the US ceded it to the state of Hawai'i. Hundreds of ancient sites have been found here, and although access is strictly limited, Hawaiians have begun to reclaim their heritage.

The tiny island of Molokini, popular for underwater exploration

Molokini ⑮

Maui Co. 🚢 from Mā'alaea Harbor. 🛈 MVB, Wailuku, (808) 244-3530.

An almost completely submerged volcano, Molokini rises just 160 ft (50 m) above the sea. The exposed rim is rocky and barren, but below the surface this marine reserve teems with pelagic (open-sea) fish that are comfortable with people, thanks to the many boats that anchor here for snorkeling and scuba diving.

'Ulupalakua Ranch and Tedeschi Winery ⑯

Maui Co. Hwy 37. **Tel** (808) 878-6058. 🕐 10am–5pm daily. 🗺
www.ulupalakuaranch.com &
www.mauiwine.com

High up on the slopes of Haleakalā, where this ranch and winery are located, the air is cooler and the scenery panoramic. In the 19th century this area was known as Rose Ranch because of the many rose gardens planted here by the then owner's wife. Some of the trees that she planted still stand shading the grounds today. What is today known as 'Ulupalakua Ranch is a working ranch and the site of Maui's only winery, at the Tedeschi Vineyards. The winery's tasting room is located in King's Cottage, which was built in 1874 for King David Kalakaua, a frequent visitor. Here you can sample and purchase the fruits of the winery's labor. Two free tours of the winery are offered daily.

Upcountry Farms ⑰

Maui Co. Kula District. 🛈 MVB, Wailuku, (808) 244-3530.

Upcountry is the term used to describe the verdant western slopes of Haleakalā. At these higher elevations, the views are breathtaking, the scenery is magnificent, the cool and misty air is invigorating, and the volcanic soil is fertile. Here you will find most of the island's farms and ranches, where an intriguing array of flowers, vegetables, fruits, and livestock flourish. Many welcome visitors to enjoy their beauty and their bounty.

O'o Farm is run by the owners of two leading Lahaina restaurants, Pacific'O and I'o (see p204), who are the first in the state to own and operate a farm for the sole purpose of supplying their restaurants. Their farm features orchards where citrus fruits, tropical fruits, stone fruits, and apples are cultivated, as well as extensive herb and vegetable gardens. Visitors may tour the farm with a culinary specialist, handpicking items for a one-of-a-kind lunch, with a choice of fresh fish or vegetarian fare. You are welcome to bring wine to enjoy with your lunch.

Fragrant and pastoral, **Ali'i Kula Lavender** farm cultivates 45 different varieties of lavender. Stroll through the gardens or take a 90-minute guided tour that offers information about the history, health benefits, and culinary attributes of lavender. In addition to the walking tour, a visit to this farm can include lunch and various seasonal tours, some with wreath-making and others with cooking demonstrations.

So named because there are surfboards in the pens and the goats stand on them, the **Surfing Goat Dairy** produces more than 20 different varieties of goat's cheese. The dairy offers daily tours that include information about cheese making and cheese sampling. During the "Evening Chores and Milking" tour you can help bring in the herd, feed them, and even try out your skills at hand milking the goats.

O'o Farm
651 Waipoli Road, Kula. **Tel** (808) 667-4341 🗺 🗺
www.oofarm.com

Ali'i Kula Lavender
1100 Waipoli Road, Kula. **Tel** (808) 878-3004. 🕐 9am–4pm daily. 🗺
🗺 www.aklmaui.com

Surfing Goat Dairy
3651 Omaopio Road, Kula.
Tel (808) 878-2870 🗺 🗺
www.surfinggoatdairy.com

Fertile upcountry farmland on the misty western slopes of Haleakalā

A Tour of Upcountry Maui ⑱

Sign outside the Tedeschi Winery

Between Maui's coastal towns and the mountaintop wilderness of Haleakalā, the air is cool, scented by eucalyptus groves that give way to the rolling hills of ʻUlupalakua and Haleakalā ranches. Here, roads wind through long stretches of countryside and often ascend into cloud banks, meanwhile offering stupendous views of Central Maui, the West Maui Mountains, and the surrounding island-dotted seas. While the scenery alone is worth the drive, any bend in the road can reveal a surprising bit of history – a European-style winery, a park paying homage to Chinese immigrants, or a church shaped like the Queen of Portugal's crown.

Baldwin Avenue ⑧
From Makawao to the coast at Pāʻia, this scenic road makes a pleasant drive and is used by bicycle tours descending from Haleakalā National Park (see pp128–9).

Church of the Holy Ghost ①
Built in the mid-1890s by Maui's Portuguese community, this Catholic church has an octagonal shape based on a crown worn by Queen Isabella of Portugal. Inside, opposite an exquisite wood and gold altar, sits a replica of a crown given to the church by Portugal.

Kēōkea ②
Little Kēōkea has a colorful church and charming country stores. Beyond it, the road twists through pastureland offering expansive views of West Maui and the islands of Lānaʻi, Molokaʻi, Kahoʻolawe, and tiny Molokini.

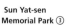

Sun Yat-sen Memorial Park ③
In this now overgrown park, stone lions guard the statue of the revolutionary Dr. Sun Yat-sen, first president of the Republic of China (1911), whose brother was among the many Chinese immigrants who settled in Kēōkea. Sun Yat-sen hid his family here during the Chinese Revolution (1911–12).

Tedeschi Winery ④
Set in the heart of ʻUlupalakua Ranch, this winery has picnic tables under grand old trees. The tasting room is in a cottage once used by King Kalākaua.

rolling hills and open spaces,
typical upcountry landscape

TIPS FOR DRIVERS

Tour length: 48 miles (77 km).
Stopping-off points: Plan half
a day to accommodate a tour of
Tedeschi Winery, a walk through
Kula Botanical Gardens, and
a stroll around Makawao.
There are good restaurants in
Makawao and Hāli'imaile (north
of Makawao) (see pp202–6);
alternatively, there are various
good picnic spots along the way.

Bronco-riding at the Makawao
Rodeo, an annual extravaganza

Hui No'eau Visual Arts Center ⑦
Set in charming grounds,
the Arts Center occupies a
1917 mansion designed for
the Baldwin family by C.W.
Dickey. A gallery and gift
shop feature pieces by
local artists, and the various art classes welcome
visitors on a drop-in basis.

KEY
▬ Tour route
═ Other roads
⁂ Vista

0 kilometers 5
0 miles 3

Small Upcountry Farms ⑥
Proteas and sweet Maui onions are
the principal crops here. Several
walk-through farms and gardens
admit visitors and sell cut proteas.

HALEAKALĀ
NATIONAL PARK

Kula Botanical Gardens ⑤
These lush, cool gardens display hydrangeas,
proteas, and other delights. There is also a collection of the world's most poisonous plants.

Makawao ⑲

Maui Co. 🏠 7,184. 🚌 MVB,
Wailuku, (808) 244-3530.
🎪 Makawao Rodeo (Jul 4).

The false-front wooden
buildings, the annual rodeo,
and the cattle ranches that surround the town give Makawao
a distinctly Old West flavor.
It has been a cowboy town
since the mid-19th century,
but gradually the *paniolo (see
p143)* have made way for an
"alternative" culture catering to
a growing artistic community.
Trendy art galleries showing
local creations cluster around
the crossroads at the town
center. Glassblowing can be
seen throughout the day at
Hot Island Glass on Baldwin
Avenue. Alternatively, you can
sit in a café to watch town life
go by, or stroll into **Komoda
Store and Bakery** (also on
Baldwin Avenue) for pastries
and old-Maui ambience.

HENRY PERRINE BALDWIN

Maui's verdant "lawn" of cane fields is due largely to the
vision of H.P. Baldwin (1842–1911), the son of prominent
Lahaina missionaries. In 1876, he and his partner S.T.

Alexander trumped their sugar
competitors by digging the
Hāmākua Ditch, an innovative
17-mile (27-km) irrigation
system that carried up to 40
million gallons (150 million
liters) of upcountry water a
day to their dry fields east of
Pā'ia. "HP" went on to develop a highly profitable sugar
company and build modern
Maui's top business power
(Alexander & Baldwin). In
effect, he ruled Maui during

**"HP" (right) and associate at
Hāmākua Poko Mill in 1898**

its transition from monarchy
to annexation *(see pp43–4).*

A glassblower demonstrating his
skills at Hot Island Glass

Windsurfers at Ho'okipa Beach County Park

Pā'ia ⑳

Maui Co. 🏘 2,700. ℹ MVB, Wailuku, (808) 244-3530.

Today, Pā'ia is a bohemian beach town with offbeat stores, an international surfing reputation, and good, rustic restaurants. Back in the 1930s, though, this little sugar town was the island's biggest population center. No longer in use, the sugar mill that once supported the town is located on Highway 390, a mile (1.5 km) southeast of Pā'ia's only traffic light. The **Mantokuji Buddhist Temple**, just east of town beside Hāna Highway (Hwy 36), speaks eloquently of those who came to work the plantations.

Environs: To the west of town, **HA Baldwin Beach County Park** is good for bodysurfing and popular with locals. Ten minutes east of Pā'ia on Hāna Highway is the world-famous windsurfing spot, **Ho'okipa Beach County Park**. Unique conditions allow windsurfers to perform spectacular aerial maneuvers over the breaking waves. This is not a swimming beach, but with five surf breaks it is certainly a spectators' spot, especially in the afternoon when the wind blows strongly.

Ke'anae Peninsula and Wailua Valley ㉒

Maui Co. ℹ MVB, Wailuku, (808) 244-3530.

Between Mile Markers 16 and 20, drivers cross an area deemed by the state a "cultural landscape." The star attraction, the ancient *lo'i* or taro ponds, can be seen from overlooks at mile markers 17 and 19. It is said that the Ke'anae Peninsula was just lava rock until the local chief, jealous of his neighbors in Wailua, sent people to bring soil down from the hills.

Wailua's Coral Miracle Church, site of **Our Lady of Fatima** shrine, was built in 1860 with sea-coral. A freak storm deposited the coral on a nearby beach. The locals gathered what they needed to build the church; later, another storm swept the unused coral back out to sea.

The Road to Hāna ㉑

MILE 1

360

Mile marker

Not until 1926 did the "Hāna Belt Road" connect the rest of Maui to its rain-forested eastern shores. The drive itself is pure fun, somehow being as suited to Jeeps as to convertible BMWs. The road is notoriously twisting and narrow, and road-handling commands every second of your attention. At the same time, the scenery demands that you stare in awe. This is one of the earth's rainiest coasts; the terrain is sliced with waterfalls and gulches choked with tropical vegetation.

Waikamoi Ridge Trail ①
An unmarked but obvious rest stop between mile markers 9 and 10 offers a picnic area, barbecues, and an easy nature walk. On the trail, labels identifythe flora, which includes species of eucalyptus and bamboo.

Ke'anae

Wailua

Hana Hig

PĀ'IA

Honomanū Bay ②
This dramatic bay with its rocky, black-sand beach is a popular surfing spot, but swimming in the turbulent waters can be risky.

0 kilometers	5
0 miles	5

KEY

▭▭ Tour route

═══ Other road

🔆 Viewpoint

Ke'anae Arboretum ③
These public gardens just before mile marker 17 provide a close-up look at working taro fields as well as a pleasant trail amid a variety of tropical flora from around the world.

Hāna ❷

Maui Co. 🏘 1,200. ✈ 🛈 MVB,
Wailuku, (808) 244-3530. 🎨 East
Maui Taro Festival (Mar/Apr).

Often called Hawai'i's most
Hawaiian town, Hāna
continues to lag lazily behind
the tempo of modernity, and
everyone here seems to think
that this is just fine. Its perfect
round bay and dreamy climate
have made Hāna a prized
settlement since time
immemorial. Kings of Maui
and Hawai'i Island fought to
possess the district, using
Ka'uiki Head, the large cinder
cone on the right flank of the
bay, as a natural fortification.
A cave at the base of the cone
was the birthplace of Queen
Ka'ahumanu *(see p42)*.

Tiny **Hāna Cultural Center**
presents a *kauhale* (residential
compound) in the precontact
style once unique to this area.
Exhibited artifacts give a sense
of local history. **Wānanalua**

TARO IN HAWAI'I

The purplish-gray root (corm) of
Colocasia esculenta was the staff
of life in ancient Hawai'i. It was
believed that taro and humans
had the same parents and that the
gods had ordered the plant to care
for humans, its siblings. This it did
by providing nutrition, mostly in
the form of *poi*, a pounded paste.
It also acted as a symbol of the
ideal *'ohana* (family): the plant
grows in clumps of *'ohā* (stems),
with the younger stems, like children, staying near the older core.

The taro plant, a traditional
source of food in Hawai'i

Church, beside Hāna Highway
(Hwy 360), was constructed
from blocks of coral in 1838.
Missionaries built it on top of
an existing *heiau* (temple),
thus symbolizing the triumph
of Christianity over paganism.

Sugar cultivation took root
in Hāna in the 1860s and continued until 1944, when San
Francisco capitalist Paul Fagan
closed the mill and converted

the area to cattle. Three years
later he built Hotel Hāna-Maui
on a plot once used by early
missionaries. Today, Fagan's
influence is still felt, and his
large memorial cross looms
on the hillside above the bay.

🏛 **Hāna Cultural Center**
Uakea Road. **Tel** (808) 248-8622.
⭕ 10am–4pm daily. ⭘ Jan 1, Dec
25. 🎫 🛗 **www.hookele.com**

...anihale Heiau ④
...beautifully preserved
...anihale Heiau is
...ai'i's largest ancient
...ple. It is well worth
...king your journey
...a closer look.

Wai'ānapanapa State Park ⑤
Plan a stop here to explore sea
caves, rocky cliffs, the black-
sand beach, and the ancient
"King's Trail," which follows
the spectacular coastline
from here to Hāna.

Ka Iwi o Pele ⑥
This large cinder cone beyond mile marker 51 is the
site of mythical struggles involving Pele, the goddess
of volcanoes. Nearby, the excellent Kōkī and Hāmoa
beaches face the waters where Maui the demigod
is said to have fished the islands out of the sea.

Hāna •

'Ohe'o Gulch ⑦
The pools in this lovely
stream are perfect for
swimming, but beware
of sudden flooding.
A 2-mile (3-km) trail
leads through a forest
to Waimoku Falls, one of
Maui's highest waterfalls.

**Palapala Ho'omau
Congregational Church** ⑧
The famous US aviator Charles
Lindbergh is buried at this beauti-
fully preserved 1864 church, along
with fellow flyer Sam Pryor.

Pi'ilani Highway

TIPS FOR DRIVERS

Tour length: *70 miles (110 km)
round trip.*
Stopping-off points: *Start
early, allowing a day for the
drive. There are no gas stations
from Pā'ia to Hāna, where most
facilities close at dusk. Hāna
has a few restaurants (see p202)
and hotels (see p184); there
are camping facilities at
Wai'ānapanapa State Park (permit
required) and 'Ohe'o Gulch (very
basic). For tours of Pi'ilanihale
Heiau, phone (808) 248-8912.*

Breathtaking waterfall at Kipahulu

Kīpahulu ㉔

Maui Co. Highway 31.
ℹ️ *Haleakalā National Park, (808) 248-7375.* www.nps.gov/hale

Reached on the winding Hāna Highway, in the Kīpahulu District of Haleakalā National Park *(see pp128–9)*, is 'Ohe'o Gulch, popularly but incorrectly called The Seven Sacred Pools. In Hawai'i all water is considered sacred and there are many more than seven pools here, all formed by the waterfalls rushing seaward from the top of Haleakalā.

About 10 miles (16 km) past Hāna you will drive over a small concrete bridge that spans the pools. A few curves after the bridge is a parking lot on your left, which is the site of the ranger station. An admission fee ($10 per car) is charged. There are restrooms, but no food, gas, or drinking water are available.

This lush, tropical area is great for hiking, swimming, and camping. The pools below the road are easy to reach along the short Kuloa Point Loop Trail that begins in the parking area. More adventurous visitors can search out the upper pools along the Waimoku Falls Trail. This trail begins across the road from the ranger station, climbs through a meadow and winds along the stream through the rainforest. After ascending for a while, it passes the magnificent Falls at Makahiku,

an 181-ft (55-m) waterfall, where you can stop for a breathtaking view down the cascading falls and pools to the ocean. Continuing for another 2 miles (3 km), beyond a fantastic bamboo forest, the trail ends at a shallow pool at the base of Waimoku Falls, which spill 400 ft (120 m) over the high cliff ledge. It is possible to swim or wade in the refreshing water here. Always be alert to the weather as flash flooding is common throughout this area.

A mile (1.5 km) past 'Ohe'o Gulch, on the ocean side of the road, stands the small, white **Palapala Ho'omau Congregational Church**, built in 1857. It is the final resting place of the famed American aviator Charles Lindbergh (1902–74), the first person to fly a plane solo across the Atlantic. He spent his last days in peaceful Hāna. Next to the cemetery is **Kīpahulu Lighthouse Point County Park**, perched on the edge of the cliff. There are shaded picnic tables here.

Kaupo ㉕

Maui Co. 8 miles (13 km) past 'Ohe'o Gulch on Highway 31.
ℹ️ *Maui VB, (808) 244-3530.*

From 'Ohe'o Gulch, the Hāna Highway winds in and out of valleys with steep rock walls and on blind curves hugging the ocean cliffs, to arrive at Kaupo. Kaupo means

"Landing at Night" and could refer to travelers from other islands, who arrived by canoe at night. Established in the mid-1920s, the quaint **Kaupo Store** was the last of the Soon family stores. These were set up by the son of an indentured Chinese laborer, Nick Soon, who also built the first electric generator in the area. The store sells cold beverages and local snacks like marlin jerky and shave ice. Opening times are erratic but if it is closed, stop and peruse the bulletin board by the door, which is plastered with business cards from all over the world.

Before the first Europeans arrived on Maui, thousands of people lived in the villages along this coast, sustaining themselves through farming the fertile land and fishing in the bountiful sea. The missionary churches that still stand here, such as **St. Joseph's Church** (built in 1862), give a clue to the large Hawaiian population they once served. Built in 1859, **Huialoha Church** fell into disrepair during the last century. However, volunteers worked to renovate the building and it was reopened in 1978, adding extra meaning to its name Huialoha, "meeting of compassion".

From Kaupo, the landscape turns into dry desert as this area is in the lee of Haleakalā and gets little rain. The impressive **Kaupo Gap** is visible from the road. It was created when an erupting Haleakalā blew away a large section of the mountain's rim.

Eventually, the highway leads to the verdant uplands of 'Ulupalakua *(see p121)*, offering spectacular scenery and serenity.

Spectacular scenery surrounding Huialoha Church, Kaupo

Beaches of South Maui

From the small harbor town of Māʻalaea to the solidified lava flows of La Pérouse Bay, South Maui's leeward coast is a playground for activities in, on, and near the water. Haleakalā's towering bulk shelters the region from trade winds and rain, while the proximity of neighboring islands and shallow waters create generally mild ocean conditions. All the beaches on Maui are public, and these along South Maui's leeward coast are particularly fine for swimming, snorkeling, scuba diving, and kayaking.

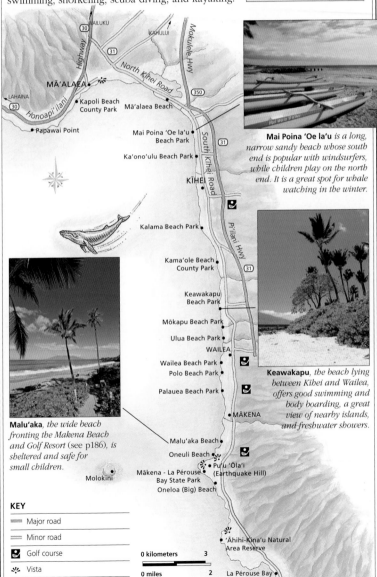

Mai Poina ʻOe laʻu *is a long, narrow sandy beach whose south end is popular with windsurfers, while children play on the north end. It is a great spot for whale watching in the winter.*

Keawakapu, *the beach lying between Kīhei and Wailea, offers good swimming and body boarding, a great view of nearby islands, and freshwater showers.*

Maluʻaka, *the wide beach fronting the Makena Beach and Golf Resort (see p186), is sheltered and safe for small children.*

KEY

▦▦▦ Major road

═══ Minor road

⛳ Golf course

✴ Vista

0 kilometers   3

0 miles   2

Haleakalā National Park ㉖

Nēnē living on
Haleakalā

The land mass of East Maui is really the top of an enormous shield volcano that begins more than 3 miles (5 km) below sea level. Haleakalā ("House of the Sun") is thought to have last erupted some 200 years ago and is still considered to be active, although not currently erupting. Its summit depression is 7.5 miles (12 km) long and 2.5 miles (4 km) wide, formed by erosional forces acting on volcanic rock. This natural wonder is preserved as part of the national park, which includes Kīpahulu valley and ʻOheʻo Gulch on the coast (see p109). In under two hours, motorists drive from sea level to the 10,023-ft (3,055-m) summit, rising from one ecosystem to the next while temperature and oxygen levels fall dramatically.

Hosmer Grove
campground has an easy, informative nature hike.

At Leleiwi Overlook
it may be possible to see your shadow on the clouds in the valley below, encircled by a rainbow.

MAKAWAO

Hōlua
Cabin

Park
headquarters

378

Haleakalā Crater Road

★ Puʻuʻulaʻula Summit
Standing on Puʻuʻulaʻula (Red Hill) is a breathtaking experience because of both the altitude – this is the highest point on Maui – and the view of the entire volcano. A glassed-in shelter provides relief from the bitterly cold winds.

Haleakalā Observatories
This off-limits, science fiction-style cluster of research stations is set in the summit's lunar landscape. Data from here help scientists map movements of the Earth's crust.

Visitor center

0 kilometers   2

0 miles   1

STAR SIGHTS

- ★ Puʻuʻulaʻula Summit
- ★ Silversword Loop
- ★ Sliding Sands Trail

Summit Depression
At one time, Haleakalā was much higher than it is now. Water eroded the peak, formed the basin you see today, and drained away through two huge gaps in the rim. Later volcanic activity filled in the valley floor and created the cinder cones.

Halemau'u Trail
This trail incorporates switchbacks and sharp drops, plus fine views, often to the ocean. The hike from the trailhead on Haleakalā Crater Road to Hōlua Cabin and back is a good but tough day trip.

VISITORS' CHECKLIST

Maui Co. Haleakalā Crater Road (Hwy 378). ⬤ 24 hrs daily. 🅿 **Park headquarters** *Tel* (808) 572-4400. ⬤ 7:30am–4pm daily. 👤 **Visitor Center** ⬤ sunrise–3pm daily. 👤 **Cabins** To reserve one of the three wilderness cabins, visit https://fhnp.org/wcr up to 90 days in advance. **www**.nps.gov/hale

★ Silversword Loop
The Haleakalā Silversword, one of the world's rarest plants, thrives here under the most hostile conditions the volcano can offer: hot days, cold nights, and porous ash soil. The soft silvery hairs on its incurved leaves protect the plant from sunlight and draft. It takes up to 50 years to flower, when it raises a spectacular spike of purplish flowers.

KO'OLAU GAP

'u Trail

Halemau'u Trail

Pele's Paint Pot is a surreal landscape of brightly colored ashes.

ing Sands Trail

Sliding Sands Trail

KAUPŌ GAP

Kaupō Trail

Palikū Cabin

KEY

═══ Minor road

- - Hiking trail

☆ Vista

★ Sliding Sands Trail
The only way to really appreciate the scale and varied terrain here is to descend 3,000 ft (900 m) into the volcano. The 10-mile (16-km) Sliding Sands Trail takes you from the visitor center through scenery that ranges from a barren cinder desert to an alpine shrubland.

Kapalaoa Cabin
One of three primitive cabins in the volcano – so popular that you must reserve well in advance.

HAWAI'I ISLAND

To understand fully the culture and spirit of the Hawaiian islands, travelers must venture to the island of Hawai'i itself – commonly called "the Big Island." This is the site of some of the earliest Polynesian settlements as well as the last heiau (temple) to be built. Here, Captain Cook met his demise, Kamehameha the Great rose to power, and the first Christian missionaries set foot on Hawaiian soil.

Being a relatively young island (a million years old, compared with Kaua'i's five million) not yet ringed with sandy beaches, Hawai'i has wisely placed its tourist-industry focus on the preservation of cultural sites. An amazing number of these are accessible to the traveler.

Spreading over 4,035 sq miles (10,450 sq km), Hawai'i Island is more than twice the size of all the other islands combined. Its bulk includes the earth's most massive mountain, Mauna Loa, which rises over 30,000 feet (9,150 m) from its base on the sea floor and is still growing. It also includes the state's tallest peak, the often snow-capped Mauna Kea, and three other mountains: Hualālai, which blocks the moist trade winds from dry north Kona; Kohala, the soft hump of the Waimea area's northern ranch lands; and Kīlauea, the

most active volcano on earth. A new mountain called Lō'ihi, currently forming 20 miles (32 km) off the southeast coast, should emerge from the sea thousands of years from now. Hawai'i Island's great bulk offers travelers the chance to see a variety of ecosystems, from alpine heights to barren desert.

Today, with only ten percent of the state's population, the Big Island is one of Hawai'i's sleepiest, most scattered communities. Hilo, its main town, was pushed into the economic background by devastating tsunamis in 1946 and 1960, and in the 1990s the island's sugar industry collapsed. Now tourism plays a big role, especially in sunny Kona. Visitors will find a land of open space, quiet towns, and a population that is friendly in the traditional Hawaiian way.

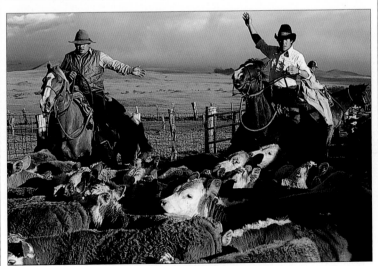

Paniolo (Hawaiian cowboys) at the Parker Ranch in the Waimea area

◁ **A cluster of astronomical domes on Mauna Kea, Hawai'i Island's tallest mountain**

Exploring Hawai'i Island

Both East and West Hawai'i Island provide good bases for touring. Hilo is well situated for excursions to the Hāmākua Coast, Mauna Kea, the Puna district, and Hawai'i Volcanoes National Park – a highlight on any visitor's itinerary, with Kīlauea Caldera and its active lava rifts. Hilo itself is charming but very rainy, averaging 130 in (330 cm) per year. Travelers who prefer their days bone dry head for Kailua-Kona on the island's burgeoning west side. From here there is access to the South Kohala resorts to the north, the Parker Ranch country of Waimea, Kona coffee country to the south, and many well-preserved ancient sites, including Pu'uhonua O Hōnaunau.

Traditional canoe at Pu'uhonua O Hōnaunau National Historical Park

TOP RECREATIONAL AREAS

The places shown here have been selected for their recreational activities. Conditions, especially those of the ocean, vary depending on the weather and the time of year, so exercise caution and, if in doubt, stay out of the water or seek local advice.

	SWIMMING	SNORKELING	DIVING	BODY-SURFING	WINDSURFING	HIKING	HORSEBACK RIDING	GOLF
AHALANUI BEACH PARK	●							
'ANAEHO'OMALU BAY	●	■	●	■				
HĀPUNA BAY	●	■	●	■				■
HAWAI'I VOLCANOES NATIONAL PARK						■		
HILO	●	■	●	■			●	■
HONOKA'A								■
HO'OKENA	●	■						
KA LAE						■		
KAHALU'U BEACH COUNTY PARK	●	■	●					
KAILUA-KONA	●	■	●	■			●	■
KALŌPĀ STATE RECREATION AREA						■		
KAPA'AU						■		
KAWAIHAE HARBOR					●			
KEALAKEKUA BAY	●	■	●				●	
KEKAHA KAI STATE PARK	●	■				■		
KOLEKOLE BEACH COUNTY PARK	●							
LAPAKAHI STATE HISTORICAL PARK	●	■	●					
MAUNA KEA						■	●	
MAUNA LANI	●	■		■			●	■
PĀHALA								■
PEPE'EKEO SCENIC DRIVE						■		
PUAKŌ		■						
PUNALU'U BEACH COUNTY PARK	●	■	●					
PU'UHONUA O HŌNAUNAU	●	■	●					
SPENCER BEACH COUNTY PARK	●	■	●	■				
VOLCANO VILLAGE								■
WAIKOLOA							●	■
WAIMEA							●	
WAIPI'O VALLEY	●					■	●	

Mo'okini Heiau

HĀWĪ 13 14
KAPA'AU
LAPAKAHI STATE HISTORICAL PARK 12   250
KOHALA MOUNTAIN ROAD 9
270
Kawaihae
PU'UKOHOLĀ HEIAU NATIONAL HISTORIC SITE 11
HĀPUNA BAY 10
MAUNA LANI 8
WAIKOLOA COAST 7   Waikoloa Village
Kīlolo Bay

19

Makalawena
190
KEKAHA KAI STATE PARK 6
Hualālai 8,271ft
Honokōhau
KAILUA-KONA 1   180
HŌLUALOA 2
Kailua Bay
Keauhou
Honalo
Kealakekua   Captain Co
KEALAKEKUA BAY 3

PU'UHONUA O HŌNAUNAU NATIONAL HISTORICAL PARK 5   HO'OKE 4

Kauhakō Bay

11
Miloli'i

Hawaii Oc
View Est.

0 kilometers   25

0 miles   20

SEE ALSO

KEY

— Major road

═══ Minor road

– – Track

— Scenic route

△ Summit

WAIPI'O VALLEY **16**

Kukuihaele

HONOKA'A **17**

WAIMEA

HĀMĀKUA COAST

Kalōpā Forest State Park

18

Laupāhoehoe

MAUNA KEA **21**

SADDLE ROAD **20**

Mauna Loa Observatory

MAUNA LOA **24**

Hawai'i Volcanoes National Park

Kolekole Beach County Park

'AKAKA FALLS STATE PARK **22**

Honomū

WORLD BOTANICAL GARDENS **19**

PEPE'EKEO SCENIC DRIVE **23**

Hilo Bay

HILO **25**

Kea'au

KAPOHO **27** Cape Kumukahi

Lava Tree State Monument

PĀHOA **26**

Abalanui Beach Park

MacKenzie State Recreation Area

PUNA LAVA FLOWS **28**

VOLCANO VILLAGE **29**

Kīlauea Caldera

HAWAI'I VOLCANOES NATIONAL PARK

32

Nāpau Crater

Kalapana Kehena Beach

Pāhala

KA'Ū DISTRICT **30**

Punalu'u

Punalu'u Beach Park

Nāʻālehu

Whittington Beach Park

Sands Beach

KA LAE

Ka Lae, the southernmost point in the United States

GETTING AROUND

Travelers can fly into Hilo International Airport or Kona International Airport, north of Kailua-Kona. From there, a rented car is essential as bus services are minimal. The island is encircled by the Hawai'i Belt Road. Its northern stretch (Hwy 19 and continuing on Hwy 190) crosses from Hilo via Waimea to Kailua-Kona, taking about two hours. The southern route (Hwy 11) crosses the Ka'ū district in around three hours. Saddle Road, a shorter middle route passing between Mauna Kea and Mauna Loa, has narrow stretches that make progress slow. Lava flows have split Highway 130 into two sections: an eastern route into the Puna area, and Chain of Craters Road, which offers a close-up view of Kīlauea's eruptions.

Aerial view of the coastline south of Kailua-Kona

Kailua-Kona ❶

Hawai'i Co. 🏠 33,000. ✈ ⛴
i Big Island VB, (808) 961-5797.
📷 Ironman Triathlon (Oct: Sat
closest to full moon).

Referred to locally as "Kona", this town is the center of the island's "Gold Coast". Within a two-block span along oceanfront Ali'i Drive are sites that played a role in some of the most important moments in Hawai'i's history, from the unification of the islands to the advent of Christianity. Kailua-Kona's tourist strip does little to obscure these vivid reminders of Hawaiian history.

Built out into Kailua Bay is **Ahu'ena Heiau**, an ancient temple dedicated to the god Lono. It was restored by Kamehameha the Great, whose residence was next to the temple. Adjoining it is **King Kamehameha Kona Beach Hotel** (see p188) – the lobby has Hawaiian artifacts: tools, handicrafts, and a feather cape.

Idyllic Kahalu'u Beach

In 1820, the first party of missionaries landed at Kailua-Kona. They built the original **Moku'aikaua Church** on Ali'i Drive. The present lofty, granite church dates from 1837. A modest museum at the rear offers a scale model of the missionaries' brig, *Thaddeus*. Across the street, **Hulihe'e Palace** was built at the same time of similar rough-stone construction. In 1885, King Kalākaua beautified the little building, which now serves as a museum. It takes a candid look at the lifestyle of the monarchy in its heyday.

Kailua-Kona, so named to distinguish it from Kailua on O'ahu, is synonymous with sportfishing. Charter boats offer year-round opportunities to fish for marlin and other ocean giants. In October the town is overrun by endurance athletes who compete in the grueling Ironman Triathlon. The sunny coastline is dotted with small beaches good for swimming, snorkeling, and diving. **Kahalu'u Beach**, 4.5 miles (7 km) south of Kailua, provides snorkelers with the island's finest natural aquarium.

Kona Coffee Cultural Festival poster

🔒 **Moku'aikaua Church**
75-5713 Ali'i Drive. **Tel** (808) 329-0655. ⬜ daily. ♿

🏛 **Hulihe'e Palace**
75-5718 Ali'i Drive. **Tel** (808) 329-1877. ⬜ 10am–3pm Tue–Sat.
⬤ public hols. 📷

Hōlualoa ❷

Hawai'i Co. 🏠 6,100. **i** Big Island
VB, West Hawai'i, (808) 885-1655.
📷 Kona Coffee Cultural Festival
(2nd week of Nov).

A 15-minute drive up the winding and scenic Hualalai Road from Highway 19, on the slopes of Mount Hualalai, lies Hōlualoa. Set in the heart of the Kona coffee belt, coffee is its main focus, as attested by the annual Kona Coffee Cultural Festival. Artists also add their flavor to the town.

Long before tourism took hold, many immigrants settled here to work on the coffee plantations and vegetable farms and Hōlualoa was a thriving town full of hotels, restaurants, and general stores to provide for their needs. Some of these stores still operate today. **Kimura Lauhala Shop** began as a general store in 1915, but became famous for its *lauhala* hats woven from the leaves of the pandanus tree. The Kimura family still runs the store.

Hōlualoa's main street is lined with galleries that present works by many of the island's most well known artists. **Studio 7** showcases the creations of Hiroki and Setsuko Morinoue. He is known for his large watercolors and woodblock prints; she is a ceramist. The studio also displays works by other artists, including turned bowls, wooden bracelets, and silk-screen prints. The pottery and paintings of Matthew and Mary Lovein are on show at their **Hōlualoa Gallery**, along with jewelry, sculptures, and glass works by other artists.

🔲 **Kimura Lauhala Shop**
Mamalahoa Highway and Hualalai
Road. **Tel** (808) 324-0053.

🔲 **Studio 7**
76-5920 Mamalahoa Highway.
Tel (808) 324-1335.

🔲 **Holualoa Gallery**
76-5921 Mamalahoa Highway.
Tel (808) 322-8484.

For hotels and restaurants in this region see pp188–9 and pp206–8

Kona Coffee

For over a century the upward slopes of the Kona district have been home to the United States' only coffee-growing region. The massive bulk of Mauna Loa, an enormous shield volcano *(see p147)*, creates a localized weather pattern that favors the crop. Sunny mornings are followed by cloudy, humid afternoons that often drench the rich, volcanic soil with rain. Over 500 independent small farms cultivate this world-class, gourmet coffee, producing a crop of about 2 million pounds (900,000 kg) a year. Roadsides are dotted with cafés, mills, and farms, and the Hawai'i Visitors and Convention Bureau in Kailua-Kona offers a driving map of the area. Every year, in the second week of November, the district celebrates its coffee with the Kona Coffee Cultural Festival.

HOW COFFEE IS HARVESTED

Coffee beans grown in the rich soil of the Kona district are picked by hand, ensuring only the best beans go into making coffee.

"Kona snow" *is the local term for the white, fragrant spring flowers. The first Coffea arabica plants were introduced to the area in 1828 by the American missionary Samuel Ruggles.*

Coffee cherries *ripen in waves, from August until March, so they must be laboriously hand-harvested. The cherries start out green in color and turn red as they ripen.*

A kuriba *(pulping mill) separates the flesh of the cherry from its hard, parchment-covered bean. After soaking and washing, beans in the "wet parchment" stage are left to dry in the sun.*

A hoshidana *is a drying deck with a wheeled cover that is rolled over the beans whenever the mountain rains move in. Beans are raked three or four times a day for up to two weeks.*

Milling *removes two outer layers from the hard beans - the tough parchment and the filmy "silver skin." Raw beans, called green coffee, are then graded and ready for roasting.*

IMMIGRANT WORKERS

The success of Kona's coffee owes as much to its people as to its weather. In the late 19th century, after decades of control by the large plantations, the crop began to be cultivated tenaciously on small-scale family farms. Many of these farmers were Japanese immigrants who fled slavelike conditions on the plantations to work their own farms. Today, their descendents continue the coffee tradition.

Kona coffee beans *are known throughout the gourmet coffee world for their rich, highly aromatic flavor. The roasting process brings out the flavor: beans that are roasted longer and at higher temperatures are darker with a more intense taste. Additional flavorings, such as chocolate or macadamia nuts, may be added immediately after roasting.*

Roasted coffee beans

The colorful interior of St. Benedict's Painted Church in Hōnaunau

Kealakekua Bay ❸

Hawai'i Co. Nāpō'opo'o Road,
4 miles (6 km) S of Captain Cook.
🚩 Captain Cook. 🛈 Big Island VB,
(808) 961-5797.

In 1778, Captain Cook sailed into this deep, protected bay, "discovering" Hawai'i. He was honored as the returning Hawaiian god Lono, but less than a month later was killed here (see p41). **Hikiau Heiau**, where Cook was honored, is at the road's end. A monument marks where he died.

The bay, a State Marine Life Preserve with an abundance of fish, sea turtles, and spinner dolphins, offers excellent diving, snorkeling, and kayaking.

Ho'okena's Kauhakō Bay, which is lined with a beach of gray sand

ENVIRONS: The bay sits at the heart of Kona coffee country, with its rustic farms and mills. In the town of **Kealakekua**, the **Kona Historical Society** gives interpretive tours of its headquarters in the 1870s-vintage **Greenwell Store** and of neighboring **Uchida Farm**, a restored 1930s coffee farm. The entire district invites exploration, from Hōnaunau in the south up to Hōlualoa (see p134) in the north. In Hōnaunau, **St. Benedict's Painted Church** is brightly illuminated with biblical scenes executed by a Belgian priest in the early 20th century.

🏛 **Kona Historical Society**
81-6551 Māmalahoa Hwy
(Hwy 11). *Tel (808) 323-3222.
🕐 9am–3pm Mon–Fri. ⬤ public
hols. 🖼 donation requested. ♿

🔒 **St. Benedict's
Painted Church**
Painted Church Road, off Hwy 160
near mile marker 1. *Tel (808) 328-
2227.* 🕐 daily. ♿

Ho'okena ❹

Hawai'i Co.
🛈 Big Island VB,
West Hawai'i, (808)
885-1655.

In 1889, when author Robert Louis Stevenson asked to see a classic Hawaiian village, King Kalākaua sent him to Ho'okena. In those days, the town could boast churches, a school, a courthouse, and a pier from which cattle were shipped to market in Honolulu. Today, besides weather-beaten houses and beach shacks, only lava walls and the ruined pier survive as reminders of its more prosperous past.

The center of life, then as now, is beautiful **Kauhakō Bay** with its gray-sand beach backed dramatically by long cliffs. The water teems with sea life, and there is excellent snorkeling and diving. However, the surf can be rough, and wearing foot protection is recommended.

Pu'uhonoua O Honaunau National Historic Park ❺

See pp138–9.

Kekaha Kai State Park ❻

Hawai'i Co. Off Queen Ka'ahumanu Highway (Hwy 19), 9 miles (14 km) N of Kailua-Kona. *Tel Division of State Parks, (808) 961-9540.* 🕐 Thu–Tue.

North of Kailua, the road runs through barren lava fields, the aftermath of an 1801 eruption of Mount Hualālai. In places, road and landscape are distinguishable only by their relative smoothness. The state park, with its picnic shelters and sinuous beach of salt-and-pepper sand, is an oasis in this distorted wasteland. It is an excellent spot for swimming, snorkeling, diving, and, when the conditions are right, surfing.

Green sea turtle swimming in the waters off the beach at Makalawena

Just before the park entrance, a dirt road on the right leads 1.5 miles (2.5 km) to isolated **Makalawena**, a beautiful beach with dunes and coves for snorkeling. Turtles, dolphins, and seals frequent these waters, as well as whales.

Waikoloa Coast ❼

Hawai'i Co. W of Queen Ka'ahumanu Highway (Hwy 19), 24 miles (39 km) N of Kailua-Kona. 🏨 Kohala Coast Resort Association, (808) 885-6414.

Waikoloa Beach Resort has built itself around one of this coast's best family recreational areas, coconut-rimmed **'Anaeho'omalu Bay**. The beach at "A-Bay" is calm, with a gradual, sandy bottom. Watersports equipment, including kayaks and sailboats, can be rented from the beach hut, and lessons in windsurfing and scuba diving are offered. Boat dives and cruises are also available.

From the beach, coastal trails lead to fish ponds, caves, and natural pools in which salt and fresh water mix to form unique ecosystems.

A short walk north of the beach is **Hilton Waikoloa Village Resort** (see p189), a 62-acre fantasy resort built in 1988 at a cost of $360 million. Silent monorails and canal boats provide transportation around the resort. Visitors can view the impressive art collection and explore the artificial beach, lagoon, and waterfall. At the dolphin pool, both guests and visitors can swim with the resort's trained dolphins. Also within the resort, the Waikoloa Beach Marriott Resort (see p189) fronts ancient fishponds along A-Bay and is a short walk from a restored *heiau* (temple).

Hilton Waikoloa Village Resort
69-425 Waikoloa Beach Drive. *Tel* (808) 886-1234. ☐ daily. 🚻 www.hiltonwaikoloavillage.com

Vacationers enjoying the lagoon at Hilton Waikoloa Village Resort

Mauna Lani ❽

68–1400 Mauna Lani Dr. *Tel* (808) 885-6622. ☐ daily. 🚻 www.maunalani.com

Petroglyph figure

The vast resort at Mauna Lani includes two luxury hotels, a couple of award-winning golf courses, several tennis courts, and small, white-sand beaches. It also encloses sites of cultural importance. **Kalāhuipua'a Trail** – a 20-minute hike, usually through blazing sunshine – winds past petroglyphs, lava tubes, and ancient habitation sites, ending at several ancient fish ponds. A coastal trail from here leads about a mile (1.5 km) south to **Honoka'ope Bay**, a sheltered swimming and snorkeling spot.

At the northern end of the resort, a shorter shady trail leads to the **Puakō Petroglyphs**. These are an expanse of crusty red lava plates that were engraved with more than 3,000 symbols between AD 1000 and 1800. Wear sturdy shoes.

Waimea ❾

Hawai'i Co. 🏨 9,200. ✈ 🚗 🏨 Waimea Visitor Center, Main St, (808) 885-6707. 🎠 Parker Ranch Rodeo (Jul 4).

Waimea's setting amid sprawling pasture land at a cool elevation of 2,700 ft (820 m) is a startling contrast to Hilo's rainforest and the Kona Coast's lava flats. By Hawai'i Island standards, Waimea is a large, modern town. On the edge of town is the **Keck Observatory Center**, with the world's most powerful telescopes (see p147).

In the middle of town, the **Parker Ranch Visitor Center** offers a short video and an eloquent collection of artifacts that tells the history of *paniolo* (cowboy) culture and provides an insight into the tempestuous and influential Parker family.

The **Historic Parker Ranch Homes** include Puopelu, a ranch house with a Regency interior and a respectable collection of European art, and Mānā Hale, the Parkers' original home, which has a display of family photographs.

🏛 **Keck Observatory Center**
65-1120 Māmalahoa Hwy (Hwy 19). *Tel* (808) 961-2120. ☐ 8am–4:30pm Mon–Fri. ● public hols. 🚻
www.keckobservatory.org

🏛 **Parker Ranch Visitor Center**
Parker Ranch Shopping Center, Māmalahoa Hwy (Hwy 19). *Tel* (808) 887-1046. ☐ 9am–5pm Mon–Sun. ● public hols. 📷 🚻

🏚 **Historic Parker Ranch Homes**
Off Māmalahoa Hwy (Hwy 190). *Tel* (808) 885-5433. ☐ 10am–5pm Mon–Sat. ● Sun, public hols. 📷 🚻 (partial access only.)
www.parkerranch.com

The façade of Puopelu, one of the Historic Parker Ranch Homes

Pu'uhonua O Hōnaunau National Historical Park 🄳

From the 11th century on, social interactions were regulated by the *kapu* (taboo) system *(see p40)*. Violent death was the consequence of infractions, which ranged from stepping on a chief's shadow to women eating bananas. Lawbreakers could escape punishment, however, by reaching a *pu'uhonua* (place of refuge). The greatest of these was at Hōnaunau, a 6-acre temple compound dating from the 16th century that offered absolution to all who managed to run or swim past the chief's warriors. The sanctuary was stripped of power in 1819, after the fall of the *kapu* system. Partially restored, it now provides a glimpse into precontact Hawai'i.

Heleipālala Fish Ponds
These two ponds were stocked with fish reserved for the royal table.

Worker in a field

Hālau
Thatched A-frame structures were used for storage and as work sheds.

Animals in enclosure

Keone'ele Cove was the royal canoe landing, making it *kapu* to all commoners.

Papamū
This carved stone board was used to play kōnane, *a Hawaiian game similar to checkers.*

Outrigger canoes

★ Hale O Keawe Heiau
The pu'uhonua's spiritual power resided in this temple compound, built in 1650. Now reconstructed, the heiau (temple) once held the bones and therefore the mana (sacred power) of great chiefs.

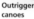

STAR SIGHTS

★ Hale O Keawe Heiau

★ The Great Wall

Wooden Ki'i
These carved images of gods outside Hale O Keawe Heiau are copies based on drawings and descriptions of the originals.

VISITORS' CHECKLIST

Hawai'i Co. Hwy 160, off
Hawai'i Belt Rd (Hwy 11).
Tel (808) 3282326. ◯ 7am–
sunset. 🏛 ♿
Visitor Center ◯ 8am–4:30pm.
www.nps.gov/puho

'Āle'ale'a Heiau
predates the 16th-
century Great Wall.
It served as the
focus of spiritual
power until the
construction of
Hale O Keawe.

A reconstructed sailing canoe with passengers

★ **The Great Wall**
*This superb example of a dry-
stone wall, built around
1550, separated the
pu'uhonua from
the palace area
inland. It is 10 ft
(3 m) high and
17 ft (5 m) wide.*

The old *heiau* **may**
have been built by
the Tahitian priest
Pā'ao in the 13th
century *(see p40)*.
It is now in ruins,
destroyed by either
tsunamis or large
storm waves.

0 meters		50
0 yards		50

The Keōua Stone was
a favorite resting spot
of Keōua, a high chief
of Kona district.

A RECONSTRUCTION

This is an artist's impression of the
pu'uhonua when the ruling chief
of the district lived here along with
his court and attendants. Some
elements have been reconstructed
by the National Park Service, and
visitors may see artisans at work.

Exposed Peninsula of Black Lava
*The peninsula's jagged shoreline made it diffi-
cult for* kapu-*breakers to approach from the sea.*

The popular white-sand beach at Hāpuna Bay, on Hawai‘i Island's south Kohala Coast

Hāpuna Bay ⑩

Hawai‘i Co. Off Queen Ka‘ahumanu Highway (Hwy 19), 7 miles (11 km) N of Waikoloa Coast.

An expanse of white sand, both broad and deep, makes Hāpuna Bay the most popular beach on Hawai‘i Island. With its clean, sandy bottom, the bay offers excellent swimming, snorkeling, and diving conditions. When the waves are active, surfers and body-boarders flock here, and it is generally a good spot for beginners to acquire some wave-riding skills. The water should be approached with caution, however; strong currents have resulted in several drownings. On the beach, there are places to rent snorkel sets and boogie boards, and posts staffed by life guards throughout the day.

Hāpuna Beach State Recreation Area, which surrounds the beach, provides cabins for overnight stays, as well as a snack bar and picnic tables at which visitors can enjoy their own food.

About 1 mile (1.5 km) north of the bay, accessed via the Mauna Kea Beach Hotel (*see p189*), is the lovely, crescent-shaped **Kauna‘oa Beach**, with fine conditions for swimming and snorkeling most of the year. One of the most photo-graphed beaches on the island, this stretch of sand was once the playground of *ali‘i* (Hawaiian royalty).

🏖 **Hāpuna Beach State Recreation Area**
Around Hāpuna Beach. *Tel* Division of State Parks, (808) 882-6206. ☐ daily.

Pu‘ukoholā Heiau National Historic Site ⑪

Hawai‘i Co. Off Akoni Pule Hwy (Hwy 270), 1 mile (1.5 km) S of Kawaihae. *Tel* (808) 882-7218. ☐ 7:30am–4pm daily. ♿ visitor center only. www.nps.gov/puhe

In 1790, Kamehameha I had reached an impasse in his drive to unify the island chain. On the advice of an oracle, he undertook the construction of **Pu‘ukoholā Heiau**, dedicated to Kūkā‘ilimoku, his family war god, which was destined to become the last such temple ever built. For the dedication ceremonies, the crafty king invited his rival Keoua, the chief of Ka‘ū.

As Keoua stepped out of his canoe, he was slaughtered and carried to the new altar to serve as its first sacrifice.

Today, the massive monument stands undamaged on a hilltop overlooking Kawaihae Bay. Below it are the ruins of **Mailekini Heiau**, built for Kamehameha's ancestors. A third *heiau*, **Haleokapuni**, dedicated to shark gods, is believed to lie submerged in the waters below. Sacrifices left here would soon have become shark fodder. An easy trail runs down past the first two *heiau* from the visitor center.

Immediately south of the *heiau* is **Spencer Beach County Park**, a popular spot for camping, snorkeling, and diving. The clean beach and calm waters make it a great area for children. Operated by the National Park Service, it includes a visitor center where park rangers provide information and you can pick up a map of points of interest.

Traditional ceremony at Pu‘ukoholā Heiau National Historic Site

Lapakahi State Historical Park ⓬

Hawai'i Co. Off Akoni Pule Hwy (Hwy 270), 12 miles (19 km) N of Kawaihae. **Tel** (808) 961-9540. ◯ daily. ⬤ public hols.

The ruins of this large settlement provide a glimpse into the daily life of an old Hawaiian fishing village. Established in the 14th century, the village was inhabited for 500 years – until a falling water table and changing economic conditions caused the natives to abandon their homes.

Some thatched walls and roofs are gone; others have been restored to their original appearance. The lava foundations, *hālau* (canoe sheds), *kū'ula ko'a* (fishing shrines), and a *kōnane* stone board-game remain undamaged.

Hāwī ⓭

Hawai'i Co. 🏘 950. 🛈 Big Island Visitors Bureau, (808) 961-5797.

The town of Hāwī had its heyday during the era of "King Cane," when five sugar plantations brought prosperity to Kohala, the island's northern district. After the mills closed in 1975, Hāwī was left to dwindle to its present size. These days it is a pleasant town to wander through, with its wooden sidewalks and brightly painted storefronts. Hāwī's grassy, windswept surroundings and relaxed

Restored thatched dwelling, Lapakahi State Historical Park

charm now attract a new breed of citizen – the town currently offers a health-food store and a handful of trendy eateries.

Environs: Reached by a rutted dirt road, lichen-covered **Mo'okini Heiau** is one of the oldest temples on the islands, possibly dating from the 5th century AD. In 1250 it was re-dedicated as a *luakini heiau* (for human sacrifice). Legend says the temple was built in one night using stones that were passed hand to hand by a human chain of 18,000 men from Pololu Valley 14 miles (23 km) away. In 1963, Mo'okini Heiau was the first Hawaiian site to be listed in the National Historical Site Registry. Today, visitors to this massive *heiau* will discover a remote and peaceful ruin.

A traditional *hale* (grass hut) at Mo'okini Heiau

🏛 **Mo'okini Heiau**
Off Akoni Pule Highway (Hwy 270) at mile marker 20, then left at airfield.

Kapa'au ⓮

Hawai'i Co. 🏘 1,300. 🛈 Big Island Visitors Bureau, (808) 961-5797.

The small town of Kapa'au contains the original statue of Kamehameha the Great, a much-photographed replica of which stands in front of Ali'iōlani Hale in Honolulu (see p54). King Kalakaua commissioned the bronze sculpture in 1878. Cast in Paris, France, the statue was thought lost when the ship carrying it to Hawai'i sank. A new statue was commissioned and cast and this is the one that now stands in Honolulu. However, the original statue was found and arrived in the islands a few weeks after the first was installed on O'ahu. So it was brought to Kapa'au, historically known as the birthplace of Kamehameha I.

A large boulder labeled **Kamehameha Rock** can be found on the roadside heading east of town. Legend has it that the big chief once carried it to prove his strength; whole road crews have failed to move it since! Nearby, the intricately painted **Tong Wo Society** building is the last of its kind on Hawai'i Island. Immigrant Chinese communities once relied on clubs like this to provide social cohesion.

Environs: At the end of Highway 270, a lookout focuses the gaze on idyllic **Pololū Valley**. Isolated by lush canyon walls, the valley's wide floor meets the ocean at a black-sand beach. It is a 20-minute walk down the steep trail to the beach.

Kapa'au's Tong Wo Society building, part of Hawai'i's immigrant heritage

Some of the dramatically varied terrain along Kohala Mountain Road

Kohala Mountain Road ⑮

Hawai'i Co. Highway 250. ⓘ BIVB, East Hawai'i, (808) 961-5797.

The 20-mile (32-km) drive from Hāwī to Waimea follows the western ridge of low, worn Kohala Mountain. It is a beautiful, cool and breezy drive. This narrow, twisting, tree-lined road provides breathtaking vistas and constantly changing scenery. The landscapes range from lush green hills and rolling pastures to black lava rock and distant beaches. A good place to stop and enjoy the dramatic panoramic views of the entire North Kohala

coastline is at the Kohala Mountain Road lookout which gives a sense of the awesome size of Hawai'i island. This is ranch land, and the scenic drive gives views of elegant ranch houses, cattle and horses grazing in deep grass, and occasional vistas of the north Kohala Coast.

Parker Ranch is the largest operation in this area, and, in fact, the largest privately owned cattle ranch in the United States. Its origins date right back to the early years of Western discovery and a young American adventurer named John Palmer Parker. In 1809, Parker befriended Kamehameha I and eventually married one of the king's granddaughters. He established a small dynasty that shaped the history of the Kohala district. Today, the ranch covers a tenth of the island and supports 35,000 head of cattle.

Waipi'o Valley ⑯

Hawai'i Co. ⓘ Big Island Visitors Bureau, (808) 961-5797.

If any particular spot could be designated the spiritual heartland of ancient Hawai'i, it would have to be Waipi'o, or the "Valley of the Kings." The largest of seven enormous amphitheater valleys that punctuate this windward stretch of

coast, Waipi'o measures 1 mile (1.5 km) wide at the sea and extends nearly 6 miles (10 km) inland. Its steep walls, laced with waterfalls, including the stupendous Hi'ilawe cascade, rise as high as 2,000 ft (600 m). Waipi'o Stream slices the lush valley floor, courses through fertile taro fields, and empties into the rough sea across a wide black-sand beach.

The road from the stunning lookout at the end of Highway 240 down to the valley floor is only a mile (1.5 km) long, but its steepness limits access to four-wheel-drive vehicles; on foot the trip takes about 30 minutes. Shuttle tours, even one in a mule-drawn surrey, are available at the tiny village of Kukuihaele, and nearby stables offer horseback trips.

In precontact days, Waipi'o supported a population of over 10,000. A sacred place, the valley contained important *heiau*, including a *pu'uhonua* (place of refuge) equal to that at Hōnaunau (*see pp138–9*). The valley was Kamehameha the Great's boyhood playground. It was here that he received the sponsorship of his terrifying war god Kūkā'ilimoku, and that he defeated his cousin and rival Keoua. Today, Waipi'o's few inhabitants cultivate taro, lotus, avocado, breadfruit, and citrus, and earnestly protect Hawai'i's ancient spirit.

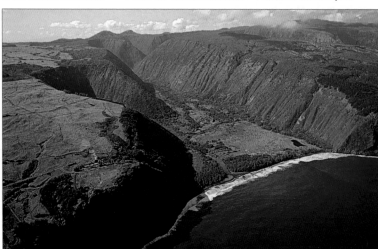

Isolated Waipi'o Valley, historically a sacred site and now a favorite of hikers and nature lovers

Honoka'a ⑰

Hawai'i Co. 🅿 👥 *3,400.*
ℹ️ *Big Island VB, East Hawai'i,
(808) 961-5797.*

A 15-mile (24-km) drive from
Waipi'o Valley, this quaint
rural town is actually one of
the largest on the Hāmākua
Coast. It has one hotel, bed
and breakfast accommoda-
tions, shops, boutiques, and
restaurants. The town also
boasts art galleries, antique
stores, a macadamia nut
factory, a movie theater,
and a nine-hole golf course.
 This small community
is home to The **Honoka'a
People's Theater**. Built in 1930
on the town's main thoroughfare, Mamane Street, the
renovated theater now shows
movies on a big screen and
also hosts the Hawai'i International Film Festival
(see p218) and the **Hāmākua
Music Festival**. Held each fall,
the music festival features
renowned Jazz, Classical, and
Hawaiian folk musicians such
as Eric Marienthal, Gene Harris,
Ray Brown, and Kenny Burrell.

🎵 **Hāmākua Music Festival**
PO Box 1757, Honoka'a.
***Tel** (808) 775-3378.*
www.hamakuamusicfestival.com
**The Honoka'a People's
Theater**
Mamane Street, Honoka'a.
***Tel** (808) 775-0000.*

Hāmākua Coast ⑱

Hawai'i Co. (Hwy 19), Waipi'o Valley
to Hilo. 🅿 *Honoka'a, Laupāhoehoe,
Honomū, and Pepe'ekeo.* ℹ️ *BIVB,
East Hawai'i, (808) 961-5797.*

The verdant cliffs lining the
island's windward coast are
stunning company on the drive
along the Hawai'i Belt Road
(Hwy 19). With dozens of side
roads begging investigation,
you can easily spend a day
traveling the 55 miles (89 km)
between Waimea and Hilo.
 This stretch has been
designated the Hilo-Hāmākua
Heritage Coast due to the
area's historic and cultural
significance. Look out for
brown-and-white signs on the
Hawai'i Belt Road as these

PANIOLO CULTURE

When George Vancouver brought
eight cattle to Hawai'i Island in
1794, the sight of the huge beasts
sent the natives running in terror.
Fifty years later, herds of wild
cattle had become such a scourge
that Kamehameha III hired three
Mexican *vaqueros* (cowboys) to
control them. The *vaqueros* introduced their own customs, which
evolved into the tradition of the
paniolo (from *español*). They also

A paniolo astride his horse

brought the guitar and the funda-
mental sound of popular Hawaiian music. There are now
ranches all over the state. Hawai'i Island has annual rodeos
at Honoka'a, Waimea, Nā'ālehu, and Waikoloa. Maui's *paniolo*
host a parade and rodeo on July 4 in Makawao *(see p123).*

indicate specific points of
interest situated along the way.
 High in the hills south of
Honoka'a is **Kalōpā State
Recreation Area**. This has a
native forest nature trail and
a small arboretum of
Hawaiian and introduced
plants. Twelve miles (19 km)
farther on is **Laupāhoehoe
Point**, a lush lava outcrop that
juts into the pounding sea,
providing stupendous views
along the coast. A sizable
village once existed here but
was destroyed by the 1946
tsunami *(see p149).*
 At **Kolekole Beach County
Park**, south of mile marker 15,
a delightful stream tumbles into
the ocean, making this a popular picnic and swimming spot.

🥾 **Kalōpā State
Recreation Area**
Off Hawai'i Belt Rd (Hwy 19),
2 miles (3 km) S of Honoka'a.
***Tel** (808) 961-9540.* ⭕ *daily.* 🏕️

World Botanical Gardens ⑲

Hawai'i Co. Off Highway 19
near mile marker 16. ***Tel** (808) 963-
5427.* ⭕ *9am–5:30pm daily.*
🖥️ **www.**wbgi.com

World Botanical Gardens,
just north of Hilo on an
expanse of former sugarcane
fields, is Hawai'i's largest
botanical garden. Featuring
5,000 species, it includes the
spectacular three-tiered 300-ft
(90-m) Umauma Falls. The
viewing area for Umauma
Falls is reached by a short
walk through the rainforest
along a flower-lined path
that follows a stream.
 Although only in development since 1995, the site is
abundant with fruits, flowers,
trees, medicinal plants, and
lush greenery. There is also
a large children's maze.

The sheer, green cliffs of the stunning Hāmākua Coast

Spectacular lava flow from Kīlauea Volcano, Hawai'i Island ▷

The route serving Mauna Loa weather station, off Saddle Road

Saddle Road ⑳

Hawai'i Co. Hwy 200 from Waimea to Hilo. 🛈 BIVB, East Hawai'i, (808) 961-5797.

To drive the 55-mile (89-km) Saddle Road linking Hilo and Waimea is to drive along the shoulders of giants. The jumbled peaks of **Mauna Kea** rise to the north, while broad **Mauna Loa** looms to the south, the road following the trough where the two mountains collide. Some car rental companies ban drivers from taking the Saddle Road, an "unimproved" two-lane highway, but the road is better than they make out. As long as you drive at a reasonable speed, and in daylight, this is not a hazardous trip.

Drivers get a close-up look at the ecological forces at work on the island's interior – the cool rain forests of Hilo district, dominated by 'ōhi'a trees, koa, and huge ferns; the subalpine lava fields at the road's 6,500-ft (2,000-m) summit; and the vast, parched grasslands on the Waimea side. Much of the traffic is generated by two sizable military installations.

The highest vantage point from which to view the imposing terrain is a weather station situated 11,000 ft (3,350 m) above sea level. It is reached along a narrow paved road that begins near the summit of Saddle Road and climbs for 17 miles (27 km) up Mauna Loa. The 45-minute drive is hard work (loosening the gas tank cap helps to prevent vapor lock at this altitude), but the reward is the spectacular view across Saddle Road to Mauna Kea. Starting at the weather station, an extremely rugged trail – a four- to six-hour hike – leads to the crater on the summit of Mauna Loa, at 13,677 ft (4,169 m).

Mauna Kea ㉑

Hawai'i Co. Off Saddle Road (Hwy 200) at mile marker 28. 🛈 BIVB, East Hawai'i, (808) 961-5797.

Midway between Hilo and Waimea, an unmarked but well-paved road climbs up Mauna Kea, winding through a native māmane forest that has been severely damaged by the predations of wild goats and sheep. The road rises so steeply that most cars crawl up the 15-minute drive to the **Onizuka Center for International Astronomy**.

Here, a small visitor center, named after the Kona-born astronaut who died in the 1986 explosion of the space shuttle *Challenger*, offers the solace of shelter with refreshments. It also has informative displays about the ecology of Mauna Kea and a video about its observatories. There are impressive views, too, but the panorama is better still from the summit. Driving to the very top of Mauna Kea is impossible, however, without a four-wheel-drive vehicle. The alternative is to go on foot. The 4,600-ft (1,400-m) climb is a tough 6-mile (10-km) hike.

The route to the summit takes in several remarkable sites: the **Mauna Kea Ice Age Natural Area Reserve**, with a quarry where the ancient Hawaiians obtained the rock used for making their axlike tools, or adzes; **Moon Valley**, where *Apollo* astronauts practiced driving their lunar rover in the 1960s; **Lake Waiau**, the third-highest lake in the US; and **Pu'u Poli'ahu**, the legendary abode of Pele's sister Poli'ahu, the goddess of snow.

Mauna Kea is crowned with a cluster of astronomical domes, including the **W.M. Keck Observatory**. Research teams from the US, Canada, France, and the UK are based here, collecting new information about the cosmos.

🏛 **Onizuka Center for International Astronomy**
6 miles (10 km) N of mile marker 28 off Saddle Road (Hwy 200). **Visitor Center** *Tel* (808) 961-2180. ⬤ 9am–10pm daily. ♿ 📷

Mauna Kea, a giant post-shield stage volcano *(see pp18–19)*, viewed from Mauna Loa weather station

THE W.M. KECK OBSERVATORY

Mauna Kea, due to its elevation, the clear air, and the absence of light and air pollution, is the best observatory site in the world – enabling the telescopes at its summit to observe the universe with minimal distortion. Keck I (built in 1992) and Keck II (1996), sitting like a pair of huge eyes on the mountain top, have four times the imaging power of the world's next largest telescope in California. Instead of just one monolithic mirror, each observatory has a mosaic of flexible mirror segments computer-guided to focus in unison.

The twin globes of the W.M. Keck Observatory on Mauna Kea

'Akaka Falls State Park ㉒

Hawai'i Co. Highway 220, 3.5 miles (5.5 km) W of Honomū. ⬛ Honomū. **Tel** Division of State Parks, (808) 961-9540. ◯ daily.

Two of the state's most hypnotic waterfalls have been packaged for easy viewing at 'Akaka Falls State Park, in the hills above the Hāmākua Coast. A loop trail, taking less than half an hour, links the 400-ft (120-m) **Kahūnā Falls** to **'Akaka Falls**, an unbroken cascade of 420 ft (130 m). At the main lookout, the roar of water almost drowns out the incessant clicking of cameras. At the edge of the path you can see the entire length of the falls from top to bottom, including the pool below, yet not get wet from the spray.

The waterfalls apart, the breezy 66-acre park alone is worth the visit. Paths wind through a rich blend of trees, vines, bamboo, ginger, orchids, and other exotic plants, accompanied by the cooling sounds of rushing streams.

The access road veers off Highway 19 at the welcoming old sugar town of **Honomū**, which has dwindled from its 1930s population of 3,000 to just over 500 today. The residents have kept the small main street alive, with the **Ishigo General Store and Bakery** (established 1910) and several other weathered wooden buildings serving as cafés and gift shops. The **Honomū Henjoji Mission**, a temple of the Buddhist Shingon Esoteric sect, was founded in the 1920s and has a sanctuary richly ornamented in black lacquer and gold. The signs inviting visitors to come in are sincerely meant.

🛕 **Honomū Henjoji Mission**
28-1668 Government Main Road, Honomū. **Tel** (808) 963-6308. ◯ call ahead for details.

Gracefully cascading 'Akaka Falls, set back above the Hāmākua Coast

Pepe'ekeo Scenic Drive ㉓

Hawai'i Co. Off Hawai'i Belt Road (Hwy 19), 4 miles (6.5 km) N of Hilo. ⬛ Pepe'ekeo. 🏋 BIVB, East Hawai'i, (808) 961-5797.

This 4-mile (6.5-km) scenic detour off the Hawai'i Belt Road plunges into tropical growth, crossing waterfall-fed streams and shaded by vine-draped palms and mango, banana, and *hala* trees.

Halfway along the drive, at beautiful Onomea Bay, the **Hawai'i Tropical Botanical Garden** has trails meandering through a patch of rainforest that includes a lily pond and a vast array of tropical plants.

🌿 **Hawai'i Tropical Botanical Garden**
2 miles (3 km) from either end of the drive. **Tel** (808) 964-5233. ◯ 9am–5pm daily. ● Jan 1, Thanksgiving, Dec 25. ◲ www.htbg.com

Mauna Loa ㉔

Hawai'i Co. 🏋 BIVB, East Hawai'i, (808) 961-5797.

Mauna Loa, or "Long Mountain", is the largest volcano on earth and one of the most active. One of five volcanoes that form Hawai'i Island, it covers the entire southern half of the island. It is 60 miles (95 km) long and 30 miles (50 km) wide and rises to 13,677 ft (4,169 m) above sea level. Mauna Loa's summit is protected as part of Hawai'i Volcanoes National Park (*see pp152–3*).

Since its first documented eruption in 1843, Mauna Loa has erupted more than 33 times, most recently in 1984. It is a shield volcano, with gently sloping inclines that have been created from successive lava flows oozing from the earth's crust. The caldera at the summit, Moku'aweoweo, is more than 3 miles (5 km) long and 1.5 miles (2.5 km) wide, with 600-ft (180-m) walls.

Kilauea (*see pp152–3*), an extremely active volcano with areas of continually moving lava, lies on Mauna Loa's southeast flank.

Hilo ㉕

With 43,000 residents, significant shipping and fishing industries out of its large bay, and a campus of the University of Hawai'i, Hilo rightfully deserves its designation as the state's second city. In spirit, though, "rainy old Hilo" couldn't be more different from sunny, urban Honolulu. The downtown buildings, many of them beautifully restored, were mostly constructed in the early 1900s; the streets are quiet, the pace is slow, and the atmosphere is low-key. Local attractions include gardens, waterfalls, beach parks, and fish ponds.

Exploring Hilo

Nature itself has checked the city's progress in two ways: the fact that rain falls 278 days of the year has not endeared Hilo to sun-worshiping vacationers; and, as though even more water were needed, the sea pounded Hilo with two destructive tsunamis in 1946 and 1960. The city has since retreated from the sea, turning the waterfront area into enormous green parks.

The Hawaiian Telephone Company building

Hilo has a friendly, relaxed, and ethnically diverse personality. The population is largely Japanese and Filipino in ancestry, and the stores and eating places reflect that heritage. The Merrie Monarch Festival, the state's most prestigious *hula* competition, takes place here every year in the week following Easter. The plentiful rain makes Hilo a natural garden, suited to orchids and anthuriums. This is a city not so much for "tourists" as for visitors.

Downtown

Many of the brightly colored, restored buildings of the old business district, clustered next to the Wailuku River, are listed with the National Register of Historic Places. Look out for the **Hawaiian Telephone Company building**, which combines aspects of the traditional Hawaiian house *(hale)* and Californian mission architecture; its designer, C.W. Dickey, is credited with developing Hawaiian Regional Architecture. Hilo Downtown Improvement Association offers visitor information.

🛒 Farmers' Market

Corner of Mamo St and Kamehameha Ave. ⬜ *Wed & Sat.*

On two mornings a week the junction of Mamo Street and Kamehameha Avenue turns into a multilingual open-air marketplace. Farmers bring exotic produce such as squash blossoms, ice cream bananas, cut orchids, and mats woven from *lauhala* (leaves of the pandanus plant). Stroll around and pick up a fresh breakfast.

🏛 Pacific Tsunami Museum

130 Kamehameha Ave. **Tel** *(808) 935-0926.* ⬜ *9am–4pm Mon–Sat.* ⬤ *public hols.* 📷 www.tsunami.org

This museum is located in the historic First Hawaiian Bank Building, designed by C.W. Dickey. Built in 1930, it survived both the 1946 and 1960 tsunamis and was donated to the museum in 1970. Exhibits focus on how tsunamis (often called tidal waves) are formed.

🏛 Mokupāpapa Discovery Center

308 Kamehameha Ave, Suite 109. **Tel** *(808) 933-8181.* ⬜ *9am–4pm Tue–Sat.* ⬤ *public hols.* **www. papahanaumokuakea.gov**

The natural science, culture and history of the remote northwest Hawaiian islands, and that of the surrounding marine environment, is explained at this free exhibition center. A 2,500-gallon salt-water aquarium provides a home for some of the fish that inhabit the region's coral reef.

🏛 Wailoa Center

In Wailoa River State Park, Piopio St. **Tel** *(808) 933-0416.* ⬜ *8:30am–4:30pm Mon–Fri, noon–4:30pm Wed.* ⬤ *public hols.* ♿

This octagonal gallery sits on a wide lawn where the Japanese quarter used to be – the town refused to rebuild here after the tsunami of 1960. Downstairs there is a photographic display showing the appalling destruction caused by the giant waves. The rest of the gallery hosts temporary exhibitions.

🏛 Lyman Museum and Mission House

276 Haili St. **Tel** *(808) 935-5021.* ⬜ *10am–4:30pm Mon–Sat.* ⬤ *Jan 1, Jul 4, Thanksgiving, Dec 25.* 📷 ♿ *museum only.* www.lymanmuseum.org

Once the home of the Reverend David and Sarah Lyman, missionaries who settled in Hilo in the early 1830s. It is well preserved with household items like a cradle and quilts. The complex also includes a

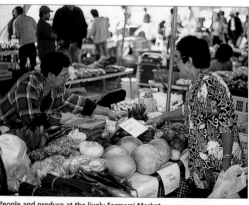

People and produce at the lively Farmers' Market

For hotels and restaurants in this region see pp188–9 and pp206–8

TSUNAMIS IN HILO

In 1946 an Alaskan earthquake triggered a tsunami that hit the unsuspecting Hawaiian Islands on the morning of April 1. Waves 56 ft (17 m) high tore Hilo's bayfront buildings off their foundations and swept them inland, killing 96 people. In 1960, another tsunami struck with a vengeance. Originating off the coast of Chile, it slammed Hilo on May 23 with three successive waves, causing damage worth $23 million. In spite of warnings, many locals refused to retreat, and 61 died.

Great devastation in the aftermath of the 1946 tsunami

modern museum housing a varied collection of Hawaiiana, including a display of volcanic geology and artifacts from the years of immigration, such as a *braginha* – the Portuguese precursor to the *'ukulele*.

🌿 Waiākea Peninsula
Banyan Drive.
Jutting into Hilo Bay, Waiākea Peninsula supports a nine-hole golf course, a row of high-rise hotels, and the 30-acre **Liliʻuokalani Gardens**. The latter is a Japanese park that blends fish ponds with small pagodas and arched bridges. A footbridge crosses to tiny **Coconut Island**, now a park and popular fishing spot but once a place of healing; the Hawaiians called it Moku Ola (Island of Life). **Banyan Drive** loops the peninsula under the dense shade of huge banyans planted by celebrities such as Amelia Earhart and Babe Ruth.

VISITORS' CHECKLIST

Hawaiʻi Co. 🏠 43,000. ✈ 3 miles (5 km) E. 🚌 Kamehameha Ave, near Mamo St, (808) 961-8744. 🎫 HDIA, 329 Kamehameha Ave, (808) 935-8850. 🎉 Merrie Monarch Festival (Mar or Apr).

🌺 Rainbow Falls
Waiānuenue Avenue, 2 miles (3 km) W of Downtown.
Rainbow ("Waiānuenue") Falls earns its name when the morning sun filters through the mist generated by the 80-ft (24-m) waterfall, creating rainbows. The hollow at its base is the legendary home of Hina, Maui's mother. The nearby trails provide many lookouts.

🏖 The Eastern Beaches
Kalanianaʻole Ave.
Kalanianaʻole Avenue, which follows the east side of Hilo Bay, passes a number of beach parks interlaced with large fish ponds. **James Kealoha Beach Park** (also called Four Mile Beach) offers excellent snorkeling and swimming on its sheltered eastern side; fishermen often cast their nets on the Hilo side, which is also a popular but challenging winter surfing hangout. Another good swimming spot is **Richardson Ocean Park**, which nature has sculpted into protected, lagoonlike pools.

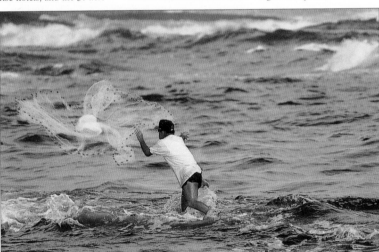

A fisherman throwing his net into the rough waters off James Kealoha Beach Park

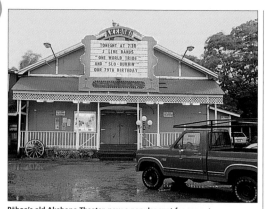

Pāhoa's old Akebono Theater, now a popular spot for concerts

Pāhoa 26

Hawai'i Co. 🏘 *1,100.* 🚌 🛈 *BIVB,
East Hawai'i, (808) 961-5797.*

The main strip of Pāhoa,
the central town of the
Puna district, offers a double
surprise – "Wild West"-style
buildings with raised boardwalks and low awnings that
have been reinterpreted along
psychedelic themes. Shops
sell hemp products, espresso
coffee, and New Age books.
The popular **Akebono
Theater** (built in 1917) has
been kept alive to host a
busy schedule of rock and
reggae concerts.

Three miles (5 km) southeast
of Pāhoa, a state-sponsored
geothermal energy project has
attempted to derive electricity
from the heat of the world's
most active volcano. However,
a public outcry over environmental damage has embroiled
the project in legal controversy.

Kapoho 27

Hawai'i Co. 🛈 *BIVB, East Hawai'i,
(808) 961-5797.*

In 1960, the town of Kapoho
was destroyed by lava that
spewed from a fire fountain
2,600 ft (795 m) wide. Today,
the eerie devastation can be
crossed on a 2-mile (3-km)
cinder road leading to **Cape
Kumukahi**, where a light-
tower was inexplicably spared
when the flow parted. Volcanic
activity in Kapoho is a source
of local legends: one tells of a

local chief who challenged a
beautiful young woman to a
sled race down Kapoho
Crater and found to his shock
that he was competing with the
volcano goddess, Pele, riding
on a wave of lava.

In 1790, one such
wave surged through a
nearby forest, leaving
'ōhi'a trunks sheathed
in black stone. Today,
only the hollowed-out
casts, or "lava trees,"
remain, but new trees
have grown back.
Together they make
up the **Lava Tree
State Monument**,
a shady park with a
trail around the casts.
This serene spot will   *Lava tree cast*
be best enjoyed if you
bring your mosquito repellent.

🏕 Lava Tree State
Monument
*Highway 132, 2.5 miles (4 km) E of
Pāhoa.* **Tel** *Division of State Parks,
(808) 961-9540.* ⬜ *daily.* ♿

*Clidemia hirta (Koster's curse)
growing in a lava tree cast*

Puna Lava Flows 28

Hawai'i Co. Hwy 137 SW of Kapoho
for 14 miles (23 km). 🛈 *County
Parks & Recreation, (808) 961-8311.*

Narrow highway 137 traces
the Puna coastline along
the base of Kīlauea's East Rift
Zone. Here, the dense foliage
occasionally breaks into solidified lava flows, mute reminders
that Puna residents live by the
grace of Madam Pele's fury.

At **Ahalanui Beach Park**,
a natural thermal spring in a
coconut grove has been
adapted into a 60-ft (18-m)
wide seaside swimming pool.
With a sandy bottom and
waves crashing against the
pool's edge, this is the best
place to swim in the district.
Isaac Hale Beach Park
features camping, a small boat
ramp, and a rugged beach
with a respectable surf break.
**MacKenzie State Recreation
Area**, a clifftop campsite set
in an ironwood forest,
gives access to an old
Hawaiian coastal trail
and a long lava tube.

Southwest of here the
Puna coastal road ends
with shocking abrupt-
ness where the road-
way, and indeed the
entire countryside,
has been obliterated
by congealed piles
of lava. In 1990, this
flow erased the town
of Kalapana and a much-loved
black-sand beach called Kaimū.

🏖 Ahalanui Beach Park
*Hwy 137, 1 mile (1.5 km) NE of junc-
tion with Pāhoa-Pohoiki Rd.* ⬜ *daily.*

🏖 Isaac Hale Beach Park
*Junction of Hwy 137 and Pāhoa-
Pohoiki Rd.* ⬜ *daily.*

🏕 MacKenzie State
Recreation Area
*Hwy 137, 2 miles (3 km) S of junction
with Pāhoa-Pohoiki Rd.* ⬜ *daily.*

Volcano Village 29

Hawai'i Co. 🏘 *2,200.* 🚌 🛈 *BIVB,
East Hawai'i, Hilo, (808) 961-5797.*

Cut into the 'ōhi'a rain
forest of Mauna Loa's high
windward slopes, this village
lies just a mile (1.5 km) outside the entrance to **Hawai'i**

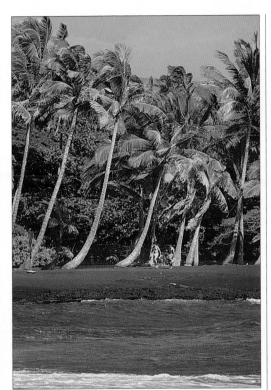

The beautiful black beach at Punalu'u Beach Park, southwest of Pāhala

Volcanoes National Park *(see pp152–3)*. The village has a general store and a gas station (the only one in the area) and makes a good provisioning stop before entering the park.

Environs: Just 2 miles (3 km) west of the park entrance, a small road leads northwest to **Volcano Golf and Country Club**, which has an 18-hole public golf course and an inexpensive restaurant. At the end of the road a winery *(see p211)* gives tastings of its unique wines, which include a guava Chablis.

A short drive east of Volcano Village are **Akatsuka Orchid Gardens**, where visitors can take a self-guided tour.

🌺 **Akatsuka Orchid Gardens**
Hawai'i Belt Rd (Hwy 11), 5 miles (8 km) E of Volcano Village. *Tel (808) 967-8234.* ◯ *9am–5pm daily.* ● *public hols.* ♿

Ka'ū District ㉚

Hawai'i Co. 🚌 Pāhala, Punalu'u, Nā'ālehu and Wai'ōhinu. 🛈 County of Hawai'i, (808) 961-8311.

The long southern arc of the Hawai'i Belt Road (Hwy 11) between Volcano Village and Kailua-Kona traverses the vast and sparsely populated Ka'ū district. Three very small towns are located here. Agricultural **Pāhala**, where macadamia nuts, sugarcane, and oranges are grown, is a quiet place where the only commotion might be the occasional crowing of roosters. **Nā'ālehu**, the most southerly town in the United States, is Ka'ū's largest town, with a few small shops. Tiny **Wai'ōhinu** is known for a monkeypod tree that Mark Twain planted in 1866. The original tree fell in a storm in 1957 but has since grown again

NAALEHU
SOUTHERNMOST COMMUNITY
IN THE U.S.A.
Road sign in Nā'ālehu

from shoots. The gem of the south coast is **Punalu'u Beach Park**, where a pure black sand beach is crowded with coconut trees. Visitors may camp here and at **Whittington Beach Park**, 5 miles (8 km) farther south.

🏕 **Punalu'u Beach Park**
Off Hwy 11, 5 miles (8 km) SW l of Pāhala. ◯ *daily.* *Tel Dept of Parks and Recreation, Hilo, (808) 961-8311.*

Ka Lae ㉛

Hawai'i Co. S Point Rd, off Hwy 11, 6 miles (10 km) W of Wai'ōhinu. 🛈 BIVB, East Hawai'i, Hilo, (808) 961-5797.

Also known as South Point, Ka Lae is as far south as you can travel in the United States. Constant fierce winds drive against a battered grassland that gives way finally to a rocky shoreline. Halfway along the 11-mile (18-km) access road, three rows of enormous, propeller-driven electricity generators emit a repetitive music of almost maddening whistles. It all feels suitably like the ends of the earth.

Although the powerful waves are daunting, these have long been prime fishing grounds. The mooring holes that ancient Hawaiians drilled into the coastal rocks so that they could keep their canoes safe while they went fishing are still visible – providing some of the earliest recorded evidence of Polynesian settlement.

A four-wheel-drive road runs 2.5 miles (4 km) northeast, to **Green Sands Beach**, which is composed of olivine sand.

Wind-powered electricity generators along the road to Ka Lae

Hawai'i Volcanoes National Park ❷

Petroglyph at Pu'u Loa, near the coast

The national park encompasses about a quarter of a million acres, including the 13,677-ft (4,169-m) summit of Mauna Loa, 150 miles (240 km) of hiking trails, and vast tracts of wilderness that preserve some of the world's rarest species of flora and fauna. But it is Kīlauea Caldera and the lava flows of its furious East Rift Zone that draw most visitors. Two roads – Crater Rim Drive, which loops around the caldera, and Chain of Craters Road, which descends through the recent outpourings – form a gigantic drive-through museum. The present eruption started in 1983. Check for viewing conditions before you visit; since lava flow, sulfur dioxide gas, and other hazards may restrict access. You should also stay out of closed areas. It is unkown how long the flow will continue or when it will next erupt.

Lava fountains spewing from Kīlauea during the 1983 eruption

Kīlauea Overlook

KIPUKA PUAULU

MAUNA LOA

Jaggar Museum

NA'ALEHU

Hawai'i Belt Road

Crater Rim Drive

Crater Rim Trail

KĪLAUEA CALDER

HALEMA'UMA'U CRATER

Halema'uma'u Trail

Crater Rim Drive

★ **Halema'uma'u Overlook**
Once a boiling lake of lava, the crater below still steams with sulfurous fumes. This is the home of Pele, the volcano goddess (see p24).

PROFESSOR JAGGAR (1871–1953)

Thomas A. Jaggar was a pioneer in the young science of volcanology. A professor of geology at Massachusetts Institute of Technology, he founded the Hawaiian Volcano Observatory (now part of the Jaggar Museum) at Kīlauea Caldera in 1912. Four years later, he and Honolulu publisher Lorrin Thurston persuaded Congress to preserve the area as a national park. Professor Jaggar developed techniques for collecting volcanic gases and measuring ground tilt, seismic activity, and lava temperatures. The work he initiated has made Kīlauea one of the best under-stood volcanoes in the world.

Professor Jaggar working at his desk in 1916

0 meters   500

0 yards   500

STAR SIGHTS

★ Halema'uma'u Overlook

★ Thurston Lava Tube

Kīlauea Iki Overlook

In 1959 the crater below this overlook filled with bubbling lava, shooting fire fountains 1,900 ft (580 m) into the air. Today a hiking trail crosses the cool crater floor to give a close-up view.

VISITORS' CHECKLIST

Hawai'i Co. Hawai'i Belt Road (Highway 11), 30 miles (48 km) SW of Hilo, 96 miles (155 km) SE of Kailua-Kona. *Tel* (808) 985-6000. 24 hours daily. www.nps.gov/havo
Jaggar Museum *Tel* (808) 985-6049. 8:30am–5pm daily.
Volcano House Hotel *Tel* (808) 967-7321.

Kīlauea Military Camp
Steam Vents
Kīlauea Visitor Center and Volcano Art Center
Volcano House Hotel

VOLCANO VILLAGE
HILO

Sandalwood Trail
Waldron Ledge
Crater Rim Drive
Crater Rim Trail
emaumau Trail
KĪLAUEA IKI CRATER
Kīlauea Iki Trail
yron Ledge Trail
Devastation Trail
KEANAKĀKO'I CRATER
Chain of Craters Road
PUU LOA
EAST RIFT ZONE
Crater Rim Trail

★ Thurston Lava Tube
This huge tunnel was left behind when a subterranean river of lava drained away. An easy trail runs through the tube and a grove of giant ferns.

KEY

Major road	
Minor road	
Hiking trail	
Vista	

Devastation Trail
This short walk passes through the ghostly remains of a rain forest wiped out by ash falling from Kīlauea Iki's 1959 eruption.

Southern Extent of the Park

Kīlauea Caldera
Pu'u 'Ō'ō
Makaopuhi Crater
Nāpau Crater
Nāpau Crater Trail
Hilina Pali Road
Chain of Craters Road
Kalapana Trail
HILINA PALI
Keauhou Trail
Puʻu Loa
HŌLEI PALI
Hōlei Sea Arch
Puna Coast Trail
HILINA PALI
Hilina Pali Trail
0 kilometers 7
0 miles 5

Exploring Hawai'i Volcanoes National Park

The impressive volcanic terrain of Hawai'i Volcanoes National Park supports diverse climates and eco-systems that range from sea level to the summit of Mauna Loa, the largest volcano on earth. The park is also the site of Kīlauea – the world's most active volcano. This dramatic volcanic landscape, including sulfur banks, steam vents, lava tubes, fern forests, lava deserts, and endangered plants and animals, attracts millions of visitors each year. Numerous hiking paths and scenic drives lead visitors from one awe-inspiring panoramic scene to another. Over half of the park is designated wilderness and, in recognition of its outstanding natural wonders, the area has been recognized as an International Biosphere Reserve and as a World Heritage Site.

Lava fountain erupting from Kīlauea

Kīlauea Visitor Center building

Kīlauea Visitor Center

Hwy 11. *Tel* (808) 985-6000.
7:45am–5pm daily.
The visitor center presents an informative overview of the environmental, historical, and cultural features of the park. Exhibits give information about island formation, ecosystems, invasive species, and resource protection. A 25-minute film about geology and volcanism, "Born of Fire, Born of the Sea", is shown throughout the day. Trail and lava viewing conditions can change rapidly so check with the park rangers at the center for the latest information. Overnight visitors must register here and permits are issued on a first-come basis.

Volcano Art Center

Crater Rim Dr. *Tel* (808) 967-8222.
9am–5pm daily. Dec 25.
www.volcanoartcenter.org
The Volcano Art Center preserves and promotes Hawaii's rich culture and traditions through *hula* performances, exhibitions,

and concerts. The center's Volcano Art Center Gallery is housed in the nearby 1877 Volcano House Hotel, listed in the National Register of Historic Places as Hawai'i's oldest visitor accommodation. The gallery features works by over 300 prominent local artists inspired by Hawaii's environmental and cultural heritage. The displays embrace a variety of media including paint, glass, metal, ceramic, fiber, wood, and photography. The center also

offers classes and workshops on Hawaiian music, dance, crafts, writing, and language as well as sponsoring a performing arts season.

Earthquake Trail (Waldron Ledge)

A section of the Crater Rim Loop Trail along Waldron Ledge, this is an easy trail that is wheelchair and stroller accessible over a paved road surface. It begins to the left of the Volcano House Hotel and follows a section of the road that was cracked and destroyed by a devastating magnitude 6.6 earthquake in 1983 on Mauna Loa. The earthquake caused many rockfalls along the caldera walls and damaged trails and roads in the park. It takes approximately 45 minutes to complete the one mile (1.6-km) roundtrip. The trail features interesting earthcracks, a rich variety of plants, birds, and insects, and spectacular views of Kīlauea Caldera and Mauna Loa.

Panorama of Kīlauea Caldera from Waldron Ledge

For hotels and restaurants in this region see pp188–9 and pp206–8

Halema'uma'u Crater

On the floor of the enormous expanse of the Kīlauea Caldera, Halema'uma'u Crater is 3,000 ft (914 m) across and 300 ft (90 m) deep. The many fumaroles found both in the crater and along the rim continue to spew a large quantity of sulphur dioxide daily so those with respiratory problems should beware. The challenging 7-mile (11-km) Halema'uma'u Trail that leads to the crater can take three to six hours to complete. It begins by the Volcano House Hotel, descends 400 ft (120 m) through lush rain forest to the barren floor of the caldera, and crosses old lava flows to the southern edge of the crater. The trail passes Halema'uma'u Overlook which offers direct views of the crater pit.

Ancient Hawaiian petroglyph depicting a human figure

Pu'u Loa Petroglyphs

This coastal trail crosses old lava flows to reach an extensive petroglyph field located on the southern flank of Kīlauea. It is an easy to moderate 2-mile (3.2-km) roundtrip hike, beginning at mile marker 16 on Chain of Craters road, that takes about one and half hours to complete. Hikers walk across rough basaltic lava to reach a wooden boardwalk that surrounds in excess of 23,000 petroglyph images etched on to the abundant lava surface. The majority of the images in this extensive field depict stylized human forms but there are also representations of the moon, canoes, ships, insects, fish, and spears. Circles, spirals, dots, and other geometric designs are also common features.

Thurston Lava Tube Trail

Thurston Lava Tube can be accessed via an easy 15-minute loop trail. The paved trail begins with a steep descent into the rain forest, dense with towering green ferns. The trail then leads visitors in to a pit crater where it is possible to enter the lava tube. Formed when the exterior of a lava flow cooled to a crust while the still-molten interior magma flowed out, the tube resembles a giant tunnel. Walking through the 600-ft (180-m) winding passage takes about ten minutes. Signs posted along the trail provide information about plants and animals that can be seen in the area.

Native *elepaio* bird

Kīlauea Ike Trail

Descending 400 ft (120 m) through tropical rain forest, this trail crosses the Kīlauea Iki Crater floor, passes Pu'u Pua'i cinder cone, and returns along the crater's rim. It is a moderate to challenging 4-mile (6.4-km) loop that takes two to three hours to hike. The trail allows visitors to explore features resulting from the 1959 Kīlauea Iki eruption, such as steam vents and cinder cones. Beginning at the Thurston Lava Tube parking lot on Crater Rim Drive, it takes 2-3 hours to complete. The contrast between the lush vegetation found on the crater rim and the barren rocky terrain of the crater floor is striking.

Devastation Trail

This easy paved trail winds through a forested area recovering from the devastating effects of the 1959 eruption of Kīlauea Iki. The eruption produced huge fountains of lava that shot up to 1,900 ft (580 m) in the air and covered the densely forested area with black pumice and falling cinder. In addition to the ghostly remains of the trees, the one-mile (1.6-km) trail features a variety of native plants, birds, tree molds, and cinder and spatter cones.

Kipuka Puaulu

A kipuka is a forested island untouched by surrounding lava flow. Vegetation has been spared by the lava flows and is therefore older and richer here. The lush green woodlands of Kipuka Puaulu bird park are home to one of the richest concentrations of rare native plants and bird life in Hawai'i. The 1-mile (1.6-km) loop trail takes about one hour to complete. It begins with a gentle hike on an unpaved forest path, surrounded by recent lava flows from Mauna Loa. Native *koa* and *'ōhi'a lehua* trees *(see p20)* grow here. It is possible to glimpse endemic birds such as the 'elepaio or 'apapane as well as other species including finches and Japanese white eyes. A bulletin board at the start of the trail provides descriptions of the diverse birds and plants species that are found here.

Kipuka Puaulu, dense forest land on the barren slopes of Mauna Loa

KAUA'I

*I*t is no coincidence that the oldest of the major Hawaiian islands is also the most beautiful. Wind and water have had six million years to carve Kaua'i into a stunning array of pleated cliffs and yawning chasms, while the rich topsoil of the "Garden Island" is cloaked in a spectacular mantle of emerald green vegetation. With its sandy beaches and large coral reefs, Kaua'i is Hawai'i's most irresistible destination.

The outline of the volcano that created Kaua'i has all but vanished, leaving a roughly circular island on which no place is more than a dozen miles (19 km) from the ocean. Although its highest point barely exceeds 5,000 ft (1,500 m), the interior remains a forbidding, waterlogged wilderness, and Kaua'i's 55,000 inhabitants are distributed fairly evenly around the coastal lowlands.

Settled by a separate wave of Polynesian voyagers – possibly the small, legendary *Menehune (see p161)* – and never conquered by the other islands, Kaua'i has its own proud history. It was here that Captain Cook first landed, and here too that the sandalwood and sugar industries were established. A trail of ancient temples can still be seen along the Wailua River on the east shore, and former plantation towns from Hanalei in the north to Hanapēpē in the south lend the island a small-town charm.

The capital Līhu'e is surprisingly sleepy, while resorts such as Princeville and Po'ipū are rare pockets of modern luxury in an otherwise timeless rural landscape.

Scenery is Kaua'i's greatest attraction. The North Shore, in particular, is stunning, with a succession of gorgeous beaches to the east and the soaring Nā Pali Coast to the west. High above lies Kōke'e State Park, where trails command views of the valleys and lace through the rain-soaked Alaka'i Swamp, home to rare flora and fauna. The road to the park climbs the flanks of mighty Waimea Canyon, an ever-changing panoply of colors.

Visitors are both intrigued by Kaua'i's fascinating history and awed by the vast array of scenic beauty that it offers. Exotic, enchanting, and welcoming, the "Garden Isle" is a memorable place to stay.

Workers picking taro, a traditional Hawaiian crop cultivated in Kaua'i's Hanalei Valley

◁ The soaring cliffs of the Nā Pali Coast, accessible only by rugged trail, or by boat or helicopter tour

Exploring Kaua'i

Tourist facilities on Kaua'i are concentrated in three main areas. Po'ipū in the south is a classic family resort, with beautiful beaches and modern hotels. On the east coast, from Līhu'e to Kapa'a, the beaches are equally stunning, and the hotels are cheaper and well placed for sightseeing. Līhu'e also has a couple of grand plantation-era mansions, while the back roads behind Kapa'a offer glimpses of both ancient history and scenic wilderness. Finally, the lush North Shore is a playground for active travelers, with surfing and golf at Hanalei and Princeville, plus hiking and canoeing on the magnificent Nā Pali Coast. No visitor should leave Kaua'i without taking in the dramatic splendor of Waimea Canyon and the breathtaking views from Kōke'e State Park.

NI'IHAU LOCATOR MAP
See p173

HĀ'ENA AND KĒ'Ē BEACHES 15 LUMAH BEA

14 LIMAHULI GARDEN

KALALAU TRAIL

16

17 KALALAU VALLEY

Nā Pali Coast State Park

Kalalau Lookout

Pu'u o Kila Lookout

Kōke'e Natural History Museum 550

Alaka'i Swamp

Māhaihai Valley

18

WAIMEA CANYON & KŌKE'E STATE PARK

Waimea Canyon Lookout

19 POLIHALE BEACH

Barking Sands

Kaulakahi Channel

50

552

550

Kekaha

20 WAIMEA

Russian Fort Elizabeth

Pākalā

Kaumakani

HANAPĒPĒ 21 Ele'ele

Salt Pond Beach County Park

Kalāh 50

TOP RECREATIONAL AREAS

The places shown here have been selected for their recreational activities. Conditions vary depending on the weather and the time of year, so exercise caution and, if in doubt, stay out of the water or seek local advice.

	SWIMMING	SNORKELING	DIVING	BODY-SURFING	WINDSURFING	HIKING	HORSE RIDING	GOLF
ANAHOLA BAY	●			■				
'ANINI BEACH	●				●			
HANALEI BAY	●			■				
KALAPAKĪ BEACH	●	■		■	●			■
KALIHIWAI BEACH	●							
KEĀLIA BEACH				■				
KĒ'Ē BEACH	●	■						
KŌKE'E STATE PARK						■		
LUMAHA'I BEACH						■		
LYDGATE STATE PARK	●	■						
NĀ PALI COAST STATE PARK		■				■		
PALI KE KUA (HIDEAWAYS) BEACH		■						
PO'IPŪ BEACH COUNTY PARK	●	■	●	■	●			■
PRINCEVILLE	●	■					●	■
PU'UPŌĀ BEACH	●	■						
SALT POND BEACH COUNTY PARK		■			●			
SECRET BEACH						■		
TUNNELS BEACH	●	■	●					

GETTING AROUND

Kaua'i's major highway is prevented from completing a loop around the island by the Nā Pali cliffs. Known as Kūhiō Highway (Hwy 56) north of Līhu'e, and Kaumuali'i Highway (Hwy 50) to the west, it is served by the regular, inexpensive Kaua'i Bus (large suitcases and backpacks not allowed). To explore the island in detail, however, rent a car at either Līhu'e or Princeville airport. You can drive anywhere in Kaua'i in three hours or less, so you can see the whole island from a single base.

Mount Wai'ale'ale, one of the wettest places on earth

NCEVILLE
Anini Beach
Secret Beach
KĪLAUEA POINT ⑨
Kīlauea
Larsen's Beach
Moloa'a Bay
KALIHIWAI
NALEI
Hanalei
Anahola Mtn
Anahola Bay
⑧ ANAHOLA
Makaleha Mountains
Donkey Beach
Keālia
MOUNT WAI'ALE'ALE
SLEEPING GIANT ⑤
⑦ KAPA'A
Waipouli
waikini Keahua Arboretum '145ft
Wailua
④ KING'S HIGHWAY
③
Lydgate State Park
WAILUA FALLS ②
FERN GROTTO
Hanamā'ulu
Kilohana
Puhi
① LĪHU'E
Nāwiliwili Bay
Hulē'ia National Wildlife Reserve
Ha'upu Ridge
'Ōma'o
wa'i
Kōloa
ALLERTON GARDEN
Māhā'ulepū Beach
PO'IPŪ ㉓
Kauai Channel

0 kilometers 10
0 miles 5

Remote Polihale Beach, with the soaring Nā Pali cliffs behind

SIGHTS AT A GLANCE

Allerton Garden ㉒
Anahola ⑧
Fern Grotto ③
Hā'ena and Kē'ē Beaches ⑮
Hanalei ⑫
Hanapēpē ㉑
Kalalau Valley ⑰
Kalihiwai ⑩
Kapa'a ⑦
Kīlauea Point ⑨
King's Highway ④
Līhu'e pp160–61 ①
Limahuli Garden ⑭
Lumaha'i Beach ⑬
Mount Wai'ale'ale ⑥
Po'ipū ㉓
Polihale Beach ⑲
Princeville ⑪
Sleeping Giant ⑤
Wailua Falls ②
Waimea ⑳
Waimea Canyon and Kōke'e State Park pp170–71 ⑱

Hikes

Kalalau Trail ⑯

SEE ALSO

• *Where to Stay* pp190–91

• *Where to Eat* pp208–9

KEY

— Major road
══ Minor road
-- Track
— Scenic route
▲ Summit

Līhu'e

Līhu'e is the administrative and business center of Kaua'i and is also the site of the island's main air and sea ports. It was built in the mid-19th century to serve the Līhu'e Sugar Mill, whose rusting machinery is being dimantled and removed from the area. Līhu'e's multi-ethnic heritage, which stems from plantation days, is reflected in some of the shops and restaurants here. Located within a few miles of central Līhu'e are several more attractive areas. The oceanfront district, is especially appealing. Though the Kaua'i Marriott Resort dominates Kalapakī Beach, visitors can also enjoy a safe swim or a surfing lesson.

Hamura Saimin Stand, an Oriental diner in central Līhu'e (see p209)

Exploring Līhu'e

The outskirts of town offer hidden delights. To the west, Hulē'ia Stream is a wildlife sanctuary, overlooked by a splendidly forbidding ridge of green mountains. To the east lies the barely distinct community of Hanamā'ulu, where a pleasant little beach lines a sweeping crescent bay.

🏛 Kaua'i Museum

4428 Rice St. *Tel (808) 245-6931.* 🕙 *10am–5pm Mon–Sat.* 🔲 *Jan 1, Labor Day, Jul 4, Thanksgiving, Dec 25.* 📷 ♿ **www**.kauaimuseum.org

This two-part museum relates the history of the island and its indigenous people. The Wilcox Building centers on a collection of traditional artifacts gathered by the missionary Wilcox family, including huge *koa*-wood bowls and *kāhili*, feathered standards once used as a sign of royalty in Hawai'i. The newer Rice Building tells *The Story of Kaua'i,* with displays ranging from ancient weapons to videos on geology. Dioramas show how the island might have looked before European contact, and the arrival of immigrants from

around the world is chronicled, with an emphasis on the harsh conditions endured by early plantation workers. A gift shop sells books, jewelery, and crafts.

🏚 Grove Farm Homestead

Nāwiliwili Rd. *Tel (808) 245-3202.* 🕙 *Mon, Wed & Thu.* 🔲 *public hols.* **Donation.** 📷 *by appointment.* **www**.grovefarm.net

No settlement existed on the site of modern Līhu'e until 1864, when George Wilcox, the son of early missionaries, established the Grove Farm Plantation. Hawai'i's sugar business was then in its first boom, and although water was scarce, Wilcox prospered by developing a network of irrigation channels that reached deep into the mountains.

He lived on until the 1930s, content with a humble cottage. His heirs built the imposing mansion, paneled throughout in dark, heavy *koa*-wood, that now forms the centerpiece of the Grove Farm Homestead.

As well as the rather formal house and cramped servants' quarters, the two-hour guided tour takes in Wilcox's private orchard. Phone a week in advance for a place on the tour; you will not be let in without a reservation.

🏖 Kalapakī Beach

Off Wa'apā Road (Hwy 51), at Kaua'i Marriott Resort & Beach Club.

Līhu'e became Kaua'i's main port during the 1920s, when a new deepwater harbor was dredged in Nāwiliwili Bay. While the breakwaters and harbor installations appeal only to avid fishermen, the gently sloping white sands of Kalapakī Beach just to the east are highly inviting.

This is one of the safest beaches in the area, making it a good choice for families, and it is also home to the top-class Kaua'i Marriott Resort & Beach Club *(see p191)* and a handful of restaurants. Expert surfers swirl right out into the bay, but the inshore waters are sheltered enough for children. The western limit of the beach is marked by the mouth of Nāwiliwili Stream. On the far side, the palm-fringed lawns of Nāwiliwili Beach County Park are ideal for picnics.

🏚 Kilohana Plantation

3-2087 Kaumuali'i Hwy (Hwy 50), 1.5 miles (2.5 km) W of Līhu'e. *Tel (808) 245-5608.* 🕙 *9:30am–9:30pm daily.* ♿ *ground floor.* 🍴 **www**.kilohanakauai.com

The grand house known as Kilohana Plantation was, like Grove Farm Homestead, built

The shady *koa*-wood veranda at Grove Farm Homestead

Kilohana Plantation Railway

by the Wilcoxes. Dating from the 1930s, its resemblance to an English country estate makes it the perfect home for one of Kaua'i's most elegant restaurants (see p175), as well as a small mall of expensive craft shops and galleries. The train offers a comfortable way of exploring the vast plantation, and allows visitors to discover Kilohana's agricultural past and present. The conductor will point out the various fruits and vegetables that grow alongside the track; this produce is used in the restaurant.

⋔ Menehune Fish Pond

Lookout Hulemalū Rd, 1.5 miles (2.5 km) S of Līhu'e. ⬤ to the public.

West of Nāwiliwili Harbor, a minor road ascends a small headland to enter an idyllic pastoral landscape that comes as a surprise so close to Līhu'e. Beneath a highway lookout, the tranquil Hulē'ia Stream makes a sharp right-angle turn. Ancient Hawaiians exploited this natural bend by constructing a 900-ft (275-m) dam of rounded boulders to create the Alekoko ("Rippling Blood") Fish Pond. Skilled fish farmers,

the Hawaiians used it to fatten mullet for the royal table; as the fish grew, they could no longer pass through the latticed sluices that had allowed them to enter the enclosure.

This ancient structure is more commonly referred to as the Menehune Fish Pond, its prehistoric stonemasonry being credited, as so often in Hawai'i, to the little *Menehune*. These mythical figures are described by popular legend as a magical people already hard at work in Hawai'i when the first Polynesian settlers arrived. Now privately owned, the fish pond can be seen only from afar.

Unless you rent a kayak, the same goes for the **Hulē'ia National Wildlife Refuge** just upstream, where former taro and rice terraces are set aside for the exclusive use of a raucously grateful population of waterbirds.

Wailua Falls ❷

Kaua'i Co. Mā'alo Road (Hwy 583), 5 miles (8 km) N of Līhu'e. ⊞ Līhu'e.

The one winding road through the old sugarcane fields, which branches left from the main highway a mile (1.5 km) north of Līhu'e, leads directly to the 80-ft (24-m) Wailua Falls.

From the roadside parking lot you can admire the white cascade as it tumbles from a sheer ledge. After heavy rain the river also bursts from a couple of natural basins hollowed into the rock wall below. Reaching the pool below the falls is forbidden. The walk down is difficult and dangerous because the hillside is all but vertical and very muddy.

The best time to visit is in the morning when the sun is glistening off the water and you are likely to be the only people viewing the falls.

The twin cascade of Wailua Falls, seen from a roadside overlook

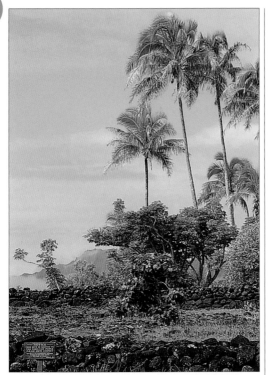

The ruins of Poli'ahu Heiau, a sacrificial temple on the King's Highway

Fern Grotto ❸

Kaua'i Co. Wailua River.
🚤 Smith's Motor Boat Service,
(808) 821-6895. 🚌 Waipouli.
⬜ daily. 🖥 www.smithskauai.com

Although a bridge makes it impossible to sail up the Wailua River from the ocean, a constant procession of pleasure barges sets out from a marina upstream for the 2-mile (3-km) excursion to the Fern Grotto. This large cave behind a fern-draped rock face is famous for its beauty. A paved path, lined with lush foliage, leads up to the grotto, where you may end up being serenaded with the *Hawaiian Wedding Song* – about three couples per day get married here. The hour-long narrated cruise up the longest navigable river in Hawai'i gives you a chance to enjoy some attractive scenery; the riverbanks are covered in palm-like pandanus plants and piri grass. There's a singalong on the return trip.

King's Highway ❹

Kaua'i Co. 🚌 Waipouli.
🏠 KVB, Līhu'e, (808) 245-3971.

The Wailua Valley was the seat of power in ancient Kaua'i, and the nearby shoreline remains the island's main population center. A trail of sacred sites known as the King's Highway ran from the ocean to the remote peak of Mount Wai'ale'ale. It started just south of the Wailua River in what is now **Lydgate State Park**, a deservedly popular

beach. Only vestiges survive here of the mighty stone walls of the **Hikinaakalā Heiau** (the name means "Rising of the Sun"), where worshipers would greet the dawn. Across the highway farther inland, Kaua'i's largest temple, **Malae Heiau**, lies buried beneath a tree-covered mound.

North of the river, a short way up Kuamo'o Road (Hwy 580), **Holoholokū Heiau** was, by contrast, so small that it could be entered only on all fours. Even so, it was the site of Kaua'i's first human sacrifices. Farther up the road lies a pair of boulders known as the **Birthing Stones**; only chiefs whose mothers gave birth while wedged between them could ever rule Kaua'i. A mile (1.5 km) farther up Kuamo'o ("lizard") Ridge, on a flat promontory with wide views, the stone walls of **Poli'ahu Heiau** remain in place, guarded by swaying coconut palms.

Half a mile (800 m) more and the ground to the right drops away to swift 'Ōpaeka'a ("rolling shrimp") Stream, which tumbles over the broad **'Ōpaeka'a Falls**. It is a fine spectacle, but do not go closer than the roadside lookout.

🏞 **Lydgate State Park**
Leho Drive, off Kūhiō Hwy
(Hwy 56), just S of Wailua River.

Sleeping Giant ❺

Kaua'i Co. 1.5 miles (2.5 km) NW of
Wailua. 🚌 Waipouli.

The east shore's principal residential district nestles 3 miles (5 km) in from the ocean, behind the undulating ridge of Nounou Mountain.

Sleeping Giant ridge, its profile reminiscent of a reclining figure

This long, low hillock is more commonly known as Sleeping Giant, thanks to an outline resembling a huge human figure lying flat on its back.

Three distinct hiking trails climb from its east, west, and south sides. They are reached from Kūhiō Highway (Hwy 56), Kāmala Road (Hwy 581), and Kuamo'o Road (Hwy 580) respectively. They converge to follow the alarmingly narrow crest, arriving at a meadow-like clearing in the forest at the top. This prime picnic spot offers panoramic views up and down the coastline, as well as westward to the sequence of parallel ridges that stretch inland. You can continue up the giant's head from here, but be extremely careful; the ridge is very steep in places and prone to rock slides.

Mount Wai'ale'ale **6**

Kaua'i Co.
11 miles (18 km) W of Wailua.

Within spitting distance of Kapa'a's sunny beaches lies one of the wettest places on earth – Mount Wai'ale'ale, or "overflowing water." An average of 440 in (1,100 cm) of rain each year cascades in huge waterfalls down its green-velvet walls. The summit, wreathed in almost perpetual mists, was the last call on the sacred King's Highway; the ancients would follow knife-edge ridges to reach a mountain-top *heiau* (temple).

These days, unless you take a helicopter tour, you can glimpse Wai'ale'ale only from below. Follow Kuamo'o Road (Hwy 580) past 'Ōpaeka'a Falls and the Keahua Forestry Arboretum, and if the clouds clear you will be confronted by astonishing views of a sheer, pleated cliff face. Dirt roads lead through the forest to its base, where the Wailua River thunders down from the 5,148-ft (1,570-m) peak. These roads are dangerous, if not impassable, after heavy rain.

The curving expanse of Donkey Beach, popular with nudists and surfers

Kapa'a **7**

Kaua'i Co. 🏠 *10,700.* 🚌
🛈 *KVB, Līhu'e, (808) 245-3971.*

Tourist development along Kaua'i's East Shore, also known as the Coconut Coast, is mostly concentrated into the 5-mile (8-km) coastal strip that stretches north of the Wailua River. Maps mark distinct communities at Wailua and Waipouli, but the only real town here is Kapa'a, farther north, home of the Coconut Festival *(see p35).* Most of the false-front buildings that line its wooden boardwalks now hold tourist-related businesses such as restaurants, souvenir stores, or equipment rental outlets, but Kapa'a still maintains the look of a late 19th-century plantation village. The fringe of sand at the ocean's edge is divided into a number of beach parks.

1920s rain gauge once used on Mt. Wai'ale'ale

Environs: The first of the more appealing beaches north of Kapa'a is tucked out of sight half a mile (800 m) from the highway and is reached by a forest trail that drops to the right not far past mile marker 11. This uncrowded, pretty stretch of sand is known as **Donkey Beach**, thanks to the beasts of burden that used to work in the adjacent sugar fields and were turned loose to graze along the beach's edges in the evenings. In their absence, wildflowers have

flourished. There are no trees to provide shade for sun-bathers, many of whom take advantage of this remote spot to go entirely naked. The surf is generally too rough to allow swimming, but is a rendezvous for expert surfers.

Anahola **8**

Kaua'i Co. 🏠 *2,200.* 🚌
🛈 *KVB, Līhu'e, (808) 245-3971.*

The small, scattered village of Anahola overlooks the sweeping, palm-fringed curve of Anahola Bay, an ancient surfing site. North of town, just inland of the highway, is the picturesque **Anahola Baptist Church**. Set against a beautiful mountain backdrop, the church makes a lovely photograph.

Nearby Anahola Beach is often relatively empty, despite its combination of beautiful setting, safe swimming, and convenient access. Reached by a spur road that loops down from Kūhiō Highway (Hwy 56) shortly after mile marker 13, the beach faces the most sheltered section of Anahola Bay. The area nearest the showers is reserved for family swimming, while the slightly more turbulent waters farther north are enjoyed by local surfers.

Hawaiian activists have sometimes staged protests on the beach, arguing that the state has failed to meet its obligation to provide native Hawaiians with affordable housing in the area. However, their campaigns have not been directed against tourists.

An inviting stretch of golden sand at secluded Secret Beach, near Kīlauea Point

Kīlauea Point ❾

Kauaʻi Co. Kīlauea Road, off Kūhiō Highway (Hwy 56), 10 miles (16 km) NW of Anahola. 🏠 *Kīlauea*. 🛈 *KVB, Līhuʻe, (808) 245-3971.*

The Hawaiian name Kīlauea ("much spewing") applies not only to the southernmost volcano on Hawaiʻi Island but also to the northernmost spot on the Hawaiian archipelago, Kauaʻi's Kīlauea Point. Here the name refers not to spouting lava, but rather to the raging waves that foam around the base of this rocky promontory.

Together with a couple of tiny offshore islets, the splendidly windswept cliff top has been set aside as the **Kīlauea Point National Wildlife Refuge**, a sanctuary for Pacific seabirds. Displays in the refuge's well-equipped visitor center enable amateur birdwatchers to pick out frigatebirds, Laysan albatrosses, and various tropic birds.

A short walk beyond the visitor center leads to the red and white **Kīlauea Lighthouse**, which marks the beginning of Kauaʻi's North Shore. When

KILAUEA LIGHTHOUSE

Colorful official marker for the lighthouse

erected in 1913, the lighthouse held the largest clamshell lens in the world, but that has now been supplanted by a much smaller and barely noticeable structure on its far side. As you approach the tip of the headland, extensive views open up to the west beyond Secret Beach and Princeville to the Nā Pali cliffs. The exposed oceanfront slopes to the east, meanwhile, are flecked with thousands of white seabirds and can be explored on ranger-led walking tours.

Environs: The most dramatic views of Kīlauea Lighthouse and, in winter especially, of the mighty waves that pound northern Kauaʻi, are from the vast but little-visited shelf of glorious yellow sand known as **Secret Beach**. To reach it, turn right onto Kalihiwai Road, half a mile (800 m) west of the Kīlauea turn-off, then follow a red-dirt track that cuts away almost immediately to the right. From its far end, a narrow trail zig-zags through the woods, coming out after ten minutes at a luscious tropical cove. Even in the summer, when the mile (1.5 km) of coarse sand at least doubles in width, the sea tends to be too rough for swimming.

However, it is worth walking the full length of the beach to see the white surf as it crashes against the black lava rocks that poke from the sand, and the glorious waterfall at the far end, nearest the lighthouse.

🦅 **Kīlauea Point National Wildlife Refuge**
Kīlauea Point. **Tel** *(808) 828-1413.* ⏰ *10am–4pm Mon–Fri.* ⬛ *Jan 1, Thanksgiving, Dec 25.* 📷 ♿

Kalihiwai ❿

Kauaʻi Co. 🏔 *1,000.* 🛈 *KVB, Līhuʻe, (808) 245-3971.*

From Kūhiō Highway (Highway 56), two successive turnings, a mile and a half (2.5 km) apart, are called Kalihiwai Road. The two parts of the road through this small settlement were connected until a tsunami washed away the bridge over the Kalihiwai River in 1957. The last few hundred yards of the eastern segment, just before the mouth of the river, run alongside the lovely **Kalihiwai Beach**. Shielded behind a grove of ironwood trees, this beach offers fine surfing and body-surfing as well as swimming. Kūhiō Highway crosses the river about half a mile (800 m) back from the ocean; glance inland from the bridge at this point to spot the beautiful, wide **Kalihiwai Falls**.

Environs: The second (western) segment of Kalihiwai Road quickly dead-ends at the Kalihiwai River, with no beach on this side. However, an unmarked spur road to the left, halfway down this segment, leads to quiet **'Anini Beach**. Here, between 3 miles (5 km) of golden sand and the coral reef that lies 200 yds (180 m) offshore, shallow turquoise waters provide the safest swimming on Kaua'i's North Shore. There is also excellent snorkeling on the coral reef itself, as well as an idyllic campsite set among the trees. The large lawns on the inland side of the road host polo matches on summer Sunday afternoons, often with boisterous crowds cheering on the players.

The Westin Princeville, set amid golf courses and ocean views

The mouth of the Kalihiwai River with Kalihiwai Beach behind

Princeville ⓫

Kaua'i Co. 🏠 *2,200.* ✈ 🏢
🛈 KVB, Līhu'e, (808) 245-3971.

The former sugar plantation and livestock ranch of Princeville, set on the rolling meadows of a headland above Hanalei Bay, was sold off in the 1960s to be developed as Kaua'i's most exclusive resort. Its centerpiece, the opulent **Westin Princeville** *(see p191),* occupies a prime site near the remains of an earthwork fort built by the German adventurer George Schäffer in 1816 *(see p172).* Its long-range views of the North Shore mountains are now shared by two golf courses, as well as several more hotels, condominiums, vacation homes, and a small shopping mall.

Below the bluffs, Princeville boasts some delightful little beaches. The best of the bunch, **Pu'upōā Beach**, is reached by trails that drop from both the Princeville Hotel and the Hanalei Bay Resort next door. Its wide sands offer dramatic views across Hanalei Bay, as well as over the wetlands to the peaks that tower behind Hanalei *(see p166),* and there's excellent family swimming in the shallow waters. Pu'upōā Beach stretches as far as the mouth of the Hanalei River, so rented kayaks can easily be paddled upstream. Princeville-based surfers and snorkelers flock to **Pali Ke Kua Beach**, also known as Hideaways Beach, by way of a trail down from the tennis courts of the Pali Ke Kua condominiums.

KAUA'I IN THE MOVIES

The fabulous scenery of Kaua'i has served as an exotic backdrop in countless Hollywood blockbusters, from a Caribbean paradise in *Islands in the Stream* (1977) to South America in *Raiders of the Lost Ark* (1981) and Vietnam in *Uncommon Valor* (1983). Ever since Esther Williams performed one of her trademark aquatic ballets in Hanalei Bay in *Pagan Love Song* (1950), the island has starred alongside the big screen's biggest names. Frank Sinatra's war-torn Pacific-island beach in *None but the Brave* (1965) was Pila'a Beach, east of Kīlauea. Meanwhile, Elvis Presley's greatest box-office hit, *Blue Hawaii* (1961), climaxed with a gloriously kitsch wedding ceremony at the Coco Palms Resort. The remote Honopū Valley on the Nā Pali coast stood in as Skull Island in the 1977 remake of *King Kong* and, before Hurricane Iniki put an abrupt end to proceedings, much of *Jurassic Park* (1993) was shot in Hanapēpē Valley. Kaua'i is probably best remembered, however, for its role in the smash-hit Rodgers and Hammerstein musical

South Pacific (1958). Of the movie's showstopping songs, *Some Enchanted Evening* was filmed at Hanalei Bay, and, most famous of all, Mitzi Gaynor sang *I'm Gonna Wash That Man Right Out of My Hair* at Lumaha'i Beach.

Publicity poster of Elvis Presley in *Blue Hawaii*

Hanalei ⑫

Kaua'i Co. 🏠 500.
🚉 ℹ️ KVB, Lihu'e,
(808) 245-3971.

Only one spot in all
the islands bears
the name Hanalei, or
"crescent bay." Nowhere
deserves it more than the
placid half-moon inlet,
fringed with golden sand
and cradled by soaring
green cliffs, that lies just
west of Princeville.

The flat valley floor of
the Hanalei River was in
ancient times a prime
area for growing taro.

The taro fields of Hanalei Valley, seen from a highway overlook

Later turned into a patchwork
of rice paddies by Chinese
settlers, it is once again dominated by taro, planted under
the auspices of the **Hanalei
National Wildlife Refuge** to
re-create the preferred habitat
of the state's increasingly
endangered waterbirds. Crisscrossed by irrigation channels
and scattered with inaccessible islands that poke from the
mud, it is home to an ever-
changing population of coots,
herons, stilts, and transient
migratory birds. The valley's
lush, green landscape is best
seen from a lookout on Kūhiō
Highway (Hwy 56), just west
of the Princeville turnoff.

The slender bridge across the
Hanalei River is the first of a
series of one-lane bridges that
slow North Shore traffic to a
virtual crawl, thereby helping
to protect the region from the
ravages of overdevelopment.
The village of **Hanalei** on the
far side is a relaxed place, still
recognizably a plantation settlement but kept busy these
days catering to the needs
of a year-round communi-
ty of surfers and Nā Pali
adventurers.

A trio of awe-inspiring mountains forms a magnificent
backdrop – Hīhimanu to the
east, Māmalahoa to the west,
and, in the center, the sublime
Nāmolokama, furrowed with
over 20 waterfalls that combine to form Wai'oli Stream.

At first glance **Hanalei Bay**
might look like an ideal harbor, but so many ships have
come to grief on its submerged
reefs that only shallow-draft
pleasure yachts now use the
old jetty on its eastern side.
Conditions for swimmers using
the 2-mile (3-km) strand west
of the jetty depend on the state
of the reef; although there are
several attractive spots for sunbathing or camping, swimming
is only really advisable from
Waikoko Beach at the western
end, beyond the mouth of the
Wai'oli Stream. Expert surfers,
untroubled by these issues,
set off from Wai'oli Beach, or
"Pinetrees Park," nearer the
center of the bay, to practice
their art amid the waves that
break at the bay's entrance.

Hanalei's most visible relic
of the past is the missionary
complex, set on landscaped
lawns west of the town
center and backed by
high, tree-clad moun-
tains. The town's earliest
Christian edifice, **Wai'oli
Church**, was put up in
1841. Dwarfed beneath a
tall, sloping roof, this large
wooden structure now
functions as a social hall,
set back to the right of
its successor, the 1912-
vintage **Wai'oli Hui'ia
Church**. With its vivid

The striking facade of Wai'oli Hui'ia Church

green shingles, shimmering
stained glass, and gray-capped
belfry, all nestled beneath a
spreading palm tree, Wai'oli
Hui'ia is without a doubt the
loveliest building on Kaua'i.
Tucked away behind it, the
Wai'oli Mission House was
home to several generations
of two missionary families,
including the Wilcoxes (see
p160), whose descendants
lived here until the late 1970s.
Although some of the original
furnishings have gone, period
replacements provide a sense
of 19th-century Hanalei.

🏛️ **Wai'oli Mission House**
Kūhiō Hwy (Hwy 56). **Tel** (808)
245-3202. ⬜ 9am–3pm Tue,
Thu & Sat. ⬤ public hols.
Donation. ♿ ground floor only.

Lumaha'i Beach ⑬

Kaua'i Co. Off Kūhiō Highway
(Hwy 56), 2 miles (3 km) W of
Hanalei. 🚌 Hanalei.

Immediately beyond Hanalei
Bay, a small roadside pull-
off marks the top of a steep,
muddy trail down to the
spell-binding Lumaha'i Beach.
Thanks to its appearance in
the movie South Pacific (see
p165), this has a reputation as
the most romantic beach in
all Hawai'i. Its golden sands
always seem to hold at least
one pair of lovers, but the
beaches are long and broad
enough to maintain the illusion
of privacy. Except on very
calm days, rolling in the surf
is not a good idea.

The mountain peak of Bali Hai may have dominated the beach on screen, but that was due to technical trickery; in fact it's a tiny outcrop called Makana at the end of a ridge, 4 miles (6.5 km) farther west.

Limahuli Garden ⓮

Kaua'i Co. Kūhiō Hwy (Hwy 56), 6 miles (10 km) W of Hanalei. *Tel* (808) 826-1053. ◷ 9:30am–4pm Tue–Sat. ◉ Jan 1, Thanksgiving, Dec 25. ⬛ ◪ **www**.ntbg.org

The lush Limahuli Garden is located a quarter of a mile (400 m) before the end of Kūhiō Highway, in a steep, high valley. In ancient times, the Limahuli Valley was part of a self-sufficient *ahupua'a* (a wedge-shaped division of land running from mountain to sea). Since then, it has barely been occupied, with the exception of the notorious "Taylor Camp," an ocean-front commune that survived from 1969 to 1977 on land owned by Elizabeth Taylor's brother.

Part of the valley remains in sufficiently pristine condition to have been set aside as a botanical sanctuary, protecting both indigenous Hawaiian plants and species brought to the islands by early Polynesian settlers. The preserve is run by the National Tropical Botanical Garden, whose aim is to preserve the native species and increase their numbers.

Visitors can explore only a 17-acre portion that begins at the road and stretches inland,

Snorkeling at Tunnels Beach

supporting reconstructed ancient taro terraces that climb the hillside. A network of trails allows one to meander through a mixed forest of unusual trees, such as the Polynesian-introduced *kukui* or candlenut, once prized for its oil, and the native *'ōhi'a 'ai* or mountain apple. The higher slopes command wonderful views of the coastline below, as well as giving glimpses of the jagged Nā Pali cliffs to the west. Inland, the strangely eroded mountains loom above slender Limahuli Stream, overshadowing the off-limits Limahuli Preserve.

Hā'ena and Kē'ē Beaches ⓯

Kaua'i Co. Off Kūhiō Hwy (Hwy 56), 7 miles (11 km) W of Hanalei.

Two separate beach parks with similar names are located near the end of the highway along the North Shore. The first one, **Hā'ena Beach County Park**, offers a pleasant campsite in a coconut grove where the shoreline is too exposed for safe swimming. Ten minutes' walk east from here is **Tunnels Beach**, whose extensive reef is one of Kaua'i's most popular snorkeling sites. The name refers not to the beautiful coral formations but to the tubular waves that lure the surfers here in winter.

Immediately west of here, the second park, **Hā'ena State Park**, is mostly inaccessible to

Hibiscus at
Limahuli Garden

casual visitors, having been set aside more to spare this section of coast from development than to make it available for public use. **Kē'ē Beach**, at the end of the road but still within the state park, is one of the most beautiful of all the North Shore beaches, its glowing yellow sands all but engulfed by rampant tropical vegetation. The turquoise inshore lagoon provides an irresistible cooling-off spot for hikers back from the Kalalau Trail (*see pp168–9*), as well as a much-loved swimming and snorkeling site. However, the often-turbulent waters around and beyond the reef hold perils for the unwary.

Many legends attach themselves to this remote beach, including one that identifies it as the original birthplace of *hula*. Pele the volcano goddess (*see p24*) is said to have been enticed here in a dream by the sweet music of the young Kauaian warrior Lohi'au. Upon waking, she sent her sister Hi'iaka to bring Lohi'au to her, but these two promptly fell in love. Beneath the undergrowth, near the start of the Kalalau Trail, crumbling walls mark the site of Lohi'au's home, while the raised headland just west of the beach holds the remains of Hawai'i's first *hālau hula* (*hula* school). Here, Hi'iaka passed on the art of *hula* to eager devotees from all the islands.

Limahuli Garden's taro terraces, where the crop is grown in the traditional way

Kalalau Trail ⑯

The precipitous cliffs of the Nā Pali Coast make it impossible for the road to continue west of Kē'ē Beach, but hardy hikers can follow the narrow Kalalau Trail 11 more miles (18 km) to isolated Kalalau Valley. One of the most dramatic hikes in the world, it threads its way through a landscape of almost primeval vastness and splendor. While this is not an expedition to undertake lightly, a half-day round trip to Hanakāpī'ai Valley is within most capabilities and provides an unforgettable wilderness experience. The trail gets progressively drier as it heads west, so the initial stretches are the muddiest, with the densest vegetation. Negotiating this tangled forest of *hala* (pandanus) trees often requires scrambling over rock falls, or picking your way among slippery tree roots.

Start of the trail ①
The trail climbs steeply from the trailhead at the end of Kūhiō Highway, affording spectacular views of the rugged coastline.

Makana Peak ②
On special occasions, the ancient Hawaiians tossed flaming logs into the night sky from this peak. Crowds would gather in boats on the sea below to watch this early form of fireworks.

Ke Ahu A Laka ③
This was once Hawai'i's most celebrated *hālau hula* (*hula* school), where students could spend several years learning their art. The ancient temple nearby is thought to have been used for graduation ceremonies.

Hanakāpī'ai Valley ④
In summer, a pristine sandy beach replaces the pebbles found in winter at the mouth of Hanakāpī'ai Valley. Swimming and wading are not recommended due to dangerous rip currents.

End of the trail ⑨
For the last 5 miles (8 km), the trail clings perilously to a sandstone cliff that turns to dust at every step, thanks to the goats that have eaten the vegetation that should bind the soil together. The view of Kalalau Valley is the reward for the long hike.

Hanakāpīʻai Falls ⑤
An energetic hour's hike inland, through a long-abandoned coffee plantation, ends up at this towering waterfall.

Pā Ma Waʻa ⑥
This vertical 800-ft (240-m) cliff stands above a protected little cove welcomed by weary canoers. The boulder at the top marks the highest point on the Kalalau Trail.

Hanging Valleys ⑦
Between Hanakāpīʻai and Hanakoa, the trail dips into a number of "hanging valleys," where the streams have yet to cut their way down to sea level.

Hanakoa Valley ⑧
The campsite here is set amid the ruins of ancient taro terraces (see p125), with no access to the sea. The mighty 2,000-ft (600-m) cascade at the head of the valley is just 600 yds (550 m) away – a short but muddy climb.

```
0 kilometers          2
0 miles          1
```

KEY

- Hiking trail
- Road
- Vista

Koʻolau the Leper (far right) with his family

Kalalau Valley ⑰

Kauaʻi Co. [i] KVB, Līhuʻe, (808) 245-3971.

Unless you persevere through the last difficult stretch of the Kalalau Trail, the majestic amphitheater of Kalalau Valley can be seen only from afar. Most visitors view it by boat or helicopter tour, or from the two lookouts at the end of Kōkeʻe Road (see pp170–71).

For well over 1,000 years this isolated valley was home to a thriving community of taro farmers. In the years after European contact, however, disease and the lure of the city thinned out the population, the last permanent inhabitant leaving in 1919. Later, Kalalau became a cattle ranch and was then briefly colonized by hippies who sneaked in during the 1960s. Attempts to evict them resulted in the creation of the Nā Pali Coast State Park, which now controls access and limits places at Kalalau's idyllic camp site.

The valley's pinnacles made a perfect refuge for the infamous Koʻolau the Leper, as immortalized by Jack London (see p25) in his story of the same name. Koʻolau, a cowboy from Waimea, fled into the valley in the 1890s rather than face exile and death at Molokaʻi's dreaded leper colony (see pp100–1). Koʻolau's wife eventually left Kalalau alone, after both her husband and son had died of leprosy.

BIRDS OF KAUAʻI

The innermost recesses of the Nā Pali valleys, and the bogs and ravines that stretch across the top of Kauaʻi, are cloaked with dense rain forest. This unique environment is the last natural sanctuary for the island's native flora and fauna. Before human contact with Hawaiʻi, only a handful of bird species

The tiny ʻanianiau

lived here – probably descendants of wind-blown stragglers lucky to find dry land. Encountering endemic plants with curved flowers, many birds developed curved bills for sipping nectar; others acquired short, strong beaks for crushing seeds and nuts. Forest birds extinct elsewhere in the state still cling to life in the ʻōhiʻa forests of the Alakaʻi Swamp. Honeycreepers abound here, the most common being the bright-red ʻiʻiwi, with its black wings and

Red-billed tropicbird

salmon-colored sickle-shaped bill; the ʻapapane, similarly colored but with a short, black bill; and the diminutive yellow ʻanianiau. Also conspicuous is the gregarious rust-colored ʻelepaio, which follows hikers through the forest.

Most prominent on the Nā Pali Coast are the soaring tropicbirds, while in the drier Kōkeʻe State Park, honking nēnē appear at the lookouts together with Kauaʻi's most ubiquitous bird, the moa, or red jungle fowl – a showy wild chicken.

Moa, red jungle fowl

Waimea Canyon and Kōke'e State Park ⑱

Waimea Canyon, known as the "Grand Canyon of the Pacific," was created by earth movements that almost split Kaua'i in two. Over time, heavy rains have helped form a gorge 3,000 ft (915 m) deep that is still being eroded today, as occasional landslides slash away layers of rich green vegetation and the Waimea River carries the red mud into the ocean. Most visitors see the canyon from the lookouts dotted along the rim, along Kōke'e Road, but hiking trails enable the more adventurous to explore in greater depth. At the north end of Waimea Canyon is Kōke'e State Park, laced through by more hiking trails and including the most accessible part of the daunting Alaka'i Swamp. The road finally ends at two stunning overlooks 4,000 ft (1,220 m) above the Nā Pali Coast.

View from Waimea Canyon Drive showing eroded, exposed earth

Kōke'e Natural History Museum
Displays on wildlife and local history are featured in the museum, while the shop has hiking information, books, and trail maps.

★ Waimea Canyon Lookout
Despite being the lowest of the lookouts, this offers the definitive canyon views: north into the gorges cut by the Waiahulu and Po'omau streams, and south to Waimea itself on the distant shoreline.

Iliau Nature Loop
Reached from mile marker 9, this roadside trail is named after the iliau *plant, which is endemic to this part of Kaua'i. Native plants along the loop are labeled.*

STAR SIGHTS
★ Alaka'i Swamp
★ Pu'u O Kila Lookout
★ Waimea Canyon Lookout

WAIMEA

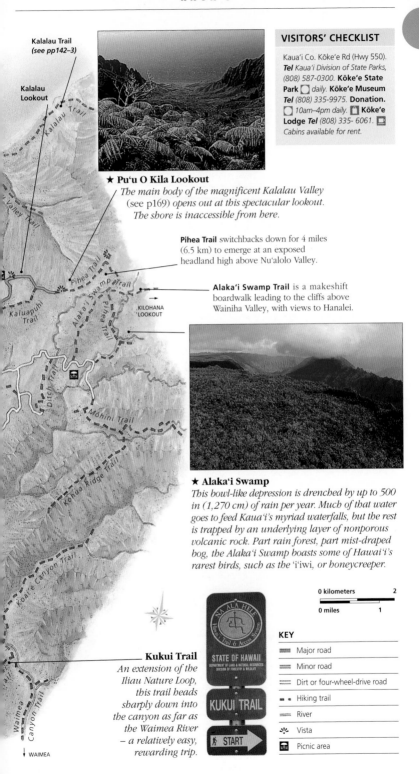

Kalalau Trail *(see pp142–3)*

Kalalau Lookout

★ Pu'u O Kila Lookout
The main body of the magnificent Kalalau Valley (see p169) opens out at this spectacular lookout. The shore is inaccessible from here.

Pihea Trail switchbacks down for 4 miles (6.5 km) to emerge at an exposed headland high above Nu'alolo Valley.

Alaka'i Swamp Trail is a makeshift boardwalk leading to the cliffs above Wainiha Valley, with views to Hanalei.

KILOHANA 'LOOKOUT

★ Alaka'i Swamp
This bowl-like depression is drenched by up to 500 in (1,270 cm) of rain per year. Much of that water goes to feed Kaua'i's myriad waterfalls, but the rest is trapped by an underlying layer of nonporous volcanic rock. Part rain forest, part mist-draped bog, the Alaka'i Swamp boasts some of Hawai'i's rarest birds, such as the 'i'iwi, or honeycreeper.

Kukui Trail
An extension of the Iliau Nature Loop, this trail heads sharply down into the canyon as far as the Waimea River – a relatively easy, rewarding trip.

NA ALA HELE
Hawaii Trail & Access System
STATE OF HAWAII
DEPARTMENT OF LAND & NATURAL RESOURCES
DIVISION OF FORESTRY & WILDLIFE
KUKUI TRAIL
🚶 START

0 kilometers 2
0 miles 1

KEY

▬▬▬	Major road
▬▬▬	Minor road
▭▭▭	Dirt or four-wheel-drive road
▪ ▪	Hiking trail
▬▬▬	River
�018	Vista
🏕	Picnic area

↓ WAIMEA

Polihale Beach ⓵

Kaua‘i Co. 5 miles (8 km) beyond the end of Kaumuali‘i Hwy (Hwy 50).

The westernmost region of Kaua‘i, shielded from the ocean winds in the rain shadow of the central mountains, is characterized by long, flat expanses of sand. A sizable chunk has been taken over by the US military, whose sophisticated installations include systems that would give early warning of another attack on Pearl Harbor.

Skirt the security fences by following the dirt roads inland, and 15 miles (24 km) northwest of Waimea you come to the vast expanse of Polihale Beach. The surf is far too ferocious for swimming, but it's a wonderful place for a walk, with the cliffs of the Nā Pali Coast rising to the north. Head west from the end of the road and you'll reach the dunes known as the **Barking Sands**, whose hollow grains are said to groan and howl when disturbed by wind or a heavy footfall.

Statue of Captain Cook in Waimea

Waimea ⓶

Kaua‘i Co. 🚶 1,700. 🚉 🛈 KVB, Līhu‘e, (808) 245-3971.

Waimea is among Kaua‘i's more historic towns. It was here in 1778 that the crewmen of Captain Cook's third Pacific voyage – after pausing to shoot a Hawaiian – became the first Europeans to set foot on Hawaiian soil. Cook stated that "I never saw Indians so much astonished," while he himself was amazed to find the natives speaking a Polynesian language similar to those in the far-off South Seas. A statue of Cook graces the town center.

However, perhaps mindful of the mixed results of Cook's visit, including rampant venereal disease, the beach where he landed is named not in his honor but after Lucy Wright, Waimea's first native teacher. Situated west of the Waimea ("reddish water") River, it is

made up largely of mud washed down from Waimea Canyon. A plaque marks the site of Cook's first landfall.

Just across Waimea River, a headland holds what's left of **Russian Fort Elizabeth**. This star-shaped edifice was built by an adventurer, George Schäffer, in 1816. A German doctor, pretending to be a naturalist but working as a spy for the Russian-American Company, he had gained the confidence of Kaumuali‘i, the chief of Kaua‘i, and decided to double-cross his employers. He and Kaumuali‘i hatched a plot to conquer the archipelago and divide it between the Tsar of Russia and the chief. Within a year, fooled into thinking that the US and Russia were at war, Schäffer fled the islands. His fort served the government for 50 more years but is now dilapidated.

Hanapēpē ⓶

Kaua‘i Co. 🚶 2,500. 🚉 🛈 KVB, Līhu‘e, (808) 245-3971.

Halfway between Waimea and Po‘ipū, Hanapēpē makes an intriguing detour off Kaumuali‘i Highway (Hwy 50). Although taro was once grown in the valley, the village owes its late 19th-century look to the Chinese laborers who farmed rice here after serving out their contracts on sugar plantations.

Later Hanapēpē was all but abandoned, but several of its timber-frame buildings have now reopened as galleries and craft shops, and there are several attractive restaurants.

Allerton Garden ⓶

Kaua‘i Co. **Tel** (808) 332-7324. ⏰ 8:30am–5pm daily. 🌐 public hols. 🎫 ♿ with prior notification. 📷 by appointment, at visitor center across from Spouting Horn parking lot, Lāwa‘i Road, Po‘ipū. **www**.ntbg.org

Lāwa‘i Valley stretches back from the pretty little cove of Lāwa‘i Kai, 2 miles (3 km) west of Po‘ipū. Occupied in antiquity by taro farmers and later used by Chinese immigrants to grow rice, the valley became Queen Emma's favorite retreat in the 1870s. In the 1930s, it was bought by the Allertons, a Chicago banking family, and a plot near the sea was exquisitely landscaped to create Allerton Garden.

Bequeathed to the National Tropical Botanical Garden by the last of the Allertons in 1987, the valley was devastated by Hurricane Iniki in 1992. Both the Allertons' oceanfront home and Queen Emma's cottage have been fully restored, and the Allerton Garden is once more a showpiece. Unlike its counterpart at Limahuli (see p167), it aims to delight the eye rather than concentrate on native plants.

Visitors are transported from the visitor center near Po‘ipū to the otherwise

The pool and pavilion of the Diana Fountain at Allerton Garden

inaccessible site via a mandatory 15-minute tram ride, and from there tour the garden on foot. The Allertons conceived the design as a series of separate "rooms," and each section, such as the serene Diana Fountain or the Italianate Art Deco Mermaid Fountain, has its own character. The plants are the real stars, however, from heliconias and bromeliads to assorted tropical fruits in the orchards. Species familiar as house plants in chillier climes run riot, while graceful palms line the placid stream that glides through the heart of the valley.

Serious botanists will appreciate the chance to see rare species in the nursery, including *Kanaloa kahoolawensis*, a woody shrub whose only two known wild specimens were first identified on Kaho'olawe *(see p121)* during the 1980s. Prior reservation is required for the tour, and children under five are not admitted. A visitor center, surrounded by 10 acres of gardens near the parking lot, was opened in 1997.

Po'ipū ㉓

Kaua'i Co. 🏠 1,000. 🚐 2 a day. 🛈 KVB, Līhu'e, (808) 245-3971.

Sprawling to either side of the mouth of the Waikomo Stream, at the southern tip of Kaua'i, Po'ipū remains the island's most popular beach

Spouting Horn sending up a jet of water

resort. In 1992, Hurricane Iniki ripped the roofs off its plush oceanfront hotels and filled their lobbies with sand and ruined cars. Give or take the odd derelict property, Po'ipū is now back to normal: a strip of hotels, condos, and restaurants.

The prime spot in the center of the beach is **Po'ipū Beach Park**, complete with vigilant lifeguards and a kids' playground. There's safe swimming directly offshore, and great snorkeling around the rocks at its western end. To the east, **Brennecke's Beach** is more of a haunt for young surfers, while farther along, beyond Makahū'ena Point, the shoreline becomes a wilderness of sand dunes. The fossilized

bones of long-extinct flightless birds known as Māhā'ulepū have been found in this area, and several native plant species survive here and nowhere else.

Environs: Po'ipū itself is a modern creation, but the rudimentary jetty at the mouth of Waikomo Stream has been in use since the mid-19th century. Known as Kōloa Landing, it was built to serve Hawai'i's first sugarcane plantation, established 2 miles (3 km) inland at **Kōloa** in 1835. Kōloa now plays second fiddle to Po'ipū, but with its wooden boardwalks and false-fronted stores, it's a pleasant place for a stroll. A huge sugar mill dominates the area a mile (1.5 km) east of town. Built in 1913, it finally shut down in 1996.

The coastal road west of Po'ipū ends after only a mile (1.5 km) at **Spouting Horn**, a natural blow-hole in a ledge of black lava a few steps back from the sea. The waves that break against the rock are channeled underground and then forced up in fountains of white spume that can reach a height of 50 ft (15 m) before raining down onto the usual crowd of spectators. It is very dangerous to approach closer than the roadside lookout.

NI'IHAU, THE "FORBIDDEN ISLAND"

Lying 15 miles (24 km) southwest of Kaua'i, but just visible from the coast at Waimea, Ni'ihau is the smallest populated island in the chain, with 250 inhabitants. Owned by the Robinson family – descendants of Elizabeth Sinclair, who paid Kamehameha V $10,000 for the island in 1864 – it is little affected by tourism. You can visit only by a costly helicopter tour that avoids the inhabited areas *(see p243)*. It has no hotel, airport, or cars.

Although Ni'ihau's original inhabitants were furious at the sale of their homeland to an outsider, the isolation has since turned the island into the last stronghold of Hawaiian culture – Hawaiian is still the first language here. When not tending cattle for the Ni'ihau Ranch, locals support themselves with fishing, farming, and threading necklaces of the delicate *pūpū* (shells) that wash up on the beaches.

With annual rainfall of just 12 in (300 mm) Ni'ihau is able to support only minimal agriculture. The only town, Pu'uwai ("heart"), is on the west coast, a grid of dirt roads dotted with bungalows and colorful gardens.

Ni'ihau's west coast and the tiny town of Pu'uwai

TRAVELERS' NEEDS

WHERE TO STAY

From thousand-room, oceanfront mega-resorts to a treehouse for two in Hawai'i Island's Waipi'o Valley, the accommodation possibilities in Hawai'i are as numerous as they are diverse. The price range, too, is vast. As the beach is the main attraction for most visitors, the hotels closest to the ocean are considered most desirable and are usually the most pricey. Air-conditioning is

Bellhop at Mauna Lani

standard, though some smaller and older properties provide ceiling fans instead. In addition to resort hotels, there are many dozens of smaller hotels, condominiums, inns, and bed & breakfasts, all with lower rates. Many of the inns and B&Bs are charming and distinctive and stress personalized service; some, like the Old Wailuku Inn at Ulupono on Maui, are historic properties.

CHAIN AND BOUTIQUE HOTELS

Most of Hawai'i's large resort hotels are run by well-known chains such as **Hilton**, **Hyatt**, and **Sheraton**. Some are so self-contained and offer such a variety of activities that many visitors choose never to leave the property. If you prefer elegance and gracious service, however, head for gems like the Halekūlani in Waikīkī *(see p180)* or Maui's Four Seasons Resort *(see p187)*.

Less expensive options include local chains such as **Aston Hotels**, **Outrigger Hotels Hawai'i**, and **Castle Resorts**, as well as smaller, individual establishments that stress service over amenities. The latter, known as "boutique" hotels, are popular with inter-island travelers.

CONDOMINIUMS

A condominium unit or "condo" – an apartment, really – is an ideal choice for a family or travelers who would prefer to spend their money

on sightseeing and activities rather than on accommodations and dining. On O'ahu, they are mostly in high-rise buildings *mauka* (inland) of Waikīkī. On the neighboring islands, they are generally in low-rise complexes often located on or near the beach.

Condos range in size from studios to three-bedroom units suitable for up to eight adults or a family. They have kitchens and are stocked with everything from china to beach towels. Most condo units are privately owned and may be booked directly, through companies such as **Sunquest Vacations** on Hawai'i Island, and **Destination Resorts Hawai'i** on Maui. Condos in smaller complexes can be booked through the building's resident manager. House-keeping service varies, but is normally provided every three or four days.

Twist Lounge, Sheraton Waikīkī *(see p180)*

INNS AND B&BS

Hawai'i's few inns are worth seeking out as an alternative to the big hotels. Because they are small and do not offer the amenities of the resorts, their staff pride themselves on service and attention to detail. Maui's Lahaina Inn, a restored Victorian-era masterpiece, is a stunning example *(see p186)*.

Nowadays there are hundreds of B&Bs (bed & breakfasts) all over Hawai'i. Many are just a room in someone's home; others are charming cottages. If a B&B suits your needs, there are two reservation services you can use, **Hawai'i's Best Bed & Breakfasts**, which represents the top 100 in the state, and **Bed & Breakfast Hawai'i** .

CAMPING AND HOSTELS

Campsites range in setting from beachfront park to volcanic crater. All county and state parks require permits, available for a small fee from **County Departments of Parks and Recreation** or the **State Department of Land and Natural Resources**. Some parks have basic cabins, which are inexpensive, but usually

Aston Waimea Plantation Cottages *(see p191)*

◁ Vacationers enjoying the sea and sun at one of Hawai'i's golden sand beaches

Idyllic seaside camp site at 'Anini Beach on Kaua'i's North Shore

booked months in advance, especially on weekends. The main islands also have hostels, with dormitory accommodations and some private rooms. Contact the Hawai'i Visitors and Convention Bureau for more information (see p235).

PRICES AND BOOKING

Hawai'i has accommodations to match every desire and wallet. Prices are highest from December to April, and lowest in May, June, September, and October. One of the more economical options is to stay in a condo. A one-bedroom unit, which can easily fit a family of four, costs between $150 and $250 per night. Some inns and B&Bs have double rooms for under $100 a night.

Cabin in Haleakalā National Park

It is simplest to book accommodations through your travel agent. The Hawai'i Visitors and Convention Bureau can help, as can resort and B&B reservation services. You can book directly over the Internet; check for good deals and packages. Most accommodations' phone numbers are toll-free in the US.

Oceanfront bungalow at the Four Seasons Resort Hualalai (see p189)

HIDDEN EXTRAS

All accommodations are subject to a combined sales and room tax of 11.42 percent. Most places allow children to share with parents at no extra charge, but check beforehand. Phone calls and faxes from hotel rooms are more expensive than normal rates, and many hotels in Honolulu charge a daily rate for parking. Extra costs can include things like towel "rental" and items from your minibar. To avoid surprises at checkout, ask beforehand. Tipping is not mandatory, but average tips for staff are as follows: $2–3 a day for housekeepers; $1–2 for bellmen and parking attendants.

VISITORS WITH DISABILITIES

All hotels and many smaller properties have at least some rooms with disabled access; many ensure access to public areas as well. The Disability and Communication Access Board website (see p237) provides an up-to-date list of the most accessible hotels.

TRAVELING WITH CHILDREN

Families with children should choose a large resort with children's activities, or a condo. Most of the hotels with activities charge for the care, but some of the top hotels offer a fantastic service at no additional charge.

Choosing a Hotel

The hotels in this guide have been selected across a wide price range for their good value, facilities, and location. These listings highlight some of the factors that may influence your choice. Entries are listed by island, beginning with Honolulu and Waikiki. For information on restaurants in the area, see pages 196–209.

PRICE CATEGORIES
For a standard double room per night in high season, with all unavoidable extra charges including service and tax.

$ under $100
$$ $100-$200
$$$ $200-$300
$$$$ $300-$450
$$$$$ over $450

HONOLULU AND WAIKĪKĪ

WAIKĪKĪ Aqua Bamboo $$

2425 Kūhiō Ave, 96815 **Tel** *(808) 922-7777* **Fax** *(808) 922-9473* **Rooms** *90*   **Map** 4 E4

A block from Waikīkī Beach, this deluxe boutique hotel offers stylish rooms with kitchen facilities. The Aqua Spa, in a cabana by the pool, offers Swedish, Hawaiian *lomi-lomi,* and hot-stone massages. Shopping, dining, and attractions are within walking distance. **www.aquaresorts.com**

WAIKĪKĪ Aqua Island Colony $$

445 Seaside Ave, 96815 **Tel** *(808) 923-2345* **Fax** *(808) 921-7105* **Rooms** *347*   **Map** 4 E4

This condo hotel is on a busy street off Kalākaua Avenue, near the Ala Wai Canal. Although small, units have private *lānai* (verandas). Studio units have kitchenettes and one-bedrooms have full kitchens. The great views are of either Diamond Head and the ocean, or nearby mountains. **www.aquaresorts.com**

WAIKĪKĪ Aston Waikīkī Beachside Hotel $$

2452 Kalākaua Ave, 96815 **Tel** *(808) 931-2100* **Fax** *(808) 931-2129* **Rooms** *79*   **Map** 4 E5

This elegant boutique hotel is lavishly furnished with art and antiques reflecting the many influences that shape the islands' culture. Guest rooms are decorated in oriental style and feature luxurious private bathrooms. Continental breakfast is included. The hotel is just across the street from Waikīkī Beach. **www.astonhotels.com**

WAIKĪKĪ Aston Waikīkī Joy Hotel $$

320 Lewers St, 96815 **Tel** *(808) 923-2300* **Fax** *(808) 924-4010* **Rooms** *47*   **Map** 4 D4

One of the smaller boutique hotels, this has pleasant rooms and interesting extras, including Jacuzzis, state-of-the-art stereo systems, and soundproofing. Complimentary continental breakfast is served on the tropical veranda off the lobby. It is within walking distance of Waikīkī Beach, shopping, dining, and activities. **www.astonhotels.com**

WAIKĪKĪ The Breakers Hotel $$

250 Beach Wlk, 96815 **Tel** *(808) 923-3181* **Fax** *(808) 923-7174* **Rooms** *64*   **Map** 4 D4

A 1950s-vintage, Hawaiian-style oasis amid towering neighbors, this hotel prides itself on real Hawaiian hospitality. A patio with tropical flowers surrounds the pool, which has a bar and grill right next to it. Every room overlooks the shady courtyard and has a kitchenette, air-conditioning, television, and telephone. **www.breakers-hawaii.com**

WAIKĪKĪ Diamond Head Bed & Breakfast $$

3240 Noela Dr **Tel** *(808) 923-3360* **Fax** *(808) 923-3360* **Rooms** *3*   **Map** 4 F5

On the side of Kapi'olani Park *(see pp72–3)* farthest from Waikīkī, Joanne Trotter has been welcoming guests into her home since 1986. Her tasteful house, with its big *lānai* (veranda), is filled with heirlooms. One room features a carved bed that once belonged to a Hawaiian princess. Breakfast is included. **www.diamondheadbnb.com**

WAIKĪKĪ Ewa Hotel Waikīkī $$

2555 Cartwright Rd, 96815 **Tel** *(808) 922-1677* **Fax** *(808) 922-8538* **Rooms** *92*   **Map** 4 F5

Tucked between Kalākaua and Kūhiō Avenues, the attractions here are a check-in time of 2pm (the usual is 3pm), particularly good kitchen facilities in many rooms, and low rates. One block from the beach, it is as close to Kapi'olani Park *(see pp72–3)* as you can get. **www.ewahotel.com**

WAIKĪKĪ Holiday Inn Waikīkī Beachcomber $$

2300 Kalākaua Ave, 96815 **Tel** *(808) 922-4646* **Fax** *(808) 923-4889* **Rooms** *494*   **Map** 4 E5

The main attractions here are proximity to the beach, live entertainment, and shopping. The hotel has modern decor throughout and hosts the dazzling Magic of Polynesia. Macy's department store occupies the ground floor and The Royal Hawaiian Shopping Center is across the street. **www.ohanahotels.com**

WAIKĪKĪ Ramada Plaza Waikīkī $$

1830 Ala Moana Blvd, 96815 **Tel** *(808) 955-1111* **Fax** *(808) 947-1799* **Rooms** *199*   **Map** 3 B4

This 17-story hotel is at the gateway to Waikīkī, two blocks from the beach. Rooms have telephones with voicemail. A pool and sundeck, complimentary fitness equipment, laundry facilities, business services, and a gift shop are all on site. The China Buffet Restaurant offers bountiful, affordable Asian fare. **www.ramadaplazawaikiki.com**

Key to Symbols *see back cover flap*

WAIKĪKĪ Aqua Waikīkī Marina

1700 Ala Moana Blvd, 96815 **Tel** *(808) 942-7722* **Fax** *(808) 942-1873* **Rooms** *103*   **Map** *3 B4*

This 40-story high-rise offers affordable condominium accommodations within walking distance of the Hawai'i Convention Center and Ala Moana Shopping Center. Guest rooms have kitchenettes and panoramic views of the Pacific Ocean, Honolulu, Waikīkī Beach, or Diamond Head. Tennis courts are available. **www.aquaresorts.com**

WAIKĪKĪ Aston Waikīkī Sunset

229 Paoakalani Ave, 96815 **Tel** *(808) 922-0511* **Fax** *(808) 923-8580* **Rooms** *435*   **Map** *4 F4*

Just a block from the beach and two from the zoo, this all-suite hotel has a pool, a sauna, and a tennis court. Dining and shopping are a step away. Decorated in tropical style, the one- and two-bedroom suites have kitchens and private *lānai* (verandas) with views of the ocean, mountains, or Diamond Head. **www.waikikisunset.com**

WAIKĪKĪ Coconut Waikīkī Hotel

450 Lewers St, 96815 **Tel** *(808) 923-8828* **Fax** *(808) 923-3473* **Rooms** *80*   **Map** *4 D4*

A favorite of inter-island business travelers, this boutique hotel is just 10 miles (16 km) from Honolulu Airport. Near the Ala Wai waterway, it is ideal for a scenic early morning walk or jog. There are hotel rooms, studio rooms, and suites, most with kitchenettes. **www.coconutwaikikihotel.com**

WAIKĪKĪ Hilton Hawaiian Village Waikīkī Beach Resort

2500 Kūhiō Ave, 96815 **Tel** *(808) 922-0811* **Fax** *(808) 921-5507* **Rooms** *601*   **Map** *4 E4*

A block from the beach and two from Kapi'olani Park *(see pp72–3)*, this hotel nevertheless seems a long way from the Waikīkī crowds. Rooms offer high-speed Internet access, work areas, refrigerators, and telephones with voicemail. There is a fitness center. **www.hiltonwaikikibeach.com**

WAIKĪKĪ Hyatt Regency Waikīkī Resort & Spa

2424 Kalākaua Ave, 96815 **Tel** *(808) 923-1234* **Fax** *(808) 926-3415* **Rooms** *1230*   **Map** *4 E5*

Located in the center of Waikīkī, this impressive resort consists of two 40-story towers joined by an elaborate atrium with an intriguing waterfall. There are lots of things to do at the Hyatt, including working out at the fitness center in the Na Ho'ola Spa, using the pool that overlooks Waikīkī Beach, and, for the kids, Camp Hyatt. **www.hyatt.com**

WAIKĪKĪ Ilima Hotel

445 Nohonani St **Tel** *(808) 923-1877* **Fax** *(808) 924-2617* **Rooms** *98*   **Map** *4 E4*

Many believe this condominium-style hotel offers the best value in Waikīkī. All the studios, one-, two-, and three-bedroom suites are spacious, with kitchens and *lānai* (verandas). HBO, The Disney Channel, and even local calls are included in the low prices. There is a pool, an exercise room, a sauna, and limited free parking as well. **www.ilima.com**

WAIKĪKĪ 'Ohāna East

150 Ka'iulani Ave, 96815 **Tel** *(808) 922-5353* **Fax** *(808) 954-8800* **Rooms** *441*   **Map** *4 E4*

'Ohāna means family in Hawaiian and this is a good choice for family vacations. Standard hotel rooms, and studios with kitchenettes, are available. The Nintendo games in each room will keep the kids busy when you are not out or using the pool or restaurants. It is a short walk to the beach, shopping, and attractions. **www.ohanahotels.com**

WAIKĪKĪ Outrigger Reef on the Beach

2169 Kālia Rd, 96815 **Tel** *(808) 923-3111* **Fax** *(808) 924-4957* **Rooms** *858*   **Map** *4 D5*

This beachfront hotel is a good mid-price option; with oustanding decor in the guest rooms, reception and communal areas. Guests from nearby Outrigger hotels share the amenities, including restaurants, a pool, a spa, a fitness center, wedding planning services, and beach activities. **www.outrigger.com**

WAIKĪKĪ Outrigger Waikīkī on the Beach

2335 Kalākaua Ave, 96815 **Tel** *(808) 923-0711* **Fax** *(808) 921-9749* **Rooms** *530*   **Map** *4 E5*

This flagship of the Outrigger chain has a prime oceanfront location and plenty of amenities. It has five restaurants and three lounges, some with popular live entertainment nightly. Rooms are large and views determine prices. The hotel offers a wide range of Hawaiian cultural programs, displays, and workshops. **www.outrigger.com**

WAIKĪKĪ Outrigger Waikīkī Shore

2161 Kālia Rd, 96815 **Tel** *(808) 922-3871* **Fax** *(808) 922-3887* **Rooms** *37*   **Map** *4 D5*

The only resort condominium on Waikīkī Beach has studio units with kitchenettes and one- and two-bedroom units with full kitchens; all have washer-dryers. Guests can make use of the amenities at the Outrigger Reef on the Beach next door, including the pool, restaurants, Serenity Spa Hawai'i, and weekly activities. **www.outrigger.com**

WAIKĪKĪ Pacific Beach Hotel

2490 Kalākaua Ave, 96815 **Tel** *(808) 922-1233* **Fax** *(808) 922-8061* **Rooms** *837*   **Map** *4 F5*

The main attraction at this twin-tower hotel is the three-story Oceanarium, containing nearly 400 marine creatures. It is possible to dine beside the Oceanarium at all three restaurants. Every room has a private *lānai* (veranda) with a panoramic view, digital telephone, Internet access, and video games. **www.pacificbeachhotel.com**

WAIKĪKĪ Queen Kapi'olani Hotel

150 Kapahulu Ave, 96815 **Tel** *(808) 922-1941* **Fax** *(808) 922-2694* **Rooms** *312*   **Map** *4 F5*

Overlooking Kapi'olani Park *(see pp72–3)* and Diamond Head, this simple high-rise is good value. Named for the wife of Hawai'i's last king, it has an ambience that recalls the grandeur of her era. As well as being across the street from Kapi'olani Park, it is a short walk to the beach and close to other major attractions. **www.aquaresorts.com**

WAIKĪKĪ Royal Garden at Waikīkī $$$

440 Olohāna St, 96815 **Tel** *(808) 943-0202* **Fax** *(808) 945-7407* **Rooms** *220*   **Map** *4 D4*

This boutique hotel is a luxurious breath of fresh air. Located on a peaceful, tree-lined street, a half block from the Ala Wai Canal, it is quiet and beautifully appointed. Rooms have one king, one queen, or two twin beds, a small refrigerator, and Internet access. There is a pool, a sauna, and a restaurant. **www.royalgardens.com**

WAIKĪKĪ Sheraton Princess Ka'iulani $$$

120 Ka'iulani Ave, 96815 **Tel** *(808) 922-5811* **Fax** *(808) 931-4577* **Rooms** *1147*   **Map** *4 E4*

Named for Hawai'i's last princess (her royal estate was located here), this comfortable hotel has all the advantages of a Sheraton without the oceanfront prices. Every room has a *lānai* (veranda). A huge swimming pool, shops, restaurants, and the popular cocktail-dinner show "Creation - A Polynesian Journey" are on offer. **www.princess-kaiulani.com**

WAIKĪKĪ Sheraton Waikīkī Hotel $$$

2255 Kalākaua Ave, 96815 **Tel** *(808) 922-4422* **Fax** *(808) 931-8883* **Rooms** *1764*   **Map** *4 D5*

Sleek and modern, this towering 1,764-room hotel has a prime location on the beach at Waikīkī. Most rooms have fantastic ocean views. An exterior glass elevator rises up to the Leahi Club, from which, at night, guests can view the sparkling lights of the city below. A pool, fitness center, and shops are on site. **www.sheraton-waikiki.com**

WAIKĪKĪ Waikīkī Sand Villa Hotel $$$

2375 Ala Moana Blvd, 96815 **Tel** *(808) 922-4744* **Fax** *(808) 926-7587* **Rooms** *214*   **Map** *4 E4*

Near Waikīkī Beach, this ten-story hotel has affordable, good-sized rooms and studio apartments. The kidney-shaped swimming pool is the setting for the complimentary continental breakfast. Each room has free unlimited high-speed Internet access and there is also an Internet center. **www.waikikisandvillahotel.com**

WAIKĪKĪ Moana Surfrider $$$$

2365 Kalākaua Ave, 96815 **Tel** *(808) 922-3111* **Fax** *(808) 924-4799* **Rooms** *791*   **Map** *4 E5*

This stunning "First Lady of Waikīkī," whose central section was built in 1901, combines modern comforts with high elegance. The hotel has retained many of its Victorian features, such as the *porte-cochère*, or replicated them, as in the case of the ornate plasterwork. On-site acitivites include a children's program. **www.moana-surfrider-com**

WAIKĪKĪ Waikīkī Beach Marriott Resort & Spa $$$$

2552 Kalākaua Ave, 96815 **Tel** *(808) 922-6611* **Fax** *(808) 921-5255* **Rooms** *1310*   **Map** *4 F5*

Once the site of Queen Liliu'okalani's summer homes, this large resort is next to Kūhīo Beach in the heart of Waikīkī. Two towers house attractively decorated rooms and many amenities. The resort includes several restaurants, two swimming pools, and a spa created by world-famous hairstylist Paul Brown. **www.marriottwaikiki.com**

WAIKĪKĪ Waikīkī Parc $$$$

2233 Helumoa Rd, 96815 **Tel** *(808) 921-7272* **Fax** *(808) 923-1336* **Rooms** *297*   **Map** *4 D5*

This friendly, intimate hotel offers affordable luxury in a great location. Guests here enjoy privileges at the Halekulani, the Waikīkī Parc's sister hotel, which is right across the street on Waikīkī Beach. The Parc's comfortable rooms have sitting areas, desks, and *lānai* (verandas), with either ocean, mountain, or city views. **www.waikikiparc.com**

WAIKĪKĪ Aston Waikīkī Beach Tower $$$$$

2470 Kalākaua Ave, 96815 **Tel** *(808) 926-6400* **Fax** *(808) 926-7380* **Rooms** *98*   **Map** *4 F5*

These one- and two-bedroom suites, with kitchens and washer-dryers, are well-furnished and have spacious *lānai* (verandas) overlooking Waikīkī Beach. A twice daily maid service is provided. Amenities include a heated outdoor pool, jet spa, paddle tennis court, and billiards area. Complimentary valet parking is a plus. **www.astonhotels.com**

WAIKĪKĪ Halekulani $$$$$

2199 Kālia Rd, 96815 **Tel** *(808) 923-2311* **Fax** *(808) 926-8004* **Rooms** *456*   **Map** *4 D5*

The Halekulani is the epitome of elegance. Everything is perfect: the impeccable service, the manicured tropical grounds, the tasteful decor, the spacious rooms, the luxurious spa, and the superb cuisine at La Mer *(see p197)*. The hotel stands on extensive grounds on Waikīkī Beach Front and almost all rooms face the ocean. **www.halekulani.com**

WAIKĪKĪ The Royal Hawaiian $$$$$

2259 Kalākaua Ave, 96815 **Tel** *(808) 923-7311* **Fax** *(808) 931-7098* **Rooms** *528*   **Map** *4 D5*

This elegant Waikīkī hotel, affectionately known as the Pink Palace of the Pacific, has been restored to its original grandeur. Right on the beach and surrounded by lush tropical gardens, the hotel has been a Waikīkī landmark since 1927, hosting movie stars and heads of state. **www.royal-hawaiian.com**

WAIKĪKĪ Trump International Hotel & Tower $$$$$

223 Saratoga Rd, 96815 **Tel** *(808) 683-7495* **Rooms** *462*   **Map** *4 D5*

The first luxury property to be built in Waikīkī in many years, Trump Waikīkī has almost all the high-end amenities imaginable. The 38-story tower provides magnificent views from sumptuously appointed studio, one-, two- and three-bedroom suites. The term "Ritzy" may now be replaced by "Trumpy." **www.trumpwaikiki.com**

GREATER HONOLULU Ala Moana Hotel $$

410 Atkinson Dr, 96814 **Tel** *(808) 955-4811* **Fax** *(808) 944-6839* **Rooms** *1058*   **Map** *3 A4*

Set near the popular Ala Moana Beach Park, the Hawai'i Convention Center, and the Ala Moana Shopping Center, this 36-story hotel offers many amenities at reasonable prices. These include three restaurants, a nightclub, a good fitness center, a swimming pool, and direct access to the Ala Moana Shopping Center. **www.outrigger.com**

Key to Price Guide *see p178* **Key to Symbols** *see back cover flap*

GREATER HONOLULU Aloha Bed & Breakfast

$$

909 Kahauloa Pl, 96825 **Tel** *(808) 395-6694* **Fax** *(808) 396-2020* **Rooms** *3*   **Map** *4 F5*

Comprised of three guest rooms with a shared bath, this affordable B&B in residential, upscale Hawai'i Kai has panoramic ocean views. One room has a king-sized bed, one a queen, and one two twin beds. It is a 15-minute drive from Waikīkī Beach Front and close to local dining and shopping. **http://home.roadrunner.com/~alohaphyllis**

GREATER HONOLULU Doubletree Alana Hotel-Waikīkī

$$

1956 Ala Moana Blvd, 96815 **Tel** *(808) 941-7275* **Fax** *(808) 949-0996* **Rooms** *268*   **Map** *3 C4*

This small boutique hotel located at the gateway to Waikīkī has a reputation for hospitality and offers the amenities of a luxury hotel at affordable prices. These include a poolside fitness center, a business center, room service, and in-room massage. Guest rooms are compact, but well equipped. **http://doubletree1.hilton.com**

GREATER HONOLULU Manoa Valley Inn

$$

2001 Vancouver Dr, 96822 **Tel** *(808) 947-6019* **Fax** *(808) 946-4664* **Rooms** *7*   **Map** *4 D1*

Set in beautiful grounds just minutes from Waikīkī, this 1912 home retains its old-fashioned charm. There are seven rooms and also one cottage. Each is distinctively decorated and named for a prominent Hawaiian historical figure. Some rooms share a bath. Rates include continental breakfast. **www.manoavalleyinn.com**

GREATER HONOLULU Pagoda Hotel and Floating Restaurant

$$

1525 Rycroft St, 96814 **Tel** *(808) 941-6611* **Fax** *(808) 955-5067* **Rooms** *360*   **Map** *3 A3*

The Pagoda offers rooms that are unadorned but good value. Close to shopping at the Ala Moana Center, this hotel is a favorite with local residents. Accommodations are standard, studios, and suites. Facilities include free parking, laundry facilities, and a shop. The floating restaurant and water gardens are notable. **www.pagodahotel.com**

GREATER HONOLULU Diamond Head Beach Hotel

$$$

2947 Kalākaua Ave **Tel** *(808) 922-1928* **Fax** *(808) 924-8980* **Rooms** *45*   **Map** *4 F5*

No frills here, but the serene oceanfront setting away from the crowds of Waikīkī makes up for the simplicity. Rooms come with refrigerators and coffee makers; one-bedroom suites have full kitchens. All are air-conditioned and many have large private *lānai* (verandas). Kalākaua Avenue is a short walk away. **www.obrhihotel.com**

GREATER HONOLULU Hawai'i Prince Hotel Waikīkī

$$$

100 Holomoana St, 96815 **Tel** *(808) 956-1111* **Fax** *(808) 946-0811* **Rooms** *578*   **Map** *3 A4*

Every room at this marina-front hotel has a panoramic ocean view, but only a few have a *lānai* (veranda). There are two award-winning restaurants, a day spa, a fitness center, a business center, and tennis courts. Located near the Ala Moana Shopping Center, the hotel is also close to Waikīkī and downtown Honolulu. **www.princeresortshawaii.com**

GREATER HONOLULU Hotel Renew

$$$

129 Paoakalani Ave, 96815 **Tel** *(808) 687-7700* **Fax** *(808) 687-7701* **Rooms** *72*   **Map** *4 F4*

A short walk from Waikīkī beach, this small boutique hotel has much to offer. The decor is Asian-inspired and is sleek, modern, and minimalist. Complimentary amenities include breakfast, cocktail parties, beach gear use, and Wi-Fi. Children under 18 can stay with parents free of cost and small dogs are welcome. **www.hotelrenew.com**

GREATER HONOLULU Ilikai Hotel & Suites

$$$

1777 Ala Moana Blvd, 96815 **Tel** *(808) 949-3811* **Fax** *(808) 947-0892* **Rooms** *696*   **Map** *3 B4*

This hotel is convenient for Waikīkī beaches, the Ala Moana Shopping Center, and Beach Park. Its main attractions are Sarento's Top of the I Restaurant, and 24-hour fitness center. Most of the rooms have *lānai* (verandas) and kitchens. All have televisions with on-demand movies and Internet access. **www.ilikaihotel.com**

GREATER HONOLULU The New Otani Kaimana Beach Hotel

$$$

2863 Kalākaua Ave, 96815 **Tel** *(808) 923-1555* **Fax** *(808) 922-9404* **Rooms** *125*   **Map** *4 F5*

On beautiful San Souci beach, across from Kapi'olani Park *(see pp72–3)*, this boutique hotel has small, but nicely appointed rooms. Choose from tasteful rooms and suites, or studios and one-bedroom suites with kitchenettes. Two seaside restaurants include a Japanese one. Honolulu Zoo and other attractions are nearby. **www.kaimana.com**

GREATER HONOLULU Aqua Lotus at Diamond Head

$$$$$

2885 Kalākaua Ave, 96815 **Tel** *(808) 922-1700* **Fax** *(808) 923-2249* **Rooms** *51*   **Map** *4 F5*

Situated at the base of Diamond Head, this small boutique hotel is only a few minutes away from the activities and attractions of Waikīkī. Each guest room has views of Diamond Head or the ocean. Amenities include high-speed Internet access, cable television, video games, and CD/DVD player. **www.aqualotus.com**

GREATER HONOLULU Hilton Hawaiian Village Beach Resort & Spa

$$$$$

2005 Kālia Rd, 96815 **Tel** *(808) 949-4321* **Fax** *(808) 951-5458* **Rooms** *3886*   **Map** *3 C4*

More like a small city than a hotel, the Hilton has it all: a beach, five pools, 90 shops, a spa, a wedding chapel, tropical gardens, and penguins and other wildlife in the lobby. There are 16 lounges and restaurants. Rooms, in six towers, are equipped with cable television and *lānai* (verandas). **www.hiltonhawaiianvillage.com**

GREATER HONOLULU The Kahala Hotel & Resort

$$$$$

5000 Kahala Ave, 96816 **Tel** *(808) 739-8888* **Fax** *(808) 739-8800* **Rooms** *338*   **Map** *4 F1*

Set in an upscale district, this modern, stylish hotel is fronted by a great swimming beach. There are six restaurants, notably Hoku's, a state-of-the-art fitness center, and a full spa. The property is famous for its lagoon, where guests can get up close and personal with six Atlantic bottlenose dolphins. **www.kahalaresort.com**

O'AHU

HALE'IWA Kē Iki Beach Bungalows   🚶 P $$$

59-579 Kē Iki Rd, 96712 **Tel** *(808) 638-8829* **Fax** *(808) 637-6100* **Rooms** *11*

These modest, yet clean and comfortable beach cottages occupy their own stretch of white sand between the famous surfing beaches of Waimea Bay and Banzai Pipeline. Run by a local resident, they have televisions and kitchens. Outdoors, there are barbecues and hammocks; tennis courts are nearby. **www.keikibeach.com**

HALE'IWA North Shore Vacation Homes   🚶 P $$$

66-250 Kamehameha Hwy, 96712 **Tel** *(808) 637-3507* **Fax** *(808) 637-8881* **Rooms***10*

You will feel like a local staying at one of these beach houses along the North Shore. Furnished rentals have large *lānai* (verandas), spectacular sunset views, and all the comforts of home. The fabled surf of Sunset Beach and Waimea Bay is nearby as are shopping, dining, golf, and other attractions. **www.teamrealestate.com**

KAHUKU Turtle Bay Condominiums   ▦ 🚶 🍴 P $$

55-565 Kamehameha Hwy, 96731 **Tel** *(808) 293-2800* **Fax** *(808) 293-2169* **Rooms** *52*

About an hour away from the bustle of Waikīkī, these large one- and two-bedroom condominium units have full-size kitchens, washer-dryers, telephones, and cable television, making them perfect for families. They are on the golf courses in the Turtle Bay Resort, near famous surfing beaches and major North Shore attractions. **www.turtlebay-rentals.com**

KAHUKU Turtle Bay Resort   🏨 ▦ 🚶 📺 🍴 P $$$$

57-091 Kamehameha Hwy, 96731 **Tel** *(808) 293-6000* **Fax** *(808) 293-9147* **Rooms** *448*

Stretching for 5 miles (8 km) along the coastline, this is the only full-service resort on the North Shore. Amenities include a spa, a fitness center, two championship golf courses, a tennis complex, riding, and water sports. All luxury guest rooms, suites, beach cottages, and villas have ocean views and *lānai* (verandas). **www.turtlebayresort.com**

KAILUA Hawaii's Hidden Hideaway   ▤ P $$$

1369 Mokolea Dr, 96734 **Tel** *(808) 262-6560* **Fax** *(808) 262-6561* **Rooms** *3*

A short walk from Lanikai and Kailua beaches, this privately-owned house is comfortable and well equipped. Choose between a suite with an ocean view and private outdoor Jacuzzi and a studio with a garden view. Both have private entrances, baths, kitchenettes, and televisions. A minimum three-night stay is required. **www.ahawaiibnb.com**

KAILUA Ingrid's Place   ▤ ▦ P $$$

571 Pauku Street **Tel** *(808) 262-8133* **Fax** *(808) 262-5030* **Rooms** *1*

Located in a residential neighborhood just a mile from Kailua Beach, this one-bedroom apartment is decorated in dramatic Japanese style. It has a kitchenette complete with dishwasher, a television, high-speed Internet access, and a large deck. Rates include continental breakfast. A minimum five-night stay is required. **www.bestbnb.com**

KAILUA Lanikai Bed & Breakfast   P $$$

1277 Mokolua Dr, 96734 **Tel** *(808) 261-7895* **Fax** *(808) 262-2181* **Rooms** *2*

In a chic neighborhood across from Lanikai Beach, this bed and breakfast has warm and knowledgeable hosts. The upstairs apartment has a kitchenette, living-dining area, and den. There is also a small, secluded room with a kitchenette. Beverages, breakfast pastries, and chairs and coolers for the beach are provided. **www.lanikaibb.com**

KAILUA Lanikailua Beach Rentals   ▦ 🚶 P $$$

P.O. Box 4731 Kaneohe, 96744 **Tel** *(808) 342-1586* **Rooms** *2*

This rental company offers a wide variety of vacation homes, located along a white, sandy beach. Properties range from studios, one-, and two-bedroom units to private houses with several bedrooms and fully functional kitchens, they are ideal for a peaceful family holiday. **www.lanikailuabeachrentals.com**

KAILUA Pat's Kailua Beach Properties   🍴 P $$$

204 S. Kalāheo Ave, 96734 **Tel** *(808) 261-1653* **Fax** *(808) 261-0893* **Rooms** *34*

The O'Malley's have island-style homes in the beautiful residential areas of Kailua and Lanikai. Ranging from fully-furnished studios to four-bedroom units, they are perfect for families and sleep up to eight people. Some have ocean views and some are beachfront. Weekly rentals are preferred; three nights is the minimum stay. **www.patskailua.com**

KĀNE'OHE Ali'i Bluffs Windward Bed & Breakfast   ▦ P $

46-251 Iki Iki St, 96744 **Tel** *(808) 235-1124* **Fax** *(808) 236-4877* **Rooms** *2*

This European-style bed and breakfast is a short drive from Oahu's best beach. Overlooking Kāne'ohe Bay, it offers two double bedrooms, each with private bath. The Victorian Room is in period style, while the Circus Room has antique circus toys and posters. Continental breakfast and afternoon tea are included. **www.aliibluffshawaii.com**

KĀNE'OHE Paradise Bay Resort Hawaii   ▦ P $$$

47-039 Llihikai Dr, 96744 **Tel** *(808) 239-5711* **Fax** *(808) 239-6658* **Rooms** *22*

In a rural setting on a peninsula 30 minutes from Waikīkī, these modest cottages include complimentary snorkeling and kayaking expeditions. One-, two-, three-, and four-bedroom accommodations with kitchenettes are available. Picnic tables, barbecues, and a pool set the scene for a fun vacation. **www.schradersinn.com**

Key to Price Guide *see p178* **Key to Symbols** *see back cover flap*

WAI'ANAE Aulani, A Disney Resort ⏩ 🛏 🍽 💺 🛁 🛗 🅿 ⑤⑤⑤⑤⑤
92-1185 Ali'inui Dr, Ko Olina Resort **Tel** *(808) 674-6200* **Fax** *(808) 674-6313* **Rooms** *359*

This fabulous resort blends Hawaiian flair with Disney magic. Fantastic water features include slides, lazy rivers, and a private snorkelling lagoon. Rooms at this family friendly resort are comfortable and contemporary; get the kids to look out for Mickey Mouse hidden in the decor. **http://resorts.disney.go.com**

WAI'ANAE JW Marriott 'Ihilani Resort & Spa at Ko Olina Resort 🛏 🍽 💺 🛁 🛗 🅿 ⑤⑤⑤⑤⑤
92-1001 Olani St **Tel** *(808) 679-0079* **Fax** *(808) 679-0080* **Rooms** *423*

This enormous, sprawling property is on the island's leeward side. The rooms are large and luxurious, with marble baths and high-tech systems to control the interior environment. There is an 18-hole championship golf course with clubhouse. The resort's huge spa offers massages, facials, soaks, and scrubs. **www.ihilani.com**

MOLOKA'I AND LĀNA'I

EAST END (MOLOKA'I) Wavecrest 🍽 🛁 🅿 ⑤⑤
Kamehameha V Hwy, Mile Marker 13 **Tel** *(808) 553-8334* **Fax** *(808) 553-8332* **Rooms** *126*

In the lush East End of the island, 13 miles (21 km) past Kaunakakai, are these waterfront condominiums with a pool, cabanas, and tennis courts. Units are individually owned, and reservations are made through an agency. Laundry facilities and Internet access are available on site. **www.molokai-vacation-rental.net**

EAST END (MOLOKA'I) Aloha Beach House 🖥 🅿 ⑤⑤⑤
Kamehameha V Hwy, Mile Marker 19, 96770 **Tel** *(808) 828-1100* **Fax** *(808) 828-2199* **Rooms** *2*

This Hawaiian-style beach house sits right on Waialua's white sand, in the lush East End. It has two bedrooms, an open living-dining area, a complete kitchen (including a dishwasher), a DVD with video library, and beach toys. Its location close to the neighborhood store is a plus on this remote side of the island. **www.kauaisunrise.com**

KALUAKO'I (MOLOKA'I) Kaluako'i Villas 🍽 🛁 🅿 ⑤⑤⑤
1131 Kaluakoi Rd, 96770 **Tel** *(808) 552-2721* **Fax** *(808) 552-2201* **Rooms** *40*

These studio and one-bedroom condos are set in the Kaluakoi Resort on the west coast of Moloka'i. Each has a spacious private *lānai* (veranda) and kitchenette. Guests can sunbathe on the glistening white-sand beach, or stroll in the beautifully landscaped grounds. **www.castleresorts.com**

KALUAKO'I (MOLOKA'I) Ke Nani Kai Resort 🖥 🍽 🅿 ⑤⑤⑤
50 Kepuhi Pl, 96770 **Tel** *(808) 533-3666* **Fax** *(808) 533-3867* **Rooms** *57*

This complex of low-rise condominiums lies along the fairways of the old golf course, within the planned Kaluakoi Resort. Every unit has a private *lānai* (veranda), color television, telephone, kitchen, and washer-dryer. Amenities include a free-form pool, heated whirlpool, tennis courts, and barbecue area. **www.molokai-vacation-rental.net**

KALUAKO'I (MOLOKA'I) Paniolo Hale 🍽 🛁 🅿 ⑤⑤⑤
Lio Pl, 96770 **Tel** *(808) 553-8334* **Fax** *(808) 552-2288* **Rooms** *15*

Situated within the Kaluako'i Resort, these studio, one- and two-bedroom condominiums are individually owned but booked through a rental pool. All are fully furnished and most have a *lānai* (veranda). Tropical landscaping and a pool add island flavor. It is a short walk to the 3-mile (5-km) Papohaku Beach. **www.molokai-vacation-rental.net**

KAUNAKAKAI (MOLOKA'I) Dunbar Beachfront Cottages 🖥 🅿 ⑤⑤
Kamehameha V Hwy, just past Mile Marker 18, 96748 **Tel** *(808) 558-8153* **Fax** *(808) 558-8153* **Rooms** *4*

The two green and white plantation-style cottages sit right at the water's edge on their own secluded beach. Each has two bedrooms, a kitchen, television with VCR, and ceiling fans. Their large decks have views of the nearby islands of Maui, Lānai, and Kaho'olawe. They are truly idyllic and peaceful. **www.molokai-beachfront-cottages.com**

KAUNAKAKAI (MOLOKA'I) Hotel Moloka'i 🛏 🍽 🛁 🅿 ⑤⑤
Kamehameha V Hwy, 96748 **Tel** *(808) 553-5347* **Fax** *(808) 553-5047* **Rooms** *45*

Not fancy, but right on the water and affordable, this is the only centrally located hotel on the island. The oceanfront dining room, Hula Shores *(see p201)*, provides a gathering place for local residents on Friday nights, when everyone brings their 'ukuleles and joins in a Hawaiian jam session by the pool. **www.hotelmolokai.com**

KAUNAKAKAI (MOLOKA'I) Moloka'i Shores 🍽 🛁 🅿 ⑤⑤
Kamehameha V Hwy, 96748 **Tel** *(808) 553-5954* **Fax** *(808) 553-3241* **Rooms** *102*

A few minutes outside of Kaunakakai are these comfortable but basic oceanfront condominiums. One- and two-bedroom units, they have full kitchens and large living rooms. The great view from the swimming pool and barbecue area makes this a perfect whale-watching spot. There are no phones and no air-conditioning. **www.castleresorts.com**

LĀNA'I CITY (LĀNA'I) Dreams Come True 🅿 ⑤⑤
1168 Lāna'i Ave **Tel** *(808) 565-6961* **Fax** *(808) 565-7056* **Rooms** *4*

Built in 1925 in picturesque Lānai City, this bed and breakfast is shaded by papaya, banana, lemon, and avocado trees. The hosts, both jewelers, decorated it with the Asian antiques they collected on their travels. There are four bedrooms and a common area that overlooks the garden. Continental breakfast is included. **www.dreamscometruelanai.com**

LĀNAʻI CITY (LĀNAʻI) Hotel Lānaʻi
🏨 🍴 🅿️ $$

828 Lānaʻi Ave, 96763 **Tel** *(808) 565-7211* **Fax** *(808) 565-6450* **Rooms** *11*

Built in 1923 as a home for plantation executives, this hotel has simple, plantation-style Hawaiian architecture, and tall Cook pines still stand out front. The rooms in this charming rustic place are small, but clean and comfortably furnished. All have private baths. There is an excellent hotel restaurant and a full bar. **www.hotellanai.com**

LĀNAʻI CITY (LĀNAʻI) Four Seasons Resort Lanai, The Lodge at Koʻele
🏨 🏊 🍴 📺 🔧 🅿️ $$$$

1 Keomuku Hwy, 96763 **Tel** *(808) 565-4000* **Fax** *(808) 565-4561* **Rooms** *102*

Here at the edge of Lānai City, 1,700 ft (520 m) above sea level and 8 miles (13 km) from the nearest beach, the air is cool and misty. Rooms have an upcountry elegance and spacious bathrooms. The hotel offers restaurants, two 18-hole championship golf courses, horseback riding, and sporting clays. **www.fourseasons.com/koele**

LĀNAʻI CITY (LĀNAʻI) Captain's Retreat
🅿️ $$$$$

504 Nininiwai Circle, 96763 **Tel** *(914) 275-2628* **Rooms** *4*

Surrounded by towering Cook pine trees in the misty cool air of Lānai City, this two-story cedar home has an upstairs master suite with private bath, and three bedrooms and two bathrooms downstairs. A fireplace, big-screen television, stereo, and VCR are in the living room. Outside, there is a large redwood deck with barbecue. **www.lanairental.com**

MĀNELE BAY (LĀNAʻI) Four Seasons Lānai at Mānele Bay
🏨 🏊 🍴 📺 🔧 🅿️ $$$$$

1 Mānele Bay Rd, 96763 **Tel** *(808) 565-2000* **Fax** *(808) 565-2483* **Rooms** *236*

This hotel commands the sparkling crescent beach at Mānele Bay. Averaging a spacious 700 sq ft (65 sq m), rooms have *lānai* (verandas), LCD televisions, and high-speed Internet access. Bathrooms offer Four Seasons amenities: plush bathrobes, a marble double basin, deep-soaking tub, and separate shower. **www.fourseasons.com/manelebay**

MAUI

HAIKU Maui Vacation Hideaway
🏊 🔧 🅿️ $$

240 N Holokai Rd, 96708 **Tel** *(808) 283-8526* **Fax** *(808) 573-2775* **Rooms** *3*

Surrounded by lush tropical vegetation, these uniquely decorated units have kitchens and Wi-Fi. The hostess lives on-site and provides an eco-friendly environment by not using chemicals or pesticides on the property. Gentle breezes and a saltwater pool fed by a waterfall add to the natural experience. **www.mauivacationhideaway.com**

HAIKU Puʻu Koa
🅿️ $$

66 Puʻukoa Place, 96708 **Tel** *(808) 573-2884* **Rooms** *7*

With a great location for access to the North Shore waves, these affordable studio and one-bedroom apartments in a shady garden setting are a short drive from Pāʻia and Baldwin Beach. The large studios have kitchenettes; the one-bed units have fully equipped kitchens. Haiku town is close by for groceries and restaurants. **www.puukoa.com**

HĀNA Hāna Kai Maui
📺 🏊 🅿️ $$$

1533 Uakea Rd, 96713 **Tel** *(808) 248-8426* **Fax** *(808) 248-7482* **Rooms** *18*

These studio and one-bedroom condominiums are set in a sheltered cove overlooking a black-sand beach. The spacious furnished units have fully equipped kitchens, private *lānai* (verandas), and come with a daily maid service. Children aged six or younger stay free. Discounts are also offered for stays of at least seven nights. **www.hanakaimaui.com**

HĀNA Travaasa Hāna
♿ 🏨 🏊 📺 🅿️ $$$$

5031 Hāna Hwy, 96713 **Tel** *(808) 248-8211* **Fax** *(808) 248-7202* **Rooms** *70*

Located in the serene environs of Hāna, Travaasa Hāna is built in the low-rise, Hawaiian plantation-era style. It offers two accommodation plans: the all-inclusive "Total Travaasa", which includes meals and resort activities such as spa treatments and horseback riding, and the customized 'Your Travaasa'. **www.travaasa.com/hana**

HONOKŌWAI Aston at Papākea Resort
🏊 🔧 📺 🔧 🅿️ $$$$

3543 Lower Honoapiʻilani Rd, 96761 **Tel** *(808) 669-4848* **Fax** *(808) 665-0662* **Rooms** *463*

Five four-story beachfront condominiums offer simple studios to luxurious two-bedroom suites. Amenities include two pools, two huge Jacuzzis, two saunas, floodlit tennis courts, a putting green, and a barbecue area. There are *koi* ponds and tropical gardens that meander down to the beach. It is great for families. **www.astonhotels.com**

KĀʻANAPALI Royal Lahaina Resort
🏨 🏊 🔧 📺 🔧 🅿️ $$$

2780 Kekaʻa Dr, 96761 **Tel** *(808) 661-3611* **Fax** *(808) 661-6150* **Rooms** *516*

The first hotel built in the Kaʻanapali resort in 1962, this property offers up-to-date hotel rooms in high-rise towers, low-rise plantation-style cottages, and a budget inn. Its poolside restaurant serves *mai tais* in an oceanfront setting. Guests can also enjoy a nightly *luʻau* and an 11-court tennis ranch on the property. **www.hawaiihotels.com**

KĀʻANAPALI Aston Kāʻanapali Shores
🏨 🏊 🔧 📺 🔧 🅿️ $$$$

3445 Honoapiʻilani Hwy, 96761 **Tel** *(808) 667-2211* **Fax** *(808) 661-0836* **Rooms** *463*

All studios and suites offer fully equipped kitchens; washer-dryers are available in one- and two-bedroom suites. Guests can enjoy the Ocean Pool and Beach Club Restaurant, the Garden Pool (ideal for kids), three tennis courts, a fitness-massage center, two jet spas, complimentary scuba lessons, and a beautiful beach. **www.astonhotels.com**

KĀ'ANAPALI Kā'anapali Beach Hotel

2525 Kā'anapali Pkwy, 96761 **Tel** (808) 661-0011 **Fax** (808) 667-5978 **Rooms** 432

Right on the beach in the Kā'anapali Resort, this is known as Maui's most Hawaiian hotel. Rooms and suites are furnished island-style and have *lānai* (verandas) looking onto a lush tropical garden. The six-story Maui, Lāna'i, and Kaua'i wings have elevators; the three-story Moloka'i does not. Hawaiian cultural activities abound. **www.kbhmaui.com**

KĀ'ANAPALI Marriott's Maui Ocean Club

100 Nohea Kai Dr, 96761 **Tel** (808) 667-1200 **Fax** (808) 667-8300 **Rooms** 442

One of the first hotels on Maui to spend millions on renovations in order to become vacation ownership properties, the Maui Marriott is a great place to take the kids, with fully equipped apartments, resort amenities, and one of the best locations on Kā'anapali Beach. **www.marriott.com**

KĀ'ANAPALI Hyatt Regency Maui Resort & Spa

200 Nohea Kai Dr, 96761 **Tel** (808) 661-1234 **Fax** (808) 667-4497 **Rooms** 806

The impressive beachfront grounds feature works of art, tropical flowers and plants, exotic birds, a meandering pool with waterfalls, a swinging rope bridge, and an underwater grotto bar. An upscale shopping arcade, restaurants, spa and nightly *lu'au*, are also on site. Rooms have a sitting area and a private *lānai* (veranda). **www.maui.hyatt.com**

KĀ'ANAPALI Kā'anapali Ali'i

50 Nohea Kai Dr, 96761 **Tel** (808) 667-1400 **Fax** (808) 661-5686 **Rooms** 264

This elegant property right on the beach offers one- and two-bedroom condominium units. They are spacious, with full kitchens and sometimes two bathrooms. Nicely furnished, all have air-conditioning, washer-dryers, and a daily maid service. There are tennis courts, a pool, an exercise room, and a beach activity center. **www.kaanapaliali.com**

KĀ'ANAPALI Sheraton Maui

2605 Kā'anapali Pkwy, 96761 **Tel** (808) 661-0031 **Fax** (808) 661-0458 **Rooms** 508

Kā'anapali's first luxury resort hotel sits above Black Rock, but the original 1950s-style decor is gone. Now the furnishings are reminiscent of Hawai'i's plantation era, using natural materials and pastel shades. Almost all guest rooms face the ocean and have air-conditioning, a *lānai* (veranda), and small refrigerator. **www.sheraton-maui.com**

KĀ'ANAPALI The Westin Maui

2365 Kā'anapali Pkwy, 96761 **Tel** (808) 667-2525 **Fax** (808) 661-5764 **Rooms** 758

The rooms are small, but well-appointed at this opulent oceanfront hotel. Asian artwork is found throughout the public areas and the lush tropical grounds, which also have a collection of exotic birds. There are five pools and a huge waterslide, along with restaurants, exclusive boutiques, beach activities, and a spa. **www.westinmaui.com**

KĀ'ANAPALI The Whaler on Kā'anapali Beach

2481 Kā'anapali Pkwy, 96761 **Tel** (808) 661-4861 **Fax** (808) 661-8315 **Rooms** 360

This luxury condominium is situated next to Whalers Village Shopping Center. All suites have fully equipped kitchens and are generously sized. A beachfront swimming pool, five tennis courts, a fitness-massage center, and the beautiful beach are at hand. Fine shops, galleries, and restaurants are in nearby Whalers Village. **www.astonhotels.com**

KAHANA Kahāna Sunset

4909 L Honoapi'ilani Hwy, 96761 **Tel** (808) 669-8700 **Fax** (808) 669-1488 **Rooms** 90

Kahana Sunset has a great location on a white-sand beach surrounded by tropical gardens. Six two- and three-story buildings house 90 units, with modern kitchens, cable television, washer-dryers, and DVDs. Each has a *lānai* (veranda) linked to those of its neighbors. A heated pool, barbecues, and Internet access are on site. **www.kahanasunset.com**

KAPALUA Kapalua Villas

200 Village Rd, 96761 **Tel** (808) 665-5400 **Fax** (808) 669-5234 **Rooms** 280

These spacious one- and two-bedroom condominiums offer oceanfront, ocean-view and fairway-view units in three complexes: The Bay Villas, The Ridge, and the Golf Villas. Guests have full use of Kapalua golf and resort amenities, such as complimentary tennis and discounts in resort shops and restaurants. **www.outrigger.com**

KAPALUA The Ritz-Carlton Kapalua

1 Ritz-Carlton Dr, 96761 **Tel** (808) 669-6200 **Fax** (808) 669-2028 **Rooms** 463

This Ritz is set apart by its Hawaiian cultural program, including hands-on activities, entertainment, special events, seminars, and exhibits. Elegance abounds in the guest rooms and sumptuous Residential Suites. Spa, golf course, a variety of cafés, bars and restaurants, and stunning ocean views complete the picture. **www.ritzcarlton.com**

KĪHEI Hale Hui Kai

2994 S Kīhei Road, 96753 **Tel** (808) 879-1219 **Fax** (808) 875-8242 **Rooms** 59

With two-bedroom, two-bath units in a Hawaiian-style condomium right on the beach, this property is great for families. Units have kitchens and cable television. Laundry facilities on each floor, shuffleboard, a putting green, barbecues, and a recreation area are provided. Dining, shopping, and golf are nearby. **www.halehuikaimaui.com**

KĪHEI Punahoa

2142 Ili'ili Rd, 96753 **Tel** (808) 879-2720 **Fax** (808) 875-9147 **Rooms** 15

All these individually owned studio, one-, and two-bedroom condominium units are oceanfront. Each has one bathroom, a kitchen, a big *lānai* (veranda), cable television, and DVD. The units are in a four-story building with an elevator and laundry facilities. Kama'ole and Kalama Parks flank the property. **www.punahoabeach.com**

KĪHEI Kama'ole Sands Condominiums $$$$

2695 S Kīhei Rd, 96753 **Tel** *(808) 874-8700* **Fax** *(808) 879-3273* **Rooms** *315*

Across the street from the popular Kama'ole Beach Park, this complex offers studios and one-, two-, and three-bedroom suites. All units have a kitchen and *lānai* (veranda). Four tennis courts, a swimming pool, a sun deck, two jet spas, and barbecue areas are set in vast tropical gardens, with ponds, fountains, and waterfalls. **www.castleresorts.com**

KĪHEI Mana Kai Maui Resort $$$$

2960 S Kīhei Rd, 96753 **Tel** *(808) 879-2778* **Fax** *(808) 879-7025* **Rooms** *98*

This high rise is on beautiful, white-sand Keawakapu Beach, right before Wailea. The accommodations are not spectacular, but the location is. One- and two-bedroom condos have kitchens and private *lānai* (verandas). Hotel rooms have baths. An open-air restaurant, general store, and beauty shop are on site. **www.crhmaui.com**

KĪHEI Maui Coast Hotel $$$$

2259 S Kīhei Rd, 96753 **Tel** *(808) 874-6284* **Fax** *(808) 875-4731* **Rooms** *265*

The only full-service hotel in Kīhei offers a reasonably priced alternative to Wailea. Just across the street from a 6-mile (9-km) stretch of sandy beach parks, it has a restaurant, pool, tennis courts, and laundry facilities. Rooms are small, but have fridges, coffee makers, Internet access, air-conditioning, and *lānai* (verandas). **www.mauicoasthotel.com**

KUAU The Inn at Mama's Fish House $$$$

799 Pono Place, off Hana Highway, 96779 **Tel** *(808) 579-9764* **Rooms** *9*

These comfortable, tropical one- and two-bedroom cottages are well appointed with retro Hawaiian-style rattan furniture, local artworks, and fully equipped kitchens. They are situated in a quiet oceanfront neighborhood right next to one of the island's best and most popular restaurants, Mama's Fish House. **www.mamasfishhouse.com**

KULA Kula Lodge $$

15200 Haleakalā Hwy, 96790 **Tel** *(808) 878-1535* **Fax** *(808) 878-2518* **Rooms** *5*

Not what you would expect on a tropical island, this rustic lodge is set in cool, upcountry Maui, where nights can be chilly – two units have gas fireplaces. There's a restaurant with scenic views and an art gallery on site. It's a long ride to the beach, but Kula Lodge is a great romantic getaway. **www.kulalodge.com**

LAHAINA Lahaina Inn $$

127 Lahainaluna Rd, 96761 **Tel** *(808) 661-0577* **Fax** *(808) 667-9480* **Rooms** *12*

This small boutique hotel in the heart of Lahaina has nine rooms and three parlor suites lovingly decorated with authentic Victorian furnishings. There are no televisions in the rooms. The Lahaina Grill restaurant *(see p204)* occupies the first floor; the ocean is half a block away. **www.lahainainn.com**

LAHAINA The Makai Inn $$

1415 Front St, 96761 **Tel** *(808) 662-3200* **Fax** *(808) 661-9027* **Rooms** *18*

A quiet retreat on the edge of Lahaina town, this good-value inn sits right on the beach. The Makai has modest one-bedroom units with kitchens. Shops, restaurants, and the action of Front Street are just a few blocks away. Clean and comfortable, if not luxurious (there are no TVs or air-conditioning in the rooms). **www.makaiinn.net**

LAHAINA The Pioneer Inn $$

658 Wharf St, 96761 **Tel** *(808) 661-3636* **Fax** *(808) 667-5708* **Rooms** *34*

The Pioneer Inn's colorful history dates back to 1910, when a Canadian Mountie came to Maui to catch his man. Now managed by Best Western, its rooms are not deluxe, but the location is: right at the water's edge in scenic Lahaina Harbor. Rooms are on the second floor. There is a pool, a rowdy bar, and a restaurant. **www.pioneerinnmaui.com**

LAHAINA The Plantation Inn $$

174 Lahainaluna Rd, 96761 **Tel** *(808) 667-9225* **Fax** *(808) 667-9293* **Rooms** *19*

Steps from the waterfront, this charming inn combines plantation style with modern convenience. Romantic island-style guest rooms have *lānai* (verandas); suites have kitchenettes. Breakfast is served around the pool, a delightful garden oasis in hot Lahaina town. Gerard's Restaurant *(see p204)* is on the first floor. **www.theplantationinn.com**

LAHAINA Lahaina Shores Beach Resort $$$$

475 Front St, 96761 **Tel** *(808) 661-4835* **Fax** *(808) 661-4696* **Rooms** *200*

This hotel is right on the beach and offers great value. Accommodations include studios, one-bedroom, and penthouse suites with full kitchens, *lānai* (verandas), and ocean or mountain views. Right next to the 505 Front Street shopping village, with restaurants and boutiques, the hotel is a short walk from the center of town. **www.lahainashores.com**

MAKAWAO Banyan Tree House $$

3265 Baldwin Ave, 96768 **Tel** *(808) 572-9021* **Fax** *(808) 573-5073* **Rooms** *7*

Accommodations here are in a classic Hawaiian pineapple plantation home and four cottages. The historic main house has three bedrooms and three baths. The cottages have bathrooms and phones; some have kitchens. Between Pā'ia and Makawao, the location offers sweeping views of the ocean and nearby islands. **www.banyantreehouse.com**

MĀKENA Mākena Beach & Golf Resort $$$$

5400 Mākena Alanui, 96753 **Tel** *(808) 874-1111* **Fax** *(808) 879-8763* **Rooms** *310*

Standing alone in Mākena, this gleaming, wing-shaped hotel fronts a big, beautiful beach. The guest rooms are stylishly simple in their design. Some are oceanfront and all have an ocean view. Three restaurants, two pools, six tennis courts, and 18 holes of championship golf are some of the amenities on offer. **www.makenaresortmaui.com**

Key to Price Guide *see p178* **Key to Symbols** *see back cover flap*

NĀPILI Outrigger Napili Shores Resort   ⬛🏊♿🛏🅿 $$$

5315 Lower Honoapi'ilani Rd, 96761 **Tel** *(808) 669-8061* **Fax** *(808) 669-5407* **Rooms** *152*

Perched at one end of crescent-shaped Napili Bay, these studio and one-bedroom units have *lānai* (verandas) and full kitchens. There is a restaurant and a grocery store, along with two pools, an adult hot tub, a croquet lawn, and a barbecue area. This is a great location for viewing sunsets and seasonal whale watching. **www.outrigger.com**

NĀPILI Napili Kai Beach Resort   ⬛🏊♿🛏🅿 $$$$

5900 Lower Honoapi'ilani Rd, 96761 **Tel** *(808) 669-6271* **Fax** *(808) 669-0086* **Rooms** *163*

This older, spacious and graceful property commands one of the best beach locations on the island. It offers hotel rooms, studios and one- and two-bedrooms suites, almost all with ocean views. There are four pools, a Jacuzzi, putting greens, an exercise room, and an oceanfront restaurant in the lush, tropical grounds. **www.napilikai.com**

WAILEA Paia Inn Hotel   ♿🏊🅿 $$

93 Hāna Hwy, 96779 **Tel** *(808) 579-6000* **Fax** *(808) 579-6001* **Rooms** *15*

Located in the heart of Paia, a former plantation town, this hotel was built in 1927 as a boarding house, and it reopened in 2008 as a hip property. The rooms although small, are well-furnished complete with flatscreen TVs and minibars. Shops, restaurants and beaches lie close by. No elevator facility to rooms on the second floor. **www.paiainn.com**

WAILEA Mākena Surf   🏊🛏🅿 $$$$

96 Mākena Alanui, 96753 **Tel** *(808) 891-6249* **Fax** *(808) 874-3554* **Rooms** *107*

Managed by Destination Resorts Hawai'i, these one, two-, three-, and four-bedroom condominiums are big, have huge *lānai* (verandas), and feel secluded. They offer all the comforts of home, including pleasant furnishings and full kitchens, plus extras such as a wet bar and a housekeeping service. **www.drhmaui.com**

WAILEA Palms at Wailea   🏊🛏🅿 $$$$

3200 Wailea Alanui, 96753 **Tel** *(808) 879-5800* **Fax** *(808) 874-3723* **Rooms** *150*

These spacious one- and two-bedroom units in the upscale resort of Wailea offer great value. Each is well decorated, has a big kitchen, washer-dryer, comfortable living and dining areas, and a private *lānai* (veranda). There are verdant tropical gardens and a pool. The beach is a short downhill walk away. **www.outrigger.com**

WAILEA 'Ekahi, 'Elua and 'Ekolu   🏊📺🛏🅿 $$$$$

3750 Wailea Alanui, 96753 **Tel** *(808) 891-6249* **Fax** *(808) 874-3554* **Rooms** *594*

Many of these individually owned condominium units (managed by Destination Resorts Hawaii) in upscale Wailea offer contemporary furnishings and custom appliances. All have air-conditioning, high-speed Internet, and daily housekeeping. A good-value option in this pricey resort community. **www.drhmaui.com.com**

WAILEA The Fairmont Kea Lani Maui   ⬛🏊🛏📺🛏🅿 $$$$$

4100 Wailea Alanui, 96753 **Tel** *(808) 875-4100* **Fax** *(808) 875-2250* **Rooms** *450*

With its stark, onion-domed exterior, it looks like a castle from the Arabian Nights. Inside, it has a cool, luxurious island ambience. All rooms are suites with sitting rooms and huge marble bathrooms. There are 37 oceanfront one-, two-, and three-bedroom villas, each with a private pool. Three restaurants and a spa are here, too. **www.fairmont.com/kealani**

WAILEA Four Seasons Resort Maui   ⬛🏊🛏📺🛏🅿 $$$$$

3900 Wailea Alanui, 96753 **Tel** *(808) 874-8000* **Fax** *(808) 891-7086* **Rooms** *301*

Huge guest rooms, imposing furnishings, elegant decor, and incredible service: all trademarks of Four Seasons resorts are available on a sparkling beach in Wailea. There are three restaurants, including Spago *(see p206)*, a spa, and a beauty salon. At the two pools, an attendant will, on request, cool your face with a water spritz. **www.fourseasons.com**

WAILEA Grand Wailea Resort, Hotel & Spa   ⬛🏊🛏📺🛏🅿 $$$$$

3850 Wailea Alanui, 96753 **Tel** *(808) 875-1234* **Fax** *(808) 874-2411* **Rooms** *780*

Grand is the word for this opulent beachfront resort, a fantasy land of art and ambience set in sprawling tropical grounds with awesome water features: waterfalls, streams, rapids, slides, reflecting pools, swimming pools, and a saltwater lagoon. Rooms are on a grand scale too, as are the bathtubs. The spa is legendary. **www.grandwailea.com**

WAILEA Wailea Beach Marriott Resort & Spa   ⬛🏊🛏📺🛏🅿 $$$$$

3700 Wailea Alanui, 96753 **Tel** *(808) 879-1922* **Fax** *(808) 875-4878* **Rooms** *423*

Set on a rocky promontory between two sparkling white-sand beaches, this sprawling property has restaurants, pools (infinity and children's), and a spa. Rooms are quite large, with refrigerators, cable television, and an ocean view in most cases. An oceanfront *lu'au* rounds out the resort experience here. **www.marriott.com**

WAILUKU Banana Bungalow   🅿 $

310 N Market St, 96793 **Tel** *(808) 244-5090* **Rooms** *28*

The Banana Bungalow offers probably the least expensive accommodation on Maui. It has both private and dorm rooms. Kitchen facilities, a Jacuzzi, and high-speed Internet are available on-site. Not large or luxurious, but excellent value. Daily free tours are offered to Hana, beaches, and Haleakala. **www.mauihostel.com**

WAILUKU Old Wailuku Inn at Ulapono   🖉🛏🛏🅿 $$

2199 Kaho'okele St, 96793 **Tel** *(808) 244-5897* **Fax** *(808) 242-9600* **Rooms** *10*

Built in 1924 by a wealthy banker as a wedding gift for his daughter, this historic home has been lovingly restored by hosts Tom and Janice Fairbanks. The ambience of an earlier gracious time is prevalent throughout. This cool, open, and airy house has guest rooms named for Hawaiian flowers, with quilts to match. **www.mauiinn.com**

HAWAI'I ISLAND

HILO Hilo Hawaiian Hotel ⊞⛱🏃👤🅿 $$
71 Banyan Dr, 96720 **Tel** *(808) 935-9361* **Fax** *(808) 961-9642* **Rooms** *286*

The views from the guest rooms here are the best in Hilo. All have air-conditioning, televisions, on-demand movies, coffee makers, and baths. Suites offer good value for families as they include a kitchen and living-dining area. Guest services include a laundromat, free parking, a pool, restaurants, and a day spa. **www.castleresorts.com**

HILO Hilo Seaside Hotel ⊞⛱🏃👤🅿 $$
126 Banyan Dr, 96720 **Tel** *(808) 935-0821* **Fax** *(808) 969-9195* **Rooms** *135*

Rooms here are not fancy, but affordable, clean, and well kept; all have refrigerators, televisions, air-conditioning, ceiling fans, and *lānai* (verandas). The pretty tropical gardens include *koi* ponds and colorful flowers, and there is a pool. It is a 45-minute drive from Hawai'i Volcanoes National Park *(see pp152–5)*. **www.seasidehotelshawaii.com**

HILO Naniloa Volcanoes Resort ⊞⛱🏃📺👤🅿 $$
93 Banyan Dr, 96720 **Tel** *(808) 969-3333* **Fax** *(808) 969-6622* **Rooms** *383*

This affordable resort is a Hilo landmark. Rooms are air-conditioned and have TVs and refrigerators. There are two pools, a spa, and a restaurant on the property. Right on Hilo Bay, it is well placed for a trip to Hawai'i Volcanoes National Park *(see pp152–5)*. **www.hottours.us**

HILO Uncle Billy's Hilo Bay Hotel ⊞⛱🏃👤🅿 $$
87 Banyan Dr, 96720 **Tel** *(808) 935-0861* **Fax** *(808) 935-7903* **Rooms** *143*

Uncle Billy's is the least expensive place to stay on Hilo Bay. The rooms have televisions and air-conditioning; some have kitchenettes. The on-site general store offers deli-style food, souvenirs, sundries, and resort apparel. This is the place for a fun, island-style experience. **www.unclebilly.com**

KAILUA-KONA Outrigger Royal Sea Cliff Resort ⛱🏃👤🅿 $$
75-6040 Alii Dr, 96740 **Tel** *(808) 329-8021* **Fax** *(808) 326-1887* **Rooms** *148*

Rising high above a lava rock bluff looking out toward the sea, the terraced design here provides uninterrupted ocean views from balconies that are a feature of the one- and two-bedroom villas. Units have kitchens and washer-dryers. The lush tropical grounds include a cascading water feature and two oceanfront pools. **www.outrigger.com**

KAILUA-KONA Royal Kona Resort ⊞⛱🏃📺🅿 $$
75-5852 Ali'i Dr, 96740 **Tel** *(808) 329-3111* **Fax** *(808) 329-2230* **Rooms** *436*

Perched oceanfront on Kailua Bay, there are the usual resort amenities to enjoy, such as a multi-level swimming pool and a saltwater lagoon. Guest rooms have granite countertops and marble showers; all have *lānai* (verandas). Don the Beachcomber restaurant is on the property. **www.royalkona.com**

KAILUA-KONA King Kamehameha Kona Beach Hotel ⊞⛱🏃👤🅿 $$$
75-5660 Palani Rd, 96740 **Tel** *(808) 329-2911* **Fax** *(808) 329-4602* **Rooms** *460*

This hotel has a fabulous location, with its own beach in downtown Kailua-Kona. This is an old property now totally renovated with modern amenities including a restaurant, a pool, Jacuzzi, tennis courts, a shopping arcade, and a Hawaiian cultural activity center. **www.konabeachhotel.com**

KAILUA-KONA Aston Kona By The Sea ⛱🏃👤🅿 $$$$
75-6106 Alii Dr, 96740 **Tel** *(808) 327-2300* **Fax** *(808) 327-2333* **Rooms** *56*

Situated along a rocky shoreline, this four-story condominium complex has an oceanfront swimming pool and Jacuzzi. Redecorated to reflect a casual Hawaiian style, the large one- and two-bedroom suites have kitchens and *lānai* (verandas) with ocean views. Golf, tennis, shops, and restaurants are nearby. **www.astonhotels.com**

KAILUA-KONA Holualoa Inn ♿⛱🅿 $$$$
76-5932 Mamalahoa Hwy, 96725 **Tel** *(808) 324-1121* **Fax** *(808) 322-2472* **Rooms** *6*

Set amid a lush tropical coffee estate, this Inn offers rooms with comfortable sitting areas and a shared guest kitchen-ette. The breakfast is created from homegrown produce and includes coffee, fresh fruits, eggs, and homemade breads and jams. Guests can explore old Hawaiian trails or relax in a rooftop gazebo. **www.holualohainn.com**

KEAUHOU Outrigger Keauhou Beach Resort & Spa ⊞⛱🏃📺👤🅿 $$
75-6740 Ali'i Dr, 96740 **Tel** *(808) 332-3441* **Fax** *(808) 322-3117* **Rooms** *309*

This hotel sits right on the ocean and has easy-to-explore tidepools full of fascinating marine life, such as reef fish and sea turtles. There are interesting spots on land, too, including the remains of three Hawaiian *heiau* (ancient temples) and a replica of King David Kalākaua's summer cottage. Resort amentities include a spa. **www.outrigger.com**

KEAUHOU Outrigger Kanaloa at Kona ⛱🏃👤🅿 $$$$
78-261 Manukai St, 96740 **Tel** *(808) 322-9625* **Fax** *(808) 322-3818* **Rooms** *166*

These oceanfront apartments range in size from one bedroom to two bedrooms with a loft. They are roomy and have open-beamed ceilings, family-sized kitchens, washer-dryers, and covered *lānai* (verandas). There are three pools, two tennis courts, and barbecue grills. Golf and shopping are available nearby. **www.outrigger.com**

Key to Price Guide *see p178* **Key to Symbols** *see back cover flap*

KEAUHOU Sheraton Keauhou Bay Resort & Spa · ⊞ ≋ ⧊ ⊠ ⬛ ⊞ $$$$$$
78-128 Ehukai St Tel (808) 930-4900 Fax (808) 930-4800 Rooms 509

Perched on an old lava flow, this resort has modern rooms and the latest amenities: a fantasy pool with the island's largest waterslide, a spa, golf, tennis, restaurants, and children's programs. Just about everything is modern, but in time honored tradition the manta rays still come for their nightly visits. **www.sheratonkeauhou.com**

KOHALA COAST Waikoloa Beach Marriott Resort · ⊞ ≋ ⧊ ⊠ ⬛ ⊞ $$$
69-275 Waikoloa Beach Dr, 96738 Tel (808) 886-6789 Fax (808) 886-3601 Rooms 555

The location of this resort on 'Anaeho'omalu Bay (or A-Bay, as it is known locally) is its most outstanding feature. The beach is good for swimming, snorkeling, diving, kayaking, windsurfing, and exploring ancient royal fish ponds. This hotel is not as luxurious as some of its Kohala Coast neighbors, but lower room rates reflect this. **www.marriott.com**

KOHALA COAST Fairmont Orchid Hawaii · ⊞ ≋ ⧊ ⊠ ⬛ ⊞ $$$$$$
1 North Kanikū Dr, 96743 Tel (808) 885-2000 Fax (808) 885-5778 Rooms 483

The spacious rooms in this luxury hotel have big *lānai* (verandas), sitting areas, and marble bathrooms, each with a double sink and separate shower. Active travelers will love the outdoor spa, fitness center, oceanfront pool, canoe paddling, 36 holes of championship golf, 10 tennis courts, and many cultural activities. **www.fairmont.com/orchid**

KOHALA COAST Four Seasons Resort Hualalai · ⊞ ≋ ⧊ ⊠ ⬛ ⊞ $$$$$$
72-100 Ka'upulehu Dr, 96740 Tel (808) 325-8000 Fax (808) 325-8053 Rooms 243

Luxurious oceanfront accommodations are available here in bungalows that surround three swimming pools. There are five pools on the property; one of them is a saltwater pond containing colorful reef fish. An award-winning spa and further luxurious resort amenities pamper the guests at this beautiful resort. **www.fourseasons.com/hualalai**

KOHALA COAST Hāpuna Beach Prince Hotel · ⊞ ≋ ⧊ ⊠ ⬛ ⊞ $$$$$$
62-100 Kaunaoa Dr, 96743 Tel (808) 880-1111 Fax (808) 880-3142 Rooms 350

This stylish, low-key resort nestles beside the island's best beach. Guest rooms face the ocean and have private *lānai* (verandas), entertainment centers, refrigerators, and bathrobes. Amenities include a spa, golf, tennis courts, five restaurants. **www.princeresortshawaii.com**

KOHALA COAST Hilton Waikoloa Village Resort · ⊞ ≋ ⧊ ⊠ ⬛ ⊞ $$$$$$
69-425 Waikoloa Beach Dr Tel (808) 886-1234 Fax (808) 886-2902 Rooms 1,240

Set in extensive and beautiful grounds, this is the giant among Kohala's resorts. There are the usual activities – tennis, golf, and a pool – and a program in which guests can swim with Atlantic bottlenose dolphins. The resort transportation takes the form of Swiss-made trams and mahogany boats. **www.hiltonwaikoloavillage.com**

KOHALA COAST Mauna Kea Beach Hotel · ⊞ ≋ ⧊ ⊠ ⬛ ⊞ $$$$$$
62-100 Mauna Kea Beach Dr, 96743 Tel (808) 882-72222 Fax (808) 882-5700 Rooms 258

The Big Island's first big resort, the Mauna Kea is still one of the best in Hawai'i. It has been extensively renovated and upgraded with fewer, more spacious rooms. Rooms have *lānai* (verandas), and residents can enjoy the remarkable collection of museum-quality Pacific and Asian art and artifacts. **www.princeresortshawaii.com**

KOHALA COAST Mauna Lani Bay Hotel & Bungalows · ⊞ ≋ ⧊ ⊠ ⬛ ⊞ $$$$$$
68-1400 Mauna Lani Dr, 96743 Tel (808) 885-6622 Fax (808) 885-1484 Rooms 355

The rooms here are large and all but 27 have ocean views. Every room has a *lānai* (veranda), air-conditioning, robes, coffee, and other high-end touches. Amenities include five restaurants, a spa, a sports and fitness club, tennis courts, two golf courses, water sports, and a Hawaiian cultural program. **www.maunalani.com**

VOLCANO VILLAGE Chalet Kīlauea – The Inn at Volcano · ⧊ ⬛ ⊞ $$$
Wright Rd & Laukapu Rd, 96785 Tel (808) 967-7786 Fax (808) 967-8660 Rooms 5

The rooms at this charming, affordable place are individually decorated and have names such as Out of Africa. They are adorned with art and memorabilia from the travels of the chalet's owners. Guests begin their day with the sounds of the rain forest, and enjoy afternoon tea in the living room. **www.volcano-hawaii.com**

VOLCANO VILLAGE Kīlauea Lodge · ⊞ ⧊ $$$
19-3948 Old Volcanco Rd, 96785 Tel (808) 967-7366 Fax (808) 967-7367 Rooms 17

Built as a YMCA camp in 1938, this refurbished lodge is just a mile (1.6 km) from Hawai'i Volcanoes National Park *(see pp152–5).* There are 12 rooms and three vacation cottages. Some rooms have fireplaces or wood-burning stoves; stained-glass windows feature throughout. Cottages have kitchens and two bedrooms. **www.kilauealodge.com**

WAIMEA Kamuela Inn · ⧊ ⬛ ⊞ $$
65-1300 Kawaihae Rd, 96743 Tel (808) 885-4243 Fax (808) 885-8857 Rooms 31

At this tranquil, private bed and breakfast, old-world charm is combined with all the modern conveniences of home. Rooms and suites have private baths; some have kitchenettes. The inn's location in the quaint town of Waimea is 30 minutes from the island's finest white-sand beaches and 10 minutes from golf courses. **www.hawaii-bnb.com/kamuela**

WAIMEA Waimea Gardens Cottages · ≋ ⊞ $$$
Mamalahoa Hwy Tel (808) 265-3100 Fax (808) 962-6560 Rooms 4

Three cozy cottages set alongside a meandering stream on rolling pasture land. The Waimea Cottage has a fireplace; the Kohala Wing a Japanese-style soaking tub and a private enclosed garden. Both are furnished with antiques and come with plenty of special touches, such as plush robes, bedside mints, and fresh flowers. **www.waimeagardens.com**

KAUA'I

HANALEI Hanalei Colony Resort
5-7130 Kūhiō Hwy, 96714 **Tel** *(808) 826-6235* **Fax** *(808) 826-9893* **Rooms** *52*

This seaside village of two-bedroom condominium units on Kaua'i's north shore offers a peaceful retreat: there are no private phones or televisions. These are, however, available in an oceanfront community room, along with computers and Internet access. Complimentary weekly breakfasts and *mai tai* cocktail parties are held, too. **www.hcr.com**

KALĀHEO Kalāheo Inn
4444 Paplina Rd, 96741 **Tel** *(808) 332-6023* **Fax** *(808) 332-5242* **Rooms** *15*

These one-, two-, and three-bedroom suites are decorated in comfortable island style. They are situated in lush, tropical landscaping, with fruit trees and colorful flowers. Each unit has an equipped kitchenette, television, and DVD. There are laundry facilities and free on-island phone calls. It is a 10-minute drive to Po'ipū beaches. **www.kalaheoinn.com**

KALĀHEO Plantation Hale Suites
525 Aleka Loop, 96746 **Tel** *(808) 822-4941* **Fax** *(808) 822-5599* **Rooms** *110*

Ideal for a peaceful family holiday, this property offers comfortable one-bedroom suites with kitchenettes in attractive, low-rise plantation style buildings. Other features include three pools, barbecue grills, air-conditioning, and a daily maid service. Dining options and places to shop can be found close by. **www.plantation-hale.com**

KAPA'A Kaua'i Sands
420 Papaloa Rd, 96746 **Tel** *(808) 822-4951* **Fax** *(808) 822-0998* **Rooms** *200*

Offering spartan, yet clean beachfront accommodations, this is part of the only Hawaiian-owned hotel chain in the world. Its grounds feature native plants and a walking-jogging path extends for a mile (1.6 km) along the white-sand beach. Golf, tennis, and shopping are nearby. There are self-service laundry facilities. **www.kauaisandshotel.com**

KAPA'A Aloha Beach Resort
3-5920 Kūhiō Hwy, 96746 **Tel** *(808) 823-6000* **Fax** *(808) 823-6666* **Rooms** *216*

Situated on Wailua Bay, this resort is convenient for the airport and many Kaua'i attractions. An affordable full-service, family oriented property, it has rooms, suites, and cottages, plus several restaurants, a spa, a fitness room, two pools, and more. It is close to Lydgate State Park *(see p162)* and a playground. **www.alohabeachresortkauai.com**

KAPA'A Hotel Coral Reef
4-1516 Kūhiō Hwy, 96746 **Tel** *(808) 822-4481* **Fax** *(808) 822-7705* **Rooms** *48*

One of the first hotels built on Kauai's spectacular Royal Coconut Coast, the Coral Reef has been remodeled and offers affordable accommodations. The tropical oceanfront setting on white sandy beaches in the heart of charming Kapa'a is only 10 miles (16 km) from Līhue International Airport. **www.hotelcoralreefresort.com**

KAPA'A Kapa'a Sands Resort
380 Papaloa Rd, 96746 **Tel** *(808) 822-4901* **Fax** *(808) 822-1556* **Rooms** *20*

This affordable oceanfront property offers individually owned studio and two-bedroom condominium units. All are fully furnished and have telephones, televisions, microwaves, and ceiling fans. Shops and restaurants at nearby shopping plazas, hiking trails, waterfalls, and outdoor activities are all close by. **www.kapaasands.com**

KAPA'A Courtyard Kauai at Coconut Beach
650 Aleka Loop, 96746 **Tel** *(808) 822-3455* **Fax** *(808) 822-1830* **Rooms** *315*

Sitting right on the beach and nestled among ancient coconut groves, this luxurious property offers spacious rooms, two restaurants, and a poolside bar. A golf course, places to shop, and other restaurants are in close proximity. The traditional torch lighting ceremony at sunset is a highlight. **www.marriott.com**

KAPA'A Kaua'i Coast Resort at the Beachboy
4-484 Kūhiō Hwy, 96746 **Tel** *(808) 822-3441* **Fax** *(808) 822-0843* **Rooms** *108*

Fronting a long beach, this property offers one- and two-bedroom units, each with a *lānai* (veranda), full kitchen, washer-dryer, air-conditioning, telephone, and television. Studio units have a mini-bar and coffee maker. Choose from the heated pool or the oceanside Jacuzzi. There are shopping and dining options nearby. **www.shellhospitality.com**

KŌKE'E Kōke'e State Park Lodge
3600 Kōke'e Road (Hwy 550), 96796 **Tel** *(808) 335-6061* **Fax** *(808) 335-3519* **Rooms** *12*

Located in Kōke'e State Park *(see pp170–71)*, the Kōke'e Lodge contains a gift shop and restaurant and maintains a dozen cabins. Reservations for the cabins are a must and should be made months in advance. They accommodate up to six and come with bed linens, cooking utensils, and wood for the woodstoves. **www.thelodgeatkokee.net**

KŌLOA Kaua'i Condominiums at Po'ipū Kai Resort
1941 Poipu Rd, 96756 **Tel** *(808) 742-7400* **Fax** *(808) 742-9121* **Rooms** *200*

Set amid extensive tropical gardens, these condominium units have *lānai* (verandas), kitchens, washer-dryers, cable television, stereos, CD players, and telephones with voicemail. Tennis courts, a swimming pool, Jacuzzi, and restaurant are on the resort. Brennecke and Shipwreck beaches are easily accessible. **www.suite-paradise.com**

Key to Price Guide *see p178* **Key to Symbols** *see back cover flap*

LĪHU'E Garden Island Inn   P $$

3445 Wilcox Rd, 96766 **Tel** *(808) 245-7227* **Fax** *(808) 245-7603* **Rooms** *21*

This economically priced inn is conveniently located in the heart of Kauai's bustling Kalapakī Beach-Nāwiliwili Harbor area, minutes from Līhue Airport and only a two minute stroll from Kalapakī Bay. All rooms come with air-conditioning, refrigerators, microwaves, wet bars, cable television, and a daily maid service. **www.gardenislandinn.com**

LĪHU'E Kaua'i Beach Resort $$

4331 Kauai Beach Dr, 96766 **Tel** *(808) 245-1955* **Fax** *(808) 246-3956* **Rooms** *351*

Fronting 3 miles (5 km) of beautiful beach on the east coast of Kaua'i, this plantation-style resort set in its own lush grounds boasts spa, fitness centre, four pools – including two lagoons with waterfalls, and a lava tube waterslide – and much else besides. **www.kauaibeachresorthawaii.com**

LĪHU'E Kaha Lani Resort $$$

4460 Nehe Rd, 96766 **Tel** *(808) 822-9331* **Fax** *(808) 822-2828* **Rooms** *35*

Oceanfront in the heart of Līhue, surrounded by miles of white sandy beaches and lush tropical gardens, these one- and two-bedroom units feature kitchens, views of the Pacific Ocean, and the comforts of home. The resort has barbecue areas, putting greens, tennis, and a pool. Shops and dining are a short drive away. **www.castleresorts.com**

LĪHU'E Kaua'i Marriott Resort & Beach Club $$$$

3610 Rice St, 96766 **Tel** *(808) 245-5050* **Fax** *(808) 245-5049* **Rooms** *345*

This resort stretches along a white-sand beach, just a mile (1.6 km) from Līhue Airport. A spectacular pool, two Jack Nicklaus-designed golf courses, and several restaurants, including the casual Duke's Canoe Club *(see p209)*, are available to guests. In-room amenities include a mini-refrigerator and cable television. **www.marriott.com**

PO'IPŪ Outrigger Kiahuna Plantation $$$

2253 Po'ipū Rd, 96756 **Tel** *(808) 742-6411* **Fax** *(808) 742-1698* **Rooms** *204*

Comfortable and spacious one- and two-bedroom units, in quaint wooden apartments reminiscent of Hawai'i's 19th-century past, are set on an historic expanse of former sugar cane plantation. Units have *lānai* (verandas), fully equipped kitchens, and daily maid service. Shopping and championship golf are nearby. **www.outrigger.com**

PO'IPŪ Sheraton Kauai Resort $$$

2442 Ho'onani Rd, 96756 **Tel** *(808) 742-1661* **Fax** *(808) 742-9777* **Rooms** *394*

Commanding a premier location on famous Po'ipū Beach, and no taller than the coconut trees on the property, this resort offers a full array of services and amenities in a beautiful tropical setting. Hawaiian culture is showcased in the art work dotted around and in activities such as *lei* making and *hula* lessons. **www.sheraton-kauai.com**

PO'IPŪ Aston at Po'ipū Kai $$$$

1775 Po'ipū Rd, 96756 **Tel** *(808) 742-7424* **Fax** *(808) 742-8798* **Rooms** *372*

This resort complex is set on vast grounds in sunny Po'ipū. Accommodations are in five individual communities, each with its own style. All suites are tropically decorated and have kitchens and *lānai* (verandas). Shopping, dining, activities, and sightseeing are nearby. Brennecke and Shipwreck Beaches are a stroll away. **www.astonhotels.com**

PO'IPŪ Grand Hyatt Kauai Resort & Spa $$$$$

1571 Po'ipū Rd, 96756 **Tel** *(808) 742-1234* **Fax** *(808) 742-1557* **Rooms** *602*

Grand is the key word at this elegant and luxurious large oceanfront resort. The lush, tropical grounds include three pools (one with waterfalls), water slides, and meandering saltwater swimming lagoons. A full-service spa, championship golf, tennis, and several restaurants add to the experience. **www.kauaihyatt.com**

PRINCEVILLE Hanalei Bay Resort & Suites $$$

5380 Honoiki Rd, 76722 **Tel** *(808) 826-6522* **Fax** *(808) 826-6680* **Rooms** *182*

Perched above Hanalei Bay, this resort has all the tropical amenities one would want, including fabulous views, lagoon pools with waterfalls, open-air restaurants, tennis courts, and superb golf. The rooms are light and airy, with tropical furnishings, *lānai* (verandas), air-conditioning, telephones, and a daily maid service. **www.hanaleibayresort.com**

PRINCEVILLE The Westin Princeville Ocean Resort Villas $$$

3838 Wyllie Rd, 96722 **Tel** *(808) 827-8700* **Fax** *(808) 827-8701* **Rooms** *346*

This splendid property lies close to the spectacular Nā Pali Coast. It offers studios, one-, and two-bedroom villas featuring kitchens as well as the signature Westin Heavenly beds and Heavenly showers. A small on-site market offers prepared dishes for takeaway or delivery. **www.westinprinceville.com**

PRINCEVILLE St. Regis Princeville Hotel & Resort $$$$$

5520 Ka Haku Rd, 96722 **Tel** *(808) 826-9644* **Fax** *(808) 826-1166* **Rooms** *252*

This elegant resort, built on a bluff above Hanalei Bay, offers exquisite panoramas, spacious rooms, and splendid dining. Uniquely, the lobby is up on the ninth floor and the buildings terrace down to the beach. The views are of waterfalls cascading down verdant cliffs and the sparkling blue Pacific Ocean. **www.princeville.com**

WAIMEA Waimea Plantation Cottages $$$$

9400 Kaumuali'i Hwy, 96796 **Tel** *(808) 338-1625* **Fax** *(808) 338-2338* **Rooms** *47*

Step back into old Hawai'i at these wonderful seaside plantation cottages, set in a coconut grove at the gateway to Waimea Canyon. Situated on the western coast of Kauai, these cottages have all been individually restored, with period-inspired furnishings, kitchens, and a front porch overlooking the grassy lawn. **www.waimea-plantation.com**

WHERE TO EAT

From local-style drive-ins to elegant dining rooms, the opportunities for eating well in Hawai'i are endless. In addition to hundreds of restaurants of every description, there are informal outlets – such as street stalls, delis, and coffeehouses – that sell delicious, cheap food, which is perfect for a quick bite between bouts of sightseeing. In large shopping malls, food courts offer a wide,

Colorful sign in Kaua'i

surprisingly good array of ethnic and American food, and for those with late-night cravings, some supermarkets and convenience stores offer food 24 hours a day. There are many open-air restaurants, and indoor places are usually air-conditioned. Unless you stick to the mainstream fast-food outlets, you cannot fail to taste the full range of exotic flavors that influence cooking in Hawai'i.

Beach Bar at the Sheraton Moana Surfrider Hotel (see p180)

MEAL TIMES

Some visitors to Hawai'i may be surprised by the state's early meal times. You will find places open for breakfast at 5am; lunch starts at 11am; and dinner begins at 5pm and is often over by 9pm. Many local-style establishments do not serve dinner and close by 2pm.

Cocktail hour begins early, too, around 4pm. Most hotels and restaurants serve *pūpū* (Hawaiian-style hors d'oeuvres) with the drinks, sometimes at no additional charge.

Many restaurants are closed on Sunday or Monday, but hours and closing days often change. You should phone if you have your heart set on a particular restaurant (it is a good idea to book anyway).

HAWAI'I REGIONAL CUISINE

The days of Hawai'i as a gastronomic wasteland are long gone – thanks, in no small part, to the advent of the Hawai'i Regional Cuisine

movement. Peter Merriman *(see p208)* is widely acknowledged as the leader of a pack of chefs who were determined to put Hawai'i on the culinary map. Other chefs, including Roy Yamaguchi on O'ahu *(see p198)* and Bev Gannon at Joe's Bar & Grill on Maui *(see p206)*, quickly followed suit – until a core group of 12 chefs formed a nonprofit organization dedicated to the promotion of Hawai'i Regional Cuisine.

The cuisine takes its ingredients directly from local farms and the surrounding Pacific, but its influences come from the many ethnic groups that make up Hawaiian society. The results – dishes such as breadfruit vichyssoise, tempura of Keāhole baby lobster, and Kona coffee cheesecake, as well as the upsurge of interest in Hawaiian cooking – have been of benefit to everyone,

from local producers to the dining public. Whichever name you use – Hawai'i Regional, Island Regional, East Meets West, or Pacific Rim – this new cuisine makes the most of what the islands have to offer.

LOCAL FOOD

Those dishes collectively known as "local food" are as diverse as the population that has created them. This style of cooking is filling, inexpensive, and unbeatable in the eyes of local people and those who acquire a taste for it.

The "plate lunch" is the most traditional local-style meal and consists of a meat or poultry main course – such as teriyaki beef, two scoops of sticky rice, and a scoop of macaroni or potato salad heaped onto a paper plate or molded tray. These lunches are dispensed from street carts or diners,

Chef Roy Yamaguchi at his restaurant in Honolulu (see p198)

The oceanfront Pacific'O in Lahaina *(see p204)*

and there are often dozens of food choices – of Japanese, Chinese, Korean, Filipino, and even American origin. Expect to pay in the region of $8–10.

Poi (a gray paste made from pounded taro root and definitely an acquired taste); *kālua* pork (from a whole pig baked in leaves, especially at *lū'au*); sweet potato; *limu* (seaweed); and *laulau* (fish, pork, and taro leaf stems wrapped in *ti* leaves and then steamed) are all easy-to-find Hawaiian staples.

You will see sushi everywhere, and *bento* is a Japanese version of the plate lunch, served cold. *Saimin,* a Japanese-style bowl of broth brimming with pork, fish cake, green onions, and noodles, is popular for breakfast, lunch, or dinner. Another common dish is *manapua,* the local version of Chinese steamed buns filled with seasoned pork.

Local sweet treats include shave ice (or "snow cones"), shavings of ice flavored with syrup, and crack seed – dried fruits and chewy candies seasoned with Chinese five-spice known as *li hing mui.*

FAST FOOD AND TAKE-OUT MEALS

Hawai'i is part of the United States, after all, so don't be surprised to find Burger King, McDonald's, Pizza Hut, Taco Bell, and the rest. How-ever, you will find things on

the menu that are particular to Hawai'i: most notably *saimin,* sticky rice and Portuguese sausage. Local-style fast food is sold at numerous drive-ins throughout Hawai'i, and at the many branches of Zippy's on O'ahu; most of the Zippy's outlets are open 24 hours. Another local com-pany, L & L Drive-In, is expanding fast and has many outlets on O'ahu, too.

Few restaurants will not do food to take out. Many groceries and super-markets have delis and salad, Chinese food, or *bento* bars offering take-out meals. Health food stores often have deli bars, too. All these places are good for picnic food – Hawai'i being ideal picnicking territory.

Delivery, on the other hand, is rarely available in Hawai'i. Your choices will be limited to large chains like Pizza Hut and Domino's Pizza.

Mock-Victorian Burger King, Waikīkī

COFFEEHOUSES

Just like on the US mainland, coffeehouses have opened up all over the islands. The difference in Hawai'i is that they are not chains, and they feature aromatic home-grown Kona coffee *(see p135).*

Most coffeehouses sell delicious pastries, mostly home-baked, and many provide light meals as well.

ALCOHOL

Most restaurants have bars and wine lists offering a good choice from around the world. Restaurants without a bar will usually allow patrons to bring in their own beer or wine, and there is rarely a charge for opening the bottle.

VEGETARIANS

Although there are only a few vegetarian restaurants in Hawai'i, many places have a vegetarian section on their menu and will accommodate vegetarians with a plate of steamed vegetables and rice or a vegetarian pasta dish. All you have to do is ask.

CHILDREN

Hawai'i is an extremely child-friendly place, and the only restaurants that do not welcome children with open arms are the few very formal dining rooms – mostly located in fancy resort hotels. But even here, children should never be turned away.

Many restaurants provide a children's menu, with small portions of the food kids love, such as pizzas and burgers.

ETIQUETTE

Smoking is prohibited in restaurants in Hawai'i, so those wanting to light up during a meal will have to step outside before doing so.

A standard restaurant tip is 15 percent of the check. Depend-ing upon the service and style of restaurant, you may wish to tip more or less than this.

Casual dress is acceptable in all but the most formal of Hawai'i's restaurants, and then jackets are usually requested rather than required.

Local-style diner on Hawai'i Island

The Flavors of Hawai'i

The diet of ancient Hawaiians consisted of fish, shellfish, pork, fresh fruit – mostly bananas – tubers like sweet potatoes, and, most importantly, taro (*kalo*). Since the migration of many ethnic groups to Hawai'i in the 1820s, island food has evolved to embrace various new recipes and ingredients. The fusion of these traditional cuisines has brought delicious modern offerings with a Hawaiian twist. Although Hawaiian food is often modified to appeal to Western palates, it is still possible for visitors to experience truly authentic local dishes at a *lū'au*.

Macadamia nuts

Worker tending plants in a taro field, Maui

TRADITIONAL HAWAIIAN FOOD

Hawaiians once got everything they needed from ancient land divisions that ran from mountain to sea known as *ahupua'a*. These plots of land provided them with sweet potatoes, bananas, dozens of types of *limu* (seaweed), fish and seafood from fresh, brackish, and ocean water, and of course taro, of which there were also dozens of varieties. Many foods were eaten raw, but ancient Hawaiians had several ingenious cooking methods including the *'imu*, or underground oven, which is still widely used today. In this, everything from a whole pig to individual sweet potatoes are slow-cooked at a very low temperature. The heat is generated from extremely dry, hot rocks that fill the pit. The rocks are covered with banana stalks and *ti* leaves onto which the food is laid. It is then covered with more leaves and earth and left to bake. A whole pig takes about nine hours to cook and "the opening of the *'imu*" is a ceremony enjoyed to this day by *lū'au* guests.

Papaya Pineapple Mango Bananas
Coconut Passion fruits
Lychees Kiwi fruits

Lusciously ripe tropical fruits from the Hawaiian islands

THE HAWAIIAN LŪ'AU

Traditional Hawaiian *lū'au* (feasts) are still held to mark special occasions with friends and family, as they have been for centuries. It is not unusual to have in excess of 400 guests at a wedding, family reunion, or baby's first birthday. The *lū'au* was originally a spiritual event when islanders thanked the gods for bountiful harvests whilst enjoying traditional entertainment, such as *hula* performances. It takes its name

Breadfruit

from the taro tops served at the feast. The main event is the preparation of the *kālua* pig, but certain dishes are also central, including *laulau*, *lomi lomi* salmon, chicken long rice, *haupia*, and, most important of all, *poi*. This thick, purple-gray paste is made from steamed and pounded taro root (*kalo*). *Poi* is the absolute staple of the Hawaiian diet and is meant to be eaten with the fingers.

Laulau *Meat or fish, plus taro tops, are wrapped in* ti *leaves and baked in the* 'imu, *often served with* poi.

Colorful haul of typical Hawaiian fish

Despite so much culinary integration there are still many ethnic restaurants, so visitors can sample everything from sashimi and sushi to Portuguese sausage, bean soup, and sweet bread – and even some pretty great all-American hamburgers.

Over the last two decades, top island chefs have gathered to promote the use of locally grown and produced ingredients. They have pioneered modern Hawaiian regional cuisine, emphasizing creative methods and presentation.

HAWAIIAN FOOD TODAY

Mix traditional Hawaiian produce and preparations with foods from Japan, China, Portugal, Korea, the Philippines, Europe, and the mainland United States, and you get what can best be described as today's "local" food. These diverse ethnic groups began arriving in Hawai'i in the mid- to late 19th century, bringing their traditional foods with them. Perhaps the most obvious example of the resulting combinations is that ubiquitous local staple, the "plate lunch". From lunch wagons to beachside kiosks and neighborhood eateries, plate lunch ingredients are unmistakable – meat or fish, plenty of carbohydrate (usually two scoops of white

sticky rice), and a scoop of macaroni salad. However, in the interests of a healthier lifestyle, the protein may now be tofu, the white rice may be replaced by brown, and the macaroni salad by a fresh green salad.

Roasted *kālua* pig, the highlight at a traditional *lū'au*

WHAT TO DRINK

From colorful cocktails festooned with orchids and paper parasols, to tropical fruit juices and world-renowned Kona coffee, there are many beverages that are synonymous with Hawai'i.

Perhaps the most ubiquitous of the Polynesian cocktails is the Mai Tai. Many claim to have invented this potent rum concoction, the name of which means "good" in Tahitian. Other favorites include the Blue Hawai'i, Chi-Chi, and Banana Daiquiri.

Freshly-squeezed tropical juices, like pineapple, papaya, lychee, mango, and coconut, are a perfect start to breakfast on the *lanai* (veranda).

In addition to Kona coffee, other islands – notably Maui, Molokai, and Kauai – grow, roast, and sell their own high-end, "estate" coffees. All are rich and delicious, and make an ideal gift or souvenir.

Lomi lomi salmon *Finely sliced raw salmon is marinated with green onions and tomatoes.*

Chicken long rice *A cross between a stew and a soup. The "rice" is actually long cellophane noodles.*

Haupia *A simple coconut-flavored custard pudding – the dessert of choice at every* lū'au.

Choosing a Restaurant

The restaurants in this guide have been selected across a wide price range for their exceptional food, good value, and location. These listings highlight some of the factors that may influence your choice, such as whether you can eat outdoors or if the venue offers live music. Entries are alphabetical within each price category.

PRICE CATEGORIES
For a three-course meal for one, a glass of wine, and all unavoidable extra charges including service and tax.
⑤ under $15
⑤⑤ $15–$30
⑤⑤⑤ $30–$55
⑤⑤⑤⑤ $55–$80
⑤⑤⑤⑤⑤ over $80

HONOLULU AND WAIKĪKĪ

DOWNTOWN HONOLULU Gordon Biersch Brewery Restaurant 👤♿🚻🎵🍷🅿️✸   ⑤⑤⑤
1 Aloha Tower Dr, 96813 **Tel** *(808) 599-4877*   **Map** *1 A3*

A popular after-work hangout, Gordon Biersch has the distinction of being Hawai'i's very first brewpub, producing its own lagers on the premises. The food is good bar fare, such as garlic fries and drunken *poki* (raw fish). Located in the Aloha Tower Marketplace, it provides the option of dining in or out. There is live entertainment on weekends.

DOWNTOWN HONOLULU Legend Seafood Restaurant 👤♿🍷🅿️   ⑤⑤⑤
100 N Beretania St, 96817 **Tel** *(808) 377-6735*   **Map** *1 A2*

Choices are plentiful when it comes to a weekend dim-sum brunch in Chinatown. Many in-the-know locals consider this to be the best. Servers circulate trolleys stacked high with dozens of different bite-sized delicacies, ranging from egg custard to pork hash cups. An extensive à la carte lunch and dinner menu is also available.

DOWNTOWN HONOLULU Indigo Eurasian Cuisine ♿🚻🍷   ⑤⑤⑤⑤
1121 Nu'uanu Ave, 96813 **Tel** *(808) 521-2900*   **Map** *1 A2*

This place started the culinary transformation of Honolulu's Chinatown. Its series of rooms brings the tropical outdoors inside in a very real way. The menu features an exotic blend of Asian cuisines and the food is artistically served, as is fitting in this district full of galleries. The bartenders mix a mean martini.

DOWNTOWN HONOLULU Ruth's Chris Steakhouse ♿🍷🅿️   ⑤⑤⑤⑤⑤
500 Ala Moana Blvd, 96813 **Tel** *(808) 599-3860*   **Map** *1 B4*

Ruth's Chris Steakhouse is located in Restaurant Row, in the heart of Honolulu's business district, near the Hawaiian Convention Center. Steaks are, unsurprisingly, the specialty of the house. Choose between filet, ribeye, New York strip, or Porterhouse – they're all as fabulous as they are expensive. Dinner only.

WAIKĪKĪ Duke's Canoe Club ♿👤🚻🎵🍷🅿️✸   ⑤⑤⑤
2335 Kalākaua Ave, 96815 **Tel** *(808) 922-2268*   **Map** *4 E5*

Named after famed Hawaiian surfing champion Duke Kahanamoku, this is a good spot for live Hawaiian music and spirited crowds at sunset. Located on the beach at the Outrigger Waikīkī *(see p179)*, it is a steak-and-seafood restaurant, but offers breakfast as well as lunch and dinner, and a light, inexpensive menu at its Barefoot Bar.

WAIKĪKĪ Keo's in Waikīkī ♿👤🍷🅿️   ⑤⑤⑤
2028 Kūhiō Ave, 96815 **Tel** *(808) 951-9355*   **Map** *3 C4*

Although he is Laotian, Keo Sananikone's name is synonymous in Hawai'i with Thai food. His restaurants are award winning: *Bon Appetit* magazine voted Keo's America's Best Thai Restaurant and *Gourmet* named it one of America's top tables. Specialties include the stir-fried shrimp with peanut sauce. Usefully, dishes are rated for spiciness.

WAIKĪKĪ Wailana Coffee House 🍴♿👤🍷   ⑤⑤⑤
1860 Ala Moana Blvd, 96815 **Tel** *(808) 955-1764*   **Map** *3 B4*

This 24-hour diner provides both locals and tourists with reliable food and fast service. The inexpensive but hearty meals, especially breakfast, are great for families and those traveling on a budget. The jamboree breakfast costs under $6 and features all the pancakes you can eat. There is also a cocktail lounge with karaoke.

WAIKĪKĪ Japengo ♿👤🍷🅿️   ⑤⑤⑤⑤
Hyatt Regency Waikīkī, 2424 Kalākaua Ave, 96815 **Tel** *(808) 923-2426*   **Map** *4 E5*

This stylish, contemporary restaurant offers Asian-inspired cuisine prepared from fresh local produce. Try the extensive sushi offerings and wok-fired or roasted fish. For the adventurous diner, there is an interesting side dish called "Forbidden Black Rice" – which is a delicious, purple-colored grain.

WAIKĪKĪ Sansei Seafood Restaurant & Sushi Bar ♿👤🚻🍷🅿️   ⑤⑤⑤⑤
2552 Kalākaua Ave, 96815 **Tel** *(808) 931-6286*   **Map** *4 F5*

Million-dollar views of world-famous Waikīkī Beach, and the expansive space it shares with d.k. Steak House, make this Sansei dining experience unforgettable. Dozens of signature dishes – from creative New-Wave sushi sporting surprise ingredients like foie gras to award-winning contemporary Japanese specialties – draw a steady crowd.

Key to Symbols *see back cover flap*

WAIKĪKĪ d.k. Steak House ♿ 🚻 📷 🍷 🅿 ⭐ $$$$$
2552 Kalākaua Ave, 96815 Tel (808) 931-6280 **Map 4 F5**

This restaurant is named for, and owned and run by, one of Hawai'i's most celebrated chef-restauranteurs, DK Kodama. With the island's only dry-aging room, the restaurant's signature is a huge rib-eye steak. The menu is classic American steak house, with an Asian twist. The service is pure class and the view incredible.

WAIKĪKĪ Hiroshi Eurasion Tapas ♿ 🚻 🍷 $$$$$
500 Ala Moana Blvd Tel (808) 533-4476 **Map 1 B4**

A calm and comfortable space, this restaurant puts the distinctive fusion cuisine of award-winning chef Hiroshi Fukui into the spotlight. Although based on traditional Japanese techniques and flavors, it is the modern European twists that make the food memorable. This downtown hot spot features a menu of small plates designed for sharing.

WAIKĪKĪ La Mer at Halekulani ♿ 🍷 🅿 $$$$$
2199 Kālia Rd, 96815 Tel (808) 923-2311 **Map 4 D5**

Choose this elegant, romantic, and expensive French restaurant when you are in the mood to savor each exquisite bite. Dishes are impeccably prepared. On the second floor of the Halekulani *(see p180)*, it has a magnificent ocean view and is one of the best places in Waikīkī for watching the sun set. Gentlemen are required to wear jackets.

GREATER HONOLULU Akasaka 🍷 $$
1646B Kona St, 96814 Tel (808) 942-4466

A trip to this tiny sushi bar promises a savory adventure. Located behind the Ala Moana hotel, Akasaka offers a variety of authentic Japanese delicacies including grilled specialties such as scallops and tofu. The spicy tuna and the other hand-made sushi rolls are favorites with the regulars.

GREATER HONOLULU California Beach Rock n' Sushi ♿ 🍷 🅿 $$
404 Ward Ave, 96814 Tel (808) 597-8000 **Map 2 D4**

California Beach Rock n' Sushi serve traditional and new wave sushi at reasonable prices, in a friendly, casual atmosphere. Tempura Combo meals include miso soup, salad, and rice. For a real deal, drop by between 5 and 6:30pm for early-bird specials. The Ward Center is nearby, with movies and shopping.

GREATER HONOLULU California Pizza Kitchen ♿ 🚻 🍷 🅿 $$
4211 Wai'alae Ave, 96816 Tel (808) 737-9446 **Map 4 E1**

Pizzas topped with everything from barbecue chicken to pear and Gorgonzola cheese are on offer here in the Kahala Mall. This chain began in California and now has more than 180 outlets. Salads that are large, fresh, and delicious, sandwiches, and other non-pizza choices round out a superb menu, with something to satisfy everyone.

GREATER HONOLULU Eggs 'n' Things 🍴 🚻 🅿 $$
343 Saratoga Rd, 96815 Tel (808) 923-3447 **Map 3 C4**

Boasting some of the best omelets, pancakes and waffles on the island, this popular Honolulu institution is still the best place to satisfy your cravings. Locals line up happily, newspapers in hand, to wait. The staff are very friendly and the food is simple yet delicious.

GREATER HONOLULU Hale Vietnam Restaurant ♿ 🍷 🅿 $$
1140 12th Ave, 96816 Tel (808) 735-7581 **Map 4 F2**

Steaming noodle soups are the highlight of the menu at this simple restaurant in Kaimuki. It offers no frills, but the service is fast and friendly and the atmosphere pleasant. Authentic Vietnamese vegan and vegetarian dishes are the fare. If it is available, try the *bun* (cold noodles heaped with sliced vegetables and herbs).

GREATER HONOLULU Helena's Hawaiian Food 🍴 ♿ $$
1240 N School St, 96817 Tel (808) 845-8044 **Map 1 A1**

These days octogenarian Helen Chock is at the cash register rather than the stove in this Kalihi eatery. Grandson Craig Katsuyoshi continues the tradition of smoking *pipikaula*-style spare ribs. Always buzzing, it serves its trademark *'opihi* (short ribs), hard to find elsewhere. The *kālua* pork and cabbage are straight from grandma's kitchen.

GREATER HONOLULU Little Village Noodle House ♿ 🍷 🅿 $$
1113 Smith St, 96817 Tel (808) 545-3008 **Map 1 A2**

Not too long ago this fabulous Chinatown restaurant was a local secret, but it became so popular that it has expanded to twice its original size. Fans typically use the same words to describe the food – clean and fresh, with brilliant flavors. All the noodle and fresh vegetable dishes are musts.

GREATER HONOLULU Makai Market Food Court 🍴 ♿ 🍷 🅿 $$
1450 Ala Moana Blvd, 96816 Tel (808) 955-9517 **Map 3 A4**

The huge seating area at the Ala Moana Center *(see p214)* is surrounded by kiosks offering every conceivable type of food: from pizzas to Korean barbecue fare; sub sandwiches to Japanese *bentos*; and salads to ice cream. The variety illustrates the multi-ethnic mix of Hawai'i. Almost everything you can order is under $10.

GREATER HONOLULU Ono Hawaiian Foods 🍴 🚻 $$
726 Kapahulu Ave, 96816 Tel (808) 737-2275 **Map 4 F2**

This eatery is always busy serving delicious Hawaiian dishes such as *poi* (taro paste), *laulau* (leaf-wrapped meat or fish bundles), and *lomi-lomi* salmon. You know it is genuinely Hawaiian because the combo plates come with a small cup of raw onion and Hawaiian *'alaea* salt. This restaurant is clean, basic, and inexpensive. It is closed on Sundays.

GREATER HONOLULU Spalding House Café

                                                  $$

2411 Makiki Heights Dr, 96822 **Tel** *(808) 532-8700*   **Map** *2 F1*

A perfect complement to the world-class Honolulu Museum of Art Spalding House *(see p71)*, this café has a short menu of tasty and good-value soups, salads, and sandwiches. Ask for the popular daily specials menu. You can dine inside or out surrounded by inspiring artworks. It is closed for dinner and on Mondays.

GREATER HONOLULU 12th Ave Grill

 $$$

1145C 12th Ave, 96816 **Tel** *(808) 732-9469*

This award-winning neighborhood restaurant serves contemporary American cuisine made from locally sourced and organic produce, including grass-fed beef. Fresh salads, macaroni and cheese, and grilled pork chop are just some of the dishes on offer. Closed Sunday.

GREATER HONOLULU Assaggio

 $$$

1450 Ala Moana Blvd, 96814 **Tel** *(808) 942-3446*   **Map** *3 C4*

Italian favorites are the specialties of the house at Assaggio, and the menu features a wide selection of tasty pasta dishes, in addition to fresh fish and chicken options, all offered at reasonable prices. Located inside the Ala Moana Shopping Center. Open daily.

GREATER HONOLULU Mariposa

 $$$

1450 Moana Blvd, 96814 **Tel** *(808) 951-3420*   **Map** *2 F4*

Located on the third level of the Neiman Marcus store in the Ala Moana Shopping Center, this restaurant offers sophisticated dining and really good service. Lunch and dinner are served daily, brunch on the weekends, and tea in the afternoons. Outdoor seating provides good views of Ala Moana Beach Park.

GREATER HONOLULU Side Street Inn

 $$$

1225 Hopaka St, 96814 **Tel** *(808) 591-0253*   **Map** *3 A4*

The Side Street Inn might look like just another bar with neon beer signs and a TV playing sports, but this is where Honolulu's best chefs gather after they close their own restaurants to enjoy great food in a funky setting. Highlights on the menu include blackened ahi and barbecued baby back ribs. Closed for lunch Saturdays and Sundays.

GREATER HONOLULU Singha Thai Cuisine

 $$$

1910 Ala Moana Blvd, 96815 **Tel** *(808) 941-2898*   **Map** *3 C4*

Award-winning Singha Thai is an exotic haven, its atmosphere heightened by original Thai artwork, fresh orchids, and colorful silk-clad Royal Thai dancers performing every evening. The magnificent dishes served at this Thai-Hawaiian fusion restaurant make use of local ingredients, alongside those of traditional Thai cuisine.

GREATER HONOLULU 3660 on the Rise

 $$$$

3660 Wai'alae Ave, 96816 **Tel** *(808) 737-1177*   **Map** *4 F1*

This unassuming restaurant in a refurbished building was one of the original pioneers in the gentrification of the Kaimuki neighborhood. Now a popular spot, 3660 offers creative island cuisine with a European twist. Ahi katsu is the restaurant's signature dish.

GREATER HONOLULU Alan Wong's Restaurant

 $$$$

1857 King St, 96826 **Tel** *(808) 949-2526*   **Map** *3 B2*

Considered by many to be the best restaurant in town, this place is owned by one of Hawai'i regional cuisine's original chefs, Alan Wong. Innovative dishes are fashioned out of traditional Hawaiian ingredients. The contemporary menu changes periodically, but is always great. The friendly staff make up for the restaurant's odd location.

GREATER HONOLULU Chai's Island Bistro

 $$$$

1 Aloha Tower Dr, 96813 **Tel** *(808) 585-0011*   **Map** *1 A3*

Owned and run by one of Hawai'i's most beloved chefs, Chai Chaowasaree, this bistro combines his Thai heritage and delicious local ingredients to create his own signature style. The entertainment is as good as the food, and as lovely as the atmosphere. Hawai'i's top contemporary entertainers all perform regularly at Chai's.

GREATER HONOLULU Chef Mavro

 $$$$

1969 S King St, 96826 **Tel** *(808) 944-4714*   **Map** *3 B2*

Mavro is an award-winning chef, originally from France, who is known for his culinary creativity. In his restaurant you can dine prix-fixe or à la carte, with or without wine pairings. Menus change to take advantage of the freshest local seasonal ingredients. This is an expensive option, but worth it. It is closed for lunch and on Mondays.

GREATER HONOLULU Kincaid's Fish, Chop & Steakhouse

 $$$$

1050 Ala Moana Blvd, 96814 **Tel** *(808) 591-2005*   **Map** *2 D5*

A terrific place at which to take a break from shopping in Ward Warehouse, Kincaid's offers excellent food along with first-rate service. The menu is varied, with choices across a wide price range. At the end of the work day, this is a lively party bar, and it also gets extremely busy around noon.

GREATER HONOLULU Roy's Restaurant

 $$$$

6600 Kalaniana'ole Hwy, 96825 **Tel** *(808) 396-7697*   **Map** *4 F5*

The first of chef Roy Yamaguchi's restaurants in Hawai'i (there are more than 20 worldwide) serves his signature Euro-Asian cuisine in a characteristically loud, busy atmosphere. This restaurant is extremely popular and menus offer Roy's classics, which are longtime favorites, as well as daily specials and a nightly prix-fixe selection.

Key to Price Guide *see p196* **Key to Symbols** *see back cover flap*

GREATER HONOLULU Sam Choy's Breakfast, Lunch, and Crab   👍 🧍 🍸 🅿️ $$$$

580 N Nimitz Hwy, 96817   **Tel** *(808) 545-7979*   **Map** *1 A1*

A big chef needs a big restaurant: this former warehouse now serves up several varieties of fresh crab, all manner of local fish dishes, and Sam's signature style of local cuisine. At breakfast, make sure someone at the table orders the fried rice. Portions are generous. Sam also brews beer on the premises and his brewpub is open nightly.

GREATER HONOLULU The Pineapple Room   👍 🧍 🍸 🅿️ $$$$$

1450 Ala Moana Blvd, 96814   **Tel** *(808) 945-6573*   **Map** *3 A4*

The third floor of Macy's Department Store at the Ala Moana Center *(see p214)* is not a place you would expect to find a great restaurant, but chef Alan Wong's Pineapple Room is, some say, one of the best in town. Inviting yet elegant, it offers the world-renowned chef's excellent Hawai'i regional cuisine.

O'AHU

AIEA Champa Thai   👍 🧍 🍸 🅿️ $$

98-199 Kamehameha Hwy, 96701   **Tel** *(808) 488-2881*

This award-winning Thai restaurant in Pearl Kai Shopping Center has a dozen types of curry and in excess of 20 vegetarian choices on the menu. Dishes are made as spicy as you want them: either hot, medium, or mild. Everyone loves the steamed rice served in woven baskets.

HALE'IWA Shave Ice Shops: Matsumoto's and Aoki's   📋 👍 🧍 🍴 🅿️ $

Kamehameha Hwy, 96712   **Tel** *(808) 637-4827, (808) 637-7017*

These neighboring places serve sweet, drippy shave ice. A legacy from the days when ice was shipped to Hawai'i from Alaska, the chipped ice flavored with fruit syrups is a local favorite. Matsumoto's (66-087 Kam Hwy) and Aoki's (66-117 Kam Hwy) are still there. Join the shortest line and enjoy.

HALE'IWA Ted's Bakery   📋 🍴 🅿️ $

59-024 Kamehameha Hwy, 96712   **Tel** *(808) 638-8207*

This is the source of heavenly cream pies sold all over the island. The chocolate-*haupia* (coconut) pie is Ted's signature creation. Stop by from 7am to pick up fresh pastries and coffee. There are inexpensive breakfasts and a selection of sandwiches and plate lunches, too. Food is take-out only. Open daily.

HALE'IWA Coffee Gallery   👍 🧍 🅿️ $$

66-250 Kamehameha Hwy, 96712   **Tel** *(808) 637-5355*

This North Shore eatery has a classic surf-beach atmosphere. Popular with surfers and local residents, its breakfasts are legendary. The huge omelets have surf-lingo names like Off the Wall and Off the Lip. There is also an espresso bar featuring a large selection of fresh roasted gourmet coffee, including Kona and organically grown beans.

HALE'IWA Kua-Aina Sandwich   📋 👍 🧍 🍴 🅿️ $$

66-214 Kamehameha Hwy, 96712   **Tel** *(808) 637-6067*

Try this humble surfer hangout on O'ahu's North Shore. It is a popular local landmark with some of the best food around, especially if you love chargrilled burgers and shoestring French fries. If it is too crowded, take your food to the beach and enjoy it there.

HALE'IWA Hale'iwa Joe's Seafood Grill   👍 🧍 🍴 🍸 🅿️ $$$

66-011 Kamehameha Hwy, 96712   **Tel** *(808) 637-8005*

The original Hale'iwa Joe's is a lively North Shore spot, with a terrific view of the Hale'iwa harbor and glorious sunsets. A surf-and-turf restaurant, it specializes in fresh fish and seafood, and steaks. There is a full bar and live music on weekends. The outdoor seating takes advantage of the scenery.

HALE'IWA Jameson's by the Sea   👍 🧍 🍴 🅿️ $$$

62-540 Kamehameha Hwy, 96712   **Tel** *(808) 637-6272*

At the north end of Hale'iwa, this is a good place for cocktails and sashimi. The outdoor deck is perfect for watching the sun set and indoor dining is romantic, too. The more expensive upstairs dining room serves fresh fish and *filet mignon*; the pub on the lower level does sandwiches. Reservations are recommended: ask for a window seat.

HAU'ULA Papa Ole's   📋 👍 🧍 🍴 🅿️ $

54-316 Kamehameha Hwy, 96717   **Tel** *(808) 293-2292*

A great place for families, this casual eatery serves burgers and sandwiches, but the local favorites offered at breakfast, lunch, and dinner are what really draw people here. The plate lunches (two scoops of rice, macaroni salad with meat or fish) are huge and satisfying. Try to save room for the freshly baked desserts. Closed on Wednesday.

HAWAI'I KAI Cha Cha Cha Salsaria   👍 🧍 🍸 🎵 🅿️ $$

377 Keahole St, 96825   **Tel** *(808) 395-7797*

The fare here is predominantly Mexican, with some Caribbean dishes thrown in. Nightly specials, homemade desserts, big margaritas, and a good happy hour are all plus points. The live entertainment often features Hawaiian "slack key" *(see p34)* as well as acoustic guitar.

HAWAI'I KAI Kona Brewing Co
7192 Kalaniana'ole Hwy, 96825 **Tel** (808) 394-5662

The Hawai'i Island-based Kona Brewing Company opened this O'ahu brewpub in the Koko Marine Center, adorned with the company's beer logos and brewing equipment. Besides the handcrafted ales and lagers, there are imported and specialty beers. The menu includes hand-tossed pizzas, burgers, salads, and other casual fare.

KAHALA Chin's Kahala
4230 Wai'alae Ave, 96816 **Tel** (808) 739-8760

The Chin in Chin's Kahala is owner Chin Tsai, who started his first restaurant in Honolulu in the 1970s before moving to San Diego, where Chin's has grown into a small chain. The typically expansive menu offers classic Szechwan and Cantonese fare alongside more unusual signature dishes, like salt and pepper quail, and roast cognac pigeon.

KAHALA Hoku's
5000 Kahala Ave, 96816 **Tel** (808) 739-8760

Hoku's is about as good as a restaurant gets – especially a hotel restaurant. The food is consistently fantastic, the service is exactly what people expect of Hawaiian hospitality, and the ocean views are gorgeous. Sunday brunch is a particular treat. The incredible desserts are truly mouthwatering. The dress code prohibits shorts and T-shirts.

KAHUKU 21 Degrees North
Turtle Bay Resort, 57-091 Kamehameha Hwy, 96712 **Tel** (808) 293-8811

Without question, the best evening dining on this side of the island is to be had here. The East-West fusion cuisine is innovative and focuses on fresh seasonal ingredients. Overlooking the sparkling water of Turtle Bay, this restaurant is quite romantic and a perfect place to watch the sun set. Diners are asked to dress up a little.

KAILUA Buzz's Original Steakhouse
413 Kawailoa Rd, 96734 **Tel** (808) 261-4661

A few feet from Kailua Beach Park, this Buzz's is the original of the chain. It is the quintessential surf (or, in this case, windsurf) fine-dining restaurant: shirt and shoes are required. Burgers are served at lunch and steaks at dinner. Not unexpectedly, everything is chargrilled. Credit cards are not accepted.

KAILUA The Grove
33 Aulike St, 96734 **Tel** (808) 262-2898 **Fax** (808) 262-2894

Savor scrumptious island cuisine and American-style food at this friendly neighborhood bistro. Formerly known as Lucy's Grill 'n Bar, The Grove serves flatbreads, ribs, sliders, and other dishes. Don't miss out on the popular "shady hour" (3–5:30pm), where you can try out tasters of some of the restaurant's specials. No reservations are accepted.

KANE'OHE Koa Pancake House
1139 12th Ave, 96816 **Tel** (808) 739-7778

Bring the paper on Sunday morning and have a leisurely read while you wait in line for stacks of light, fluffy pancakes. They come with a variety of toppings including bananas, blueberries, strawberries, and whipped cream; the orange syrup is homemade. The omelets are amazing, too. Once you get in, the service is fast and friendly.

KANE'OHE Hale'iwa Joe's
46-336 Haiku Rd, 96744 **Tel** (808) 247-6671

Overlooking a botanical garden with colorful foliage and lily ponds, this steak-and-seafood restaurant serves fresh local fish and beef from the Hawai'i Island's Parker Ranch (see p137). There are bar specials and a *pūpū* (appetizer) menu, too. Seating is on a first-come, first-served basis; no reservations are accepted. It is open for dinner only.

KO OLINA Azul
92-101 Olani St, 96707 **Tel** (808) 679-0079

This is the fine-dining signature restaurant at the JW Marriott 'Ihilani Resort (see p183) outside of Honolulu. The lovely, cool space opens onto a tropical lagoon. The Mediterranean menu manages to be both refined and rustic, and is complemented by a wonderful wine list. Evening resort attire is suggested. It is open for dinner only.

PEARL CITY Gyotaku Japanese Restaurant
98-1226 Ka'ahumanu St, 96782 **Tel** (808) 487-0091

This bright, casual restaurant offers a wide range of authentic Japanese dishes such as sushi, tempura, and teriyaki. It is the perfect place for the uninitiated to try their first taste of Japanese cuisine (with or without chopsticks). For those in a hurry, there are sushi and *pūpū* (appetizer) platters to take out.

PEARL HARBOR Shiro's Saimin Haven & Family Restaurant
98-020 Kamehameha Hwy 96701 **Tel** (808) 488-8824

This shrine to Japanese-style noodle soup, and immense local plate lunches, has to be seen to be believed. Founder and patriarch Shiro Matsuo has lined the walls with scribbled notes expressing his philosophy of life. A cultural icon, he is best known as "Mistah Saimin". Hawai'i's governor titled him Statesman of Goodwill of Hawai'i.

WAIMĀNALO Keneke's
41-857 Kalaniana'ole Hwy 96795 **Tel** (808) 259-9811

Next to the 7-Eleven and post office, this is part fast-food joint and part youth center. Ignore the shabby look as the people are pleasant and the food superb and inexpensive. Plate lunches, burgers, sandwiches, shave ice, and smoothies are all offered through the window. It is a favorite with the local crowd.

Key to Price Guide see p196 **Key to Symbols** see back cover flap

MOLOKA'I AND LANA'İI

KAUNAKAKAI (MOLOKA'I) Kanemitsu Bakery
79 Ala Malama St, 96748 **Tel** *(808) 553-5855*

Famous for its Molokai sweet bread, this bakery offers an array of fresh baked goods, snacks, and beverages. In the adjoining coffee shop, local-style breakfasts and lunches are served. You can take out, or eat in at a 1950s booth table. On Friday nights a line forms for the hot French bread stuffed with cream cheese, jam, and cinnamon butter.

KAUNAKAKAI (MOLOKA'I) Moloka'i Burger
3 Kamehameha V Hwy, 96748 **Tel** *(808) 553-3533*

The first and only drive-through restaurant on Moloka'i serves up great-tasting, fresh hamburgers, French fries, and milkshakes. A teenager's heaven, it makes a nice change from all the offerings of local, island-style *grindz* (food) found in Kaunakakai.

KAUNAKAKAI (MOLOKA'I) Hula Shores
Mile Marker 2, Kamehameha V Hwy, 96748 **Tel** *(808) 553-5347*

Right on the ocean at the Hotel Moloka'i *(see p183)*, this restaurant also fronts the swimming pool. The ribs and the coconut shrimp are divine. On Friday evenings, cowboys, grandmas, and everyone in between tune up their 'ukuleles and get down for a good old-fashioned *kanikapila* (Hawaiian jam session).

KAUNAKAKAI (MOLOKA'I) Moloka'i Drive-In
Kamehameha V Hwy, 96748 **Tel** *(808) 553-5655*

The Moloka'i Drive-In has the 1950s ambience that pervades downtown Kaunakakai. It is a drive-up eatery serving the favorite foods of teenagers – floats, shakes, chili dogs, burgers, and honey-dipped chicken, as well as an island delicacy, fresh *akule* (mackerel). Clean and affordable, it is open from 6am to 10pm.

KAUNAKAKAI (MOLOKA'I) Moloka'i Pizza Café
Wharf Rd, 96748 **Tel** *(808) 553-3288*

This bright, efficiently run restaurant is perfect for families: salads and ice-cream treats round out a mostly pizza menu. There are ethnic daily specials, such as Mexican on Wednesdays and Hawaiian on Thursdays. You can eat in, take out, or have your food delivered.

KAUNAKAKAI (MOLOKA'I) Outpost Natural Food Store & Juice Bar
Ala Malama St, 96748 **Tel** *(808) 553-3377*

The juice bar at this quaint country-style store provides wholesome and nutritious all-vegetarian burritos, salads, sandwiches, and smoothies. The store sells fresh local produce, natural foods, and vitamins, and is a good place to get groceries for your stay on the island. The juice bar is closed on weekends; the store is closed on Saturdays.

PUKO'O (MOLOKA'I) Mana'e Goods and Grindz
Near Mile Marker 16, close to Puko'o, 96729 **Tel** *(808) 558-8498*

The lunch counter at this convenience store serves breakfasts as well as lunches. There are shady picnic tables for enjoying the local favorite ethnic and vegetarian dishes available here. The store is the only place where it is possible to get groceries on the east end of the island.

LĀNA'I CITY (LĀNA'I) Blue Ginger Café
409 7th St, 96763 **Tel** *(808) 565-6363*

Probably the most popular restaurant on the island, Blue Ginger Café is reminiscent of a simpler time, with its oilcloth table coverings and home cooking. Casual and inexpensive, it offers a full breakfast menu, local favorites at lunch, and varying specials at dinner. It is a great alternative to the island's hotel restaurants.

LĀNA'I CITY (LĀNA'I) Café 565
408 Eighth St, 96763 **Tel** *(808) 565-6622*

There are outdoor tables with umbrellas at this colorful eatery, which is named after Lāna'i's phone prefix. The pizzas are cooked in special pizza ovens on the premises and the sub sandwich rolls are baked fresh every day. Salads and plate lunch specials are also available. It is closed on Saturdays and Sundays.

LĀNA'I CITY (LĀNA'I) Canoes
419 7th St, 96763 **Tel** *(808) 565-6537*

This casual spot offers big breakfasts such as omelets, pancakes, and fried rice. The lunch specials include fresh fish and baby back ribs. Canoes was formerly Tanigawa's, a local restaurant that had been a landmark since the 1920s. It is not fancy or stylish, but good value and charming, with lots of friendly Hawaiian spirit.

LĀNA'I CITY (LĀNA'I) Pele's Other Garden
811 Houston St, 96763 **Tel** *(808) 565-9628*

Lunch and dinner are available at this popular deli by day and bistro by night. Offerings are predominantly vegetarian, with daily soup and menu specials. Outdoor tables with umbrellas and tablecloths at dinner are unexpected luxuries. You can bring your own wine. Pele's Garden is the health food store next door.

LĀNA'I CITY (LĀNA'I) Lāna'i City Grille   🔥♫Ⓟ★ $$$$$
*828 Lāna'i Ave, 96763 **Tel** (808) 565-4700*

Celebrity chef Bev Gannon, one of the original founders of the Hawai'i Regional Cuisine movement, is lending her talents to this restaurant. The atmosphere is relaxed and the food is Pacific fusion, featuring fresh local fish, prime meats, and rotisserie chicken. Reservations recommended. Open for dinner only; closed Mon, Tue.

MĀNELE (LĀNA'I) Fresco   🔥🔲Ⓟ $$$$
*Four Seasons Lāna'i at Mānele Bay, 1 Mānele Bay Rd, 96763 **Tel** (808) 565-2296*

Enjoy pleasant outdoor dining at Fresco while you appreciate the spectacular view of the beach and the vast ocean expanse. Contemporary Italian offerings include pizzas and pastas prepared using fresh seafood and local produce. Try the Hawaiian snapper (seasonal) with risotto and caramelized fennel, or the spaghetti made with Kauai shrimp.

MĀNELE (LĀNA'I) Hulopo'e Court   🔥🏃🔲♈Ⓟ $$$$
*Four Seasons Lāna'i at Mānele Bay, 1 Mānele Bay Rd, 96763 **Tel** (808) 565-2290*

The more casual of two fine-dining restaurants at the Four Seasons Lānai at Mānele Bay *(see p184)*, Hulopo'e Court serves breakfast and dinner. The high ceilings, rows of colonnades, and open-air feel give this graceful restaurant a Classical, yet island-style ambience. The menus feature contemporary Hawai'i regional cuisine.

MAUI

HA'IKŪ Colleen's at the Cannery   🔥♈Ⓟ $$
*810 Ha'iku Rd, 96708 **Tel** (808) 575-9211*

Two miles off Hāna Highway in the small center of Ha'ikū, this casual bistro is popular with local residents and visitors staying in north-shore rentals. Juicy burgers, fresh fish and salads top the menu at lunch. For dinner, choose from a menu including filet mignon, pan-seared *ahi*, or wild mushroom ravioli.

HA'IKŪ Hāna Hou   🔥🏃🔲♫♈Ⓟ★ $$
*810 Ha'ikū Rd, 96708 **Tel** (808) 575-2661*

About 2 miles (3 km) off the Hāna Highway, this is one of few places on Maui to serve Hawaiian foods like *kālua* pork, *poi* (taro paste), and *laulau* (leaf-wrapped meat or fish bundles). A good mix of ethnic dishes, like pasta and sashimi, are also featured. There are shady outdoor tables. Live music may be Hawaiian, folk, or bluegrass.

HĀLI'IMAILE Hāli'imaile General Store   🔥🏃♈Ⓟ $$$$
*900 Hāli'imaile Rd, 96768 **Tel** (808) 572-2666*

Smack in the middle of a pineapple plantation, this restaurant is located in a historic building that was once the plantation's general store. Beverly Gannon renovated it and is now the chef and manager here. Her superb Hawai'i regional cuisine, with international influences, ensures that this is a trek well worth making.

HĀNA Waianu Fruit Stand   🍴🔥🏃Ⓟ $
Mile Marker 18, Hāna Hwy, 96713

Usually open daily, this roadside stand is typical of the low-key island-style stops along the curvy Hāna Highway. Here you can stock up on snacks, fresh island fruit, and soft drinks for the rest of the drive to Hāna. It is just a casual thing and very old-style Hawai'i, so stop by to get some refreshments and enjoy the local feeling.

HĀNA Hāna Ranch Restaurant   🔥🏃🔲Ⓟ $$$
*5301 Hāna Hwy, 96713 **Tel** (808) 248-8255*

Opposite the bank and post office, in what passes for the hub of Hāna town, the Ranch Restaurant offers hearty servings of wholesome food in a fittingly rustic setting. Lunch includes salads and sandwiches; dinner brings pasta and barbecued ribs. Indoor and outdoor tables have ocean views.

HĀNA Ka'uiki   🔥🏃♫♈★ $$$$
*Hāna Hwy, 96713 **Tel** (808) 248-8211*

Located in an enchanting tropical setting, chef Barry Villarimo's excellent culinary skills promise a delightful dining experience. Barry's "Hana Fusion" style combines traditional ingredients with innovative cooking techniques, creating healthy and tasty dishes made using seasonal, local vegetables and fruits.

KĀ'ANAPALI CJ's Deli & Diner   🍴🏃 $$
*2580 Keka'a Dr, 96761 **Tel** (808) 667-0968*

Located in the Fairway Shops within the Kā'anapali Resort, CJ's is good value and offers generous portions of food. The extensive choices range from breakfast items to sandwiches, and plate lunches to pot roast. Highlights of this friendly neighborhood eatery include Internet access, a good children's menu, and homemade pastries.

KĀ'ANAPALI Hula Grill   🔥🏃🔲♫♈Ⓟ★ $$$
*Whalers Village, 96761 **Tel** (808) 667-6636*

This lovely reproduction of a *kama'aina* architecture beach house will transport you back to the gentility of 1930s Hawai'i. Its beachfront Barefoot Bar has palm-thatched umbrellas over tables that actually sit directly on the sand. Menu favorites include *ono* (wahoo) and *ahi* (tuna) steak, sweet potato ravioli, and banana barbecue ribs.

Key to Price Guide *see p196* **Key to Symbols** *see back cover flap*

KĀ'ANAPALI Leilani's on the Beach   🅿 $$$

Whalers Village, 96761 **Tel** *(808) 661-4495*

This is a beachfront, island-style fish restaurant and steakhouse. The upstairs dining room has panoramic ocean views, while the downstairs cocktail *lānai* (veranda) has umbrella-shaded tables just steps from the beach. Leilani's is a great spot for drinks and *pūpū* (appetizers), watching people on the beach, or viewing Maui's fabulous sunsets.

KA'ANAPALI Son'z $$$

Hyatt Regency Hotel, 96761 **Tel** *(808) 667-4506*

Arguably the most romantic restaurant in all Hawai'i, this gorgeous alfresco room in the Hyatt Regency Maui Resort *(see p185)* now has food as sublime as the surroundings. The chefs prepare creative Hawai'i regional cuisine using mostly local produce. Enjoy the ambience as you watch the swans glide lazily on a lagoon surrounded by lush foliage.

KĀ'ANAPALI Roy's Ka'anapali Bar & Grill   🅿 $$$$

2290 Ka'anapali Pkwy, 96761 **Tel** *(808) 669-6999*

Serving up the trademark East-meets-West fusion cuisine of chef Roy Yamaguchi, this restaurant is always buzzing, so book ahead. The Hawaiian fusion cuisine Yamaguchi is famous for is prepared in an open kitchen. There is an award-winning wine list and the menu has nightly specials. Crowded and noisy it can be, but this makes it fun.

KAHULUI Koho's Grill & Bar   🅿 $$

Queen Ka'ahumanu Center, 96732 **Tel** *(808) 877-5588*

Shopping center restaurants come and go yet Koho just keeps on going. The food, atmosphere, and service are consistently good and the place is as family-friendly as they come. There is something to suit every taste for breakfast, lunch, and dinner. Choices include above average plate lunches, salads, burgers, fish, and desserts.

KAHULUI Maui Coffee Roasters   🅿 $$

444 Hāna Hwy, 96732 **Tel** *(808) 877-2877*

If you believe, as the staff t-shirts here say, "Corporate Coffee Sucks," this is your kind of place. It has been around for a long time, with good reason – it serves fantastic coffee at great proces. The light menu of salads and sandwiches is as good as the coffee, as is the service and atmosphere. You can eat in or get a cappucino to go.

KAHULUI Stillwell's Bakery   🅿 $$

1740 Ka'ahumanu Ave, 96732 **Tel** *243-2243*

One of the best bake shops on Maui, pastry chef Roy Stillwell's clean, well-lit place serves up perfect lunches as well as amazing bread, rolls, cakes, pies, cookies, and pastries. The homemade soups, hearty sandwiches, and salads are all wonderful. Do not leave without something either chocolatey or creamy.

KAHULUI Bistro Casanova   🅿 $$$

33 Lono Ave, 96732 **Tel** *(808) 873-3650*

This casual bistro is of the few restaurants open for dinner in Kahului. Local ingredients such as beef and fish, are used to create a variety of Mediterranean dishes including pastas and tapas. A great spot if you're looking for good food on the way to the airport, or after a show at the Maui Arts & Cultural Center.

KAPALUA Pineapple Grill   🅿 $$$

200 Kapalua Dr, 96761 **Tel** *(808) 669-9600*

Overlooking the lush greens of the Kapalua Golf Club, this tropically decorated restaurant offers Pacific cuisine that blends local ingredients and Asian style. A truly global wine list offers selections by the glass that are affordable and pair well with the food. It is open for breakfast, lunch, and dinner.

KAPALUA Sansei Seafood Restaurant & Sushi Bar   🅿 $$$

600 Office Rd, 96761 **Tel** *(808) 669-6286*

This first, wildly successful Sansei celebrated its 10th anniversary in 2006. After many years of rave reviews locally, statewide, nationally, and internationally, the award-winning Asian rock shrimp cake, mango and crab salad handroll, and Japanese calamari salad are among the signature dishes that continue to delight diners nightly.

KAPALUA The Banyan Tree   🅿 $$$$

Ritz-Carlton Kapalua, 1 Ritz-Carlton Dr, 96761 **Tel** *(808) 669-6200*

The Ritz-Carlton Kapalua's signature restaurant offers exquisite service and panoramic views. Diners can enjoy Asian-inspired world cuisine from tasting menus that change daily. Fresh fish and local produce (especially Kapalua pineapple) are highlighted. Closed for lunch and Mon, Sun.

KAPALUA The Plantation House Restaurant   🅿 $$$$

2000 Plantation Course Dr, 96761 **Tel** *(808) 669-6299*

Perched above the blue Pacific and the Kapalua Resort area, this lovely restaurant is refered to by chef Alex Stanislaw as "the last house on the right." Open for breakfast, lunch, and dinner, it is evening when the menu shines brightest. Island food with Mediterranean influences dominates and there is an excellent wine list, too.

KĪHEI Stella Blues Café   🅿 $$$

1279 South Kīhei Rd, 96753 **Tel** *(808) 874-3779*

Located in Azeka Mauka Shopping Center, this is a bustling breakfast, lunch, and dinner spot, with a menu that has something for everyone. They label their fare New American comfort food, with dishes such as meatloaf, pot roast, stir fries, pizzas, salads, and sandwiches. Economical and good for family dining, it also serves wine and beer.

LAHAINA Aloha Mixed Plate   🛇 🛆 📷 🍸 $$
1285 Front St, 96761 **Tel** *(808) 661-3322*

Mixed plate is a term Hawai'i's plantation workers of yesteryear used to describe the result of sharing their various ethnic foods. This restaurant bases its menu on that tradition, with award-winning results. Try the teriyaki beef or the Hawaiian plate. The open-air oceanfront location is a wonderful respite in hot Lahaina town.

LAHAINA Cheeseburger in Paradise   🎵 🍸 ⭐ $$
811 Front St, 96761 **Tel** *(808) 661-4855*

Located on the second story of a building right over the water, this open-air restaurant certainly lives up to its name, offering unparalleled views of the ocean and nearby islands, as well as of the action on lively Front Street. Giant juicy burgers are the main reason for coming here. Open daily until late.

LAHAINA Penne Pasta Café   🛇 🛆 🍸 P $$
180 Dickenson St, 96761 **Tel** *(808) 661-6633*

A block off Front Street in Dickenson Square, Penne Pasta Café serves up good, filling Italian food in Maui's famous tourist town. There are pastas, pizzas, salads, sandwiches, and nightly seafood specials. All are affordable as nothing on the menu is over $13.95. Most choices are large enough to share and the desserts are sublime.

LAHAINA Kimo's   🛇 🛆 📷 🎵 🍸 ⭐ $$$
845 Front St, 96761 **Tel** *(808) 661-4811*

Right on the waterfront in historic Lahaina town, Kimo's has a panoramic view of the ocean, neighboring islands, and glorious sunsets. Fresh Hawaiian fish, seafood, and prime rib are the mainstays. Dinners come with Kimo's caesar salad, bread, and rice. Popular with visitors and residents alike, this place is always busy, so make reservations.

LAHAINA Lulu's Lahaina Surf Club & Grill   🛇 📷 🍸 P $$$
Lahaina Cannery Mall, 1221 Honoapi'ilani Hwy, 96761 **Tel** *(808) 661-0808*

The party atmosphere makes this a fun late-night spot for casual dining and drinks. There are endless surf-videos and sports playing on the big flatscreen televisions, and the pool tables are free. Pizza, sandwiches, burgers, and four kinds of fries top the menu.

LAHAINA Mala An Ocean Tavern $$$
1307 Front St, 96761 **Tel** *(808) 667-9394*

The idea here is to order a selection of gorgeous food in small portions. It comes this way so that it can be shared. Clams in black bean sauce, whole wok-fried *moi* (a type of fish), and an incredible fruit and ice-cream dessert named Carmel Miranda are just some of the satisfying offerings. The oceanfront setting affords wonderful sunset views.

LAHAINA Gerard's Restaurant   🛇 🛆 📷 🍸 P $$$$
174 Lahainaluna Rd, 96761 **Tel** *(808) 661-8939*

Located a block off busy Front Street on the first floor of The Plantation Inn *(see p186)*, Gerard's serves French food in a charming country setting. Chef Gerard Reversade remains true to his classical culinary roots, while incorporating island ingredients into his original recipes. It is open for dinner only.

LAHAINA I'o Restaurant   🛇 🛆 📷 🍸 P $$$$
505 Front St, 96761 **Tel** *(808) 661-8422*

The second restaurant from the Pacific'O team focuses on contemporary Pacific cuisine with elements of European style. The extraordinary interior is as eye-popping as executive chef James McDonald's plates. In addition to this space, there is patio dining so close to the blue Pacific that you may get your feet wet.

LAHAINA Lahaina Grill   🛇 🛆 🍸 P $$$$
127 Lahainaluna Rd, 96761 **Tel** *(808) 667-5117*

A few steps off Front Street in the Lahaina Inn *(see p186)*, this is a casual yet elegant modern restaurant offering exquisitely prepared and presented food. Signature dishes include tequila shrimp with firecracker rice and Kona-coffee-roasted rack of lamb. On the pricey side, but with reason, it is open for dinner from 6pm.

LAHAINA Longhi's   🛇 🛆 🍸 P $$$$
888 Front St, 96761 **Tel** *(808) 667-2288*

Longhi's is famous. In business at the same location for 30 years, it is still an "in" spot. The food is Italian, well prepared, and pricey. Most tables are next to a window, so you can enjoy the hustle and bustle of Maui's busiest town along with your food. There is a good wine list and an espresso bar. The valet parking is a plus.

LAHAINA Pacific'O   🛇 🛆 📷 🎵 🍸 P $$$$
505 Front St, 96761 **Tel** *(808) 667-4341*

Creative contemporary Pacific cuisine with some delicious Asian twists is served in a setting fit for a king. The incredible oceanfront location was, in fact, a royal Hawaiian playground in ancient times. Dishes here include fresh greens and vegetables grown in the restaurant's upcountry O'o Farm.

LAHAINA Feast at Lele   🛇 🛆 📷 🎵 🍸 P ⭐ $$$$$
505 Front St, 96761 **Tel** *(808) 667-5353*

A divine oceanfront location complements this unique concept in dining and entertainment. A musical tour through four Pacific Island nations accompanies a sit-down dinner of modern interpretations of their cuisines. The menu was designed by multi-award-winning chef James McDonald of adjacent Pacific'O and I'o restaurants.

Key to Price Guide *see p196* **Key to Symbols** *see back cover flap*

LAHAINA Old Lahaina Lu'au

🔵🔵🔵🔵🔵 ⑤⑤⑤⑤⑤

1251 Front St, 96761 Tel (808) 667-1998

Maui's best *lu'au (see pp216–17)*, this nightly show and dinner takes place on the beach, under the palm trees and the starry skies. Traditional Hawaiian music and dance are presented. Authentic foods including *kālua* pig, *poi* (taro paste), and *lomi-lomi* salmon are served buffet style.

MĀ'ALAEA Seascape Ma'alaea Restaurant

🔵🔵🔵🔵 ⑤⑤

Maui Ocean Center, 192 Ma'alaea Rd, 96793 Tel (808) 270-7043 Fax (808) 270-7070

Located in the picturesque village of Ma'alaea this ocean-view restaurant is a great choice for many reasons. It has open-air seating arrangements, serves delicious and healthy sustainable seafood, and has an entire menu dedicated to trans-fat-free food. Open for lunch only.

MAKAWAO Komoda's Store and Bakery

🔵🔵 ⑤

3674 Baldwin Ave, 96768 Tel (808) 572-7261

For almost a century, the same family has been running Komoda's Store and Bakery in the heart of Makawao and making the goodies for it. It is always the favorite local spot for early morning specialties, especially the cream puffs and doughnuts on sticks. Arrive early as the daily supply of these outrageously tasty delights does not last long.

MAKAWAO Casanova Italian Restaurant and Deli

🔵🔵🔵🔵🔵 ⑤⑤⑤

1188 Makawao Ave, 96768 Tel (808) 572-0220

Enjoy coffee, drinks, breakfast omelets, home-baked pastries, and homemade deli specialties on the porch here as you watch people parade through Makawao town. At night, a full menu of Italian specialties is served in the restaurant. Both the pizzas, from the centerpiece wood-burning oven, and the pastas come recommended.

NĀPILI The Gazebo

🔵🔵🔵🔵 ⑤⑤

5315 Lower Honoapi'ilani Rd, 96761 Tel (808) 669-5621

The Gazebo is an indoor-outdoor restaurant right on the ocean that is a favorite breakfast place with the local residents and the tourists who find it. Macadamia nut pancakes are the most popular, but the pineapple and banana ones are equally delicious. There may be a wait for a table, but if so the superb view is compensation.

NĀPILI Sea House Restaurant

🔵🔵🔵🔵🔵🔵🔵 ⑤⑤⑤

5900 Honoapi'ilani Rd, 96761 Tel (808) 669-1500

You have to wind your way along the paths through Napili Kai Beach Resort *(see p187)* to get to the oceanfront Sea House Restaurant. From here, the view of the ocean and nearby islands is truly breathtaking. It is a great place for sunset watching. There is Hawaiian entertainment nightly and once a week a *hula* show is performed by children.

PĀ'IA Charley's Restaurant and Saloon

🔵🔵🔵🔵🔵🔵 ⑤⑤

142 Hāna Hwy, 96779 Tel (808) 579-9453

Named for the owner's pet dog, a Great Dane, Charley's serves meals of suitably large proportions. The service can be slow, but that gives you time to enjoy the *huevos rancheros* (Mexican eggs) at breakfast, fresh fish sandwiches at lunch, and pasta or pizzas later on. A long bar in the back has pool tables and occasional live music.

PĀ'IA Moana Bakery & Cafe

🔵🔵🔵🔵🔵 ⑤⑤

71 Baldwin Ave, 96779 Tel (808) 579-9999

Delicious pastries are baked daily on the premises. Breakfast, lunch, and dinner choices are all fresh and well prepared. Diners can sit either in booths or at window-side tables. The live evening entertainment at this casual café ranges from the blues to flamenco, and from jazz to Hawaiian slack key.

PĀ'IA Mama's Fish House

🔵🔵🔵🔵 ⑤⑤⑤⑤⑤

799 Poho Place, 96779 Tel (808) 579-8488

This restaurant is not only famous because it has been at its oceanfront location for more than 25 years. The fresh fish dishes it serves are excellent and extremely expensive. Even so, it is usually crowded so be sure to call ahead to reserve a table, preferably a window one. Valet parking is available.

WAILEA Tommy Bahama

🔵🔵🔵🔵🔵 ⑤⑤⑤

3750 Wailea Alanui, 96753 Tel (808) 875-9983

This chain of shops bills itself as the "purveyor of island lifestyles." Several, like this one, also have restaurants. The fare – fresh fish, salads, burgers, and lots of appetizers, all prepared island-style – is consistently excellent. The fun, tropical drinks are great, too. Portions are generally large, which at these prices they should be.

WAILEA Gannon's

🔵🔵🔵🔵🔵 ⑤⑤⑤⑤

100 Wailea Golf Club Dr, 96753 Tel (808) 875-8080

Gannon's is an elegant and spacious restaurant offering award-winning cuisine and deluxe service. Located on a hill along Wailea Golf Club's gold course *(see p227)*, the dining rooms have panoramic ocean views of the islands of Molokini and Kaho'olawe. The restaurant offers a casual fine-dining experience at breakfast, lunch, and dinner.

WAILEA Joe's Bar & Grill

🔵🔵🔵🔵 ⑤⑤⑤⑤

131 Wailea Iki Place, 96753 Tel (808) 875-7767

Joe's wife is the acclaimed Hawai'i regional cuisine chef Bev Gannon, so the food here is simply delicious. It is not just trendy, but hearty, as in the meatloaf with garlic mashed potatoes. Bev is not the only famous one in the family; Joe had his time in the limelight, as evidenced by the show-biz memorabilia that decorates the restaurant.

WAILEA Mala Wailea ⬤⬤⬤⬤⬤ $$$$

Marriott Wailea Beach Hotel, 3700 Wailea Alanui, 96753 **Tel** *(808) 875-9394*

Mala Wailea is another restaurant created by noted Maui chef Mark Ellman, one of the founders of the Hawai'i Regional Cuisine movement. His innovative dishes incorporate fresh island seafood and organic produce. Mala Wailea serves breakfast and dinner, with brunch on the weekends. Open daily.

WAILEA Spago ⬤⬤⬤⬤⬤ $$$$

3900 Wailea Alanui, 96753 **Tel** *(808) 879-2999*

The menu at celebrity chef Wolfgang Puck's Spago offers Puck's classics and locally inspired dishes that fuse Hawaiian and Californian cuisines, such as spicy ahi tuna poke in sesame-miso. Of course, it is elegant, as befits its location in the Four Seasons Resort Maui *(see p187)*.

WAILUKU A.K.'s Cafe ⬤⬤⬤ $$

1237 Lower Main St, 96793 **Tel** *(808) 244-8774*

Great tasting, local-style food that is good for you and affordable: this is what chef Elaine Rothermel set out to provide when she opened her pleasant small restaurant. She has succeeded. The Thai chicken, baked chicken, and turkey meatloaf are not to be missed. It is closed on weekends.

WAILUKU Asian Star ⬤ $$

1764 Wili Pa Loop, 96793 **Tel** *(808) 244-1833*

Tucked away in Wailuku's Millyard commercial area, this place is definitely worth seeking out. The efficient service makes it a popular lunch choice with folks who work nearby. Flavors are intense – try the curry lemongrass with chicken. The crispy tangerine beef is a specialty, salads are fresh, and noodle dishes are sure to please.

WAILUKU Tokyo Tei ⬤⬤⬤⬤ $$

1063 Lower Main St #C101, 96793 **Tel** *(808) 242-9630*

In business for more than 50 years, Tokyo Tei does local-style Japanese food exceedingly well and, somehow, cheaply. Every single dish on the menu is outstanding – the teriyaki fish, salmon, pork, and tempuras are particularly good. The sashimi is the freshest and most affordable you will find. It is not a fancy eatery, but comfortable.

WAILUKU A Saigon Cafe ⬤⬤⬤⬤ $$$

1792 Main St, 96793 **Tel** *(808) 243-9560*

Not easy to find because it is tucked away under a bridge without a sign, this is one of the most popular restaurants in central Maui. The eclectic menu features Vietnamese cuisine, with something for every appetite, including a good selection of vegetarian dishes. You may well find owner Jennifer Nguyen greeting diners when you arrive.

HAWAI'I ISLAND

HILO Bears' Coffee ⬤⬤⬤⬤⬤ $

106 Keawe St, 96721 **Tel** *(808) 935-0708*

Hilo's hippest little place is where locals gather to gossip, read the paper, and enjoy coffee, tasty breakfasts of Belgian waffles, or quick lunches such as a Greek salad or a burrito. Open daily, the coffee shop has outdoor sidewalk bistro tables that are in an ideal spot for watching the people of Hilo go by.

HILO Café 100 ⬤⬤⬤⬤⬤ $

969 Kīlauea Ave, 96721 **Tel** *(808) 935-8683*

Named for an all-Japanese fighting battalion that became famous during World War II, Café 100 has been serving Hilo folk at outdoor picnic-style tables for more than 50 years. The huge menu features items like beef teriyaki, beef curry, *laulau* (leaf-wrapped meat or fish bundles), *kālua* pig, and soda-fountain treats. It is closed on Sundays.

HILO Ken's House of Pancakes ⬤⬤⬤ $

1730 Kamehameha Ave, 96721 **Tel** *(808) 935-8711*

This 24-hour 1950s-style diner is best known for its incredible all-day breakfasts – exceptional omelets, potent coffee, and warm, friendly service. A favorite with local residents, Ken's House of Pancakes also offers a separate children's menu. A good selection of vegetarian dishes is available.

HILO Café Pesto ⬤⬤⬤ $$

308 Kamehameha Ave, 96721 **Tel** *(808) 969-6640*

Occupying a 1910 building that has survived more than one tsunami, this causal café is in a lovely setting near Hilo Bay. Hawai'i regional cuisine is featured here, including island fish prepared in a variety of ways, fresh organic salads, innovative pastas, and creative pizzas. This restaurant has a reputation for quality food and good service.

HILO Nihon Restaurant & Cultural Center ⬤⬤⬤⬤⬤ $$

123 Lihiwai St, 96721 **Tel** *(808) 969-1133*

Japanese in design, Nihon gives you culture with your sushi. This upstairs restaurant offers a beautiful view of Hilo Bay and Lili'uokalani Gardens. It is decorated with Japanese art and guests are greeted by traditional Japanese music. The food is authentic, delicious, and good value. It is closed on Sundays.

HILO Royal Siam Thai Restaurant $$
70 Mamo St, 96721 **Tel** *(808) 961-6100*

Fresh herbs and vegetables from the owner's garden enhance the Thai curries, noodles, soups, and other specialties on offer here, including Buddha Rama (a mix of spinach, chicken, and peanut sauce). This place is small, simply decorated, and inexpensive, and the food is consistently good. Closed for lunch on Sundays.

HILO Hilo Bay Café $$$
315 Maka'ala St, 96720 **Tel** *(808) 935-4939*

Its location near a strip mall, the pleasant decor, and its great food make Hilo Bay Café popular with both residents and visitors alike. The daily specials are made with local ingredients and include a choice of vegetarian, meat, and fish dishes. This trendy eatery is air-conditioned and provides separate tables for non-smokers.

HILO Ponds Hilo $$$
135 Kalanianaole Ave, 96721 **Tel** *(808) 934-7633*

Visitors to Hilo will find a delightful restaurant on Reed's Pond. The menu is American, with classics including prime rib, lobster, and escargot. Diners can enjoy the view of the pond as they chat with the chef, who visits each table personally.

HILO Seaside Restaurant $$$
1790 Kalanianole, 96721 **Tel** *(808) 935-8825*

The Nakagawa family has run this Hilo institution for more than 70 years. Dining here is an experience as the restaurant sits in the middle of Hilo ponds; the trout, mullet, and *aholehole* fish are caught right before you arrive. Reservations are recommended as its long-standing reputation as one of the island's best eateries draws crowds.

KAILUA-KONA Big Island Grill $
75-5702 Kuakini Hwy, 96745 **Tel** *(808) 326-1153*

Serving big portions at reasonable prices, the Big Island Grill is always packed. Worth the wait (reservations are not taken), the menu includes island favorites such as *loco moco* (egg-topped hamburger with rice and gravy) for breakfast, chicken katsu for lunch, and beef teriyaki for dinner. The drive-up window is great for those in a hurry.

KAILUA-KONA Boston Basil's $$
75-5707 Ali'i Dr, 96740 **Tel** *(808) 326-7836*

Right across from Hulihee Palace, this oceanview restaurant is all Italian, as evidenced by the tantalizing aroma of garlic in the air. Pizza, pasta, *parmigiana*, *cacciatore*, and an assortment of other fine Italian foods are tasty and reasonably priced. There are two large dining rooms, providing seating for 100.

KAILUA-KONA Sombat's Fresh Thai Cuisine $$
88 Kanoelehua Ave, 96720 **Tel** *(808) 969-9336*

"Fresh" is the key word here; Sombat grows a lot of the ingredients used in her flavorful dishes. Choose your heat level – mild, medium hot, or Thai hot – and enjoy traditional Thai offerings such as Green Papaya Salad, Summer Rolls, and curries. This place is small and popular, so take-out is a good option.

KAILUA-KONA Huggo's $$$
75-5828 Kahakai Rd, 96740 **Tel** *(808) 329-1493*

A Kona tradition, this family-run oceanside restaurant has been a favorite with locals for more than 35 years. Its spectacular setting affords diners a fabulous view of Kona Bay, making it a great place to watch sunsets, while enjoying live entertainment, cocktails, and *pūpū* (appetizers).

KAILUA-KONA Kona Inn Restaurant $$$
75-5744 Ali'i Dr, 96740 **Tel** *(808) 329-4455*

This is a sound choice for open-air dining in the heart of Kailua. The restaurant is set in a historic property built by the Inter-island Steam Navigation Company in 1928 and has retained a Hawaiian theme. A nice view of Kona Bay adds to the old-fashioned charm. Island fish, seafood, prime rib, and steak are featured on the menu.

KAILUA-KONA Krua Thai Cuisine $$$
75-5705 Kuakini Hwy, 96740 **Tel** *(808) 327-5782* **Fax** *(808) 327-5783*

A great spot for the experimental diner, this eatery serves reinvented versions of traditional Thai dishes. Popular offerings include curries, noodles, salads, dumplings, Thai-style chicken noodle soup, wontons, and spring rolls. For dessert try the sweet stick rice served with fresh mango.

KAILUA-KONA Pahu i'a $$$$
100 Kaupulehu Dr, 96740 **Tel** *(808) 325-5000*

The signature restaurant at the Four Seasons Resort Hualalai *(see p189)*, this beachfront spot is just steps away from the gently lapping waves of the Pacific. Terraced indoor and outdoor seating makes the most of the magnificent views. The cuisines of the Pacific are featured. Evening attire is suggested and reservations are recommended.

KEAUHOU Jackie Rey's Ohana Grill $$$
75-5995 Kuakini Hwy, 96740 **Tel** *(808) 327-0209*

Popular with the locals, this eatery serves great American food, with a good selection of American dishes. The atmosphere is lively and casual, while the service is impeccable. The mouth-watering offerings include fresh fish, salads, tacos, chops, ribs, and steaks. Reservations are recommended.

KOHALA COAST Canoe House
68-1400 Mauna Lani Dr, 96743 **Tel** *(808) 885-6622* $$$$

Set in the grounds of the Mauna Lani Bay Hotel *(see p189)*, the Canoe House combines a magnificent open-air setting with impressive Pacific Rim cuisine. A traditional *koa* canoe hangs from the ceiling. This is an expensive place, but the breathtaking location and marvelous sunset views make it worthwhile.

KOHALA COAST Roy's Waikoloa Bar & Grill
250 Waikoloa Beach Dr, 96738 **Tel** *(808) 886-4321* $$$$$

Although you would not think a venue of this caliber would be found in a strip mall, this is another one of celebrity chef Roy Yamaguchi's top-notch restaurants. His signatures are evident: an exhibition kitchen, trendy Hawaiian fusion cuisine, good service, and the roar of the crowd. Roy's is always packed, so it is best to make reservations.

VOLCANO Volcano Golf and Country Club
99-1261 Pi'i Mauna Dr, 96785 **Tel** *(808) 967-8228* $$

This restaurant is located in the golf-course clubhouse at the Volcano Golf and Country Club *(see p227)*. It serves burgers and sandwiches, along with local-style dishes such as *saimin* (noodles in broth), chili and rice, and teriyaki chicken. The service is friendly and the atmosphere casual, with the dining room overlooking the fairway.

VOLCANO Kilauea Lodge & Restaurant
Highway 11, 96785 **Tel** *(808) 967-7366* $$$

Cozy mountain decor, with a huge and historic fireplace, sets the scene for hearty European cooking. *Hasenpfeffer* (rabbit stew) is a house specialty; other favorites include freshly caught fish, duck, and venison. Dinners come with soup, freshly baked bread, and salad, and there's a good wine list. Brunch on Sundays.

WAIMEA Merriman's
65-1227 Opelo Rd, 96743 **Tel** *(808) 885-6822* $$$$$

Probably the best, and certainly the busiest, restaurant in Waimea, Merriman's is owned by one of the original Hawai'i regional cuisine chefs, Peter Merriman, who also operates Hula Grill Restaurant *(see p203)* on Maui. The menu features island-reared beef, fresh seafood (sometimes caught by Merriman himself), and other local produce.

KAUA'I

ANAHOLA Duane's Ono Char-Burgers
4-4350 Kūhiō Highway (Hwy 56), 96703 **Tel** *(808) 822-9181* $$

If you blink you will miss this Kaua'i burger institution, so keep your eyes peeled on the drive north from the airport. It is a roadside stand with a few concrete tables outside, but the burgers are big, juicy, and delicious. The fries are great too. Deservedly popular, it can attract a line at lunchtime.

HANAMAULU Hanamaulu Restaurant, Teahouse & Sushi Bar
3-4291 Kūhiō Hwy, 96715 **Tel** *(808) 245-2511* $$$

Off the beaten track, this eatery is still a local landmark. Although it is a typical Japanese teahouse, both Japanese and Chinese food, as well as plate lunches, are served. Diners can sit at the sushi bar, or at low tables on tatami floors in the teahouse (call ahead). Good Asian food has been served here for more than 75 years. Families enjoy this place.

KAPA'A Ono Friendly Restaurant
4-1292 Kuhio Hwy, 96746 **Tel** *(808) 822-1710* $

The big attraction at this diner-style restaurant is their hearty breakfast; the menu is extensive, but the pancakes and Portuguese sausage are two of the most popular options. The other big draw is the shave ice served through a takeaway window. Choose from one of the myriad flavors and enjoy.

KAPA'A Papaya's Natural Foods
4-831 Kūhiō Hwy, 96746 **Tel** *(808) 823-0190* $

This is the biggest health food store on Kaua'i and the food it serves is in keeping with the organic ingredients it sells. Tofu, hummus, tempeh, and all the usual health food fare is on the menu, along with baked goods, coffee, drinks, and smoothies. Order at the counter, then enjoy your food at the outdoor tables. It is closed on Sundays.

KAPA'A Eggbert's Family Specialty Restaurant
4-484 Kūhiō Hwy, 96746 **Tel** *(808) 822-3787* $$

Eggbert's has been a local favorite for over 25 years. In an open, airy corner of the Coconut Market Place *(see p214)*, it serves breakfast until 3pm, as well as lunch and dinner. There are more than 150 styles of omelet to choose from – and then there are the Eggs Benedict and the banana pancakes. Senior and *keiki* (children's) portions are available.

KAPA'A Hukilau Lanai
520 Aleka Lp, 96746 **Tel** *(808) 822-3441* $$$

Located in the Kauai Coast Resort, this eatery serves gluten-free healthy dishes. It also has a wine tasting menu and a happy hour tasting menu featuring items made from local produce such as Molokai sweet potato ravioli, Swiss chard, Hamakua mushroom tart, and Big Island vanilla bean crème brulée.

Key to Price Guide *see p196* **Key to Symbols** *see back cover flap*

KĪLAUEA The Kīlauea Bakery & Pau Hana Pizza

2484 Keneke St, 96746 **Tel** (808) 828-2020

This small and unassuming place is located in the Kong Lung complex on Kaua'i's North Shore. There are surely no better baked goods or pizzas anywhere on the island. Get there early for the best selection of breakfast goodies. Enjoy your delicious treat inside, or outside under the shade of an umbrella. Stock up for a picnic while here, too.

KOKE'E The Lodge at Koke'e

3600 Kokee Rd, 96796 **Tel** (808) 335-6061

Set within Koke'e State Park (see pp170–71), about 4,000 ft (1,220 m) above sea level, this welcoming place is open daily from 7am–6pm and serves breakfast, lunch, and desserts. The hearty Portuguese bean soup, a house specialty, is a delicious way to warm up. The luscious *lilikoi* (passionfruit), guava chiffon, and coconut pies are home-made.

LĪHU'E Hamura Saimin & Halo Halo Shave Ice

2956 Kress St, 96766 **Tel** (808) 245-3271

Though not particularly attractive to look at, this place is famous for having the best *saimin* (noodles and broth) around. Crowded even late at night, it is affordable as the most expensive item on the menu costs $5. Fresh *lilikoi* (passionfruit) pie is the specialty dessert. Go through the side entrance for shave ice, another local treat.

LĪHU'E Tip Top Café & Motel

3173 Akahi St, 96766 **Tel** (808) 245-2333

This spotlessly clean, large dining room has 1950s-style booths and orchids on every table. Breakfasts and lunches are hearty. The macadamia pancakes are legendary at breakfast, while the oxtail soup is the highlight at lunch. This café-bakery has been in business since 1916 and is still a local favorite. It is closed on Mondays.

LĪHU'E Café Portofino

3481 Ho'olaulea Way, 96766 **Tel** (808) 245-2121

Café Portofino serves Italian fare created with authentic ingredients imported from Italy. Breads, ice cream, and desserts are made on the premises. Located in the Kaua'i Marriott, the restaurant has a romantic atmosphere, with candelit tables, and soft music performed by a harpist or classical guitarist. Open for dinner only.

LĪHU'E Duke's Canoe Club Barefoot Bar & Restaurant

3610 Rice St, 96766 **Tel** (808) 246-9599

Named for legendary Hawaiian surfer and Olympic champion Duke Kahanamoku, this place is decorated with his memorabilia, including three of his surfboards. Oceanfront at the Kaua'i Marriott Resort (see p191), it is one of the busiest spots in town. The sunset views are incredible, the menu is affordable, and the music is live.

LĪHU'E JJ's Broiler

3416 Rice St, 96766 **Tel** (808) 246-4422

JJ's at Anchor Cove Shopping Center has a simple winning feature: open-air dining with a great ocean view. Burgers, sandwiches, and vegetarian dishes are served at lunch; seafood, steak, and pasta at dinner. Slavonic steak (tenderloin in butter, wine, and garlic) is the signature dish. Portions are large and there are daily specials at reasonable prices.

LĪHU'E Gaylord's at Kilohana

3-2087 Kaumuali'i Hwy, 96766 **Tel** (808) 245-9593

Located at Kilohana, Kaua'i's legendary plantation estate, Gaylord's offers gracious open-air dining matched by unhurried service and a menu ranging from pasta to prime rib. Sunday brunch is served here and there is an extensive wine cellar. Today the historic estate includes a complex of shops and galleries.

PO'IPŪ Casa Blanca at Kiahuna

2290 Po'ipū Rd, 96756 **Tel** (808) 742-2929

This small, open-air restaurant is located at the Kiahuna Swim and Tennis Club. The best food on offer here has Mediterranean and African influences: such as Basque *piperrada* (pepper omelet) at breakfast, Algerian chicken skewers, and North African lamb with fennel and harissa. Tapas and children's menus are available.

PO'IPŪ Casa Di Amici

2301 Nalo Rd, 96756 **Tel** (808) 742-1555

Italian-Mediterranean fare and alfresco dining make this a hidden delight. Tucked away in a residential neighborhood in Po'ipū, Casa Di Amici serves risottos, pastas, and specials, all prepared by the owner-chef. Diners come for the relaxing atmosphere, tasty food, and fairly reasonable prices. It is open for dinner only.

PO'IPŪ The Beach House

5022 Lawai Rd, 96756 **Tel** (808) 742-1424

With a spectacular oceanfront setting, The Beach House is one of the best spots on Kaua'i for sunset drinks, appetizers, and dinner. The excellent menu offers the chef's creative twists on island favorites, made with fresh local ingredients. The outstanding food, good service, and fantastic location make this one of the island's top restaurants.

PO'IPŪ Roy's Po'ipū Bar & Grill

2360 Kiahuna Plantation Dr, 96756 **Tel** (808) 742-5000

Chef Roy Yamaguchi has become internationally known and operates restaurants across the US. Most are crowded and noisy and have exhibition kitchens so that diners can watch their food being prepared. The food is typically creative, delicious, and worth the price. This one, in the Po'ipū Shopping Village (see p214), is no exception.

SHOPPING IN HAWAI'I

Pineapples, macadamia nuts, Kona coffee, alohawear, T-shirts, tropical flowers – these are the things that top visitors' shopping lists, and they are easy to find. Traditional Hawaiian crafts, such as *kapa* cloth, pandanus baskets, and Ni'ihau shell *lei*, are harder to find and usually more costly – but beautiful, and worth the hunt. You will find many things that look like they could be made in Hawai'i but actually come from Taiwan, Bali, China, or the Philippines. If you are determined to purchase "the real thing," check carefully. The addresses and telephone numbers of all the shops mentioned in the text are given on page 213.

Coconut frond hat

A woman weaving traditional *lei* garlands, a popular Hawaiian souvenir

SHIPPING

For a charge, most stores and galleries will ship goods worldwide. Alternatively, you can use the **United States Postal Service** to send purchases home. Courier companies such as **DHL**, **FedEx**, and **UPS** are another option and can be contacted by phone or email. They provide insurance, delivery confirmation, and tracking, and offer a range of delivery times and costs. Some restrictions may apply to the type of item that can be sent and the destination of the package. You will be asked to fill out a form giving a short description of the goods and stating their monetary value. Keep receipts of the transaction in case any items should get lost in transit.

WHERE TO SHOP

Supermarkets, grocery shops, Longs Drugs stores, and discount shops, such as ABC Stores and K-Mart, have the best prices for things like macadamia nuts, jam, and coffee. These are the best places for cheap souvenirs, too, while museum shops are often good for Hawaiian crafts.

Anyone who likes secondhand shops should enjoy scouring shops and home sales for collectibles ("Hawaiiana"), from aloha shirts to vintage postcards, at bargain prices. The islands are big on secondhand shops and private garage sales. Check the Friday edition of the newspapers for weekend garage sales. The papers also list crafts fairs and market days.

WHEN TO SHOP

You can shop 24 hours a day, seven days a week if you wish – some supermarkets and convenience stores never close.

Malls and large stores are normally open from 10am to 9pm, Monday to Saturday, and often on Sunday (but the hours are usually shorter). Small stores open from about 9am to 5 or 6pm, Monday to Saturday, and are closed on Sundays.

HOW TO PAY

Travelers' checks in US dollars and credit cards are accepted more or less everywhere in Hawai'i *(see p240)*. However, it is a good idea to carry at least some cash for purchases at roadside stands and small, family-run stores.

Remember that sales tax of 4.17 percent is added to every purchase made in Hawai'i, and that this tax will be added to the total bill by the cashier.

FRUIT AND FLOWERS

Many visitors take the fresh flavors and aromas of Hawai'i home with them. You can take coconuts, pineapples, and papayas (but no other fruit) through customs, as long as they are passed by the **US Department of Agriculture (USDA)** inspection.

It is best to buy such fruit prepackaged at airport shops or other reputable stores that specialize in "take home" fruits. There are many of these stores in Hawai'i, such as the **Maui Tropical Plantation & Country Store** near Wailuku. Someone at your hotel should know the best place on any particular island. These same places sell sterile cuttings and

Roadside stand selling tropical Hawaiian fruit on Maui's windward coast

seeds of tropical plants that have been passed by USDA. You can have your purchases delivered to the airport from which you are leaving or sent directly to your home address.

You can export all fresh flowers, subject to agricultural inspection, apart from jade vines, gardenias, and *mauna-loa*. Hawai'i Island is the best place for anthuriums, while you should buy protea and exotics in Maui. You can export *lei*, but most last only a very short time; check with the florist or *lei*-maker, because some *lei* are very attractive when dried. Alternatively, you could consider buying a nonperishable *lei* made of nuts, feathers, seeds, or shells, for example (*see p29*). The best places to buy flower *lei* are the small shops in Honolulu's China-town, but the stands at Honolulu International Airport have a good selection, too.

If you are unsure whether or not you'll be able to take a particular item home with you, check first by telephoning the USDA.

Macadamia nuts, in easy-to-pack cans

FOOD AND DRINK

Although mangoes, guava, and *liliko'i* (passion fruit) are not permitted out of the islands, chutneys, jams, jellies, and other products made with these fruits are great buys.

World-famous Kona coffee comes from Hawai'i Island, but coffee is now grown on Maui and Kaua'i too. All coffees are available in whole-bean or ground, flavored, instant, and decaffeinated varieties. Macadamia nuts also come in many forms, from dry-roasted and salted to honey-flavored or chocolate-covered. Adventurous gastronomes may like to try taro chips and "crack seed" – preserved and seasoned nuts, fruits, seeds, and sweets. All these products are sold at supermarkets, grocery stores, convenience stores, and specialty shops throughout the islands. **Shirokiya** (Honolulu), a Japan-based department store, also sells a great variety of unusual prepared food.

Hawai'i has two wineries. The **Tedeschi Winery** on Maui makes a couple of good red table wines, one sparkling wine, and, its most famous product, Maui Blanc – a light pineapple wine. The **Volcano Winery** on Hawai'i Island is producing some interesting wines from various tropical fruits while waiting for its grapevines to mature.

ART

Like Gauguin, many artists have followed their muse to the Pacific. Unlike Gauguin, the majority are not very good. There are literally dozens of "galleries," mostly in tourist shopping areas. Some specialize in sales of very expensive work that has no investment value – in spite of what the resident "consultants" tell you. If you need advice, someone at your hotel should be able to direct you to a reliable source; museums can often be of help, too.

There is some wonderful art to be found in Hawai'i. And much of it – in the form of lithographs, posters, and even cards – is affordable. Dietrich Varez of Volcano (on Hawai'i Island), for example, lovingly creates earth-brown linoleum block prints depicting local legends. They are glorious, easy to find, and cheap, at about $20 apiece. You will find his work in the **Volcano Art Center**. Another reputable gallery on Hawai'i Island is **Studio 7** in Hōlualoa.

The **Viewpoints Gallery** in Makawao (Maui) is a collective representing some fine local artists.

One of the many art galleries on Front Street in Lahaina, Maui

You can also rely on good quality at the **Village Gallery** and **Lahaina Arts Society** in Lahaina, **Gecko Trading** in Makawao, and **Nohea Gallery** in Honolulu.

COLLECTIBLES

Just about anything Hawaiian from the 1940s to the 1970s is now considered collectible: postcards, Matson steamship menus, even kitsch ceramic *hula* girls, and especially old aloha shirts known as "silkies."

You'll find such things in the shops on Wailuku's Market Street and in "antique" shops such as **Bailey's Antiques** and **Aloha Antiques & Collectibles** in Honolulu, and **The Only Show in Town** in Kahuku (O'ahu); **Mauna Kea Galleries** in Kamuela; **Story of Hawai'i Museum**; and the **Pā'ia Trading Company** on Maui. You may find it more fun, however, to go hunting for collectibles in secondhand stores and garage sales.

Display of blown-glass vases and other objects in a Maui gallery

Man weaving a coconut-leaf hat on a Hawai'i Island street

CRAFTS

Hawai'i teems with artisans. Hand-crafted bowls of mango, monkeypod, or *koa* wood make beautiful presents and mementos. You can also buy *koa* hair ornaments, chopsticks, and key chains. Wooden objects can be found in craft shops in most big towns.

Hawai'i also has many expert weavers. Coconut leaf is often used, but *hala* (pandanus) is better quality. Mats, bags, and hats are all popular buys. Ceramic bowls, vases, and plates are also popular. **The Island's Best** in Honolulu is a good bet for these.

It is virtually impossible to find any vintage Hawaiian quilts to buy (most are treasured family heirlooms), but new quilts, quilt kits and other crafts can be found at the **Maui Crafts Guild** in Pā'ia or the **Gallery of Great Things** on Hawai'i Island. Hawaiian kapa (bark cloth) is hard to find and most *kapa* goods for sale are imported from Samoa or Tonga.

Combing the crafts fairs is a fun and rewarding way to see what is available. Museum shops are also good sources, as are the many specialty shops, including **Sand & Sea** on Maui and **Ola's Hanalei** on Kaua'i.

JEWELRY

Costume jewelry is made from everything you can think of – ceramic, paper, plastic, metals, and more – and can be found at crafts fairs. Fine jewelry made of pearls, coral, jade, silver, and gold is sold in department stores and in the dozens of specialty shops, such as **Precision Goldsmiths** in Wailuku and Kaua'i's **Jim Saylor Jewelers**. "Heritage jewelry," Victorian gold jewelry with names and designs inscribed in black enamel, is popular. It is also expensive, so be sure to buy from a reliable dealer.

The most precious pieces of Hawaiian jewelry available are Ni'ihau shell *lei*. The shops on Kaua'i are the best places to buy them, but be sure to do some advance research before you make a purchase. A simple choker may cost as little as $25, while museum-quality, multi-strand, waist-length *lei* typically cost thousands of dollars.

BOOKS AND MUSIC

The only major bookstore still operating in the Island is **Barnes & Noble**, which has the best choice of books, CDs, DVDs, and more items about Hawai'i. Museum shops will also have a good selection of Hawaiian books for sale. **Native Books Na Mea Hawaii**, in Honolulu, has a wide range of Hawaiian-language books.

In most music stores, including the locally based **Requests**, both traditional and contemporary Hawaiian music is available.

Wooden bowl from the Maui Crafts Guild

CLOTHES AND FABRIC

The days of tourists strolling down the street dressed in matching polyester *mu'umu'u* and aloha shirts seem to have gone. Even the state's biggest producer of alohawear, **Hilo Hattie**, now sells attractive cotton or cotton-blend island fashions in its many fashion centers. **Jagger's** (Pā'ia, Maui), **Sig Zane Designs** (Hilo, Hawai'i Island), and **Reyn's** and **Macy's** (both are state-wide department stores) stock some stunning Hawaiian-style clothing in the latest fashions, colors and subtle prints. However, you might want to think about whether you will be able (or want) to wear your expensive *mu'umu'u* back home.

Sarongs are popular beachwear among local women and men. They are sold everywhere and cost $10–35, depending on the fabric and design. Most places offer tips on how to wear what is basically a couple of yards of material finished on all four sides.

Hawai'i is a great place to stock up on swimsuits, and it can surely claim to be the T-shirt capital of the world. T-shirts are sold everywhere, emblazoned with every imaginable design and logo. In particular, **Crazy Shirts**, which has a number of stores statewide, is considered by many to stock the highest quality shirts with the best designs.

Sarongs displayed outside a shop on O'ahu's North Shore

DIRECTORY

SHIPPING

DHL
Tel (800) 225-5345.
www.dhl.com

FedEx
Tel (800) 463-3339.
www.fedex.com

United States Postal Service
Tel (800) 275-8777.
www.usps.gov

UPS
Tel (800) 742-5877.
www.ups.com

FRUIT & FLOWERS

Dole Plantation
64-1550 Kamehameha Hwy, Wahiawā, O'ahu.
Tel (808) 621-8408.
www.dole-plantation.com

Maui Tropical Plantation & Country Store
1670 Honoapi'ilani Hwy, Wailuku, Maui.
Tel (808) 244-7643.
www.mauitropical plantation.com

Take Home Maui
121 Dickenson St, Lahaina, Maui.
Tel (808) 661-8067.
www.takehomemaui.com

US Department of Agriculture (USDA)
Honolulu International Airport, Honolulu, O'ahu.
Tel (808) 861-8494.

FOOD AND DRINK

Shirokiya
Ala Moana Center, Honolulu, O'ahu.
Map 3 A4.
Tel (808) 973-9111.
www.shirokiya.com

Tedeschi Winery
'Ulupalakua, Maui.
Tel (808) 878-6058.
www.mauiwine.com

Volcano Winery
35 Pi'imauna Drive, Volcano, Hawai'i Island.
Tel (808) 967-7772.
http://volcanowinery.com

ART

Gecko Trading Co.
3621 Baldwin Ave, Makawao, Maui.
Tel (808) 572-0249.

Lahaina Arts Society
Old Lahaina Courthouse, Lahaina, Maui.
Tel (808) 661-0111.
www.lahaina-arts.com

Nohea Gallery
Ward Warehouse, 1050 Ala Moana Blvd, Honolulu, O'ahu. **Map** 2 D5.
Tel (808) 596-0074.
www.noheagallery.com

Studio 7
Māmalahoa Hwy, Hōlualoa, Hawai'i Island.
Tel (808) 324-1335.

Viewpoints Gallery
3620 Baldwin Ave, Makawao, Maui. *Tel (808) 572-5979.* www.viewpointsmaui.com

Village Gallery
120 Dickenson St, Lahaina, Maui. *Tel (808) 661-4402.* www.villagegallerymaui.com

Volcano Art Center
Hawai'i Volcanoes National Park, Hawai'i Island.
Tel (808) 967-7565.
www.volcanoartcenter.org

COLLECTIBLES

Bailey's Antiques
517 Kapahulu Ave, Honolulu, O'ahu.
Tel (808) 734-7628.
www.alohashirts.com

Mauna Kea Galleries
2005 S King St, Honolulu, O'ahu. *Tel (808) 941-4901.* www.maunakea galleries.com

The Only Show in Town
56-901 Kamehameha Hwy, Kahuku, O'ahu.
Tel (808) 293-1295.

Pā'ia Trading Company
106 Hāna Hwy, Pā'ia, Maui. *Tel (808) 579-9472.*

Story of Hawai'i Museum
Maalaea Shops, Maalaea, Maui. *Tel (808) 242-6938.* www.storyof hawaiimuseum.com

CRAFTS

Gallery of Great Things
Parker Square, Waimea, Hawai'i Island.
Tel (808) 885-7706.
www.galleryofgreat thingshawaii.com

Maui Crafts Guild
69 Hāna Hwy, Pā'ia, Maui.
Tel (808) 579-9697.
www.mauicrafts guild.com

Ola's Hanalei
5016 Kūhiō Hwy, Hanalei, Kaua'i.
Tel (808) 826-6937.
www.olashanalei.com

Sand & Sea
83A Hāna Hwy, Pāia, Maui. *Tel (808) 579-9377.*

The Island's Best
Ala Moana Center, Honolulu, O'ahu.
Tel (808) 949-5345.

JEWELRY

Jessica's Gems
Whalers Village, Kā'anapali, Maui. *Tel (808) 661-4223.*

Jim Saylor Jewelers
1318 Kūhiō Hwy, Kapa'a, Kaua'i. *Tel (808) 822-3591.*

Precision Goldsmiths
16 N Market St, Wailuku, Maui. *Tel (808) 986-8282.* www.precision goldsmiths.com

BOOKS AND MUSIC

Bailey House Museum Gift Shop
2375 A Main St, Wailuku, Maui.
Tel (808) 244-3326.
www.mauimuseum.org

Barnes & Noble
Kahala Mall, 4211 Wai'alae Ave, Honolulu, O'ahu.
Tel (808) 737-3323.

Mission Houses Museum Gift Shop

533 King St, Honolulu 96813. *Tel (808) 447-3910.* www.museumhouses.org

Native Books Na Mea Hawaii
Ward Warehouse, 1050 Alamoana Blvd, Honolulu O'ahu. **Map** 2 D5. *Tel (808) 596-8885.* www.nativebookshawaii.com

Requests
10 N Market St, Wailuku, Maui. *Tel (808) 244-9315.* http://requestshawaii.com

CLOTHES AND FABRIC

Crazy Shirts
Ala Moana Center, Honolulu, O'ahu. **Map** 3 A4. *Tel (808) 973-4000.* Call for the nearest branch. www.crazyshirts.com

Hilo Hattie
700 N Nimitz Hwy, Honolulu, O'ahu.
Tel (808) 535-6500. Call for the nearest branch. www.hilohattie.com

Jagger's
100 Hana Hwy, Pā'ia, Maui. *Tel (808) 579-9221.*

Macy's
Ala Moana Center, Honolulu, O'ahu.
Tel (808) 941-2345. Call for the nearest branch.

Mamo Howell
Ward Warehouse, 1050 Ala Moana Blvd, Honolulu, O'ahu. **Map** 2 D5.
Tel (808) 591-2002.
www.mamohowell.com

Reyn's
Ala Moana Center, Honolulu, O'ahu. **Map** 3 A4.
Tel (808) 949-5929. Call for the nearest branch. www.reynspooner.com

Sig Zane Designs
122 Kamehameha Ave, Hilo, Hawai'i Island.
Tel (808) 935-7077.
www.sigzane.com

Malls and Shopping Centers

There are literally hundreds of shopping options in
Hawai'i, including huge malls and shopping centers
that stay open late. While shopping centers do not
dominate the landscape as they do in parts of the
United States, they are still a common feature of
Hawai'i's main towns. Most malls have one large
department store, together with smaller shops and
boutiques, as well as restaurants, movie theaters,
and a beauty salon or day spa. Some even have
stages for performances and present a full calendar
of entertainment, including *hula* shows, concerts,
and amateur talent contests.

HONOLULU AND WAIKĪKĪ

Honolulu and Waikīkī's many
shopping centers offer an outstanding selection of goods
and services. The largest and
most well-known is the **Ala
Moana Center**, with department stores such as Macy's,
Sears, Nordstrom's,
and hundreds of
other outlets. The
**Royal Hawaiian
Shopping Center** is
home to designer
boutiques like Cartier
and Hermès. The
International Marketplace is
an open-air bazaar offering
jewelry, apparel, and
souvenirs. Other popular
shopping spots include the
waterfront complex **Aloha
Tower Marketplace**, **Kahala
Mall**, **King's Village**, and **Koko
Marina Center**.

O'AHU

Bargain hunters can follow
their instincts at **Waikele
Premium Outlets**, with 50
discount outlets including
Banana Republic, Guess, and
Tommy Hilfiger. The **Windward Mall** has more than 80
gift, clothing, and food outlets.
Pearl Highlands Center has
stores such as Payless Shoe
Source, Old Navy, Pier 1, and
Sam's Club, movie theaters,
and a fitness center. At **Pearlridge**, a monorail connects
two shopping centers.

MOLOKA'I AND LĀNA'I

Both Moloka'i and Lāna'i each
has one large town whose
main street has most of its
shops. On Moloka'i, shoppers
can find everything from

fishing gear to clothing and
food on Ala Malama Street in
Kaunakakai. Check out **Friendly
Market Center**. Shopping on
Lāna'i is centered around Dole
Park, Lāna'i City. Visit **Pine
Isle Market** and **Richard's
Shopping Center**, an old-
fashioned general store.

The well-known
Hilo Hattie logo

MAUI

Maui's largest
department store,
Macy's, is in the
island's biggest mall,
**Queen Ka'ahumanu
Center**. Others, such as
Whalers Village and **The
Shops at Wailea**, offer upscale
shopping on the oceanfront.
Pi'ilani Shopping Village in
Kīhei has the state's largest
Safeway and Hilo Hattie for
souvenirs. **Lahaina Cannery
Mall**, housed in a refurbished
pineapple cannery, sells
everything from aloha wear
to fine art. **Maui Marketplace**
offers Borders Books & Music,
The Sports Authority, and Old
Navy. Other shopping spots
include **Kukui Mall** and **Nāpili
Plaza**, a neighborhood-style
center with a military museum.

Entrance to the Aloha Tower
Marketplace, Honolulu

HAWAI'I ISLAND

The main shopping districts
on Hawai'i Island are in the
towns of Kailua-Kona,
Waimea, and Hilo. In Kailua-
Kona there are several small
shopping centers, including
Coconut Grove Market Place
and **Kona Coast Shopping
Center**. Just outside Kailua-
Kona, the **Keauhou Shopping
Center** is home to one-off
shops selling hand-blown
glass, ceramics, mermaid
ornaments, and *hula* dolls.
Waimea Center has a supermarket, a bakery, and apparel
and gift stores. The upscale
Kings' Shops in Waikoloa are
comprised of art galleries,
boutiques, and designer stores.
In Hilo, **Prince Kūhiō Plaza**, the
island's largest mall, includes
mainland brand stores, such as
Sears and Macy's, and smaller
outlets that carry apparel,
crafts, and surf gear. WalMart,
Borders Books & Music, Hilo
Hattie, and a food court are
found in the **Waiakea Center**.

KAUA'I

The **Po'ipū Shopping Village**
features an open-air garden
setting and an array of services, eateries, and specialty
stores selling jewelry, art,
apparel, and accessories.
In Kapa'a, the open-air
Coconut Market Place is a
good spot for searching
out resort wear, collectibles,
and local arts and crafts. In
addition to the shops and
galleries at **Kaua'i Village**,
look out for a heritage center
and the Kaua'i Children's
Discovery Museum.
Kukui Grove Center is
Kaua'i's largest shopping
center. Included here are
well-known stores such
as Macy's, Sears, K-Mart,
Long's Drugs, a variety of
smaller shops, and a Fun
Factory. The plantation-
themed **Princeville Center** has
more than 35 shops and
restaurants, along with
a supermarket, a bank,
a hardware store, a post
office, and a clinic. Other
popular shopping centers
include **Ching Young Village
Shopping Center** and **Rice
Shopping Center**.

DIRECTORY

HONOLULU AND WAIKĪKĪ

Ala Moana Center
1450 Ala Moana Blvd,
Honolulu, O'ahu.
Map 2 F4.
Tel (808) 955-9517.
www.alamoana
center.com

Aloha Tower Marketplace
1 Aloha Tower Dr,
Honolulu, O'ahu.
Map 1 A3.
Tel (808) 528-5700.
www.alohatower.com

International Marketplace
2330 Kalākaua Ave,
Waikīkī, O'ahu.
Map 4 E5.
Tel (808) 971-2080.
www.international
marketplacewaikiki.com

Kahala Mall
4211 Wai'alae Ave,
Honolulu, O'ahu.
Map 4 F5.
Tel (808) 732-7736.
www.kahalamall
center.com

King's Village
131 Ka'iulani Ave,
Waikīkī, O'ahu.
Map 4 E4.
Tel (808) 944-6855.
www.kings-village.com

Koko Marina Center
7192 Kalaniana'ole Hwy,
Honolulu, O'ahu.
Map 4 F5.
Tel (808) 395-4737.
www.kokomarina
center.com

Royal Hawaiian Shopping Center
2201 Kalākaua Ave,
Waikīkī, O'ahu. **Map** 4 D4.
Tel (808) 922-0588.
www.royalhawaiian
center.com

O'AHU

Pearl Highlands Center
1000 Kamehameha Hwy,
Pearl City, O'ahu.
Tel (808) 456-1000.
www.pearlhighlands
center.com

Pearlridge Mall
98-1005 Moanalua Rd,
Aiea, Hawai'i Island.
Tel (808) 488-0981.
www.pearlridge
online.com

Waikele Premium Outlets
97-790 Lumiaina St,
Waipahu, O'ahu.
Tel (808) 676-5656.
www.premiumoutlets.
com/waikele

Windward Mall
46-056 Kamehameha
Hwy, Kane'ohe, O'ahu.
Tel (808) 235-1143.
www.windwardmall.com

MOLOKA'I AND LĀNA'I

Friendly Market Center
90 Ala Malama St,
Kaunakakai, Moloka'i.
Tel (808) 553-5595.

Pine Isle Market
356 Eighth St,
Lāna'i City, Lāna'i.
Tel (808) 565-6488.

Richard's Shopping Center
434 Eighth St,
Lāna'i City, Lāna'i.
Tel (808) 565-6047.

MAUI

Kukui Mall
1819 South Kīhei Rd,
Kīhei, Maui.
Tel (808) 877-7073.

Lahaina Cannery Mall
1221 Honoapi'ilani
Hwy, Lahaina, Maui.
Tel (808) 661-5304.
www.lahainacannery
mall.com

Maui Marketplace
270 Dairy Rd,
Kahului, Maui.
Tel (808) 873-0400.

Nāpili Plaza
509 Nāpilihau St,
Nāpili, Maui.
Tel (808) 872-4318.

Pi'ilani Shopping Village
297 Pi'ikea Ave,
Kīhei, Maui.
Tel (808) 874-8900.

Queen Ka'ahumanu Center
275 Ka'ahumanu Ave,
Kahului, Maui.
Tel (808) 877-4325.
www.queenkaahumanu
center.com

The Shops at Wailea
3750 Wailea Alanui,
Wailea, Maui.
Tel (808) 891-6770.
www.shopsatwailea.com

Whalers Village
2435 Kā'anapali Pkwy,
Kā'anapali, Maui.
Tel (808) 661-4567.
www.whalersvillage.com

HAWAI'I ISLAND

Coconut Grove Market Place
75-5818 Ali'i Dr, Kailua-
Kona, Hawai'i Island.

Keauhou Shopping Center
78-6831 Ali'i Dr,
Kailua-Kona, Hawai'i.
Tel (808) 322-3000.
www.keauhou
villageshops.com

Kings' Shops
250 Waikoloa Beach Dr,
Waikoloa Beach Resort,
Hawai'i Island. *Tel (808)
866-8811.* www.
waikoloabeachresort.com

Kona Coast Shopping Center
74-5588 Palani Rd,
Kailua-Kona,
Hawai'i Island.
Tel (808) 326-2262
www.konashopping.com

Prince Kūhiō Plaza
111 E Puainako St,
Hilo, Hawai'i Island.
Tel (808) 959-3555.
www.princekuhio
plaza.com

Waiakea Center
324 Maka'ala St,
Hilo, Hawai'i Island.
Tel (808) 961-9115.

Waimea Center
65-1158 Mamalahoa Hwy,
Waimea, Hawai'i Island.
Tel (808) 885-7727.

KAUA'I

Coconut Market Place
4-484 Kūhiō Hwy,
Kapa'a, Kaua'i.
Tel (808) 822-3641.
www.coconutmarket
place.com

Ching Young Village Shopping Center
5-5190 Kūhiō Hwy,
Hanalei, Kaua'i.
Tel (808) 826-7222.
www.chingyoung
village.com

Kaua'i Village
4-831 Kūhiō Hwy,
Kapa'a, Kaua'i.
Tel (808) 822-3777.

Kukui Grove Center
3-2600 Kaumuali'i Hwy,
Līhu'e, Kaua'i. *Tel (808)
245-7784.* www.
kukuigrovecenter.com

Po'ipū Shopping Village
2360 Kiahuna Plantation
Dr, Po'ipū, Kaua'i.
Tel (808) 742-2831.

Princeville Center
5-4280 Kūhiō Hwy,
Princeville, Kaua'i.
Tel (880) 826-9497.

Rice Shopping Center
4303 Rice St, Līhu'e, Kaua'i.
Tel (800) 246-0311.

ENTERTAINMENT IN HAWAI'I

Music, song, and dance are as important to Hawaiians as the food that they eat and the air they breathe. From the musicians strumming in virtually every hotel lounge to the Merrie Monarch Festival (known as the "Olympics of *hula*"), Hawai'i is alive with the sounds of music. Besides Hawaiian rhythms, all kinds of

Hawaiian *hula* dancer

music from country to rock, jazz, and reggae can be enjoyed, and world-class places stage both rock and classical concerts, opera, and even Broadway musicals. For information on the Hawaiian nightlife scene, from dancing the night away in Honolulu to the hotels and bars offering live music elsewhere, see pages 220–21.

Hawaiian tourist magazines, a good source of entertainment information

PRACTICAL INFORMATION

The Friday edition of *The Honolulu Advertiser* has the most complete entertainment listings; the neighboring islands' newspapers also have entertainment sections once a week. Local radio stations and posters plastered all over town are other sources, along with free local newspapers such as *Honolulu Weekly*. Your hotel should have up-to-date listings.

TICKET OUTLETS

It is best to buy tickets in advance for major events such as the Broadway shows that are occasionally put on in Honolulu. You can charge tickets to a major credit card for many events by telephoning **Ticket Master**.

If you're buying tickets in person, there is sure to be a convenient ticket outlet near your hotel for almost any event; check with the hotel's guest services department. Music stores sell most concert tickets, for example.

Local people are not known for making plans a long way in advance, so there are usually tickets to be had at the door for smaller events.

If you want to attend the really big shows – the Merrie Monarch Festival in April or February's NFL Pro Bowl, for example – you should plan your holiday around them. Tickets for these must be purchased months in advance. You should also note that hotel rooms are at a premium during particularly big events.

HAWAIIAN MUSIC, HULA, AND LŪ'AU

A great deal of the Hawaiian entertainment that is most popular with visitors – from the sounds of traditional chants and slack-key guitar (*kī hō'alu*) to traditional foods and *hula* costumes – has been "adjusted" for Western tastes. However, as a result of the cultural renaissance that has occurred in the state over the last decade, traditional Hawaiian entertainment is now accessible to anyone who wishes to experience it. Virtually every hotel offers Hawaiian music of some description on a regular, if not daily, basis, and many put on *hula* shows, too. Such performances are usually free.

The **Waikīkī Shell** in Kapi'olani Park is a magnificent outdoor spot that hosts many concerts of Hawaiian music and *hula* throughout the year.

"The Shell" was once home to the famous Kodak Hula Show, which was started by Kodak in 1939. Although the show no longer exists the Waikīkī Shell has not lost its fame and continues to be one of O'ahu's top entertainment venues.

Small shows staged at island shopping centers are often the most authentic. They usually feature students of Hawaiian music and dance from *hālau hula* (*hula* schools) and are almost always free.

For a unique treat, enjoy the remarkable talent of the two Brothers Cazimero, whose extraordinary voices and skill on the guitar and bass combine to produce one of Honolulu's best shows. Check the listings in the newspapers or tourist magazines for details of shows.

Most of the major hotels offer *lū'au* – the traditional feasts of the islands. Prices

The impressive sight of a traditional Hawaiian feast or *lū'au* in Lahaina, Maui

Colorful pageant at the Polynesian Cultural Center on O'ahu *(see p92)*

are approximately $85–125 for adults and half that for kids. On O'ahu, try the **Paradise Cove Lū'au** in 'Ewa, about 25 miles (40 km) from Waikīkī; tickets include the bus from town. The best place to go on Maui is, without doubt, **Old Lahaina Lū'au**, in a lovely setting overlooking the ocean.

The only waterfront *lū'au* in Kailua-Kona (Hawai'i Island) is held at **King Kamehameha's Kona Beach Hotel**, **The Gathering of Kings** show takes place at the **Fairmont Orchid**. On Kaua'i, be sure to make reservations in advance for the **Tahiti Nui Lū'au** in Hanalei, which takes place every Wednesday night and is perhaps Hawai'i's most "local-style" – that is, most boisterous – *lū'au*.

You can also enjoy a more authentic and inexpensive experience by checking the local newspaper for fundraisers and other *lū'au* put on by civic groups. If you get really lucky and are invited to a big Hawaiian family party, accept the invitation. You will have the experience of a lifetime.

POLYNESIAN SHOWS

These shows are Hawai'i's real extravaganzas, and usually include a *lū'au*-style meal as well as exhibitions of music and dance from Pacific islands like Tahiti, Samoa, Tonga, and Fiji. All the islands have them. While they may vary in scale, Polynesian shows are broadly similar in content – never failing to deliver women wearing grass skirts.

The **Polynesian Cultural Center** in Lā'ie (O'ahu) stages several shows daily, including "*Manai*," an evening show featuring a cast of over 100, and the newest and most Hawaiian show, the *Ali'i Lū'au*. An alternative on O'ahu is **Creation: A Polynesian Odyssey**, staged at the Sheraton Princess Ka'iulani Hotel in Waikīkī.

The Hyatt Regency Maui offers **Drums of the Pacific**, and the *lū'au* at the **Royal Lahaina Resort** features a Polynesian show. Finally, you can also try the show at the **Hilton Waikoloa Village Resort** on Hawai'i Island.

EVENING SHOWS

In Honolulu, mimicry features in the lively Las Vegas-style show put on by the **Society of Seven**, a group of veterans who have been appearing at Outrigger Waikīkī on the Beach for more than 30 years. **Cirque Polynesia** blends Hawaiian culture with dazzling acrobatics, including thrilling high-wire routines.

On Maui, evening shows are inspired by Hawaiian myths, legends, and lore. The **Feast at Lele** is an exquisite evening dinner show on the beach that showcases the cultures of the South Pacific. Magic is the focus at **Warren & Annabelle's**, where guests are entertained by the piano-playing ghost of the wife of a 19th-century whaler, as well as mystified by a modern magician in an interactive show. Cocktails and appetizers are available for an extra charge.

Kahuā Ranch on Hawai'i Island draws from another part of Hawai'i's heritage, the *paniolo* (cowboy) experience. After enjoying a hearty chuck-wagon barbecue, you can dance to live music and participate in ranch games such as roping and horseshoes.

On Kaua'i, you can enjoy an enchanted evening of musical theater, entertainment, and dining featuring a full production of the Broadway musical **South Pacific** at the Kaua'i Beach Hotel.

Concerts by big international names from Tony Bennett to Sting and legendary rock bands like the Eagles appear at major O'ahu venues such as the spectacularly restored **Hawai'i Theatre**, the **Neal Blaisdell Concert Hall**, and **Aloha Stadium**. Maui's top spot is the impressive $32-million **Maui Arts & Cultural Center**, with an outdoor amphitheater and several different auditoriums for concerts, plays, and art-house films.

The biggest stars of all are of course up in Hawai'i's night sky. Almost all the heavenly bodies in the southern hemisphere are visible from Hawai'i. Operators of star-gazing tours include **Mauna Kea Stargazing Tour** and **Haleakalā National Park**. Some hotels and charter boats also offer excursions for viewing the night sky.

The thrilling Cirque Polynesia show, a multi-million dollar spectacular

Hula at the Maui Ukulele Festival, Maui Arts & Cultural Center

THEATER

For anything other than small community theater, Honolulu is the place to be. At least a couple of Broadway musicals show up each year, usually at the **Neal Blaisdell Concert Hall**. Past shows include *Les Miserables*, *Cats*, and *Phantom of the Opera*. The **Mānoa Valley Theatre** presents local productions of the cream of Broadway and off-Broadway. Hawai'i's oldest company, the **Diamond Head Theatre**, offers a mixed bag of performances each season, as does the **Kumu Kahua Theatre** – some of whose shows are written locally.

On weekends, at any time of year, it should be possible to see a performance by at least one of Maui's four community theater groups – the Maui Academy of Performing Arts, Maui Community Theatre, the Baldwin Theater Guild, and Studio Hāmākua Poko. Most often the place is one of the two theaters inside the **Maui Arts & Cultural Center** in Kahului, although the Maui OnStage Theater uses the lovingly restored 'Iao **Theater** in historic Wailuku.

Hawai'i Island has several community theater groups, too: Akebono Theater, Aloha Community Players, and Hilo Community Players. The lovely **Kahilu Theatre** in upcountry Waimea is a wonderful spot.

On the Garden Isle, the Kaua'i Community Players offer an almost continuous program of performances throughout the year. There is a beautiful performing arts center on the campus of **Kaua'i Community College**.

OPERA, CLASSICAL MUSIC, AND DANCE

The state's resident opera company, **Hawai'i Opera Theatre**, stages three or four operas from January to April each year. These are held in Honolulu's **Neal Blaisdell Concert Hall**, where Broadway productions such as *Phantom of the Opera*, *Les Miserables*, *Miss Saigon*, and *Chicago* have also been staged. You should also look out for performances by the **Hawai'i Youth Symphony Association**, made up of student musicians from all the islands.

Every year at least one of the mainland's most reputable ballet companies travels across the Pacific to perform in Hawai'i, usually at the Neal Blaisdell Concert Hall. The **Ballet Hawai'i** – the islands' oldest ballet troupe – presents the *Nutcracker Suite* every winter for the holiday crowds, plus another ballet in summer. The **Iona Contemporary Dance Theatre** perform unique works that combine dance with theater.

The **Maui Arts & Cultural Center**, which is also known

Sign for the top cultural place on Maui

as the "MACC," is Maui's premier venue for performing and visual arts. The complex includes two theaters, an outdoor amphitheater, and a gallery. Performances include classical music, rock, pop, and many other styles by an array of nationally and internationally famous artists.

The Classical Music Festival takes place every June at various Maui venues, with a series of classical concerts performed over two weekends.

FILMS AND FILM FESTIVALS

A large and, for the most part, free film festival, the **Hawai'i International Film Festival**, takes place each November. Scores of films are shown at various theaters on O'ahu (some of which charge admission) in the first week, and on the neighboring islands the second week; even tiny communities are included.

New films normally open in Honolulu at the same time as on the mainland. In addition to the many spots that specialize in big Hollywood movies, the University of Hawai'i, community colleges, and other venues present art-house, foreign, and classic films on a regular basis. Check the Friday edition of *The Honolulu Advertiser* for the latest listings. You can go to the movies on the neighboring islands, too, but the choice there is a great deal more limited. It was not that long ago that Maui got its first multiplex cinema. The **Maui Arts & Cultural Center** presents seasons of foreign and art-house films.

On the island of Hawai'i, the Big Island Film Festival, devoted to independent narrative film, presents screenings, workshops, and celebrity appearances. On the neighboring islands, there are special showings of non-blockbuster films, often presented by community colleges, civic organizations, and various nonprofit groups.

DIRECTORY

TICKET OUTLETS

Ticket Master
Tel (808) 521-2101.
www.ticketmaster.com

MAJOR VENUES

Aloha Stadium
99-500 Salt Lake Blvd,
'Aiea, O'ahu. *Tel (808)
486-9300. www.aloh
astadiumhawaii.gov*

Hawai'i Theatre
1130 Bethel St, Honolulu,
O'ahu. **Map** 1 A2.
Tel (808) 528-0506.
www.hawaiitheatre.com

Maui Arts &
Cultural Center
1 Cameron Way, Kahului,
Maui. *Tel (808) 242-
7469. www.mauiarts.org*

Neal Blaisdell
Concert Hall
777 Ward Ave, Honolulu,
O'ahu. **Map** 2 D3.
Tel (808) 591-2211.
www.blaisdellcenter.com

Waikīkī Shell
2805 Monsarrat Ave,
Kapi'olani Park, Honolulu,
O'ahu. *Tel (808) 591-2211.*
www.blaisdellcenter.com

HAWAIIAN MUSIC, HULA, AND LŪ'AU

King Kamehameha's
Kona Beach Hotel
75-5660 Palani Road,
Kailua-Kona, Hawai'i
Island. *Tel (808) 329-2911.*
www.konabeachhotel.com

Fairmont Orchid
Hawai'i
1 Kaniku Dr, Kohala Coast,
Hawai'i Island.
Tel (808) 885-2000.
www.fairmont.com/orchid

Old Lahaina Lū'au
1251 Front St,
Lahaina, Maui.
Tel (808) 667-1998.
www.oldlahainaluau.com

Paradise Cove Lū'au
92-1089 Ali'inui Drive,
Kapolei, O'ahu. *Tel (808)
842-5911. www.
paradisecovehawaii.com*

Tahiti Nui Lū'au
5-5134 Kūhiō Highway,
Hanalei, Kaua'i.
Tel (808) 826-6277.

POLYNESIAN SHOWS

Creation: A Poly-
nesian Odyssey
Sheraton Princess Ka'iulani
Hotel, 120 Ka'iulani Ave,
Waikīkī, O'ahu. **Map** 4 E4.
Tel (808) 922-5811.

Drums of the
Pacific
Hyatt Regency Maui,
200 Nohea Kai Dr,
Kā'anapali, Maui.
Tel (808) 667-4420.
www.maui.hyatt.com

Hilton Waikoloa
Village Resort
425 Waikoloa Beach Dr,
Kohala Coast, Hawai'i
Island. *Tel (808) 886-1234.*
*www.hiltonwaikoloa
village.com*

Polynesian
Cultural Center
55-370 Kamehameha
Hwy, Lā'ie, Oahu.
Tel (808) 293-3333.
www.polynesia.com

Royal Lahaina
Resort
2780 Keka'a Dr,
Kā'anapali, Maui. *Tel
(808) 661-3611. www.
royallahainaluau.com*

EVENING SHOWS

Cirque Polynesia
Hyatt Regency Maui, 200
Nohea Kai Dr, Lahaina,
Maui. *Tel (808) 667-4540.*
www.cirquepolynesia.com

Feast at Lele
505 Front St,
Lahaina, Maui.
Tel (808) 667-5353.
www.feastatlele.com

Kahuā Ranch
Waikoloa, Hawai'i Island.
Tel (808) 987-2108.
www.kahuaranch.com

Haleakalā
National Park
PO Box 369,
Makawao, Maui.
Tel (808) 572-4400.
www.nps.gov/hale

Mauna Kea
Stargazing Tour
737 Kanoelehua Ave,
Hilo, Hawai'i Island.
Tel (808) 969-9507.
www.jackshawaii.com

Society of Seven
Outrigger Waikīkī on the
Beach, 2335 Kalākaua
Ave, Waikīkī, O'ahu.
Tel (808) 922-6408.
www.outrigger.com

South Pacific
4331 Kaua'i Beach Dr,
Līhu'e, Kaua'i. *Tel (808)
245-1955. www.
kauaibeachresort.com*

Warren &
Annabelle's
900 Front St, Lahaina,
Maui. *Tel (808) 667-6244.*
*www.warrenand
annabelles.com*

THEATER

Diamond Head
Theatre
520 Makapu'u Ave,
Honolulu, O'ahu.
Tel (808) 733-0274.
*www.diamondhead
theatre.com*

'Īao Theater
68 N Market St, Wailuku,
Maui. *Tel (808) 244-8680.*
www.mauionstage.com

Kahilu Theatre
67-1185 Māmalahoa Hwy,
Waimea, Hawai'i Island.
Tel (808) 885-6868.
www.kahilutheatre.org

Kaua'i Community
College Performing
Arts Center
3-1901 Kaumuali'i Hwy,
Līhu'e, Kaua'i. *Tel (808)
245-8311. www.kauai.
hawaii.edu/pac*

Kumu Kahua
Theatre
46 Merchant St,
Honolulu, O'ahu. **Map** 1
A3. *Tel (808) 536-4441.*
www.kumukahua.org

Mānoa Valley
Theatre
2833 E Mānoa Rd,
Honolulu, O'ahu. *Tel (808)
988-6131. www.
manoavalleytheatre.com*

OPERA, CLASSICAL MUSIC, AND DANCE

Ballet Hawai'i
650 Iwiler Rd, Honolulu,
O'ahu. *Tel (808) 521-8600.*
www.ballethawaii.org

Hawai'i Opera
Theatre
848 S Beretania St, Hono-
lulu, O'ahu. **Map** 2 E4.
Tel (808) 596-7858.
www.hawaiiopera.org

Hawai'i Youth
Symphony
Association
Suite 201, 1110 University
Ave, Honolulu, O'ahu.
Map 4 D1. *Tel (808) 941-
9706. www.hiyouth
symphony.org*

Iona Contemporary
Dance Theatre
130 Ulupa St,
Kailua, O'ahu.
Tel (808) 262-0110.
www.iona360.com

FILMS AND FILM FESTIVALS

Big Island
Film Festival
68-1851 Lina Poepoe St,
Waikoloa, Hawai'i Island.
Tel (808) 883-0394.
*www.bigislandfilm
festival.com*

Hawai'i
International
Film Festival
680 Iwilei Rd, Suite 100,
Honolulu, O'ahu.
Map 1 A3.
Tel (800) 447-0577.
www.hiff.org

Maui Film Festival
16 Baldwin Ave, Pa'ia,
Maui. *Tel (808) 572-
3456. www.mauifilm
festival.com*

Nightlife

Traditionally, Hawai'i is an early-to-bed, early-to-rise place. Night owls may, however, find enough to keep them occupied, especially in Honolulu and Waikīkī on O'ahu. There is a fair bit of nightlife on Maui as well, but do not expect to find much on the other islands. Having said that, many bars and hotel lounges provide live entertainment. On any night of the week you can find almost any kind of music – rock, pop, blues, jazz, country, reggae, and, of course, Hawaiian – either performed live or spun by a DJ. Check listings in each island's local newspapers for an up-to-date guide to what is on while you are there.

Partying goes on well into the night at the fashionable Ocean Club, Honolulu

HONOLULU AND WAIKĪKĪ

Honolulu has a flourishing club scene. **Pearl Ultra Lounge** is a swanky night club with unusual theme parties. Dance outdoors at pier-side **Gordon Biersch**, or enjoy the casual atmosphere at the **Mai Tai Bar**. For lively parties, head to the fun Polynesian themed **Tiki's Grill & Bar**.

Waikīkī's clubs stay open late – the **Jazz Minds Art & Café**, for example, closes at 2am. **Zanzabar** features themed nights, the latest dance music, and cutting-edge DJs. **The Dragon Upstairs** has hot live jazz. For chilled-out live jazz, try **Lewer's Lounge**.

Some hotels also host hip dance clubs, such as **RumFire** at the Sheraton Waikīkī Hotel (see p179), where you can dine and dance with a view. Restaurants also double up as nightclubs later in the evening: **Indigo** (see p196) serves dinner until 9:30pm; then the club is open every night until 1am. **Chai's Island Bistro** (see p198) becomes a club on Saturdays from 10pm to 2am.

MOLOKA'I AND LĀNA'I

Not much nightlife is to be found on either of these quiet islands. What there is takes place in the hotels. **Hotel Moloka'i** (see p183) hosts live entertainment in its oceanfront dining room and once a week everyone and anyone brings their ukuleles and joins in a local-style jam session. It is a casual, fun, and unique island experience.

On Lāna'i, you will also find a relaxed scene. Check out entertainment at the **Four Seasons Lodge at Kō'ele** or the **Hale Aheahe Lounge**.

MAUI

Most of Maui's nightspots are in Lahaina and Kīhei, where there are lots of bars and lounges offering live entertainment. **Mulligan's On the Blue** in Wailea offers a Hawaiian dinner show a few nights a week, live jazz or rock on other nights, and traditional Celtic music on weekends.

In Lahaina, the **Hard Rock Café** presents a live reggae band weekly, while **Paradice Bluz** features a lively schedule of local bands and dancing to DJ-spun grooves.

The popular nightspots from the last century have been replaced by modern clubs such as **Timba** in Lahaina and **Ambrosia** in Kihei, where DJs spin discs for the late-night set, with state-of-the-art video, sound, and lighting technology.

HAWAI'I ISLAND

The Big Island's nightlife centres on Kailua-Kona and Hilo. However, there are great bars with DJs and dancing, and some with live bands, around the island. Again, you will find musical variety: country and western, reggae, rock, hip hop, and Hawaiian.

There is a host of bars and restaurants that feature live music and dancing at night. Among these are **Bongo Ben's**, **Lulu's**, **Huggo's on the Rocks**, and **Blue Dragon**.

Just about every hotel has a lounge offering live Hawaiian music; choose from the chic **Honu Bar** at the Mauna Lani Bay Hotel (see p189), the open-air **Reef Lounge** at Hāpuna Beach Prince Hotel (see p189), and **Hawaii Calls** at the Waikoloa Beach Marriott (see p189).

KAUA'I

Kaua'i is not known for its nighttime scene, but live entertainment and dancing can be found in restaurants, bars, and clubs, as well as in the resort hotels. **Hanalei Gourmet** serves dinner and then has live entertainment after dark, usually modern Hawaiian or R&B. The open-air **Casablanca** restaurant at the Kiahuna Tennis Club has a schedule of local entertainers every Wednesday and Thursday. **Café Portofino** in Lihue offers a varied mix of Hawaiian, classical, and DJ dance nights. There is also a sports bar, with DJs and dancing, at **Rob's Good Times Grill** in Līhu'e's Rice Shopping Center. **The Landing Pad** at Princeville Airport has live entertainment on weekends and a DJ dance night on Thursdays.

Hawaiian dancer at a dinner show

DIRECTORY

HONOLULU AND WAIKĪKĪ

Chai's Island Bistro
1 Aloha Tower Dr,
Honolulu, O'ahu.
Map 1 A3.
Tel (808) 585-0011.
www.chaisisland
bistro.com

The Dragon Upstairs
1038 Nu'uana Ave,
Honolulu, O'ahu.
Map 1 A2.
Tel (808) 526-1411.

Gordon Biersch
Aloha Tower Marketplace,
1 Aloha Tower Dr,
Honolulu, O'ahu.
Map 1 A3.
Tel (808) 599-4877.
www.gordonbiersch.com

Indigo
1121 Nu'uanu Ave,
Honolulu, O'ahu.
Map 1 A2.
Tel (808) 521-2900.
www.indigo-hawaii.com

Jazz Minds Art & Café
1661 Kapi'olani Blvd,
Honolulu, O'ahu.
Map 3 A3.
Tel (808) 945-0800.
www.honolulu
jazzclub.com

Lewer's Lounge
Halekulani Hotel,
2199 Kālia Rd,
Waikīkī, O'ahu.
Map 4 D5.
Tel (808) 923-2311.
www.halekulani.com

Pearl Ultra Lounge
1450 Ala Moana Blvd,
Honolulu, O'ahu.
Map 2 F4.
Tel (808) 944-8000.
www.pearlhawaii.com

Mai Tai Bar
1450 Ala Moana Blvd,
Honolulu, O'ahu.
Map 2 F4.
Tel (808) 947-2900.

Tiki's Grill & Bar
2570 Kalakaua Ave,
Honolulu, O'ahu.
Map 4 E5
Tel (808) 923-8454.

RumFire
Sheraton Waikīkī Hotel,
2255 Kalākaua Ave,
Waikīkī, O'ahu. **Map** 4
D5. *Tel (808) 922-4422.*
www.sheratonwaikiki.com

Zanzabar
2255 Kūhiō Ave,
Honolulu, O'ahu.
Map 4 D4.
Tel (808) 924-3939.

MOLOKA'I AND LĀNA'I

Four Seasons Lodge at Kō'ele
Keōmuku Hwy,
Lāna'i City, Lāna'i.
Tel (808) 565-7300.
www.lodgeatkoele.com

Hale Aheahe Lounge
Four Seasons Resort
at Mānele Bay,
1 Mānele Bay Rd,
Mānele, Lāna'i.
Tel (808) 565-2000.
www.fourseasons
manelebay.com

Hotel Moloka'i
Kamehameha V Hwy,
Kaunakakai,
Moloka'i.
Tel (808) 553-5347.
www.hotelmolokai.com

MAUI

Ambrosia Martini Lounge
1913 S Kihei Rd,
Kihei, Maui.
Tel (808) 891-1011.
www.ambrosiamaui.com

Hard Rock Café
900 Front St,
Lahaina, Maui.
Tel (808) 667-7400.
www.hardrock.com

Mulligan's on the Blue
Wailea Blue Golf Course,
100 Kaukahi St,
Wailea, Maui.
Tel (808) 874-1131.
www.mulligansonthe
blue.com

Paradice Bluz
744 Front St,
Lahaina, Maui.
Tel (808) 667-5299.
www.paradicebluz.com

Timba
505 Front St,
Lahaina, Maui.
Tel (808) 661-9873.
www.timamaui.com

HAWAI'I ISLAND

Blue Dragon Musiquarium
61-3616 Kawaihae Rd,
Kamuela, Hawai'i. *Tel
(808) 882-7771.* **www.**
bluedragonhawaii.com

Bongo Ben's
75-5819 Ali'i Dr,
Kailua-Kona, Hawai'i.
Tel (808) 329-7366.
www.dirtyjakes.com

Hawaii Calls Lounge
Waikoloa Beach Marriott,
69-275 Waikoloa Beach
Dr, Waikoloa, Hawai'i.
Tel (808) 886-6789.
www.marriott.com

Honu Bar
Mauna Lani Bay Hotel,
68-1400 Mauna Lani Dr,
Kohala Coast, Hawai'i.
Tel (808) 881-7911.
www.maunalani.com

Huggo's on the Rocks
75-5828 Kahakai Rd,
Kailua-Kona, Hawai'i.
Tel (808) 329-1493.
www.huggos.com

Lulu's
75–5819 Ali'i Dr,
Kailua-Kona, Hawai'i.
Tel (808) 331-2633.
www.lulushawaii.com

Reef Lounge
Hāpuna Beach Prince
Hotel, 67-100 Kaunaoa
Dr, Kohala Coast, Hawai'i.
Tel (808) 880-1111.
www.princeresorts
hawaii.com

KAUA'I

Café Portofino
3610 Rice St,
Lihue, Kaua'i.
Tel (808) 245-2121.

Casablanca
2290 Poipu Rd,
Poipu, Kaua'i.
Tel (808) 742-2929.

Hanalei Gourmet
5-5161 Kūhiō Hwy,
Hanalei, Kaua'i.
Tel (808) 826-2524.
www.hanaleigourmet.
com

The Landing Pad
Princeville Airport,
5-3541 Kūhiō Hwy,
Princeville, Kaua'i.
Tel (808) 826-9561.

Rob's Good Times Grill
Rice Shopping Center,
4303 Rice St,
Līhu'e, Kaua'i.
Tel (808) 246-0311.

OUTDOOR ACTIVITIES

With its hot climate, Hawai'i is a great place for outdoor activities, many of which are focused on the ocean. All over the islands you will find people surfing, swimming, paddling, windsurfing, or fishing at all hours of the day. The abundance of coral and exotic marine life is a big attraction for divers and snorkelers, too. Whale watching is a popular activity

Hawai'i's colorful yellow tang fish

in the winter and numerous boat tours allow visitors to get up close and personal with these awesome marine mammals. On land, there are many attractive, well-maintained hiking trails, as well as paths for horseback riding, which provide a great way to enjoy the islands' fine scenery. For more information on Hawai'i's world-leading golf courses see pages 226–7.

Snorkeler enjoying a close encounter with a trumpet fish

SNORKELING, SCUBA DIVING, AND SNUBA

Snorkeling and scuba diving are at the top of the list of Hawai'i's most popular outdoor activities. Early morning is the best time to observe the fish. Some snorkel sites are dangerous during high wave action, so check the conditions first. Darting butterfly fish, rainbow parrotfish, bright yellow tangs, and sea turtles are all common sights. For equipment rental at good prices, **Snorkel Bob's** has outlets on O'ahu, Maui, Kaua'i, and Hawai'i Island.

The leeward sides of the islands have the best dive sites, most of which are only accessible only by boat. Some good dive operators are: **Aaron's Dive Shop** (O'ahu), **Bubbles Below** (Kaua'i), **Extended Horizons** (Maui), **Fair Wind Cruises** (Hawai'i Island), See pages 32–33 for more information about snorkeling and dive sites.

Another way to enjoy Hawai'i's magnificent undersea environment is

snuba, a cross between scuba diving and snorkeling. This shallow water diving system allows you to go many places that snorkelers cannot reach. The approximate depth of a snuba dive is 20 ft (6 m). Snuba is not difficult to learn, there is no certification required, and few restrictions apply. Anyone over the age of eight can snub. Many snorkel cruises offer snuba for an additional charge.

SWIMMING

The waters off Hawai'i are cool and inviting. Maui and O'ahu have the best beaches, particularly Maui's Kā'anapali Coast and the southern and windward shores of O'ahu, where the surf is usually gentle. World-famous Waikīkī Beach is one of the best

swimming spots, but locals generally prefer nearby Sans Souci. On O'ahu's windward side both Kailua Beach and Lanikai Beach are mellow and uncrowded with lovely, clear water. Hawai'i Island's Mauna Kea Beach is also good.

If you enjoy serious wave action, look out for Hawai'i's "rough-water" swimming contests, such as the demanding summer North Shore Roughwater Swim Series on O'ahu. The ocean is dangerous. Safety tips for anyone entering the water are given on page 238.

SURFING, BODY-SURFING, AND WINDSURFING

Athletes from around the globe flock to Hawai'i to test their mettle at some of the world's best surf breaks. With 7 miles (11 km) of excellent surf spots between Hale'iwa and Sunset Beach, O'ahu's North Shore is the surfing capital of the world, and site of the annual Triple Crown contest *(see p31)*. But there is a cornucopia of world-class surf breaks around the rest of the O'ahu coast, and also on the coasts of Maui and Kaua'i.

Waikīkī's gentle rollers are ideal for beginners. Beach boys offer surfing lessons, just like in the old days, and boards can also be rented here. Chun's Reef on O'ahu's North Shore

Surfer taking a break between rides on the Hawaiian surf

Novices being given a windsurfing lesson at Kailua Beach Park on O'ahu

is a good place for beginners. **Surf-n-Sea** rents boards here and also offers lessons.

The Lahaina Breakwall, east of Lahaina, is another popular spot for beginners. You can rent surfboards from **Honolua Surfco**, **Local Motion**, and other Maui surf shops. The **Nancy Emerson School of Surfing** offers lessons; **Windsurf Kaua'i** rents boards and offers lessons on Kaua'i. Call the **Surf News Network** for general information.

You can surf all year, but the waves reach their peak from November through April, when the north shore of any island can be dangerous for experienced surfers – let alone beginners. The power of the ocean in Hawai'i is beyond description and many visitors get into trouble after paddling out into big surf. The best advice is "Never surf alone."

Body-surfing, in which riders wearing flippers lie flat on a bodyboard or boogie board *(see p30)*, is also popular. At O'ahu's Makapu'u and Sandy Beach, waves crash onto a shallow sandy shore-break, and body-surfers shoot through the tube barely ahead of the lip of the wave. Point Panic in Honolulu is also a favorite spot. All three of these places are dangerous, but for spectators they are fantastic.

Beginners can get their fins wet at O'ahu's Bellows Beach and Waikīkī Beach, Maui's Wailea Beach, and Kaua'i's Shipwreck Beach. To rent body-boards, try **Aloha Beach Service** in Waikīkī, **Local Motion** in Lahaina, and **Progressive Expressions** on Kaua'i.

Windsurfing has a big following. The sport's hub is Maui's North Shore, Ho'okipa Beach being the top spot for acrobatics. On O'ahu, Kailua Bay suits all ability levels, and Diamond Head's constant winds and breaking waves make it a windsurfer's delight. Windsurfers replace surfers at Sunset Beach when the wind blows strongly.

Lessons and equipment are available from: **Naish Hawai'i** (O'ahu), which is owned and run by world-champion windsurfer Robbie Naish; **Secondwind** or **Hi-Tech Surf Sports**, both on Maui; and **Windsurf Kaua'i** in Hanalei, on Kaua'i.

KAYAKING, CANOEING, AND SAILING

Kayaking is quite popular in Hawai'i. Favorite spots include O'ahu's Kailua Bay and Kaua'i's Wailua River. The kayak is also one of the preferred ways to visit Kaua'i's great Nā Pali Coast. Kayaks can be rented from **Go Bananas** or **Twogood Kayaks Hawai'i** (O'ahu), **South Pacific Kayaks** (Maui), and **Outfitters Kaua'i** (Kaua'i).

Traditional Hawaiian canoe paddling in outrigger canoes is popular, too. The October Nā Moloka'i Hoe race *(see p35)* is the most important contest of its kind in the world. Regattas are held on weekends in several places, but the sport is run by tightly knit clubs, making it hard to participate. However,

Waikīkī beach boys will take you out to ride the waves in an outrigger near the Moana Hotel *(see p64)*.

Hawai'i is a major stopping-place for boats crossing the Pacific, and the state has a strong seafaring tradition of its own. Two of the world's biggest regattas, the VIC-Maui race and the Trans Pacific Race, take place in Hawai'i.

Kāne'ohe Bay on O'ahu is the best place for small boat sailing, though Waikīkī is also suitable. The **Hawai'i Yacht Club** and **Waikīkī Yacht Club** take on experienced deckhands for Honolulu's weekly Champagne Race (so named because the winners are given champagne). Races are held on Friday afternoons.

FISHING

Hawai'i is famous for its deep-sea fishing – above all on the Kona Coast, where record catches are often made of Pacific blue marlin, yellowfin tuna, and other gamefish. This area is the best for trips, but charters can be arranged on all the islands. **Sea Verse** operates in Honolulu while **Blue Hawai'i Sportfishing** is based in Kailua-Kona, Hawai'i Island. On Maui, you can arrange fishing trips with **Hinatea Charters** and **Aerial Sportfishing Charters**. *Hawai'i Fishing News* is a good source of infomation.

Hawai'i's long shoreline offers lots of surf casting for smaller fish, such as snapper and giant *ulua* (jack). Take care if you fish; conditions in the best surf-casting places can be hazardous.

Women kayak training on the gentle waters of Waikīkī's Ala Wai Canal

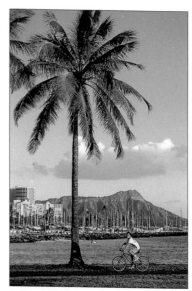

Cyclist on a scenic bike ride through Waikīkī's Ala Moana Park, away from the multitudes at the beach

CYCLING AND MOUNTAIN BIKING

Narrow shoulders and variable road quality make Hawai'i a poor place for bike riding. Mountain biking trails are limited too, but those that do exist are of good quality. Trails above Pūpūkea on O'ahu's North Shore are very popular, with ocean views and challenging riding.

South of Kula on Maui, in the Polipoli Springs Recreation Area, several miles of trails snake through ravines and forests of eucalyptus and giant ferns. An easier but extremely popular adventure is the sunrise descent down Haleakalā, a 38-mile (61-km) stretch starting in Haleakalā National Park (see pp128–9) that contains 21 switchbacks and superb views.

For quality mountain bike rentals, try **Raging Isle Sports** in Hale'iwa, O'ahu, or **Haleakalā Bike Co**, **West Maui Cycle and Sports**, or **South Maui Bicycles** on Maui.

HIKING

An extensive network of state and national parks crisscrossed by trails makes Hawai'i great hiking territory. The terrain ranges from barren volcanic desert to lush fern rainforest with waterfalls and cool swimming holes.

There are trails to suit everyone in terms of both accessibility and difficulty. Two of the finest are Kaua'i's Kalalau Trail along the stunning, rugged Nā Pali Coast (see pp168–9) and the Kaupō Trail, which descends from Haleakalā's volcanic moonscape to the lush rainforest of the Kīpahulu Valley (see p126).

Clubs and environmental groups, including the **Sierra Club**, **Nature Conservancy**, and the **Hawai'i Nature Center**, organize hikes on a number of islands. Some of the state, national, and county parks have campsites for longer stays (see p177).

Changing weather conditions can be a serious hazard when hiking; flash floods in narrow ravines are common, and hikers disappear with alarming regularity. It is dangerous to hike alone. Before you set off, leave word of your plans and your expected time of return with a friend or someone at the hotel. Pack water, a flashlight, warm clothes, and a blanket in case you become stranded.

Hiker enjoying the wild scenery of Haleakalā National Park, Maui

WHALE WATCHING

Every winter humpback whales migrate from the North Pacific to the warm waters around the Hawaiian islands to mate and bear their young. Although it is certainly possible to see whales from the shoreline, you will get a better look by getting out onto the water.

Almost every charter boat offers whale-watching cruises in the peak viewing season of January through April. Whale-watch cruises usually last two hours and many have a marine biologist or knowledgeable narrator on board. Try operators such as **Wild Side Specialty Tours** on O'ahu or **Paragon Charters** on Maui.

Tours may be on anything from large boats to kayaks. Boats may have a hydrophone, an underwater microphone, which allows you to listen to the haunting whale song. Humpback whales are protected by U.S. laws that prohibit approaching whales any closer than 300 ft (90 m).

A humpback whale, in Hawaiian waters from January to April

OTHER ACTIVITIES

Hawai'i's mild climate lends itself to all warm weather activity. In-line skating and jogging are common pastimes, particularly on O'ahu. There are busy public tennis courts on the four major islands.

Two good horseback riding trails are along the Moloka'i cliffs and in Maui's Kīpahulu Valley. Horses or rides can be organized through **CJM Country Stables**, **Moloka'i Mule Ride**, and **Paniolo Riding Adventures**.

More daring activities include caving, zipping through the tree tops, or freefalling from an airplane. Contact **Skyline Eco-Adventures** or **ATV Tours** for more information.

DIRECTORY

SNORKELING, SCUBA DIVING, AND SNUBA

Aaron's Dive Shop
307 Hahani Street, Kailua, O'ahu. *Tel (808) 262-2333.* www.hawaii-scuba.com

Bubbles Below
PO Box 157, Eleele, Kaua'i. *Tel (808) 332-7333.* www.bubblesbelow kauai.com

Extended Horizons
94 Kupuohi St, Suite A-1, Lahaina, Maui. *Tel (808) 667-0611.* www.extended horizons.com

Fair Wind Cruises
78-7130 Kaleiopapa St, Kailua-Kona, Hawai'i Island. *Tel (808) 345-0268.* www.fair-wind.com

Snorkel Bob's
700 Kapahulu Avenue, Honolulu, O'ahu. *Tel (808) 735-7944.* www.snorkelbob.com

Moanalani Dr, Kohala, Hawai'i Island. *Tel (808) 885-9499.*

3350 Lower Honoapi'ilani Road, Lahaina, Maui. *Tel (808) 667-9999.*

3236 Po'ipū Road, Kōloa, Kaua'i. *Tel (808) 742-2206.*

SURFING, BODY-SURFING, AND WINDSURFING

Aloha Beach Service
2365 Kalakaua Avenue, Waikīkī, O'ahu. *Tel (808) 922-3111.*

Hi-Tech Surf Sports
425 Kōloa Street, Kahului, Maui. *Tel (808) 877-2111.* www.surfmaui.com

Honolua Surfco
845 Front St, Lahaina, Maui. *Tel (808) 661-8848.* www.honoluasurf.com

Local Motion
Lahaina Gateway, Maui. *Tel (808) 661-7873.* www.localmotion hawaii.com

Naish Hawai'i
155A Hāmākua Drive, Suite A, Kailua, O'ahu. *Tel (808) 262-6068.* www.naish.com

Nancy Emerson's School of Surfing
505 Front St, Suite 224B, Lahaina, Maui. *Tel (808) 244-7873.* www.maui surfclinics.com

Progressive Expressions
5428 Kolōa Road, Kōloa, Kaua'i. *Tel (808) 742-6041.* www.progressive expressions.com

Secondwind
111 Hāna Hwy, Kahului, Maui. *Tel (808) 877-7467.* www.secondwind maui.com

Surf News Network
Daily updates on water conditions, weather, etc. *Tel (808) 593-2170.* www.surfnewsnetwork.com

Surf-n-Sea
62-595 Kamehameha Hwy, Hale'iwa, O'ahu. *Tel (808) 637-9887.* www.surfnsea.com

Windsurf Kaua'i
PO Box 323,Hanalei, Kaua'i. *Tel (808) 828-6838.* www.windsurf-kauai.com

KAYAKING, CANOEING, AND SAILING

Go Bananas
799 Kapahulu Avenue, Honolulu, O'ahu. *Tel (808) 737-9514.* www.gobananaskayaks.com

Hawai'i Yacht Club
1739-C Ala Moana Blvd, Suite C, Honolulu, O'ahu. *Tel (808) 944-9666.* www.hawaiiyachtclub.org

Outfitters Kaua'i
2827A Po'ipū Rd, Kōloa, Kaua'i. *Tel (808) 742-9667.* www.outfitterskauai.com

Paragon Charters
5229 Lwr Kula Rd, Kula, Maui. *Tel (808) 244-2087.* www.sailmaui.com

South Pacific Kayaks
95 Halekauai St, Kīhei, Maui. *Tel (808) 875-4848.* www.southpacific kayaks.com

Twogood Kayaks Hawai'i
134B Hamakua Dr, Kailua, O'ahu. *Tel (808) 262-5656.* www.twogoodkayaks.com

Waikīkī Yacht Club
1599 Ala Moana Blvd, Honolulu, O'ahu. *(808) 955-4405.* www.waikikiyachtclub.com

FISHING

Aerial Sportfishing Charters
Slip #9, Lahaina, Maui. *Tel (808) 667-9089.* www.aerialsportfishing charters.com

Blue Hawai'i Sportfishing
Kailua-Kona, Hawai'i Island. *Tel (808) 895-2970.* www.konamarlin fishing.com

Hawai'i Fishing News
6650 Hawai'i Kai Drive, Suite 201, Honolulu, O'ahu. *Tel (808) 395-4499.* www.hawaiifishing news.com

Hinatea Charters
Slip 27, Lahaina Harbor, Lahaina, Maui. *Tel (808) 667-7548.* www.mauisportfishing charters.com

Sea Verse
Kewalo Basin, Slip C, Honolulu, O'ahu. *Tel (808) 591-8840.* www.sea versesportfishing.com

CYCLING AND MOUNTAIN BIKING

Haleakalā Bike Co
810 Ha'ikū Rd, Suite 120, Ha'ikū, Maui. *Tel (808) 575-9575.* www.bikemaui.com

Raging Isle Sports
66-250 Kamehameha Hwy, Building B, Hale'iwa, O'ahu. *Tel (808) 637-7707.*

South Maui Bicycles
1993 S. Kīhei Road, #5, Kīhei,Maui. *Tel (808) 874-0068.* www.southmaui bicycles.com

West Maui Cycles
1087 Limahana Pl, Maui. *Tel (808) 661-9005.* www.westmauicycles.com

HIKING

Hawai'i Nature Center
2131 Makiki Heights Dr, Honolulu, O'ahu. *Tel (808) 955-0100.* www.hawaii naturecenter.org

Nature Conservancy
1040 Richards St, Rm 306, Honolulu, O'ahu. *Tel (808) 537-4508.* www.nature.org

Sierra Club
111 Bishop St, Honolulu, O'ahu. *Tel (808) 538-6616.* www.sierra clubhawaii.com

WHALE WATCHING

Paragon Charters
5229 Lwr Kula Rd, Kula, Maui. *Tel (808) 244-2087.* www.sailmaui.com

Wild Side Specialty Tours
Wai'anae Boat Harbor, A-11, Wai'anae, O'ahu. *Tel (808) 306-7273.* www.sailhawaii.com

OTHER ACTIVITIES

ATV Tours
PO Box 800, Kalaheo, Kaua'i. *Tel (808) 742-2734.* www.kauaiatv.com

CJM Country Stables
1831 Poipu Rd, Kōloa, Kaua'i. *Tel (808) 742-6096.* www.cjm stables.com

Moloka'i Mule Ride
Kualapu'u, Moloka'i. *Tel (808) 567-6088.* www.muleride.com

Paniolo Riding Adventures
Kawaihae, Hawai'i Island. *Tel (808) 889-5354.* www.paniolo adventures.com

Skyline Eco-Adventures
12 Kiopa'a St, Pukalani, Maui. *Tel (808) 878-8400.* www.zipline.com

Golf

With year-round warm, sunny weather and more than 80 challenging courses on six different islands, Hawai'i is a golfer's paradise. The courses, carved from brilliant green valleys and dramatic lava fields, are as varied as the islands. Lush fairways are bordered by tropical rain-forests and sandy beaches. Distractingly scenic panoramas reveal sparkling blue sea, neighboring islands, and even breaching whales. There are championship courses across the state, created by some of the biggest names in golf – Arnold Palmer, Jack Nicklaus, and Robert Trent Jones, Sr and Jr. *Golf Magazine* lists eight in its Top 25 US Golf Resorts; no other state boasts more than two.

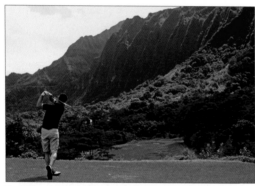

The challenging and scenic Turtle Bay Resort Golf Club, O'ahu

GENERAL INFORMATION

Most of Hawai'i's golf courses are open to the public. Municipal courses usually have low green fees. Resort courses are more expensive, but are generally open to all players, not only to resort guests. Private courses are for members only, but some set aside a day for non-members to play. Military courses are open to military personnel and their dependents.

Winner celebrates at a golf championship

Most courses have driving ranges and fully-stocked pro shops that provide equipment rental, instruction, and clinics.

Green fees usually include the use of a cart and range from less than $30 on a municipal course to in excess of $200 for a round on a plush resort course. However, many Hawai'i courses do offer discounted rates – twilight fees, junior discounts, and multiple-round discounts for those who want to play a second round on the same day or use the same course more than once in a week.

Golf packages are available at many hotels and resorts. These typically combine accommodations and golf rounds or discounted green fees with extras such as meals, instruction, video analysis, and golf logo items.

MAJOR TOURNAMENTS

In January, The Mitsubishi Electric Championship, at Hawai'i Island's Four Seasons Resort Hualālai (*see p189*), opens the Champion's tour season. Some of the biggest names in golf including Jack Niklaus have played here. Top golfers gather again for the Hyundai Tournament of Champions on Kapalua Resort's Plantation Course, Maui where the likes of Tiger Woods, Ernie Els and Vijay Singh have played a round. January also sees the return of the long-running pro tournament, the Sony Open (*see p37*), held at the Wai'alae Country Club on O'ahu. The event has been held at Wai'alae since 1965 when it began as the Hawaiian Open. Today it attracts more than 140 of the world's greatest golf professionals.

O'AHU

Ala Wai Golf Course is one of the busiest municipal courses in the world. Arnold Palmer's **Hawai'i Prince Golf Club** offers three challenging nine-hole layouts. Considered the toughest course in the US, **Ko'olau Golf Club** features extreme elevation changes and winding ravines. **Turtle Bay Resort Golf Club** has the George Fazio Course and the Arnold Palmer Course, where the back nine meander through a tropical forest and a wetlands bird sanctuary. The course at **Ko Olina Golf Club** has no parallel fairways.

MOLOKA'I AND LĀNA'I

Moloka'i offers the **Ironwood Hills Golf Club**, a municipal course along scenic hillsides. On little Lāna'i, **The Experience at Kō'ele** (upcountry) and **The Challenge at Mānele** (seaside) are top-ranked championship resort courses. In contrast, the public **Cavendish Golf Course** has nine holes and no fees (but do leave a donation in the box).

The Experience at Kō'ele, Lāna'i; one of Hawai'i's many superb courses

Putting at hole seven on the Blue Course at Wailea Golf Club, Maui

MAUI

Maui's fabulous weather and awe-inspiring beauty provide the backdrop for some of the world's most breathtaking golf experiences. The two courses at the **Kapalua Resort** are gorgeous, with long fairways and tall evergreens running down to the sea. Opened in 1993, **Mākena Golf Course** offers some of the most spectacular views of any golf course in Hawai'i. Designed by Robert Trent Jones, Jr., it winds its way up the slopes of Haleakalā *(see pp128–9)*, reaching an elevation of 800 ft (240 m) above sea level. At **Wailea Golf Club**, there are three courses – the Gold, the Emerald, and the Blue.

HAWAI'I ISLAND

Hawai'i Island boasts 20 world-class golf courses, many carved from black lava and overlooking beautiful seascapes. The first resort course built on the island is one of two in the state designed by legendary golf course architect Robert Trent Jones, Sr. **Mauna Kea Golf Course** has dramatic changes in elevation and incredible views of the snowcapped volcanic mountain from which it takes its name, as well as spectacular holes along the rugged coastline. **Volcano Golf and Country Club** is situated at a lofty 4,000 ft (1,220 m), along the rim of the active Kīlauea volcano *(see pp152–3)*. One of the

world's most unusual golf courses, it provides visiting players with a memorable experience. The par-72 course has 18 holes and you may have to look out for wild turkeys and nene geese.

KAUA'I

Kaua'i's golf courses feature waterfalls, fern forests, and flowers on lush layouts sculpted from rainforests, canyons, and sea cliffs. At **Po'ipū Bay Golf Course**, the carts have satellite navigation systems that indicate the distance to the hole and pin placement. **Princeville Golf Club** has two courses, one with three nine-hole layouts in one.

Bunkers on Mauna Kea Golf Course, Hawai'i Island

DIRECTORY

O'AHU

Ala Wai Golf Course
404 Kapahulu Ave,
Honolulu. **Map** 4 F3.
Tel (808) 296-2000.

**Hawai'i Prince
Golf Club**
91-1200 Fort Weaver Rd,
'Ewa Beach.
Tel (808) 944-4567.
www.princeresorts
hawaii.com

Ko'olau Golf Club
45-550 Kionaole Rd,
Kāne'ohe.
Tel (808) 247-7088.
www.koolaugolfclub.com

Ko Olina Golf Club
92-1220 Alii Nui Dr,
Kapolei.
Tel (808) 676-5300.
www.koolinagolf.com

**Turtle Bay Resort
Golf Club**
57-091 Kamehameha
Hwy, Kahuku.
Tel (808) 293-8574.
www.turtlebaygolf.com

MOLOKA'I
AND LĀNA'I

**Cavendish
Golf Course**
Keomoku Rd,
Lāna'i City, Lāna'i.

**The Challenge
at Mānele**
1233 Fraser Ave, Mānele,
Lāna'i. *Tel (808) 565-2222.*
www.fourseasons.com/
manelebay/golf

**The Experience
at Kō'ele**
Lāna'i Ave, Lāna'i City,
Lāna'i. *Tel (808) 565-4653.*
www.fourseasons.com/
manelebay/golf

**Ironwood Hills
Golf Club**
Kalae Hwy, Kualapu'u,
Moloka'i.
Tel (808) 567-6000.

MAUI

**Kapalua
Golf Club**
Kapalua Resort,
300 Kapalua Dr.
Tel (808) 669-8044.
www.kapalua.com/golf

**Mākena Golf
Course**
Mākena Resort,
5415 Mākena Alanui Dr.
Tel (808) 891-4000.
www.makenagolf.com

Wailea Golf Club
100 Wailea Golf Club Dr,
Wailea Resort.
Tel (808) 875-7540.
www.waileagolf.com

HAWAI'I ISLAND

**Mauna Kea
Golf Course**
62–100 Mauna Kea Beach
Dr, Kohala Coast. *Tel*
(808) 822-5400. **www.**
princeresortshawaii.com

**Volcano Golf and
Country Club**
Pi'i Mauna Road, Volcano.
Tel (808) 967-7331.

KAUA'I

**Po'ipū Bay
Golf Course**
2250 Ainako St, Kōloa.
Tel (808) 742-8711.
www.poipubaygolf.com

**Princeville Golf
Club**
Princeville.
Tel (808) 826-5001.
www.princevillegolf.com

WEDDINGS IN HAWAI'I

Beautiful and sensual, Hawai'i is the ultimate destination for lovers. Everything you could want for the perfect romantic escape is here – balmy weather year round, magnificent sunsets, star-studded night skies, brilliant rainbows, fragrant blossoms, and magical settings. In this tropical paradise there is no end to the variety of ways in which you can get married. Exchange your vows barefoot on a sparkling white sand beach or by a secluded waterfall. Have a traditional wedding in a tropical garden or a picturesque chapel. Sail into the sunset for a ceremony at sea, or fill a formal ballroom with family and friends. You can even declare your love under the waves or while falling through the air.

Conch shell, blown to signal start of ceremony

A garlanded couple exchanging rings in a traditional Hawaiian-style wedding

WEDDING DETAILS

The range of professional wedding services on offer in Hawai'i is as extensive as the choice of venues and ceremony types. Whether you want a wedding that is intimate, elegant, or unusual, wedding planners are available to assist in every way and can make recommendations to fit your personal taste and budget.

The **Hawai'i Visitors and Convention Bureau** and the individual visitors' bureaux on each island have websites with sections on weddings and honeymoons. These include directories of services provided by their members.

Many hotels offer wedding packages that include everything from a champagne toast to a private in-room dinner prepared by a top chef, and from a fragrant flower *lei* greeting to a Hawaiian blessing.

If you decide to handle the details yourself, check the *Yellow Pages* in the phone book for the island in question. Local professional associations provide useful lists of coordinators, officiants, photographers, videographers, musicians, and entertainers. They also list bridal gown boutiques, tuxedo rentals, hair, makeup, and nail stylists, caterers, florists, and more.

A HAWAIIAN WEDDING

A Hawaiian blessing is just one aspect of genuine island-style nuptials. Other special features include the blowing of the conch shell to signal the start of the ceremony, soft island music, the officiant performing the ceremony in the Hawaiian language (as well as in English), and fresh flower *lei*, worn and exchanged by the bride and groom.

It is also possible to opt for a Western ceremony and the limitless stunning locations available mean you can make your vows in a memorable setting.

GAY AND LESBIAN WEDDINGS

The State of Hawai'i does not legally recognize gay marriages and will not issue a license to same-sex couples. However, there are many gay-friendly wedding planners listed on the Internet who offer commitment ceremonies. Try www.hawaiigayweddings.com and www.mauialoha gayweddings.com

BEACH WEDDINGS

Hawai'i offers countless golden beaches that make perfect wedding settings. If you get married at **Kapi'olani Park** *(see pp72–3)* on O'ahu, your wedding photos could show the world-renowned Waikīkī Beach and Diamond Head in the background. **Hāpuna Bay** *(see p140)*, near Kawaihae on Hawai'i Island, has a gorgeous long stretch of white sand and sparkling turquoise water.

On Kaua'i, one of the most spectacular settings is **Hanalei Bay** *(see p166)*, where steep cliffs shrouded in emerald-green vegetation contrast against the dazzling white sand and deep-blue sea.

A bride and groom hand in hand on the beach at the Mākena Beach Resort, Maui *(see p186)*

Gazebo surrounded by flowers and lush greenery, an ideal garden wedding setting

Maui has mile upon mile of beautiful beaches, but it may be difficult to find one that you can have all to yourselves. The bay at **Kapalua** *(see p115)*, on the west side of the island, makes a picture-perfect wedding setting. The beach here is a white sand crescent that fronts the lovely bay, with the nearby islands of Moloka'i and Lāna'i floating on the horizon.

Hawai'i's state and county beaches allow beach wedding ceremonies without a charge, but you must obtain a permit.

GARDEN WEDDINGS

Foster Botanical Gardens, a serene oasis in Honolulu's Chinatown *(see p59)*, is a popular wedding venue. It is well stocked with beautiful plants from tropical regions around the globe. Another popular choice is **Hawai'i Tropical Botanical Garden** *(see p147)*, a short distance north of Hilo on Hawai'i Island. These gardens overlook Onomea Bay: the Twin Rocks that stand as sentinels in the bay are said to embody two legendary lovers. The **Kepaniwai Heritage Gardens** *(see p119)* on Maui are colorful and fragrant and have pavilions representing each ethnic group that has settled on the island, from the Japanese and the Chinese to the Portuguese.

Gardens that are administered by state and county parks do not charge a fee for wedding ceremonies, however it is necessary to apply for a permit in advance.

CHURCHES AND CHAPELS

Each island has a picturesque historic church built in the 1800s, when Christian missionaries first arrived. Today these churches are chosen as locations for many Hawaiian weddings. Honolulu's grand **Kawaiaha'o Church** *(see pp54–5)* once served Hawaiian royalty. On Maui, the intimate **Keawala'i Church** *(see p120)* in Mākena, built in 1832, is set on the edge of a peaceful bay and surrounded by palms gently swaying in the breeze. The oldest church on the islands, **Moku'aikaua Church** *(see p134)* on Hawai'i Island, is built of lava stone and its steeple is the highest structure in Kailua-Kona. The inter-denominational **Kōloa Church** in the Po'ipū area of Kaua'i *(see p173)* also has a beautiful steeple, as well as ornate columns, high ceilings, and seating for over 200 guests.

Old-style steepled church, Hawai'i Island

Almost every hotel in Hawai'i offers wedding packages and several have lovely chapels on their own grounds.

In Honolulu and Waikīkī, there are chapels at the **Hilton Hawaiian Village Beach Resort** *(see p181)*, the **Sheraton Moana Surfrider** *(see p180)*, and the **Ilikai Waikīkī Hotel** *(see p181)*.

Located on a magnificent stretch of O'ahu's south shore, the lovely **Kahala O Ke Kai Chapel** is part of the gorgeous Kahala Hotel *(see p181)*. At Turtle Bay Resort *(see p182)*, on the north shore of O'ahu, the **Wedding Pavilion**, located on the tip of scenic Kuilima Point, is a dramatic glass-walled sanctuary. Here wedding parties can arrive at and depart the ceremony in the utmost style, riding in Turtle Bay Resort's own horse-drawn carriage.

On Maui, the **Wailea Seaside Chapel**, part of the Grand Wailea Resort *(see p187)*, is impressive and picturesque. Its exterior resembles a New England church and inside there are chandeliers hanging majestically from the high vaulted ceiling and glorious stained-glass windows.

On Hawai'i Island, the Sheraton Keauhou Bay Resort *(see p189)* offers a romantic white seaside wedding chapel, **Bayside Chapel**, which is secluded from the rest of the property.

The striking interior of Wailea Seaside Chapel at the Grand Wailea Resort

Tying the knot underwater, in a scuba marriage ceremony

UNUSUAL WEDDINGS – LAND, AIR, AND SEA

There are many out-of-the-ordinary wedding ceremony options to be enjoyed in Hawai'i. For instance, couples can get married on the summit of one of Hawai'i's breathtaking dormant volcanoes – **Diamond Head** *(see p73)* on O'ahu, **Haleakalā** *(see pp128–9)* on Maui, or **Mauna Kea** *(see p146)* on Hawai'i Island. Permits are needed, but the location itself is free of charge.

Alternatively, you can let a helicopter whisk you away to your special beach or hidden waterfall. On Maui, Hawai'i Island, and Kaua'i **Blue Hawaiian Helicopters** can organize this.

Another heavenly option is saying your vows while skydiving. On O'ahu, you can arrange to do this with **Skydive Hawai'i** or the **Pacific Skydiving Center**.

There are a variety of possibilities for a romantic wedding at sea. You might choose to say your vows sailing into the sunset on the **Alala Catamaran** – or on a yacht provided by **Kamanu Charters** or **Shangri-La Private Sailing Charters**.

Kaua'i's legendary Fern Grotto *(see p162)*, a natural amphitheater full of luxuriant greenery, is perfect for a secluded wedding. For the journey there, **Smith's Motor Boat Service** will provide a private boat, on which

musicians can serenade you with the romantic Hawaiian Wedding Song as you cruise up the Wailua River.

In an underwater scuba ceremony, dolphins, turtles and colorful reef fish will be your witnesses as you write the words "I do" and exchange rings. **Eve Eschner Hogan** on Maui, or **Beach Weddings Hawai'i** on Hawai'i Island can arrange to make this happen for you. On O'ahu, Mau'i, and Hawai'i Island, another underwater option is to charter a private submarine cruise for your ceremony with **Atlantis Submarines**.

Musician at an Hawaiian-style wedding

LEGALITIES

Both the bride and groom must be present when the license is issued and each must provide valid picture identification (a driver's license or passport). Your birthplace, and the names of your parents will be noted on the license application. If relevant, final divorce decree information is also needed, as is written permission from a parent or legal guardian for those under 18 years of age. No waiting period, blood tests, or vaccinations are required. The license is good for 30 days and the $60 fee must be paid in cash.

The central marriage license office is located in O'ahu at the **Hawai'i State Department**

of Health. An appointment to obtain the license should be scheduled directly with a license agent. For agent contact information, call the local branch of the Hawai'i State Department of Health. After the wedding, the officiant sends the license for filing as the official marriage certificate. A certified copy is mailed to the couple around 120 days later. The license agent can speed up this process by forwarding a $10 fee.

VOW RENEWALS

Many married couples want to do it all over again and arrange a vow renewal ceremony. These can be as creative and personal as you want them to be and there is the same endless variety of locations and ceremonies available as there is for first-timers. Since the ceremony is purely symbolic, not legal, a minister or judge is not required to perform it, nor is it necessary to obtain any form of marriage license. Outrigger Waikīkī on the Beach *(see p180)* and Outrigger Reef on the Beach *(see p179)* invite guests who are newlyweds or celebrating an anniversary to renew their vows at a complimentary ceremony on Waikīkī Beach. This nondenominational Hawaiian celebration is conducted by a practicing *kahu* (priest) and includes a traditional chant, *hula* *(see pp26–7)*, song, and flower *lei* garlands.

Hawaiian dancers at a vow renewal ceremony on Waikīkī Beach

DIRECTORY

INFORMATION

Big Island Visitors Bureau
250 Keawe St, Hilo,HI 96743. **Tel** *(808) 961-5797.* **www**.gohawaii.com/big-island

Hawai'i Visitors and Convention Bureau
Suite 801, 2270 Kalākaua Ave, Honolulu, HI 96815. **Tel** *(808) 923-1811.* **www**.gohawaii.com

Kaua'i Visitors Bureau
4334 Rice St, Līhu'e, HI 96766. **Tel** *(808) 245-3971.* **www**.gohawaii.com/kauai

Kaua'i Wedding Professionals Association
www.kauaiwedpro.com

Maui Visitors Bureau (also Lāna'i and Moloka'i)
1727 Wili Pa Loop, Wailuku, Maui 96793. **Tel** *(808) 244-3530.* **www**.gohawaii.com/maui

Maui Wedding Association
www.mauiwedding association.com

O'ahu Visitors Bureau
733 Bishop St, Suite1520, Honolulu, O'ahu. **Tel** *(808) 524-0722.* **www**.gohawaii.com/oahu

BEACH WEDDINGS

Hanalei Bay
Permits: Kaua'i County Beach Parks, 4444 Rice St, Līhu'e, Kaua'i, HI 96766. **Tel** *(808) 241-6660.*

Hāpuna Bay
Permits: Hawai'i Island State Parks, P.O. Box 936, Hilo, Hawai'i Island, HI 96721.**Tel** *(808) 974-6200.*

Kapi'olani Park
Permits: 3902 Paki Ave, P.O. Box 3059, Honolulu, Oahu, HI 96815. **Tel** *(808) 545 4344.*

GARDEN WEDDINGS

Foster Botanical Gardens
Permits: Honolulu Dept of Parks and Recreation, 50 N Vineyard Blvd, Honolulu, HI 96817. **Tel** *(808) 522-7066.* **www1**.honolulu.gov/parks

Hawai'i Tropical Botanical Garden
Pepe'ekeo Scenic Dr, Hawai'i Island. **Tel** *(808) 964-5233.* **www**.htbg.com

Kepaniwai Heritage Gardens
'Iao Valley Rd, Maui. **Tel** *(808) 270-7230.*

CHURCHES AND CHAPELS

Bayside Chapel
Sheraton Keauhou Bay Resort, 78-128 Ehukai St, Kailua-Kona, Hawai'i Island. **Tel** *(808) 930-4900.* **www**.sheratonkeauhou.com

Hilton Hawaiian Village Beach Resort
2005 Kālia Rd, Honolulu, O'ahu. **Tel** *(808) 949-4321.* **www**.hilton.com

Ilikai Waikīkī Hotel
1777 Ala Moana Blvd, Honolulu, O'ahu. **Tel** *(808) 949-3811.* **www**.ilikaihotel.com

Kahala O Ke Kai Chapel
5000 Kahala Ave, Honolulu, O'ahu. **Tel** *(808) 739-8888.* **www**.kahalaresort.com

Kawaiaha'o Church
957 Punchbowl St, Honolulu, O'ahu. **Tel** *(808) 469-3000.*

Keawala'i Congregational Church
5300 Mākena Rd, Mākena, Maui. **Tel** *(808) 879-5557.*

Kōloa Church
3269 Po'ipū Rd, Kōloa, Kaua'i. **Tel** *(808) 742-6622.*

Moku'aikaua Church
75-5713 Ali'i Dr, Kailua-Kona, Hawai'i Island. **Tel** *(808) 329-0655.*

Moana Surfrider
2365 Kalākaua Ave, Waikīkī, O'ahu. **Tel** *(808) 923-3111.* **www**.moana-surfrider.com

Wailea Seaside Chapel
Grand Wailea Resort, 3850 Wailea Alanui, Wailea, Maui. **Tel** *(808) 875-1234.* **www**.grandwailea.com

Wedding Pavilion
Turtle Bay Resort, 57-091 Kamehameha Hwy, Kahuku, O'ahu. **Tel** *(808) 293-8811.* **www**.turtlebayresort.com

UNUSUAL WEDDINGS

Alala Catamaran
Ocean Sports, 69-275 Waikoloa Beach Dr, Waikoloa, Hawai'i Island. **Tel** *(808) 886-6666.* **www**.hawaiiocean sports.com

Atlantis Submarines
Maui: Suite 175, 658 Front St, Lahaina. **Tel** *(808) 667-2224.*
Hawai'i Island: 75-5669 Ali'i Dr, Kailua-Kona. **Tel** *(808) 329-6626.*
O'ahu: 1600 Kapi'olani Blvd, Honolulu. **Tel** *(808) 973-9811.* **www**.atlantis adventures.com

Beach Weddings Hawai'i
Kailua-Kona, Hawai'i Island. **Tel** *(808) 328-9239.* **www**.beach weddingshawaii.com

Blue Hawaiian Helicopters
Maui: **Tel** *(808) 871-8844.*
Hilo, Hawai'i Island: **Tel** *(808) 961-5600.*
Waikoloa, Hawai'i Island: **Tel** *(808) 886-1768.*
Līhu'e, Kaua'i: **Tel** *(808) 245-5800.* **www**.bluehawaiian.com

Diamond Head
Diamond Head Rd, Honolulu, O'ahu. **Tel** *(808) 587-0300.*

Eve Eschner Hogan
P.O. Box 943, Pu'unene, Maui. **Tel** *(808) 573-7700.* **www**.evehogan.com

Haleakalā
Haleakalā National Park, Haleakalā Crater Rd, Maui. **Tel** *(808) 572-4440.* **www**.nps.gov/hale

Kamanu Charters
P.O. Box 2021, Kailua-Kona, Hawai'i Island. **Tel** *(808) 329-2021.* **www**.kamanu.com

Mauna Kea
Hwy 200, Hawai'i Island. **Tel** *(808) 933-0734.*

Pacific Skydiving Center
68-760 Farrington Hwy, Dillingham Airfield, O'ahu. **Tel** *(808) 637-7472.* **www**.pacific-sky diving.com

Shangri-La Private Sailing Charters
Suite 109B, 5095 Napilihau St, Lahaina, Maui. **Tel** *(808) 665-0077.* **www**.sailingmaui.com

Skydive Hawai'i
68-760 Farrington Hwy, Dillingham Airfield, O'ahu. **Tel** *(808) 637-9700.* **www**.skydivehawaii.com

Smith's Motor Boat Service
Wailua Marina State Park, Wailua, Kaua'i. **Tel** *(808) 821-6887.* **www**.smithskauai.com

LEGALITIES

Hawai'i State Department of Health
1250 Punchbowl St, Honolulu, O'ahu. **Tel** *(808) 586-4545.*
Maui: **Tel** *(808) 984-8201.*
Lāna'i: **Tel** *(808) 565-6411.*
Moloka'i: **Tel** *(808) 553-3208.* Kaua'i: **Tel** *(808) 241-3498.* Hawai'i Island: **Tel** *(808) 974-6008.* **www**.hawaii.gov/health

SURVIVAL
GUIDE

PRACTICAL INFORMATION

Tourism is Hawai'i's most important industry. From the bright lights of Waikīkī, to the beaches of Moloka'i, the islands offer something for everyone. Paradise can be expensive – the cost of living is more expensive here than in the rest of the United States – but for those planning a money-no-object vacation, all kinds of luxuries await. Visitors on more

Roadside sign in Hale'iwa

modest budgets, can also enjoy a memorable trip with a little planning ahead. With its balmy climate, Hawai'i is a great all-year destination; for lower air fares and room rates, avoid peak season (mid-December to March). Throughout the year, however, many of the islands' biggest attractions are free, while most of the rest, including national parks and museums, charge low admission prices.

Aloha Week celebration at Hilton Hawaiian Village Beach Resort (see p179)

WHEN TO GO

Although Hawai'i is very much an all-year-round destination, with average daytime temperatures seldom dropping below 80° F (27° C), the weather generally turns a little cooler and wetter in winter, between November and April. Since that is precisely when visitors from North America, Japan, and Europe want to escape harsher conditions back home, however, this is still the islands' busiest time for tourism. Transportation and accommodation prices rise, and with demand high, it is a good idea to make reservations as far in advance as possible.

The most important seasonal variation is that the ocean tends to be rougher in winter. Surfers come for the big winter waves, whereas families with young children, recreational swimmers, and

snorkelers prefer the more placid summer. Winter is also prime whale-watching season, when the humpbacks return from Alaska.

Some visitors plan their stay in Hawai'i around special events and holidays, such as the Honolulu Marathon *(see p36)*, the Ironman Triathlon *(see p35)*, and Aloha Week *(see p35)*.

For more information about visiting Hawai'i and its events schedule, see the website, run by the **Hawai'i Visitors & Convention Bureau** (HVCB), or contact one of their many offices.

VISAS AND PASSPORTS

The conditions for entry into Hawai'i are the same as for the rest of the United States. All visitors are required to have a passport that is valid

for at least six months after their trip and an onward or return ticket. Citizens of the UK, most European nations, New Zealand, and Australia also need to have completed an Electronic System for Travel Authorization (ESTA) application online, for which a $14 fee is charged. Canadian citizens only need to show their passport to enter the US. Citizens of all other countries need a valid passport and a tourist visa, which can be obtained from a US consulate or embassy.

No inoculations are required unless you come from, or have stopped in, an area suffering from an epidemic, particularly cholera or yellow fever.

CUSTOMS INFORMATION

Foreign visitors staying for at least 72 hours have the following duty-free allowance: 1 liter of wine or alcohol; 200 cigarettes or 50 cigars (as long as they are not Cuban), or 4.4lb (2 kg) of smoking tobacco; and $100 worth of gifts. You are not permitted to bring foodstuffs or plants from any foreign country into Hawai'i.

All luggage is subject to an agricultural inspection on departure from the state. There are complex regulations governing which produce, foodstuffs, and flowers may be taken out of the islands – for example, the only fresh fruit you may carry with you is pineapple (also check the customs regulations of the country you are traveling to). For full details,

Coffee of Hawai'i

see the US Department of Agriculture website (www.aphis.usda.gov).

VISITOR INFORMATION

At all island airports, visitor information desks provide maps and guides, and major hotels usually have a knowledgeable and helpful guest-services desk. In major tourist areas, such as Waikīkī, or Lahaina on Maui, almost all the "information centers" on the streets are, in fact, hard-sell agencies hoping to entice you on tours and activities, but the **Hawai'i Visitors & Convention Bureau** (HVCB) runs its own office on each of the four main islands.

ADMISSION PRICES

It is impossible to generalize about admission prices in Hawai'i. Many of the best things in life, of course, are free: every beach in the state offers unrestricted public access, and much of the islands' magnificent scenery can be explored on foot.

While some museums and galleries – such as Honolulu's excellent Hawaii State Art Museum *(see p57)* – offer free admission, most charge around $5–10 for adult entry. The price for the extemely popular Bishop Museum in Honolulu *(see pp68–9)*, is $18.

Commercial attractions can be more expensive still. The standard fee at the Maui Ocean Center *(see p119)* is around $26 per person, and at the Polynesian Cultural Center on O'ahu *(see p92)* it ranges from $50 up to $230. Both those places, and many others, offer significant discounts for online bookings, and it is always worth checking websites for discounted or free days or special events.

OPENING HOURS

Typical island businesses are open on weekdays from 9am to 5pm or 6pm (for banking hours, *see p240*). The biggest shopping malls, such as Honolulu's Ala Moana Center, are open 9:30am–9pm Mon–Sat, and 10am–7pm Sun.

In resort areas, most shops remain open until 10pm or even later, while some supermarkets, convenience stores, and gas stations stay open 24 hours a day, seven days a week. In less touristy areas, stores tend to close between 5pm and 7pm.

Although the opening hours of attractions vary, most admit visitors daily. However, some close on major public holidays, such as Christmas and Thanksgiving.

ETIQUETTE, SMOKING, AND ALCOHOL

Hawai'i is a friendly, casual place where hugs are common greetings. Islanders are seldom in a hurry, so prepare yourself for their leisurely pace.

Clothing is casual, too: pack sandals, sneakers, shorts, and casual evening wear. If you plan to venture above sea level – for example, in Upcountry Maui or the Big Island – you'll also need long pants and a sweater or jacket, plus sturdy walking shoes.

While it is good manners not to trespass on private land, bear in mind that no one owns a beach in Hawaii; you're always free to walk along the oceanfront.

Smoking is prohibited in all public spaces, such as shops, theaters, nightclubs, bars, restaurants, and elevators. Hotels are allowed to designate up to 20 percent of guest rooms as smoking accommodation; however, many choose not to do so.

The minimum legal age for drinking in Hawai'i is 21. It is illegal to drink in a state or national park, and to carry an open container of alcohol in your vehicle. Grocery stores, supermarkets, and convenience stores sell beer, wine, and spirits.

ACCESSIBILITY TO PUBLIC RESTROOMS

Although public restrooms are very rare in the streets and urban areas of Hawai'i, it is usually possible to walk into any hotel or shopping mall and use a restroom there. In addition, almost every beach is equipped with toilet facilities. Most beaches have running water and showers as well, though away from the main resorts and towns a beach may have just a few portable toilets, with no water supply.

TAXES AND TIPPING

Hawai'i imposes a 4.712 percent sales tax on all goods and services, and an additional hotel tax of 9.25 percent, making a total of 13.962 percent tax on accommodation. Rates can vary slightly between islands, so if you're visiting multiple islands check in advance that tax has been included in your room rate.

It is customary to tip good service – indeed, waiters and bar staff depend on tips for a large proportion of their income. The standard restaurant tip is 15 percent of the check; tip taxi drivers 10–15 percent of the fare; baggage handlers at least $1 per piece of luggage; and valet parking attendants $2.

Whale exhibit in Maui Ocean Center

TRAVELERS WITH SPECIAL NEEDS

Hawai'i welcomes visitors with disabilities. Most hotels and restaurants, and many attractions, have wheelchair ramps, reserved parking, and specially equipped toilets.

The **Disability and Communication Access Board** website provides downloadable factsheets detailing access to beaches, parks, shopping centers and attractions, and where to rent vehicles. You can also find information about support services here, including parking permits, telecommunications, and service dogs. **Access Aloha Travel** is a Honolulu-based agency that specializes in travel plans for disabled travelers, in particular cruises, group tours and family travel.

TRAVELING WITH CHILDREN

Hawai'i is a fabulous family destination, though it is essential to remain aware of potentially dangerous ocean conditions *(see pp238–9)*. Most hotels allow up to two children to share a room with their parents at no extra charge, and many also have family suites. Larger hotels often have kids' programs and babysitters. Restaurants are child-friendly, and even if there is no special menu, they will often provide youngsters with a hamburger or even a peanut butter and jelly sandwich.

Tour operators will specify if their activities impose any restrictions on children. In cars, children must sit in a safety seat (up to age four) or wear a seat belt.

SENIOR CITIZENS

Senior citizens (which in most cases means those aged 62 and over) can claim discounts at many attractions, including national parks, and at some hotels, restaurants, and shops upon presentation of their photo ID. Always ask about discounts and check publications such as the *Honolulu Star-Advertiser* and the *Maui News*, or

A family *Lei*-making at Kā'anapali Beach Hotel, Maui

contact the **Department of Parks and Recreation** for special events.

Members of the **American Association of Retired Persons (AARP)** receive discounts on rooms, cars, and tours. The nonprofit **Road Scholar** organization offers educational trips for senior citizens that include accommodations, meals, lectures, guided tours, and activities.

GAY AND LESBIAN TRAVELERS

Hawai'i shares its *aloha* with all and is equally welcoming to gays and lesbians. Gay-friendly accommodations, restaurants, bars, and beaches can be found on all the islands, and since civil unions were legalized in 2011, many local wedding planners now arrange gay marriages.

On O'ahu, Waikīkī is the hub of gay and lesbian activity. **Hula's Bar and Lei Stand** remains the best-known gathering place. **Pacific Ocean Holidays** organizes Hawai'i vacations for gay and lesbian travelers.

TRAVELING ON A BUDGET

Although Hawai'i is an expensive place for locals and visitors alike, it's still possible to keep the costs of a visit down. The key is

careful planning. Travel in low season if you can *(see p234)*, and shop around for flights. Decide which islands you want to visit, and fly out to the first and home from the last – that is, don't fly to Honolulu unless you actually want to go there, and don't pay for a pointless flight back to the island where you arrived. Do not assume you'll get the best deal by buying your inter-island flights as part of your overall ticket; it may be cheaper to buy them separately.

In terms of accommodation, if you expect to spend your days at the beach, hiking the trails, or simply exploring the islands, then stay in a more basic property a block or two back from the ocean rather than paying premium rates for a sea view. Renting an apartment or condo is usually a cheaper option, especially for families and groups. It is also possible to camp, especially on Kaua'i and Maui.

Many budget travelers choose to stay in Waikīkī, since you don't need a fancy room or a pool when the beach is so close; you can eat cheaply in local diners; and unlike on the other islands, you don't need a rental car.

RESPONSIBLE TOURISM

For all their beauty, the Hawaiian islands are very fragile. The land, or *'āina* ("that which feeds"), is the most important element of Hawaiian culture. Traditional Hawaiians believe that humans are stewards of the

TIME

Hawai'i has its own time zone, known as Hawai'i Standard Time (HST). The West Coast of the US mainland is two hours ahead of Hawai'i, and the East Coast five. Unlike the rest of the US, Hawai'i does not put its clocks forward for summer daylight saving, so some of the time differences below increase by one hour when the respective countries switch to summer time. In the northern hemisphere, this is generally from March or April to October.

City and Country	Hours + HST	City and Country	Hours + HST
Athens (Greece)	+12	Moscow (Russia)	+13
Auckland (New Zealand)	+22	New York (US)	+5
Beijing (China)	+18	Paris (France)	+11
Berlin (Germany)	+11	Perth (Australia)	+18
Chicago (US)	+4	Rome (Italy)	+11
Dublin (Ireland)	+10	Sydney (Australia)	+20
Hong Kong (China)	+18	Tokyo (Japan)	+19
London (UK)	+10	Toronto (Canada)	+5
Los Angeles (US)	+2	Vancouver (Canada)	+2
Madrid (Spain)	+11	Washington, D.C. (US)	+5

land, put here to protect and nurture it, not to exploit it. They believe that every natural object, from a whale

Wildlife crossing sign cautions drivers to slow down

to a grain of sand, has life and a soul. You should therefore treat everything with great respect. Do not remove anything from its home – if you pick up a shell to look at it, for example, remember to put it back where you found it. Littering is both offensive and illegal.

Part of respecting the land means that locals are very careful to preserve precious resources, especially water. Most hotels and tourism

developments are sited on the drier sides of the islands, where water conservation is a major issue; follow the instructions that are posted everywhere. Some hotels are also introducing "green" door keys that turn off electrical appliances when guests are not in their rooms.

All sorts of state and federal laws aim to safeguard the islands and keep tourism responsible. Even so, it is important to be aware of the environmental consequences of your actions. Many visitors choose, for example, to eat locally sourced foods and, especially, products from the islands' many organic farms.

CONVERSIONS

US Standard to Metric
1 inch = 2.54 centimeters
1 foot = 30 centimeters
1 mile = 1.6 kilometers
1 ounce = 28 grams
1 pound = 454 grams
1 US quart = 0.947 liter
1 US gallon = 3.8 liters

Metric to US Standard
1 centimeter = 0.4 inch
1 meter = 3 feet 3 inches
1 kilometer = 0.6 mile
1 gram = 0.04 ounce
1 kilogram = 2.2 pounds
1 liter = 1.06 US quarts

DIRECTORY

VISITOR INFORMATION

Hawai'i Visitors and Convention Bureau Offices.
www.gohawaii.com

Island Tourist Offices

Hawai'i Island
250 Keawe St,
Hilo.
Tel (808) 961-5797.

Kaua'i
4334 Rice St,
Līhu'e.
Tel (808) 245-3971.

Maui
1727 Wili Pa Loop,
Wailuku.
Tel (808) 244-3530.

O'ahu
2270 Kalakaua Ave,
Suite 801, Honolulu.
Tel (808) 923-1811.

Tourist Offices Abroad

Australia
Tel (612) 9286-8951.
www.gohawaii.com/au

Germany
Tel (89) 5525 33819.
www.gohawaii.com/de

New Zealand
Tel (649) 977-2234.
www.gohawaii.com/nz

United Kingdom
Tel (020) 7644 6127.
www.gohawaii.com/uk

TRAVELERS WITH SPECIAL NEEDS

Access Aloha Travel
Tel (808) 545-1143.
www.accessaloha
travel.com

Disability and Communication Access Board
Tel (808) 586-2121.
http://hawaii.gov/health/
dcab/travel

SENIOR CITIZENS

AARP
Tel (888) 687-2277.
www.aarp.org

Department of Parks and Recreation
Aupuni Center, 101 Pauahi
Street, Suite 6, Hilo.

Tel (808) 961-8311.
www.hawaiicounty.gov/
parks-and-recreation

Road Scholar
Tel (800) 454-5768.
www.roadscholar.org

GAY AND LESBIAN TRAVELERS

Hula's Bar and Lei Stand
134 Kapahulu Ave,
Waikīkī.
Tel (808) 923-0669.
www.hulas.com

Pacific Ocean Holidays
Tel (808) 923-2400.
www.gayhawaii
vacations.com

Personal Security and Health

Lifeguard sign, Kūhiō Beach

Despite its location in the tropics, Hawai'i carries remarkably few health risks (and boasts the highest life expectancy in the US). Immunizations are not usually required (see p234), there are no land snakes to worry about, and there are only a few nasty creepy-crawlies. You should be aware of certain potential dangers if you go hiking or camping, but generally it is the sun and the ocean that pose the biggest threats to your health. Hawai'i does not have a serious crime problem, but take the normal precautions and use your common sense.

POLICE

Hawai'i is the only US state not to have a statewide police service. Instead each county – in effect, each island – runs its own police department. Your most likely contact with the police will be as a driver; each island has pretty much one main road, and local police know where speeding is most common. To report a crime, visit the nearest police station, where you can expect prompt and polite attention.

WHAT TO BE AWARE OF

While not completely crime-free, Hawai'i is still remarkably safe, and violent crime is rare.

Use common sense. Do not hitchhike; avoid hiking alone and being in dark or remote areas at night. If in doubt, ask your hotel whether or not a particular area is safe.

Carry minimal cash when you go out, and do not take your passport unless you are required to do so. Leave your best jewelry at home, and other valuables in a safe – either in your room or at the hotel front desk. The main likelihood of theft is from a rented vehicle. Never leave any valuables in the car; thieves are skilled at dealing with door and trunk locks.

IN AN EMERGENCY

In an emergency, the police, ambulance, or fire services can be reached by dialing 911. That same number will also summon help for in-shore swimming and surfing emergencies; for anything farther out at sea, call the **Coast Guard, Search and Rescue**. There is also a 24-hour **Suicide and Crisis Line**.

In the event of natural disasters, such as hurricanes or tsunamis, contact the **American Red Cross** or the **Hawai'i State Civil Defense**.

LOST AND STOLEN PROPERTY

Even though you have only a slim chance of retrieving stolen property, report all thefts to the police, and keep a copy of the police report for your insurance claim.

Most credit cards have toll-free numbers for reporting a loss (see p241). If you need a replacement passport, contact your embassy or consulate. The Department of Business, Economic Development and Tourism website has a list of consulates in Hawai'i (http://hawaii.gov/dbedt).

HOSPITALS AND PHARMACIES

Even the smallest towns in Hawai'i have medical centers, but facilities on Moloka'i and Lāna'i are less extensive than those on the main islands. Honolulu's medical services are the state's best equipped.

Ask at your hotel if you need a doctor, dentist, or other healthcare professional. All medical care is expensive; even a simple visit to a doctor can cost over $100. Hospitals take most credit cards, but doctors and dentists usually want cash. Visitors without insurance documents may have to pay in advance. Anyone on prescription drugs should take along a supply, plus a copy of the prescription. Pharmacies are plentiful (**Longs Drugs** is present on all the islands), and supermarkets and convenience stores also sell some medicines.

TRAVEL AND HEALTH INSURANCE

Travel insurance cover of at least $1 million is highly recommended, mainly because of the high cost of medical treatment. Make sure the policy covers emergency medical care, accidental death, trip cancellation, and loss of baggage or documents.

OCEAN SAFETY

The Pacific Ocean is as power-ful as it is beautiful. Always pay close attention to the ocean, regardless of how experienced a swimmer you are. If you've never surfed before, don't try it without proper instruction.

A lifeguard is stationed at the most popular beaches; always ask him or her about current conditions, and heed

Lifeguard station on Po'ipū Beach, Kaua'i

Bright-yellow Hawaiian fire engine

posted warnings. Be wary of using unguarded beaches, especially if you aren't used to identifying dangerous currents. Note: many beaches can be safe in summer but pounded by dangerous surf in winter.

When you're in the water, swim facing away from the beach, to get back, swim parallel to the shore and then make your way in; if you're snorkeling, raise your head regularly. So-called rogue waves arrive suddenly and can sweep you out to sea. Should you get carried out by a rip current, don't fight it, but stay with it until it dissipates – usually 50–100 yds (45–90 m) from shore. Always check for rocks, coral, and other potential dangers below the surface. Use protective footwear such as reef slippers whenever possible. For more information check out the **Hawaii Beach Safety** website.

If you cut yourself on coral, clean the cut thoroughly with antiseptic. If you step on a sea urchin, the spine may well break off, leaving a tip embedded in your skin. This will dissolve in several days, but applying vinegar may speed up the process.

Two kinds of jellyfish are common in Hawai'i, though you're much more likely to see them washed up on shore than to encounter them while in the ocean. Box jellyfish tend to arrive on the leeward shores of the islands nine or ten days after the full moon; their stings are best treated with vinegar. The Portuguese man o' war can swarm at any time; do not apply vinegar to stings, but irrigate them with fresh water. The website www.808jellyfish. com has more detailed advice.

NATURAL HAZARDS

Whether you're fair or dark-skinned, you must protect yourself against the harsh Hawaiian sun. Be sure to wear a hat and sunglasses, and use plenty of sunblock. Since certain sunblocks can damage coral, it makes sense to wear a T-shirt when snorkeling.

Introduce yourself to the sun slowly, and try to stay out of the sun between 11am and 2pm; even on overcast days, the ultraviolet rays penetrate the clouds. Heat can be a danger, too. Drink plenty of fluids, and avoid being out in high temperatures for long periods.

Hawaiian mosquitoes do not carry malaria but can still be a nuisance. Black widow spiders and scorpions are potential dangers when hiking or camping, while centipedes are also fairly common; check shoes before you put them on.

Warnings: currents, dangerous shore break, and big surf

DRINKING WATER

Tap water is always safe to drink in Hawai'i, and bottled water is widely available. However, you should never drink from freshwater streams or pools. A bacterial disease, leptospirosis, can be contracted by drinking untreated water or exposing cuts or abrasions to fresh water.

DIRECTORY

IN AN EMERGENCY

All Emergencies
Tel 911 to alert police, fire, and medical services, including to in-shore ocean incidents.

American Red Cross
Tel (808) 734-2101.
www.hawaiiredcross.org

Coast Guard, Search and Rescue
Tel (800) 522-6458.

Hawai'i State Civil Defense
Tel (808) 733-4300.
www.scd.hawaii.gov

Suicide and Crisis Line
Tel (808) 832-3100.

OCEAN SAFETY

Hawaii Beach Safety
http://oceansafety.ancl.hawaii.edu

HOSPITALS AND PHARMACIES

Hilo Medical Center
1190 Waiānuenue Avenue.
Tel (808) 932-3000.

Kona Community Hospital
79-1019 Haukapila St, Kealakekua, Kona.
Tel (808) 322-9311.

Lāna'i Community Hospital
628 7th Street, Lāna'i City.
Tel (808) 565-8450.

Longs Drugs
http://longs.staradvertiser.com

Maui Memorial Medical Center
221 Mahalani St, Wailuku.
Tel (808) 244-9056.

Moloka'i General Hospital
280 Homeolu Place, Kaunakakai
Tel (808) 553-5331.

Queen's Medical Center
1301 Punchbowl St, Honolulu.
Tel (808) 538-9011.

Wilcox Memorial Hospital
3420 Kūhiō Highway, Līhu'e.
Tel (808) 245-1100.

Banking and Communications

Money matters in Hawai'i are similar to those in the rest of the US, so it is not necessary to take any currency other than US dollars. And since credit and debit cards are by far the most common form of currency, there's no point carrying large amounts of cash – or for that matter, travelers' checks – with you. Communications are straightforward, too, and the postal services are very good despite Hawai'i's isolation. Internet access is readily available, you can easily got online in hotels, as well as in public spaces; and for US travelers it's possible to read the same newspapers and watch the same TV shows as back home.

BANKS AND BUREAUX DE CHANGE

The two largest local banks – First Hawaiian Bank and Bank of Hawai'i – have several branches on every island, while American Savings Bank, Central Pacific Bank, and Territorial Savings are also widely represented. If you find yourself needing to visit a bank, normal weekday opening hours are from 8:30am to 4pm; many stay open until 6pm on Fridays and also open 9am–1pm on Saturdays.

Old-style currency-exchange desks can be found at larger airports and in resort areas, and most big hotels will also change money for guests.

ATMS

Visitors to Hawai'i can expect to use their normal cards to withdraw cash from ATMs; if you are in any doubt, check with your own bank before you travel.

Many ATMs, especially those situated in convenience stores, impose surcharges, so you may have to shop around to find the best deal. In addition, it costs more to withdraw cash from ATMs using a credit card than it does with a debit card.

CREDIT AND DEBIT CARDS

You will be expected to use a credit or debit card for all major transactions, from hotel bills to restaurant meals and car rental. **VISA** and **MasterCard** are the most widely accepted cards, but most places also accept **American Express**, **Diners Club**, Discover, and JCB.

Overseas travelers should be aware that most credit and debit cards levy extra charges for foreign-currency transactions. It is also sensible to let your credit or debit card provider know you will be going away, so that they don't block your card if they see "unusual" charges.

Branch of the First Hawaiian Bank

CELL PHONES

Check with your phone provider in advance if you are hoping to use your cell (mobile) phone in Hawai'i, and be warned that, for foreign visitors in particular, the call charges can be very high.

In addition, keep in mind that while cell-phone coverage tends to be excellent in resort and urban areas, some parts of Hawai'i are very remote indeed, isolated beyond massive volcanoes or behind towering cliffs. Hikers in particular should not depend on their cell phones for emergency use.

Hawaiian Telecom pay phone

TELEPHONE CALLS

Making telephone calls in Hawai'i is easy. The area code for the state as a whole is 808. You do not need to use the area code when making local calls (that is, within one island), but inter-island calls count as long distance, so the number must be preceded by 1-808 when dialing. Calls to other US area codes have to be preceded by 1.

Many businesses have toll-free phone numbers, which are preceded by 1-800 or 1-888. Note that these are toll-free only if dialed from within the United States.

Public phones are becoming less common. Those that do exist generally charge 75 cents to make a local call. Otherwise, conventional landline rates are at their cheapest from 11pm to 8am Monday to Thursday, and from 11pm Friday to 8am Monday. Making a call from a

Post-office branch in Kīhei, Maui

hotel room always costs much more than the normal rate; for pay phones and hotel calls alike, it's worth buying a pre-paid calling card at an ABC or other convenience store. Most hotels will have a pay phone in the lobby that guests can use.

The cheapest and most convenient solution may be to bring a laptop computer, so you can hook up to an online service such as Skype – though that, of course, is dependent on having a Wi-Fi connection.

INTERNET

Almost all hotels in Hawai'i offer Wi-Fi Internet access in guests' rooms. Many establishments impose a charge for this service, however, typically in the region of $12–20 per day. Most hotels will add any fee for Internet usage to your bill at the end of your stay, but in a few cases you may have to pay the supplier direct. Since many travelers access the Internet with their own laptops and smart phones these days, there are fewer Internet cafés on the islands than there used to be, but many hotels have a few computers available for guests' use. In addition, public libraries and independent postal services also offer Internet access for a fee.

POSTAL SERVICES

Post offices are usually open from 8:30am to 4:30pm, Monday to Friday, and on Saturday morning. Smaller post offices may have shorter hours. Mailboxes can be found on the streets of all major cities and towns. You can also purchase stamps and send mail from your hotel's front desk.

Standard US postal charges apply, and sending a letter within the US costs the same, regardless of the destination. So it costs the same to post an item within any island, from one island to another, or to anywhere on the mainland. Sending ordinary mail to the US mainland from Honolulu should not take more than four days; from the other islands, it will be more like a week. Mail to the rest of the world takes longer still.

Post box

NEWSPAPERS AND MAGAZINES

Hawai'i has a single statewide daily newspaper – the *Honolulu Star-Advertiser*. Hawai'i Island, Maui, and Kaua'i each have at least one daily paper, as well as weeklies. National newspapers, such as the *Wall Street Journal*, *USA Today*, and *The New York Times*, are easy to find in Honolulu and in stores and larger hotels throughout Hawai'i. Most newspapers also have online editions; visit www.world-newspapers.com/hawaii for a list.

Local magazines worth looking out for include *Honolulu* and *Hawai'i*, a bimonthly general-interest publication. You can pick up all sorts of free glossy visitor guides at airports, on Waikīkī street corners, and at malls on the other islands. Many car-rental companies will provide you with a free local driving guide as part of the rental transaction.

TELEVISION AND RADIO

All the main US television networks – ABC, CBS, PBS, NBC, and FOX – have local affiliate stations; check listings on each island for the channel numbers. There are also a few interesting home-grown stations.

You can tune into dozens of local and state radio stations, but be prepared to lose reception as you travel around to the far side of the islands' huge volcanoes.

DIRECTORY

LOST OR STOLEN CREDIT CARDS

American Express
Tel (800) 528-4800.

Diners Club
Tel (800) 234-6377.

MasterCard
Tel (800) 627-8372.

VISA
Tel (800) 847-2911.

REACHING THE RIGHT NUMBER

- The area code for the entire state is 808
- To make a call on the same island just dial the number
- To call another island dial 1, then 808, then the number
- To make international calls from Hawai'i, dial **011** followed by the country code, the city code, and then the number (Australia: 61; Canada: 1; Ireland: 353; Japan: 81; New Zealand: 64; United Kingdom: 44; United States: 1)

TRAVEL INFORMATION

Hawai'i entertains more than seven million visitors a year (roughly seven times its resident population). Almost all travelers arrive by air, though a few cruise lines include Hawai'i on their itineraries. On any one day, half of all visitors are on O'ahu, a quarter on Maui, and the rest on Hawai'i Island, Kaua'i, Moloka'i, and Lana'i, in that order. Almost all travel between the islands is by air, although there are a couple of ferry services, and a handful of luxury cruise lines available, too. As for exploring individual islands, the only reliable way to get around is by car; public transportation is minimal, except on O'ahu.

Hawaiian Airlines plane

ARRIVING BY AIR

The Hawaiian islands are the earth's most isolated archipelago, so wherever you're coming from, be prepared for a long flight. Even the shortest flight time, from Los Angeles, is about five hours; from Europe, expect up to 18 hours' traveling.

The great majority of non-stop flights from the US to Hawai'i leave from the West Coast, especially Los Angeles and San Francisco airports. You can also catch flights to Hawai'i from other cities in the US and Canada, but be aware that most involve a stop on the West Coast. While Honolulu is the busiest airport, **American Airlines**, **United Airlines**, and **US Airlines** all fly direct from the US mainland to Maui, Kaua'i, and Hawai'i Island.

United Airlines, American Airlines, **Air Canada**, and **Air New Zealand** are just some of the airlines that fly from Europe to Hawai'i, but you'll certainly land in the mainland US en route. All foreign travelers pass through immigration and customs where they first touch down in the US, regardless of whether that is their final destination. Admission procedures involve finger-printing and taking a retina scan, and lines can be long – but all airlines allow enough time to catch your ongoing flight to Hawai'i.

AIRPORTS

Hawai'i's main transportation hub is **Honolulu International Airport**, 10 miles (16 km) west of Waikīkī, on O'ahu. Its two terminals handle 1,000 international, domestic, and inter-island flights daily.

Maui's major airport is **Kahului Airport**; it is always busy with long-haul and inter-island flights. Two smaller airports also receive a handful of flights. Kapalua-West Maui Airport, 6 miles (10 km) north of Lahaina, serves the Kā'anapali and Kapalua resort areas, while tiny Hāna Airport, on Maui's east coast, is mainly used by shuttle services from Kahului.

Kona International Airport, just north of Kailua-Kona on Hawai'i Island, has the state's prettiest terminal; its check-in counters and snack bars are housed in small thatched huts. It receives all the island's flights from the mainland, as well as plenty of inter-island services. **Hilo International Airport**, 3 miles (5 km) east of downtown Hilo, is also served by many inter-island flights. Waimea-Kohala Airport, in the grasslands outside Waimea, is used exclusively by **Pacific Wings**.

Līhu'e Airport, on the edge of Kaua'i's capital, is Kaua'i's only inter-island terminal, and it also has connections with the US mainland.

On Moloka'i, little **Moloka'i Airport** – 8 miles (13 km) northwest of the main town, Kaunakakai – is served by around 20 inter-island flights per week. There's also a tiny airstrip down on the Kalaupapa Peninsula, which receives direct flights from Honolulu and Maui, as well as "topside" Moloka'i. The latter, at seven minutes, is the world's shortest scheduled air service.

Only inter-island carriers use **Lāna'i Airport**, 4 miles (6.5 km) southwest of Lāna'i City.

Plane taxiing on the runway at Honolulu International Airport

Departure building at Kona International Airport at Keāhole, Hawai'i Island

TICKETS AND FARES

The cheapest deals on flights to Hawai'i are generally available in off-peak months: May, June, September, and October. So-called discounted fares often come with advance purchase requirements and other restrictions, particularly involving cancellations. Check these carefully before you purchase the ticket, to avoid unpleasant surprises at the last minute. Many airlines also offer cheaper deals if you can arrive on a weekday.

INTER-ISLAND AIR TRAVEL

It would be a real shame to come all the way to Hawai'i and see only one island. While traveling between the islands is very straightforward, with plentiful flight connections, it can prove expensive. Many visitors, therefore, chose to fly into one island at the start of their trip and fly home from another. It's worth shopping around for inter-island flights. The best deals can often be found online and it can be worth joining the airline's frequent flier club, as this can often add extra discounts to your ticket price.

The three main airlines with inter-island flights are **Hawaiian Airlines**, **Island Air**, and the generally cheaper **go! Airlines**. Fares are usually around $100, but you may find yourself paying as much as $200 for popular flights. Note that Island Air operates smaller, turboprop planes, which might not be as comfortable as traveling in a larger plane.

TRANSPORT FROM AIRPORTS INTO TOWN

Approximate one-way taxi fares from various airports into town are: $25–30 from Honolulu airport to Waikīkī; $15 from Hilo airport into downtown Hilo; $30 from Kona airport to Kailua-Kona; $60 from Kahului to Kā'anapali; $10 from Moloka'i airport to Kaunakakai; $10 from Līhu'e airport into Lihu'e, and $20 north to Kapa'a. Buses and shuttle vans serve some airports and resorts – many are free for resort guests.

On O'ahu, **Roberts Hawaii Express Shuttle** runs a shuttle bus from Honolulu airport to Waikīkī for about $12 per head. **SpeediShuttle** operates similar services on the major islands.

PACKAGE TOURS

Visitors have a wide range of package tours options for Hawai'i. These include air and hotel costs, car rental, inter-island travel, and often activities and meals, too. Some of the best deals are offered by the airlines themselves.

If you want to explore the natural beauty of the islands but prefer to leave the organizing to someone else, consider taking a tour with the likes of the **Sierra Club**, **Backroads**, or **The World Outdoors**.

DIRECTORY

ARRIVING BY AIR

Air Canada
www.aircanada.com

Air New Zealand
www.airnz.co.nz

Alaska Airlines
www.alaskaair.com

American Airlines
www.aa.com

British Airways
www.ba.com

Continental Airlines
www.continental.com

Delta
www.delta.com

Pacific Wings
www.pacificwings.com

Qantas Airways
www.qantas.com

United Airlines
www.united.com

US Airways
www.usair.com

AIRPORTS

Hilo International Airport
Tel (808) 961-9321.

Honolulu International Airport
Tel (808) 836-6413.

Kahului Airport
Tel (808) 872-3893.

Kona International Airport
Tel (808) 329-3423.

Lāna'i Airport
Tel (808) 565-6757.

Līhu'e Airport
Tel (808) 241-3913.

Moloka'i Airport
Tel (808) 567-6361.

INTER-ISLAND AIR TRAVEL

go! Airlines
Tel (888) 435-9462.
www.iflygo.com

Hawaiian Airlines
Tel (800) 367-5320.
www.hawaiianair.com

Island Air
Tel (800) 652-6541.
www.islandair.com

AIRPORT SHUTTLES

Roberts Hawaii Express Shuttle
Tel (808) 441-7800.

www.airportwaikiki
shuttle.com

SpeediShuttle
Tel (877) 242-5777.
www.speedishuttle.com

PACKAGE TOURS

Backroads
Tel (510) 527-1555.
www.backroads.com

Sierra Club
Tel (415) 977-5522.
www.sierraclub.org

The World Outdoors
Tel (303) 413-0946.
www.theworldout
doors.com

Getting Around Hawai'i

Birds on the highway

If you don't have a car in Hawai'i, your horizons will be limited. Having a vehicle provides both freedom of movement and the chance to be spontaneous. Most locals keep a swimsuit and towel in their car because they never know when the beach will look too good to resist. Anyone dependent on public transportation can reach only a few destinations beyond the confines of cities. Some of Hawai'i's most spectacular landscapes are out of bounds even to four-wheel-drive vehicles; that is when hiking can come into its own.

GREEN TRAVEL

Hawaiian transportation companies show considerable commitment to minimizing their environmental impact. The largest public transit network, for example, TheBus on O'ahu, has commissioned hybrid "clean diesel" buses and recycles everything, from paint to cleaning products.

For truly green travel, you can't beat getting around by bike. There are dedicated bicycle routes all over the islands. The Kauai Path (www.kauaipath.org) is a shared cycling and walking path along the east coast of Kaua'i, while Maui also has good provisions for cyclists.

BUSES AND TROLLEYS

Only O'ahu has a completely comprehensive public transit system. It is called **TheBus**, and for $2.50 you can travel almost anywhere; simply sit on a Circle Island bus to complete a full island tour. Several routes call at the airport; in theory, bulky luggage items are forbidden, but drivers rarely concern

themselves over passengers with luggage on their laps.

The more expensive **Waikīkī Trolley** loops around Honolulu and Waikīkī, charging $25 for an all-day pass, allowing you to hop on and off as desired.

On Maui, the **Maui Bus Service** runs 12 different routes. It operates seven days a week, including holidays, with a flat fare of $1. Separate routes connect Kahului with the resorts of West and South Maui; to travel between South and West Maui, you have to change buses. Only the Upcountry and Haiku routes call at Kahului Airport.

The **Kaua'i Bus** follows the main island road all the way from Hanalei in the north to Kekaha in the west, from Monday through Saturday for $2 only.

On Hawai'i Island, the **Hele-On Bus** runs various routes, connecting Kailua-Kona with Hilo via Waimea and Honoka'a; Kailua-Kona with the Kohala resorts; and Hilo with Volcanoes National Park. The fare is just $1. Schedules are built around taking employees to work rather than assisting vacationers.

GUIDED TOURS

Many companies offer guided tours of the attractions on individual islands. The largest and most reliable of these firms are **Roberts Hawai'i** and **Polynesian Adventure Tours**. They also offer packages that include inter-island flights, accommodations, bus tours, and car rental.

Your hotel's guest-services desk should know about guided tours of specific attractions and be able to make bookings for you.

TAXIS

Taxis can be found at airports and outside major hotels, but only in Honolulu is it relatively easy to hail a cab. Elsewhere, phone for a taxi. Some remote areas, such as Hāna on Maui, have no taxis.

DRIVING

Although Honolulu suffers with the traffic congestion of any major US city, driving in Hawai'i is generally a pleasure. Local people are seldom in a hurry, so allow plenty of time for any journey. Also, residents never use their horns, so on narrow roads check your mirrors regularly and pull over to let cars pass. If you break down, call the rental company. Always check the weather, since many roads wash out during or after heavy rain.

If you ask for directions, people will often suggest landmarks as reference points. Around Honolulu, you're likely to be told, "Go diamondhead" (southeast) or "Go ewa" (northwest), and on all the islands you'll hear the words *mauka* ("toward the mountain") and *makai* ("toward the sea"). If you find Hawaiian place names confusing, ask to be shown the way on a map.

PARKING

It's fairly easy to find free parking in Hawai'i; most hotels offer it, and major hotels and many restaurants also provide valet parking. The chief exception is in Waikīkī, where hotels and garages charge $20

Waikīkī Trolley, plying the streets and sights of Honolulu

Floodlit cruise ship dominating the Honolulu oceanfront

or more to park overnight. Be sure to heed all road signs. If there's no free parking, use a parking garage; you can often get a parking ticket validated by a restaurant, shopping center, or attraction.

CAR RENTAL

To rent a vehicle in Hawai'i, you must be over 21 (25 in some cases) and have a valid driver's license and credit card. Large rental companies such as **Alamo**, **Avis**, **Hertz**, and **National** have desks at the airports on the four main islands. They offer vehicles of all sizes, but for a four-wheel-drive vehicle you may need a specialist, like **Harper Car & Truck** on Hawai'i Island or **Lāna'i City Service** on Lāna'i. The only national chain on Moloka'i is Alamo.

It's usually easy to rent a car for a day or two from local agencies in Waikīkī, but you should book well in advance elsewhere. Fees start at about $35 a day or $150 a week.

Most visitors pay an extra $20 or so per day for Loss Damage Waiver (LDW). This protects you from Hawai'i's "no fault" policy, which holds the driver responsible for damage of the rental car, regardless of fault. Your insurance policy or credit card may cover damange costs to rental cars. Most rental firms forbid the use of unpaved roads.

GASOLINE

Gas is expensive in Hawai'i, but aim to keep the tank at least half full, since in certain areas, especially on Hawai'i Island, can be 50 miles (30 km) to the nearest filling station. Return rental cars with a full tank to avoid high gas prices charged by the agencies.

MOTORCYCLING AND BIKING

Mopeds and motorcycles can be rented on all four main islands. It is not mandatory to wear a helmet, but it is a good idea to do so.

You can rent bicycles easily, especially in Waikīkī. People use them more for getting about town than for touring.

CRUISES AND FERRIES

In the old days, *hula* dancers and *lei* greeters lined up on Honolulu's piers to welcome cruise ships filled with tourists. Almost all visitors now arrive by plane. However, **Norwegian Cruise Lines** offers regular week-long cruises around the islands, and luxury lines that call at Hawai'i include **Princess Cruises**, **Cunard**, and **Royal Caribbean International**.

The only inter-island ferry services are based in Lahaina Harbor on Maui. **Expeditions** sails five times daily between Maui and Lana'i, costing $30 for adults; the crossing takes about an hour and doubles as a whale-watching cruise in winter. On arrival, it's easy to get to the island's attractions.

The **Moloka'i Ferry** offers two daily sailings from Lahaina to Kaunakakai on Moloka'i for an adult fare of $40. Arrange a tour or rental car in advance, or you'll be stuck at the harbor.

DIRECTORY

BUSES AND TROLLEYS

Hele-On Bus
Tel (808) 961-8744.
www.heleonbus.org

Kaua'i Bus
Tel (808) 241-6410.
www.kauai.gov

Maui Bus Service
Tel (808) 871-4838.
www.co.maui.hi.us/bus

TheBus
Tel (808) 848-5555.
www.thebus.org

Waikīkī Trolley
Tel (808) 591-2561.
www.waikikitrolley.com

GUIDED TOURS

Polynesian Adventure Tours
www.polyad.com

Roberts Hawai'i
www.robertshawaii.com

CAR RENTAL

Alamo
www.alamo.com

Avis
www.avis.com

Budget
www.budget.com

Dollar
www.dollar.com

Enterprise
www.enterprise.com

Harper Car & Truck
Tel (808) 969-1478.
www.harpershawaii.com

Hertz
www.hertz.com

Lāna'i City Service
Tel (808) 565-7227.

National
www.nationalcar.com

Thrifty
www.thrifty.com

CRUISES AND FERRIES

Cunard
Tel (800) 728-6273.
www.cunard.com

Expeditions
Tel (800) 695-2624.
www.go-lanai.com

Moloka'i Ferry
Tel (866) 307-6524.
www.molokaiferry.com

Norwegian Cruise Lines
Tel (866) 234-7350.
www.ncl.com

Princess Cruises
Tel (800) 774-6237.
www.princess.com

Royal Caribbean International
Tel (866) 562-7625.
www.royalcaribbean.com

General Index

Acknowledgments

Dorling Kindersley would like to thank the following people whose contributions and assistance have made the preparation of this book possible.

Contributors
Gerald Carr is Professor of Botany at the University of Hawai'i, Manoa and a resident of O'ahu. Bonnie Friedman runs a public relations firm on Maui, contributes regularly to Hawaiian publications, and volunteers at a Hawaiian language immersion school. Rita Goldman is a freelance writer and editor who has lived on Maui since 1978. Clemence Mclaren is a Honolulu-based writer and teacher. Melissa Miller, a native of Honolulu, is a poet, storyteller, grant writer, and nonprofit consultant. Alex Salkever is a Hawai'i-based journalist specializing in sports. Stephen Self is Professor of Geology at the University of Hawai'i, Manoa and a resident of O'ahu. Greg Ward, an established travel writer who has written extensively on the Hawaiian islands, is also the author of *Hawaii: The Rough Guide*. Paul Wood, freelance writer, editor, writing teacher, and long-term resident of Maui, is the author of *Four Wheels Five Corners: Facts of Life in Upcountry Maui*.

Revisions Team
Emma Anacootee, Shruti Bahl, Chris Barstow, Stephen Bere, Hilary Bird, Louise Bolton, Julie Bond, Arwen Burnett, Barbara Carr, Sherry Collins, Karen Constanti, Nicola Erdpresser, Jane Ewart, Emer FitzGerald, Fay Franklin, Anna Freiberger, Emily Green, Emily Hatchwell, Des Helmsley, Kim Kemp, Shikha Kulkarni, Maite Lantaron, Nicola Malone, Linda Mather Olds, Georgina Matthews, Alison McGill, Simon Melia, Robert Mitchell, Kate Molan, Mary Ormandy, Sangita Patel, Mani Ramaswamy, Lee Redmond, Amir Reuveni, Ellen Root, Collette Sadler, Sands Publishing Solutions, Preeti Singh, Mary Sutherland, Rachel Symons, Conrad Van Dyk, Karen Villabona, Greta Walker, Greg Ward, and Stewart Wild.

Special Assistance
Alana Waikiki, Sheryl Toda and Tracey Matsushima at Bishop Museum, Four Seasons Resort Maui at Wailea, Elizabeth Anderson at Haleakalā National Park, Richard Rasp at Hawai'i Volcanoes National Park, Julie Blissett at HVCB (UK), Sharon Brown at Kalaupapa National Historical Park, www.lucies farm.com, Geraldine Bell at Pu'uhonua O Hōnaunau National Historical Park, Stouffer Renaissance Wailea Beach Resort, Bill Haig and Linda Matsunaga at TheBus, the State Parks Administrator at Waimea Canyon and Koke'e State Park, and RM Towill Corporation for artwork reference.

Additional Special Photography
Philip Dowell, DK Studio/Steve Gorton, Frank Greenaway, John Heseltine, Nigel Hicks, Dave King, James McConnachie, Andrew McKinney, Neil Mersh, David Murray and Jules Selmes, Ian O'Leary, Roger Philips, Clive Streeter, Greg Ward, Andrew Whittuck, Francesca Yorke, and Jerry Young.

Photography Permissions
Dorling Kindersley would like to thank the following for their kind permission to photograph at their establishments and for their assistance with photography: Sharon Clark at the Hawai'i Film Office, George Applegate HVCB Big Island, Connie Wright at the HVCB Moloka'i, Department of Interior and the National Park Service 106–7, 116–117 and 128–129 and all other churches, museums, hotels, restaurants, shops, galleries, and other sights too numerous to thank individually.

Picture Credits
a = above; b = below/bottom; c = center; f = far; l = left; r = right; t = top.

Works of art have been reproduced with permission of the following copyright holders: *Stage design for L'Enfant et les Sortileges 1981*, courtesy Tradhart, (c) David Hockney 1981: 71b.

The publisher would like to thank the following individuals, companies, and picture libraries for their kind permission to reproduce their photographs:

AARP: 236c; Akg, London: 25t, 45t; Museum of Mankind, London 24c; ALAMY IMAGES: Caroline Commins 126br; Hank deLespinasse 194cla; Douglas Peebles Photography/Douglas Peebles 127cra; Douglas Peebles Photography/Thomas Dove 155ca; David Fleetham 22bc, 32cl; Robert Fried 230c; Dennis Hallinan 90-91; D. Hurst 195c; Andy Jackson 121br, 127cr, 229tl; Jacques Jangoux 11br; Andre Jenny 229cr, 240bl; Jon Arnold Images/Walter Bibikow 11cl; David L. Moore 134tl; nagelestock.com 10cla; Photo Resource Hawaii/Ann Cecil 11tr; Photo Resource Hawaii/David Franzen 141tr; Photo Resource Hawaii/David Olsen 15bc; Photo Resource Hawaii/David Schrichte 32br, 134bl; Photo Resource Hawaii/Dylan Dawson 15c; Photo Resource Hawaii/Franco Salmoiraghi 142tl; Photo Resource Hawaii/G. Brad Lewis 144-145, 228bl; Photo Resource Hawaii/Jim Cazel 16c, 16bl, 120br; Photo Resource Hawaii/Mark Wilson 17c; Photo Resource Hawaii/Tor Johnson 16t, 226cl; Photo Resource Hawaii/Wayne Levin 17tr; Travis Rowan 33br; Stephen Frink Collection/James D. Watt 23bl; Stephen Frink Collection/Masa Ushioda 224cr; ALEXANDER AND BALDWIN SUGAR MUSEUM, Maui: 123bl; Allsport UK Ltd.: Vandystadt/sylvain Cazenane 31c; ARCHIVE PHOTOS: 28tr, 44b, 45b; ASTON HOTELS & RESORTS: 176bl.

Courtesy of BAMBOO RIDGE PRESS: Cover illustration From *Wild Meat And The Bully Burgers* With Kind Permission of The Artist Cora Yee 25b; BIOFOTOS: Heather Angel 21ca; BISHOP MUSEUM, Honolulu: 42c, 43t, 44c, 68br, 68cr, 69t, 152b; Charles Furneaux 135cr; Engraved By JG Woods 1878 30tr, BRIDGEMAN ART LIBRARY, London: Museum of Mankind, London 28c, 29t; National Library Of Australia, *Canberra Captain Cook C1820* by John Webber Engraved By Josef Selb C1820 41b; Scottish National Portrait Gallery *Robert Louis Stevenson (1850–94)* 1892 by Count Girolamo Pieri Nerli 25c(D); PAUL J BUKLAREWICZ: 26cl.

GERALD CARR: 20br, 21tc/bc; JEAN LOUP CHARMET: *From Voyage Autours du Monde* by Louis Choris 1822 8–9; 26tr, 40t; CIRQUE HAWAII: 217br; COFFEES OF HAWAI'I: 234crb; BRUCE COLEMAN COLLECTION: Jeff Foot Productions 115b; CORBIS UK LTD: Bettman Archive 44t, /acme 149t, /upi 63t, 65b; Mark A. Johnson 116-117; David Muench 126tl; Amos Nachoum 23cla; Douglas Peebles 56br, 118cr, 154tr, 195tl, 227tl, 230br; Randy Faris: 228tc; Roger Ressmeyer 155br; Reuters/Lucy

Pemoni 17bl; Tony Roberts 226br, 227cr; Jim Sugar 14; Karl Weatherly 10crb; Stuart Westmorland 143br. CULVER PICTURES, Inc, New York: 41c, 43c, 43b, 44c, 68tl; CURRENT EVENTS, Kailua-kona: 135cl;

RON DAHLQUIST: 20c, 31tl, 33cr, 21br, 37t, 82cb, 83tr, 100cb, 110ca, 121cl, 123tr, 127cl, 129br; DREAMSTIME.COM: Darren Brode 237cl; Robert Cravens 234tc.

ET ARCHIVE, London; National Maritime Museum *Death of Cook* by J Cleavely 41t; EXPEDITIONS INTER-ISLAND FERRIES: 245t.

FOUR SEASONS RESORT HUALALAI: 177bl; PETER FRENCH: 19b, 20tr, 21tr, 36b, 102t, 135cla, 168b, 170cb.

GETTY IMAGES: The Image Bank/Bruce Forster 10tc; CHERYL GILBERT: 135br; GO!: 242cr; GRAND WAILEA RESORT HOTEL & SPA: 229br; RONALD GRANT ARCHIVE: Paramount Pictures *Blue Hawaii* (1961) 165; GRAPEVINE PRODUCTIONS; 193tl.

ROBERT HARDING PICTURE LIBRARY: Nakamura 174–5; HAWAI'I TOURISM AUTHORITY (HTA): Robert Coello 238bl; Tor Johnson 234cl, 235br; HAWAI'I VOLCANOES NATIONAL PARK: 155cl; Dave Boyle 154cl; Norrie Judd 154br; HAWAIIAN AIRLINES: 242t; HAWAIIAN HISTORICAL SOCIETY: 14b, *From Voyage Autours du Monde* by Louis Choris 1822 38; HAWAIIAN LEGACY ARCHIVE: 24tl; HAWAIIAN TELCOM: 240cr; EVE ESCHNER HOGAN: 230tl; HONOLULU ACADEMY OF ARTS: Gift of Mrs. C. Montague Cooke, Jr, Charles M. Cooke III And Mrs. Heatin Wrenn in Memory of Dr. C. Montague Cooke, Jr 1951 *Nahienaena* Robert Dampier 111t; GEORGINA M. HUNTER: 241tl.

IMAGE BANK, London: 50; IMAGE QUEST MARINE: James D. Watt 22bl, 32tr; Masa Ushioda 22crb, 23clb; INTERNATIONAL COFFEE ORGANISATION, London: 135clb.

KA'ANAPALI BEACH HOTEL: 236br; KAPALUA RESORT ON MAUI: 226cb; © KAUA'I MUSEUM: 169t; KAUAI PLANTATION RAILWAY: 161tl; KŌKE'E NATURAL HISTORY MUSEUM: David Boynton 170ca. KONA COFFEE CULTURAL FESTIVAL: 134cr.

LAHAINA TOWN ACTION COMMITEE: 110b; JON LASIUK: 239tl; ANTHONY LIMERICK: 110tr, 112t, 153t/b, 193b, 239t, 240tl/tr, 241t, 243t, 244b.

MAUI ARTS & CULTURAL CENTER: 218h; MAUI OCEAN CENTER: Darren Jew 119br; WWW.MAUI-WEDDING-PHOTOGRAPHY: Shasta Rose 228br.

NASA, Houston: 12c; NATURE PHOTOGRAPHERS: Brinsley Burbidge 20cb/bl, 167c; James Hancock 169cr;

Paul Sterry 169cl; PETER NEWARK'S AMERICAN PICTURES: engraved by N Currier 1852 42t; NHPA: Stephen Kraseman 21cb.

MAUI CRAFTS GUILD: Randy Miller 212c.

OCEAN CLUB HONOLULU: 220cla; OSF/PHOTOLIBRARY: Botanica/Bob Stefko 23crb; David Fleetham 22tl; Pacific Stock/Dave Fleetham 22clb, 22-23, 33cl; Pacific Stock/Jim Watt 23cra.

PACIFIC STOCK: 40c; Bob Abraham 27b, 34c, 242b; Rita Ariyoshi 212b; Joe Carini 34b; Dana Edmunds 36t; Bill Schlidge 168t; Greg Vaughan 28bl, 29cb, 35b; DOUGLAS PEEBLES: 5tl, 18c, 52ca, 82ca, 84, 95b, 123tl, 142b, 143tr, 156, 171c, 224b; PHOTOLIBRARY: David Cornwell 33tl; PHOTO RESOURCE HAWAII: David Bjorn 30–1; David Boynton 26bl, 167t; Randy Jay Braun 27c; John Callahan 1, 34t, 37b, 210c; Monte Costa 45ca; Edmunds Dana 90-91, Tami Dawson 82t, 173b; David Franzen 57b; Nikiolas Konstantinou 136br; Jon Ogata 171t; Franco Salmoiraghi 83b, 131b, 157b, 140br, 192br; Joe Solem 35t; Jamie Wellner; Lani Breheme Yamasaki 12c; Photo Tropic: David S Boynton 169b; PHOTOSHOT/NHPA: Pete Atkinson 23tr; Kevin Schafer 23bc; PICTURES COLOUR LIBRARY: 27t; PLANET EARTH PICTURES: Pete Atkinson 89t; John Lythgoe 21bl; PRIVATE COLLECTION: 9 Inset, 24tr, 39b, 42brb, 47 Inset, 81 Inset, 175 Inset, 233 Inset. SCOTT ROWLAND: 18b.

SCIENCE PHOTO LIBRARY: Royal Observatory, Edinburgh 130; Soames Summerhays 152tr; MIKE SEVERNS PHOTOGRAPHY INC.: Mike Severns 22tr; THE STOCKMARKET: 26–27; SURFER PUBLICATIONS: Jeff Divine 31b; Tom Servais 30bl/bc/br, 31tr; KEVIN AND CAT SWEENEY: 135bla, 184c.

TEDESCHI VINEYARDS: 104tl; TELEGRAPH COLOUR LIBRARY: S Benbow 222b; Colorific/Jean Paul Nacivet 13t.

BRETT UPRICHARD: 29ca. Greg Ward: 18t, 101t, 168c. NIK WHEELER 216br; WORLD PICTURES: 80–81, 85b.

Front Endpaper: all special photography except Douglas Peebles: Tl/tlc; Science Photo Library: Royal Observatory, Edinburgh b.

JACKET: Front – AWL IMAGES: Travel Pix Collection. Back – ALAMY IMAGES: Craig Ellenwood cla; Rick Strange clb; DORLING KINDERSLEY: Rob Reichenfeld bl, tl. Spine – AWL IMAGES: Travel Pix Collection. Maps ERA-Maptech Ltd, Dublin, Ireland.

All other images @ Dorling Kindersley. For further information see: www.dkimages.com

SPECIAL EDITIONS OF DK TRAVEL GUIDES

DK Travel Guides can be purchased in bulk quantities at discounted prices for use in promotions or as premiums. We are also able to offer special editions and personalized jackets, corporate imprints, and excerpts from all of our books, tailored specifically to meet your own needs.

To find out more, please contact:
(in the United States) **SpecialSales@dk.com**
(in the UK) **TravelSpecialSales@uk.dk.com**
(in Canada) DK Special Sales at **general@tourmaline.ca**
(in Australia) **business.development@pearson.com.au**

Glossary of Hawaiian Terms

Hawaiian began as an oral language. It was first put into written form by the missionaries who arrived in the 1820s. The teaching and speaking of Hawaiian was banned from the early 1900s, and by the time the native cultural renaissance began in 1978 the beautiful, melodious language was almost totally lost. Immersion programs are producing new generations of Hawaiian speakers. Fluent speakers are still few, and native speakers are even more rare. Still, you will hear Hawaiian words liberally sprinkled in conversation and in the islands' glorious music, and see it written on some signs.

Summary of Pronunciation

The Hawaiian language has just 12 letters: the five vowels plus h, k, l, m, n, p, and w.

unstressed vowels:

a	as in "above"
e	as in "bet"
i	as y in "city"
o	as in "sole"
u	as in "full"

stressed vowels:

ā	as in "far"
ē	as in "pay"
ī	as in "see"
ō	as in "sole"
ū	as in "moon"

consonants:

h	as in "hat"
k	as in "kick"
l	as in "law"
m	as in "mow"
n	as in "now"
p	as in "pin"
w	as in "win" or "vine"

The 'okina (glottal stop) is found at the beginning of some words beginning with vowels or between vowels. It is pronounced like the sound between the syllables in the English "uh-oh."

ali'i	ahlee-ee
liliko'i	leeleekoh-ee
'ohana	oh-hahnah

The kahakō (macron) is a mark found only above vowels, indicating vowels should be stressed.

kāne	kah-nay
kōkua	koh-koo-ah
pūpū	poo-poo

Everyday Words

'āina	aye-nah	land
aloha	ah-loh-ha	hello; goodbye; love
hale	ha-leh	house
haole	how-leh	foreigner; Caucasian
hula	who-la	Hawaiian dance
kāhiko	kaa-hee-koh	old; traditional
kama'āina	kah-mah-aye-nah	familiar; resident
kāne	kah-nay	man
kapa	kah-pah	bark cloth
keiki	kay-kee	child
kōkua	koh-koo-ah	help
kumu	kooh-mooh	teacher
lānai	luh-nigh	porch; balcony
lei	layh	garland
lua	looah	bathroom; toilet
mahalo	muh-ha-low	thank you
mu'umu'u	moo-oo-moo-oo	long billowing dress
'ohana	oh-hahnah	family
'ono	oh-noh	delicious
pau	pow	done
puka	poo-kah	hole
wahine	w(v)ah-he-nay	woman
wikiwiki	w(v)eekee-w(v)eekee	quickly

Geographical and Nature Terms

'a'ā	ah-aah	rough, jagged lava
kai	kaee	ocean
koholā	koh-hoh-laah	humpback whale
kona	koh-nah	leeward side
ko'olau	koh-oh-lowh	windward side
kukui	kuh-kooh-eeh	candlenut tree
makai	muh-kaee	toward the sea
mauka	mau-kuh	toward the mountains
mauna	mau-nah	mountain
nēnē	nay-nay	Hawaiian goose
pāhoehoe	pah-hoy-hoy	smooth lava
pali	pah-lee	cliff
pu'u	poo-oo	hill
wai	w(v)hy	fresh water

Historical Terms

ahupua'a	ah-hoo-poo-ah-ah	a division of land, from mountains to sea
ali'i	ahlee-ee	chief; royalty
heiau	hey-ow	ancient temple
kahuna	kah-hoo-nah	priest; expert
kapu	kah-poo	forbidden; taboo
kupuna	koo-poo-nah	elders; ancestors
luakini	looh-ah-kee-nee	human sacrifice temple
maka'āinana	mah-kah-aye-nanah	commoner
mana	mah-nah	supernatural power
mele	meh-leh	song
mo'o	moh-oh	lizard
oli	oh-leeh	chant
pili	pih-leeh	grass for thatching
pu'uhonua	pooh-ooh-hoh-nuah	place of refuge

Food Words

'ahi	ah-hee	yellowfin tuna
aku	ah-koo	skipjack; bonito
a'u	ah-oo	swordfish; marlin
haupia	how-peeah	traditional coconut pudding
imu	ee-moo	underground oven
kalo	kah-loh	taro
kālua	kah-looah	food baked slowly in underground oven
kiawe	key-ah-veh	wood used for grilling
laulau	lau-lau	steamed filled ti-leaf packages
liliko'i	lee-lee-koh-ee	passion fruit
limu	lee-moo	seaweed
lomi-lomi salmon	low-me low-me	raw salmon pieces with onion and tomato
lū'au	loo-ow	Hawaiian feast
mahimahi	muh-hee-muh-hee	dorado; dolphin fish
ono	oh-no	wahoo
opah	oh-pah	moonfish
'ōpakapaka	oh-pah-kah-pah-kah	blue snapper
poi	poy	pounded taro root
pūpū	poo-poo	appetizer
uku	oo-koo	gray snapper
ulua	oo-looah	jackfish; pompano

Pidgin

Hawai'i's unofficial conglomerate language is commonly heard on playgrounds, in shopping malls, and backyards throughout Hawai'i. Here are some words and phrases you may hear:

brah	brother, pal
broke da mout'	great food
buggah	pal or pest
fo' real	really
fo' what	why
grinds	food; also to grind
howzit?	how are you?; how is everything?
kay den	okay then
laydahs	later; goodbye
li' dat	like that
li' dis	like this
no can	cannot
no mo' nahting	nothing
shoots!	yeah!
stink eye	dirty look
talk story	chat; gossip

Honolulu Bus Routes

3-11-53-54

10

9-40-40A-42-43-52-62

7-10

10-19-20

10

7-10

Kalihi

1-7

1-10

3-11-53-54

MOʻOKAULA STREET

N. SCHOOL STREET

10

10

2

3

13

LILIHA STREET

10-13

DILLINGHAM BOULEVARD

9-40-40A-42-43-52-62

Iwilei

11-53-54

2-3-13

55-56-57-57A-65

Punch Bow

6-15

15

15

NIMITZ HIGHWAY

19-20

1L-11-19-20-
40-40A-42-43-
52-53-54-62

19-20-40-
40A-42-43

11

9

1-1L-2-3-9-11-
13-53-54-62

6-55-56-
57-57A-65

4-6

7

6

1-1L-2-3-9-11-
13-40-40A-42-
43-52-53-54-62

**Downtown
Honolulu**

8

10

5

4

Sand Island

1-1L-2-3-4-9-11-
13-19-20-40-40A-
42-43-52-53-54-62

1

2

3

6

15

1-1L-2-13

*SAND ISLAND
STATE PARK*

19-20-42

42

1-1L-2-13

15

17-18-43

HONOLULU CHANNEL

6

3-9-40-40A-43-52-53-62

15

3

Kalaeola

19-20-42-55-56-57-57A

65

*KAKAʻAKO
WATERFRONT PARK*

Ala Moana

6

ALA MOANA BOULEVARD

5-6-8-
23-24-4
55-56-57

ALA MOANA S
RECREATION A

MĀMALA BAY

KEY

═	Freeway
6	Bus route and number
─	City Express route A
─	City Express route B
─	Country Express route C
─	Country Express route E
✈	Airport
⛴	Ferry port
▪	Main sightseeing areas

0 kilometers   1

0 miles   1

SIGHTS

1 King Kamehameha Statue
2 Kawaiahaʻo Church
3 Mission Houses Museum
4 ʻIolani Palace
5 State Capitol
6 St. Andrew's Cathedral

7 Fort Street Mall
8 Aloha Tower Marketplace
9 Hawaiʻi Theatre
10 Hawaiʻi State Art Museum
11 Chinatown

1 Bishop Museum
2 Oʻahu Cemetery
3 Royal Mausoleum
4 Queen Emma Summer Palace
5 National Memorial Cemetery
of the Pacific

6 Honolulu Academy of
7 The Contemporary M
8 Lyon Arboretum
9 Kapiʻolani Park
10 Pearl Harbour